Landscape Graphics

Landscape Graphics

Grant W. Reid ASLA

Whitney Library of Design
an imprint of Watson-Guptill Publications/New York

First published in 1987 in New York by Whitney Library of Design
an imprint of Watson-Guptill Publications
a division of Billboard Publications, Inc.
1515 Broadway, New York, N.Y. 10036

Library of Congress Cataloging-in-Publication Data

Reid, Grant W.
Landscape graphics.

Bibliography: p.
Includes index.
1. Landscape architectural drawing. 2. Landscape architecture—Designs and plans. I. Title.
SB476.4.R45 1986 712'.022'1 87-18884
ISBN 0-8230-7332-7
ISBN 0-8230-7331-9 (pbk.)

Distributed in the United Kingdom by The Architectural Press
9 Queen Anne's Gate, London SW1H 9BY

Manufactured in U.S.A.
First printing, 1987

12 13/00 99 98

Special thanks to

EDAW, Inc., Fort Collins, Colorado, for professional illustrations on pages 14, 15, 19, 21, 24, 29, 30, 31, 32, 34, 35, 37, 69 (right side), 79, 119 (lower), 155, 170, 177, 178, 179, 180, 181, 194, 195, 196, 197.

Winston Associates Inc., Boulder, Colorado, for professional illustrations on pages 25 and 119 (upper).

Scott Milne and Susan Alden, Colorado State University students, for their assistance with illustrations.

Contents

Foreword

Landscape Graphics is an instructional book. The emphasis is on easy, time-saving techniques. The format is how-to. Although directed primarily to the person just taking up landscape design, it also contains techniques and reference material that will be of value to established professionals who wish to refine their graphic skills.

The language of landscape graphic communication is too extensive to cover in one book. For that reason, the focus here is exclusively on black-and-white techniques. In addition, simplified techniques are featured instead of complex ones. For example, there are more technical, and perhaps more accurate, methods of perspective drawing than those shown here. But the ones demonstrated in this book have the advantage of simplicity and comprehensibility.

The very important area of computer graphics is touched very lightly here. The computer is now able to perform many graphic tasks which were formerly done only by hand, including some manual techniques described here. Yet computer graphics is far too specialized a subject for inclusion in a basic book like this one.

There will always be a need for landscape architects who can draw well and draw fast. Graphic instructional aids are, at best, only twenty percent of the learning process. The rest is confidence and practice. Improved graphic skills will have a positive effect on your ability to develop creative design ideas and on your success at selling those ideas. It is up to you. Accept the challenge; practice a lot, and have fun doing it.

How to Use This Book

If you are a beginning student or a graphics instructor, you will get the most out of this book if you study each chapter, then follow through with appropriate exercises from Appendix IV. These exercises are keyed into each chapter and follow the same sequence. The first group of exercises (1–14) do not need to be worked in any specific sequence. In fact, they are best intermixed with exercises for other chapters as a way to develop the looser, freehand expressive drawing skills.

To fully exploit the chapter on quick perspectives (Chapter 9), a different approach is necessary. Here, the exercises should be done as the text is being studied—not at the end of the chapter. Each perspective exercise builds on skills developed in previous exercises. They depend on explanations given in the preceding portion of text and follow a logical progression of skill development.

The professional or more advanced student may wish to skip over sections that seem familiar, such as drafting or lettering. Chapters 6, 7, and 8 contain the most graphic examples and may be used as a reference file. Copy the examples that suit your needs and adapt them to your own style.

Every technique shown in the book—except drafting and pencil lettering—is compatible with color rendering techniques. The reader should practice quick color applications concurrently with each black-and-white graphic technique presented here.

1 Graphic Language and the Design Process

There are five generally recognized stages, or phases, in the design process. At each of these stages, graphic products are generated to record, externalize, and communicate ideas or information.

These graphic products range from the simplest sketches to the most detailed drawings of construction details. They all have one quality in common, however. They are all products of graphic thinking—visualizations of something that does not yet exist.

The relationship between the five major design phases and their appropriate graphic products can be expressed as follows:

Design Phase	**Graphic Product**
Program development	Written program
Inventory and analysis	Site analysis drawings
Conceptual design	Concept plans and sketches
Design development	Presentation drawings
Final design	Implementation documents

In practice, the design process is often a little disorderly. Depending on the project, a stage may be repeated or even skipped. Also, these "discrete" stages sometimes overlap or blend into one another. There is, however, logic to following this specific sequence of design phases. In the following pages, we will look briefly at the purpose of each stage and how the graphic language appropriately expresses the information that must be communicated at each stage.

Program Development

Content and Purpose

Program development is a research and information-gathering phase in which data is collected from property owners, administrators, and users. The social, political, financial, and personal characteristics of a project are established at this stage. The focus is on facts, attitudes, needs, constraints, and potentials.

Graphic Character and Media

A program is often comprised of notes, completed questionnaires, and other logically organized written material. Drawings are seldom needed or made.

Inventory and Analysis

Content and Purpose
At the inventory and analysis stage, the landscape design professional gathers and records information on the physical characteristics of a site, such as lot and building dimensions, vegetation, soils, climate, drainage, views, and other pertinent affecting factors.

The purely objective recording of site data is an **inventory**. Interpretive manipulation of this data and subjective comments constitute a **site analysis**. This information, together with the written program, are the basic guidelines for design.

Graphic Character and Media
Sometimes the inventory and analysis are separate graphic items; sometimes they are combined. In all cases, they are accurate, clear, and comprehensive plan view drawings that explain site-specific conditions, constraints, and potential.

For small sites, the inventory and analysis may be done with pencil on vellum or graph paper and may be heavily annotated. Felt tip pen on marker paper is also appropriate. Large sites may require a series of maps drawn with a combination of freehand and drafting techniques. They are usually more refined, are often used as transparent overlays, and sometimes involve color. Computer-assisted site analysis techniques are valuable for larger tracts of land.

The graphic materials are generally for the designer's use only, but on regional-scale projects, site analysis drawings may be reviewed by the client. In any case, the graphics are an abstraction of the landscape features and do not need to be realistic.

Site Analysis

Outlet pipe underground

Undeveloped Pasture

Existing Post and Rail Fence

Erosion - Bank needs stabilization

House looks out of scale when viewed from road around N. side of Lake.

small existing pines

County Road

10 Miles to Fort Collins

Unpaved

Lake spring-fed No visible inlet

Seasonal Fluctuations 3-4'

Prevailing N.W. Winds
•Need shelterbelt on N.W. side

Relatively Level Area

Good Topsoil

Good Location for Vegetable garden

Neighbor is concerned that this view is not completely obstructed

Irrigation ditch

Fish mostly trash fish
•May need to poison and restock.

Lake good for small sailboats

LAKE

slopes down approx. 5'

Air Conditioner
•Needs screening

slopes down 8'

Garage

Auto access to Residence

House - Yellow with dark brown trim - cedar shake roof

Good Views across Lake to Mountains

deck

Extend outdoor living area - Needs shade.

Residence

front entry

Post and Rail fencing

sunken patio

High water table throughout site

Evaporative septic system.
•Leave open soften edges

Grade change Office 4' lower than residence

N.

Atrium

•Need an outdoor office space

Auto Access to office

Main office entry

SCALE.
0 10 20 30'

Sandy area

Mid Winter Sun Arc

Mid Summer sun Arc.

Office

Main View from office windows

air conditioner unit - needs to be screend

Client owns 3 acre feet irrigation water

Waterfowl breeding area
Cattails and reedgrasses

Property extends and encompasses a further 7 acres

Limit of intensely developed zone

Leave undeveloped

Utility access

Propane tank

Road dead ends

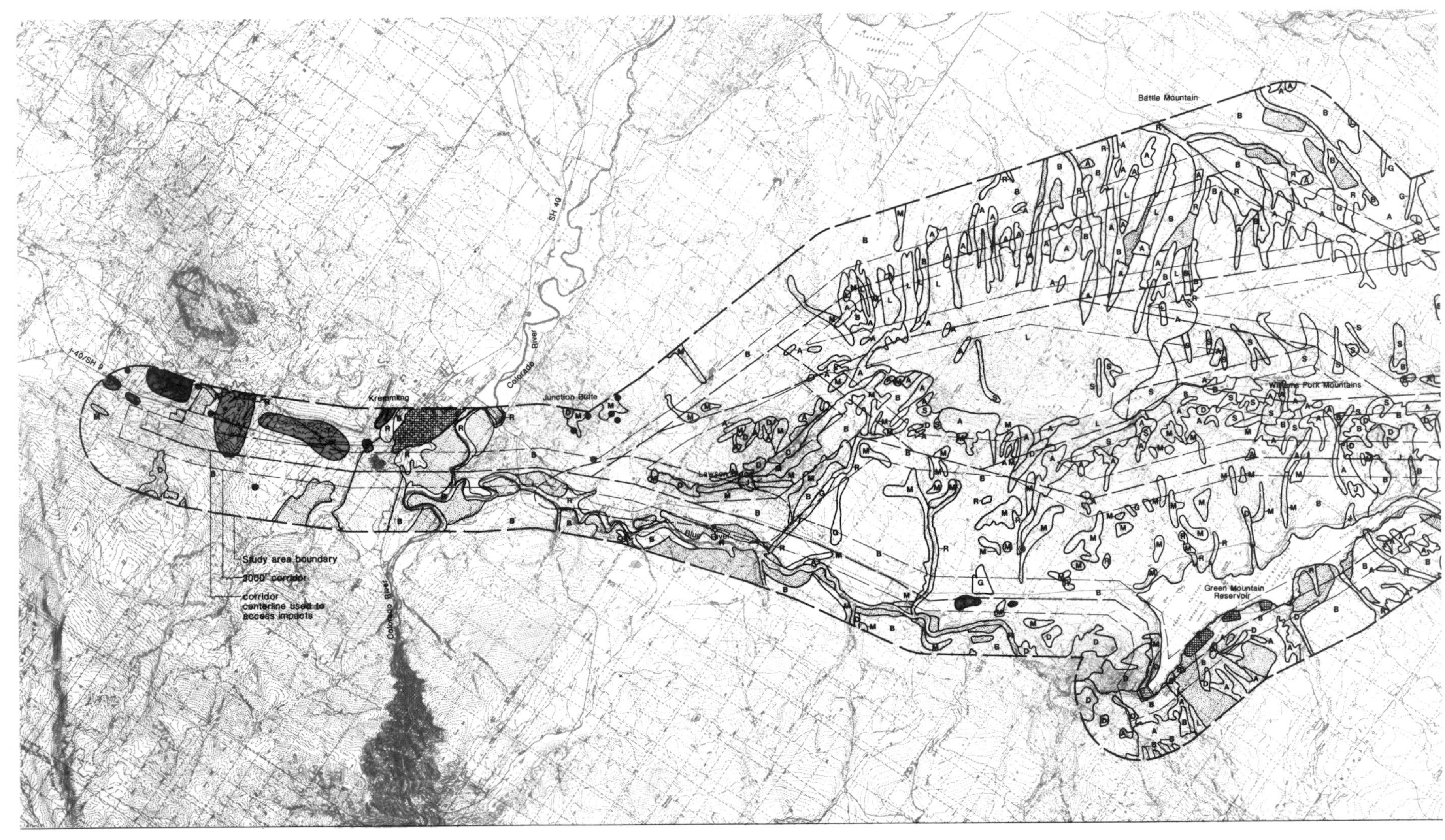

US Department of Energy
Western Area Power Administration

Blue River·Gore Pass Transmission Line

0 1 2 5 km
0 1 2 5 mi.

Figure 4-6

Vegetation

Shrub Types

- B Big Sagebrush
- M Mountain Shrub

Forest Types

- A Aspen
- S Spruce/Fir
- D Douglas-fir/Forest
- J Douglas-fir/Juniper
- L Lodgepole Pine

Other

- R Riparian/Wetland (forest, shrub & herbaceous)
- Urban
- Disturbed
- Threatend or Endangered Plant Species (under consideration for federal listing)
- Plant Association of State Interest
- Plant Species of State Interest

Herbaceous Types

- G Grassland (meadow)
- Agriculture

Sources

- Aerial Photography
  - SE of Lawson Ridge: USFS color photography, 1"-550', Sept. '81.
  - NW of Lawson Ridge, Tri-State color photography, 1:20,000, about 1979
- Field Observations
- Colorado Natural Heritage Inventory
- Bureau of Land Management

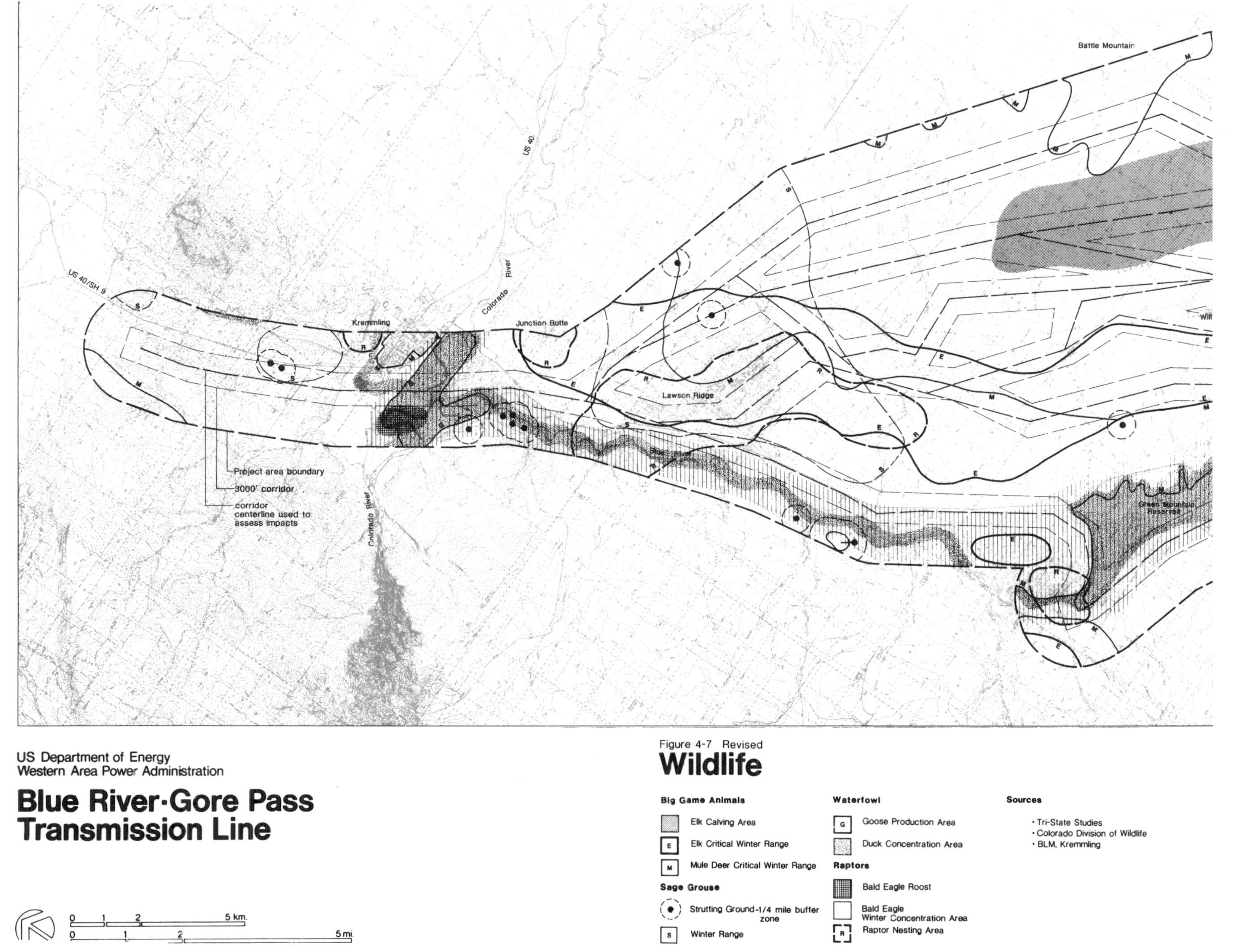

US Department of Energy
Western Area Power Administration

Blue River-Gore Pass Transmission Line

0 1 2 5 km.
0 1 2 5 mi.

Figure 4-7 Revised

Wildlife

Big Game Animals

- Elk Calving Area
- E Elk Critical Winter Range
- M Mule Deer Critical Winter Range

Sage Grouse

- Strutting Ground-1/4 mile buffer zone
- S Winter Range

Waterfowl

- G Goose Production Area
- Duck Concentration Area

Raptors

- Bald Eagle Roost
- Bald Eagle Winter Concentration Area
- R Raptor Nesting Area

Sources

- Tri-State Studies
- Colorado Division of Wildlife
- BLM, Kremmling

Conceptual Design

Content and Purpose

The conceptual design phase is when early design ideas and functional relationships are explored. The graphic products at this stage are sometimes called **functional diagrams**, **concept plans**, or **schematic plans**. They are sketches or sketch-like drawings.

For small projects, they are usually made only for the designer's self-communication: a record of ideas that forms the basis for further idea development. On larger and more complex projects, the graphic products may be presented to other designers and the client for early feedback. All are drawings that suggest more drawings.

Graphic Character and Media

Concept plans and sketches should begin as honest, open, rough freehand drawings that may be a series of creative scribbles and jumbled diagrams. Initially, they are loose and approximate and should look like the decision-making, idea-development, conflict-resolution drawings they are. Simple plan view diagrams, quick sections, or thumbnail sketches—and even cartoon-like drawings—can serve. It is common to see bubble shapes, arrows, and abstract symbols on concept drawings. These may be refined as more drawings are produced but should always remain vigorous, powerful, and direct.

For lower-budget projects, soft pencil or color felt tip pen on buff-colored sketch paper are appropriate media. Higher-budget projects may require use of colored markers on marker paper. Both should be marked by boldness and vigor. Concept graphics are supposed to be done rapidly, with ideas flowing freely. They should not be constrained by the desire to impress anyone with one's own artistry.

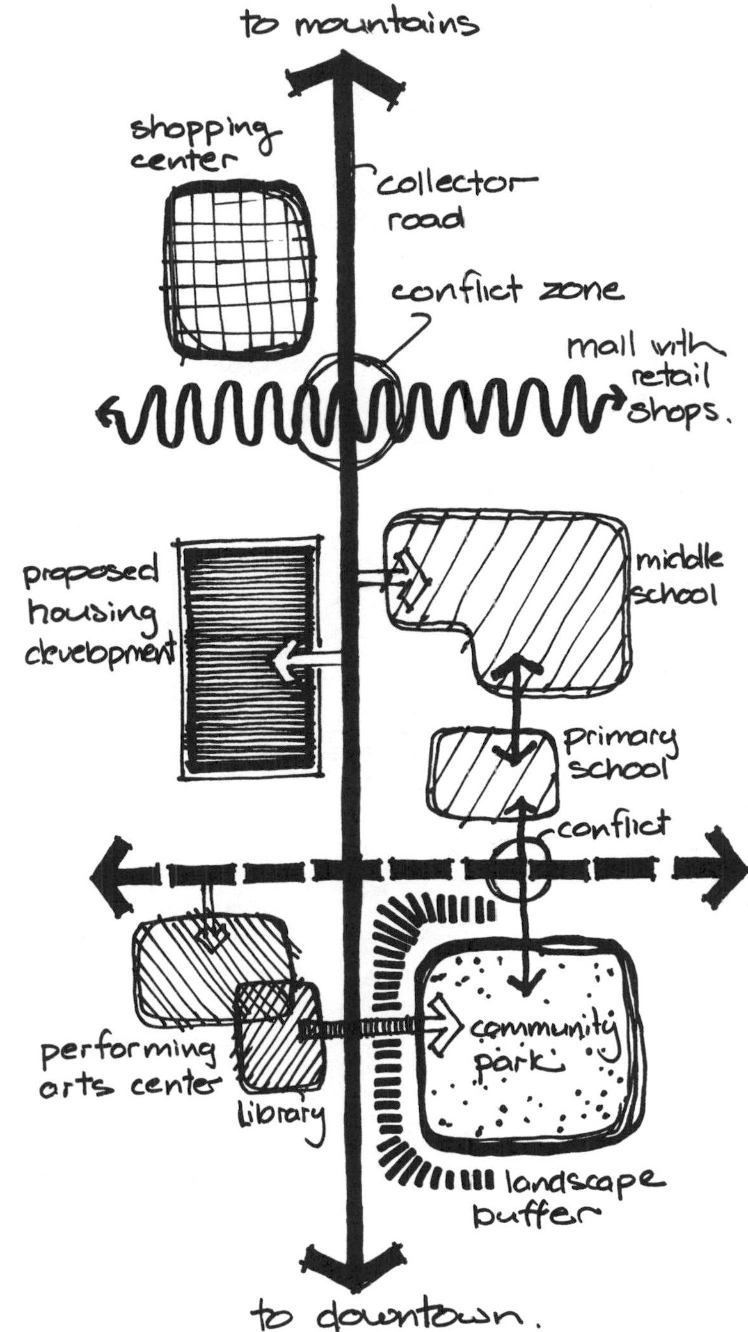
to mountains
shopping center
collector road
conflict zone
mall with retail shops.
proposed housing development
middle school
primary school
conflict
performing arts center
library
community park
landscape buffer
to downtown.

Functional Diagram

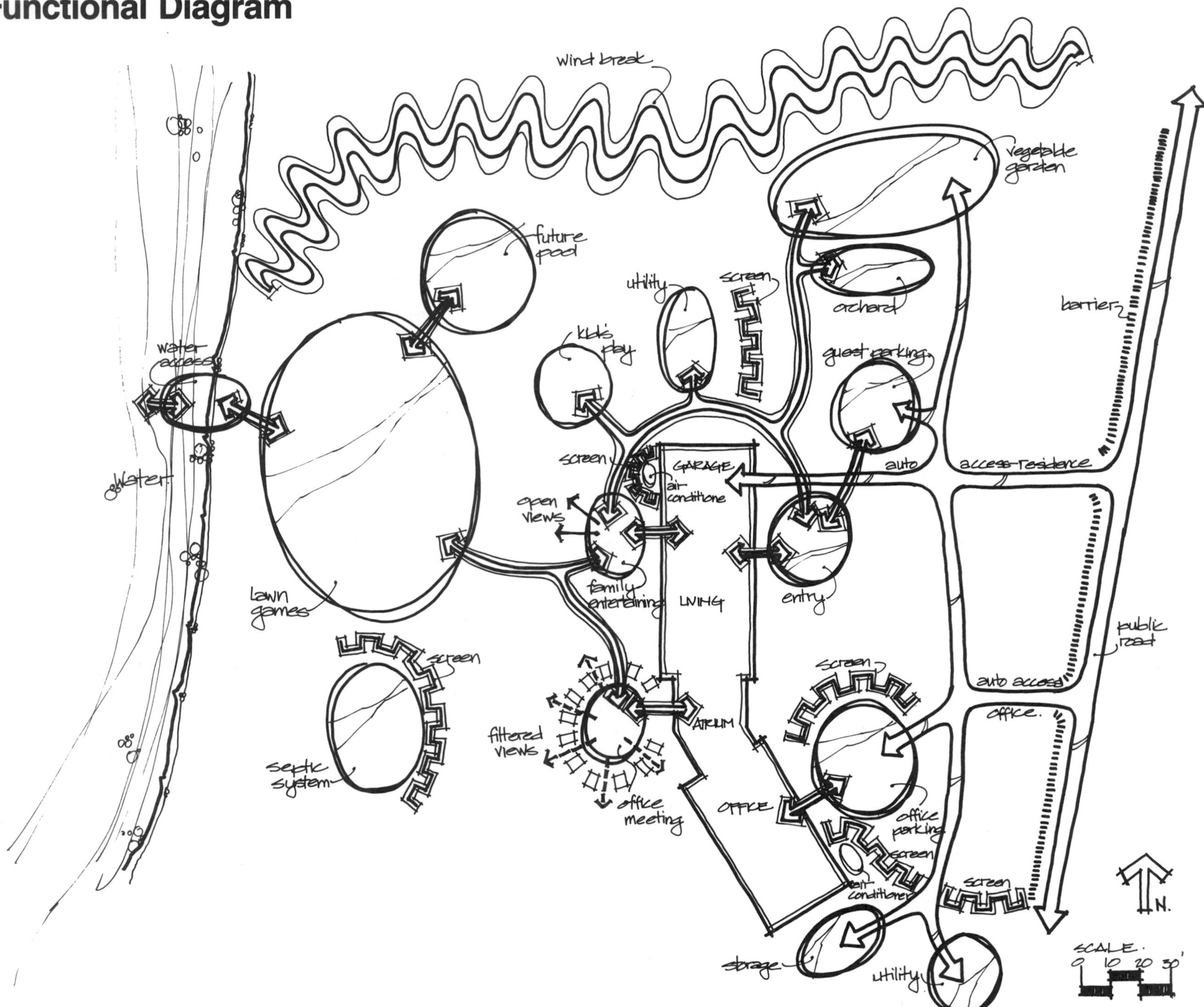

Concept Plan

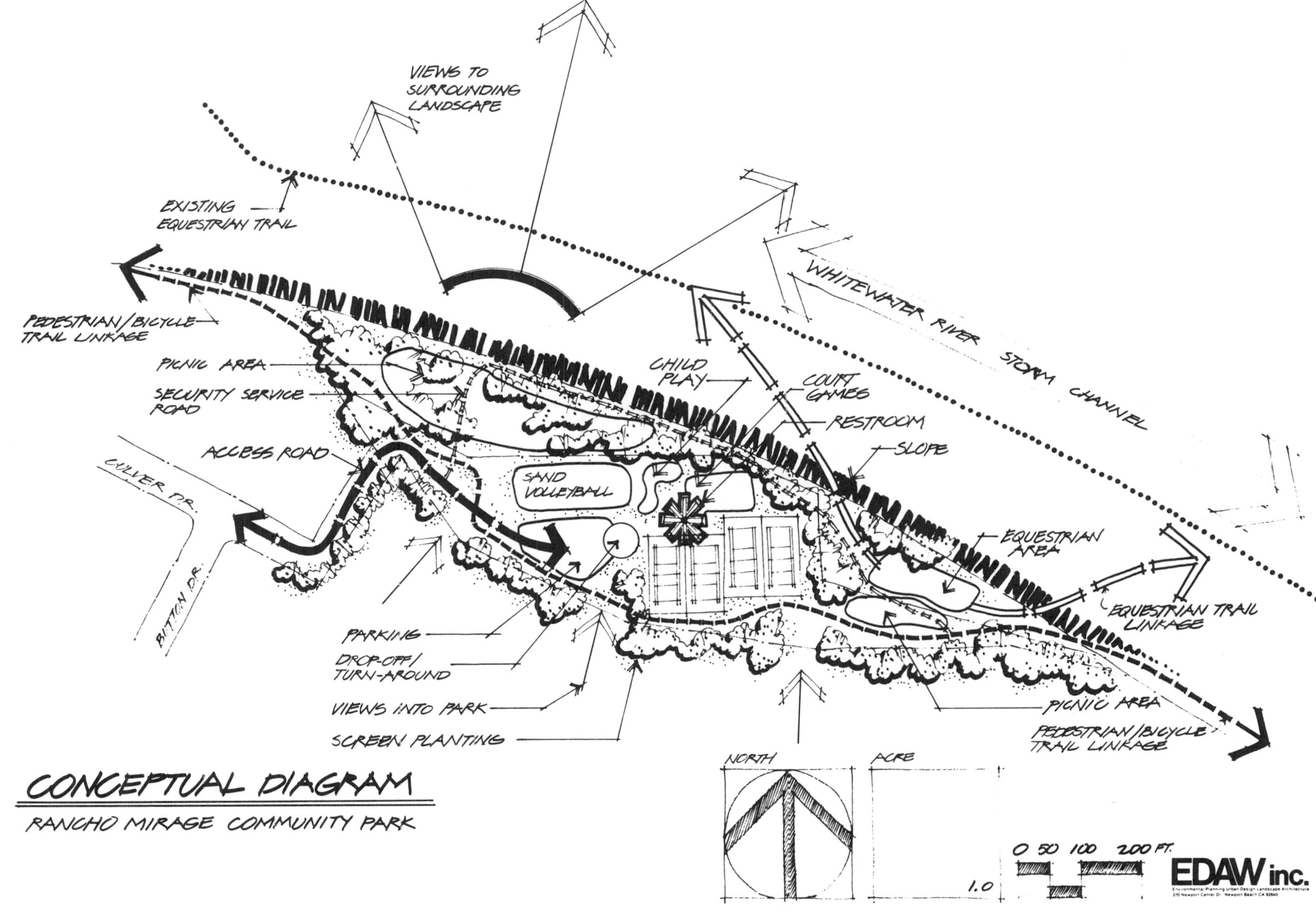

Design Development

Content and Purpose

At the design development stage, specific ideas begin to formulate. At first, the drawings are quick freehand sketches which allow the designer to evaluate solutions as they evolve. Many will be rejected outright; some will be added to, changed, and improved.

As the ideas are refined to integrate all the functional and aesthetic criteria, the more developed drawings contain specific information as to spatial organization, form, color, materials, and user potential. These more refined drawings are termed **presentation drawings** and are used by the designer to communicate ideas to the client or user group, to sell ideas, and to get additional feedback for later design refinement. Typical titles for such presentation drawings are Preliminary Plan, Master Plan, and Proposed Development Plan.

Graphic Character and Media

Although the initial drawings are usually very rough and very preliminary, they do need to show specific shapes, materials, and spaces for the designer's evaluation. (See pages 21 and 23.)

The refined presentation drawings need to be fairly realistic and convincing, because they are usually reviewed by the client. A combination of plan view, sections, and perspectives with color are most effective. They need to be self-explanatory, with script limited to brief labels. Rough models or photographic presentations are also effective. Presentation drawings require a fairly durable surface medium, such as marker paper, heavy print paper, or board-mounted artwork.

A combination of freehand and mechanical drawing techniques is necessary. Computer graphics can be very useful, especially in the rapid production of various perspective views. Computer graphics can be used as they are or can be enhanced with freehand additions.

Design Development Drawing

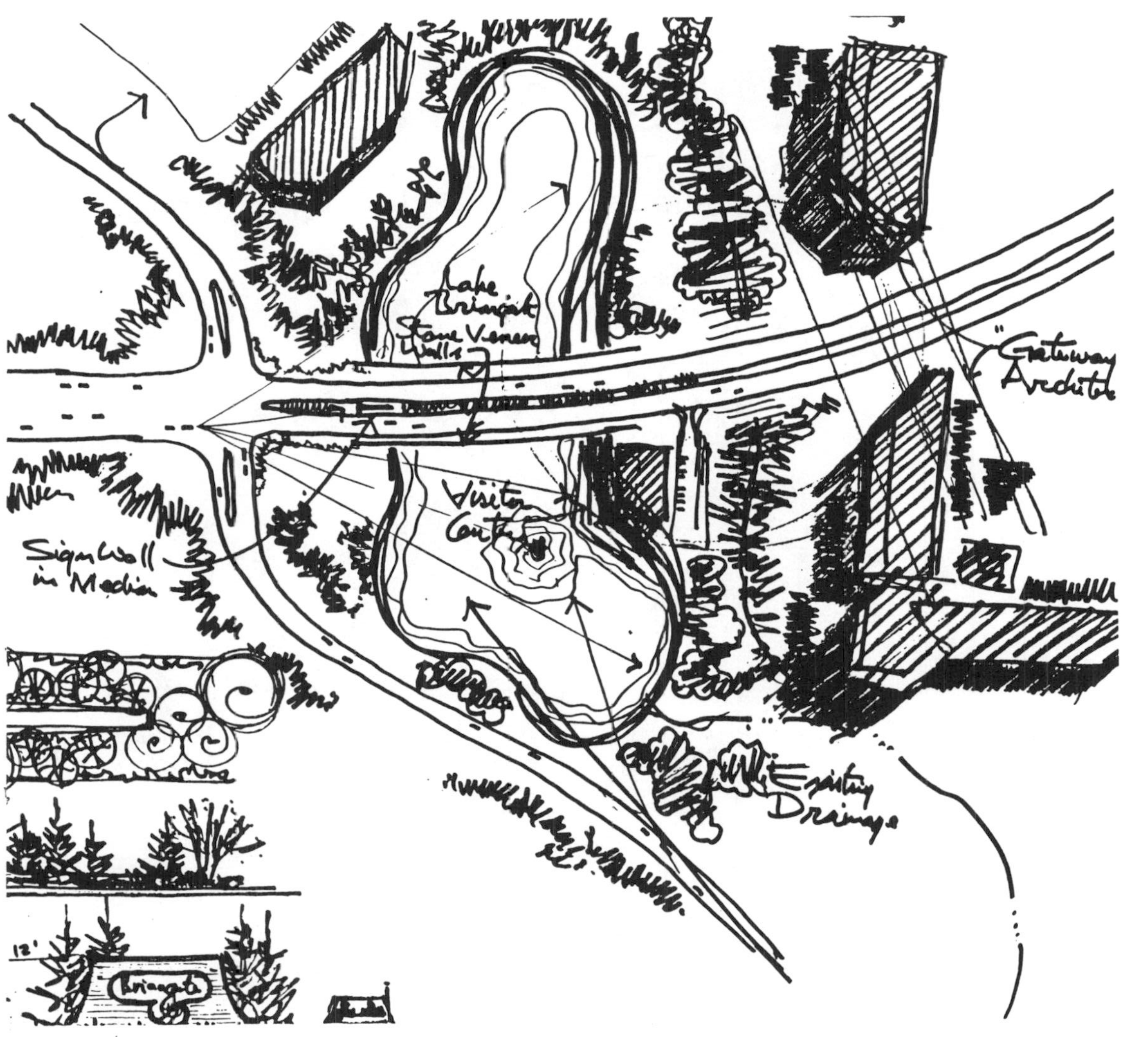

Concept Plan

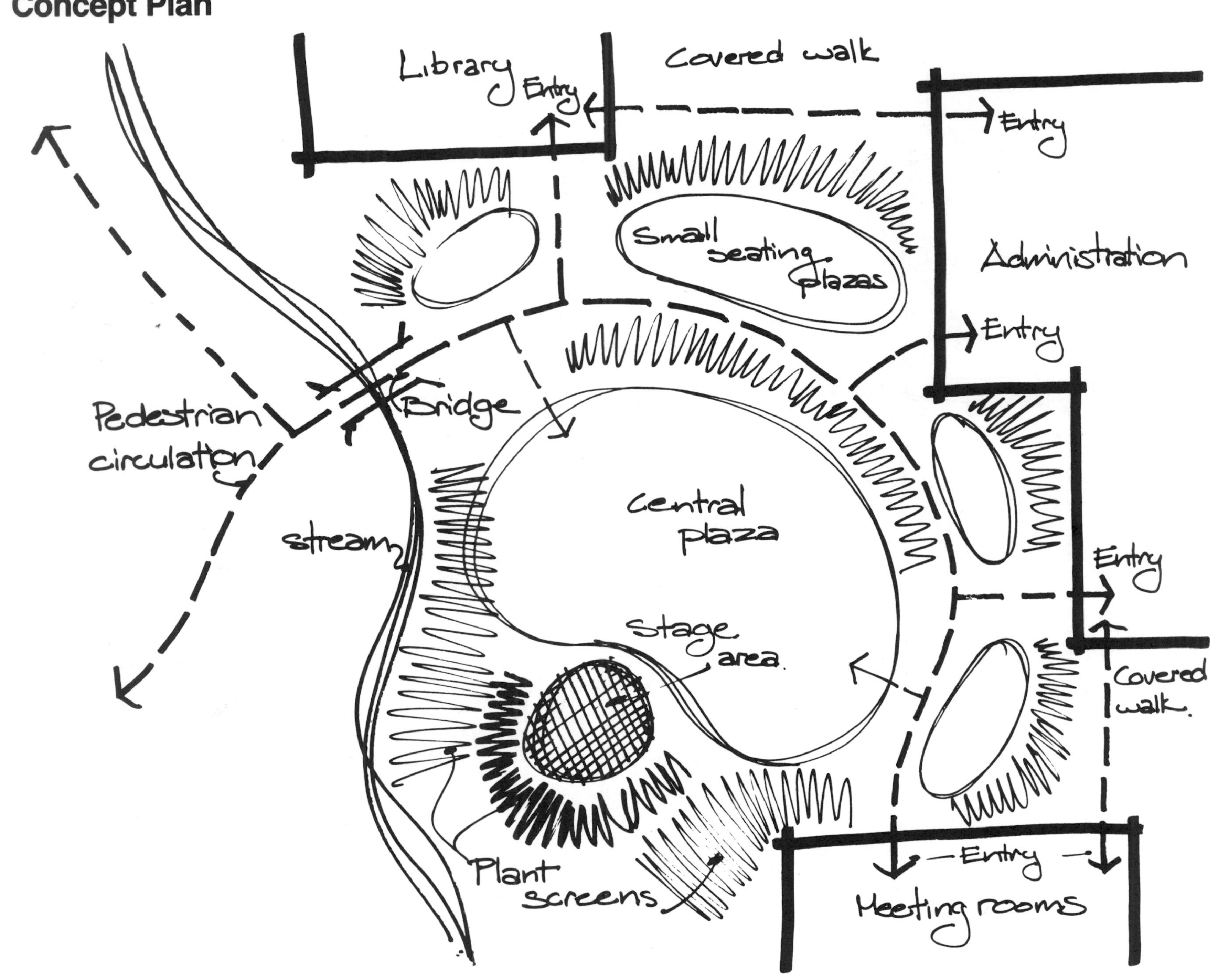

Design Development Sketch

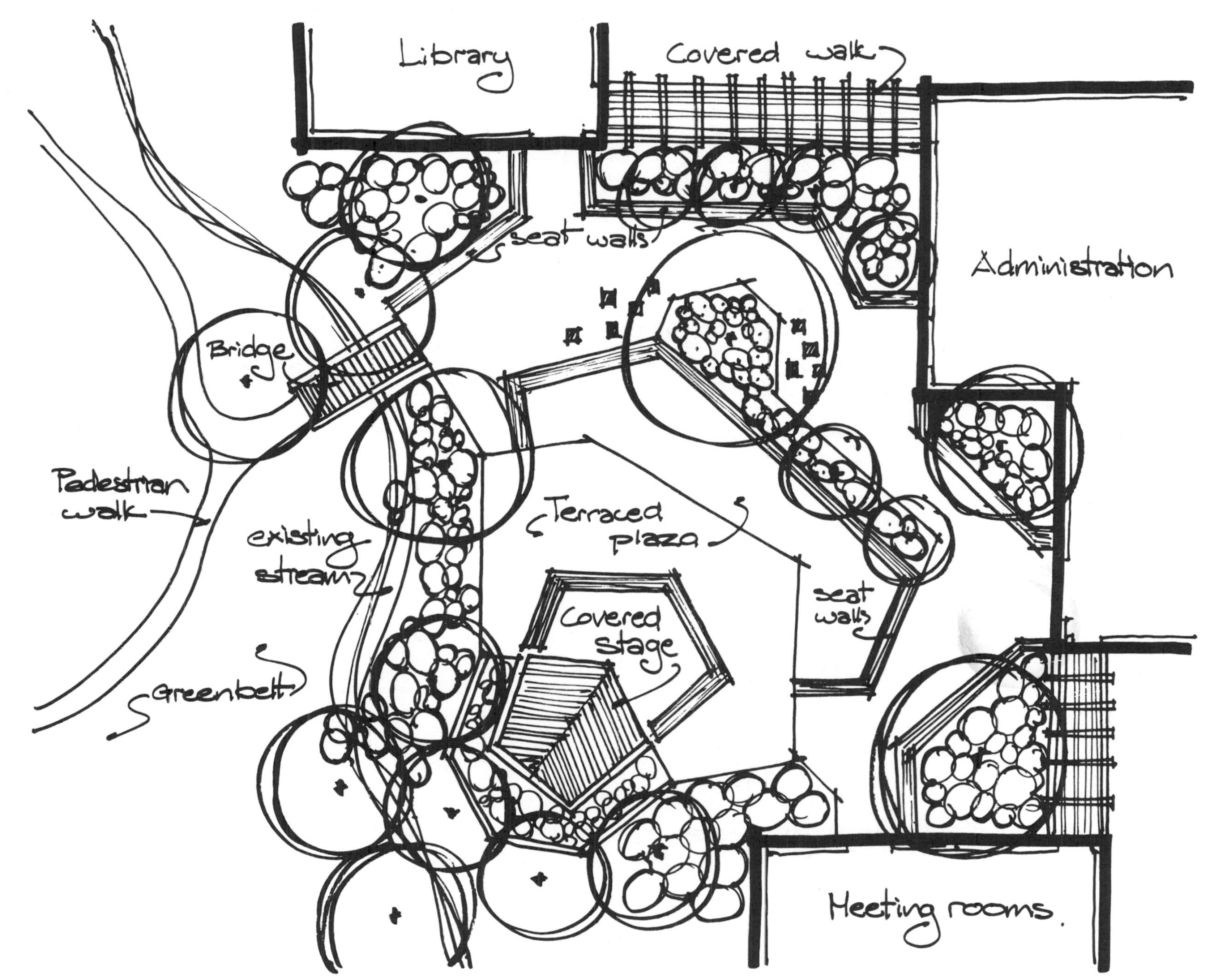

Preliminary Plan (partial)

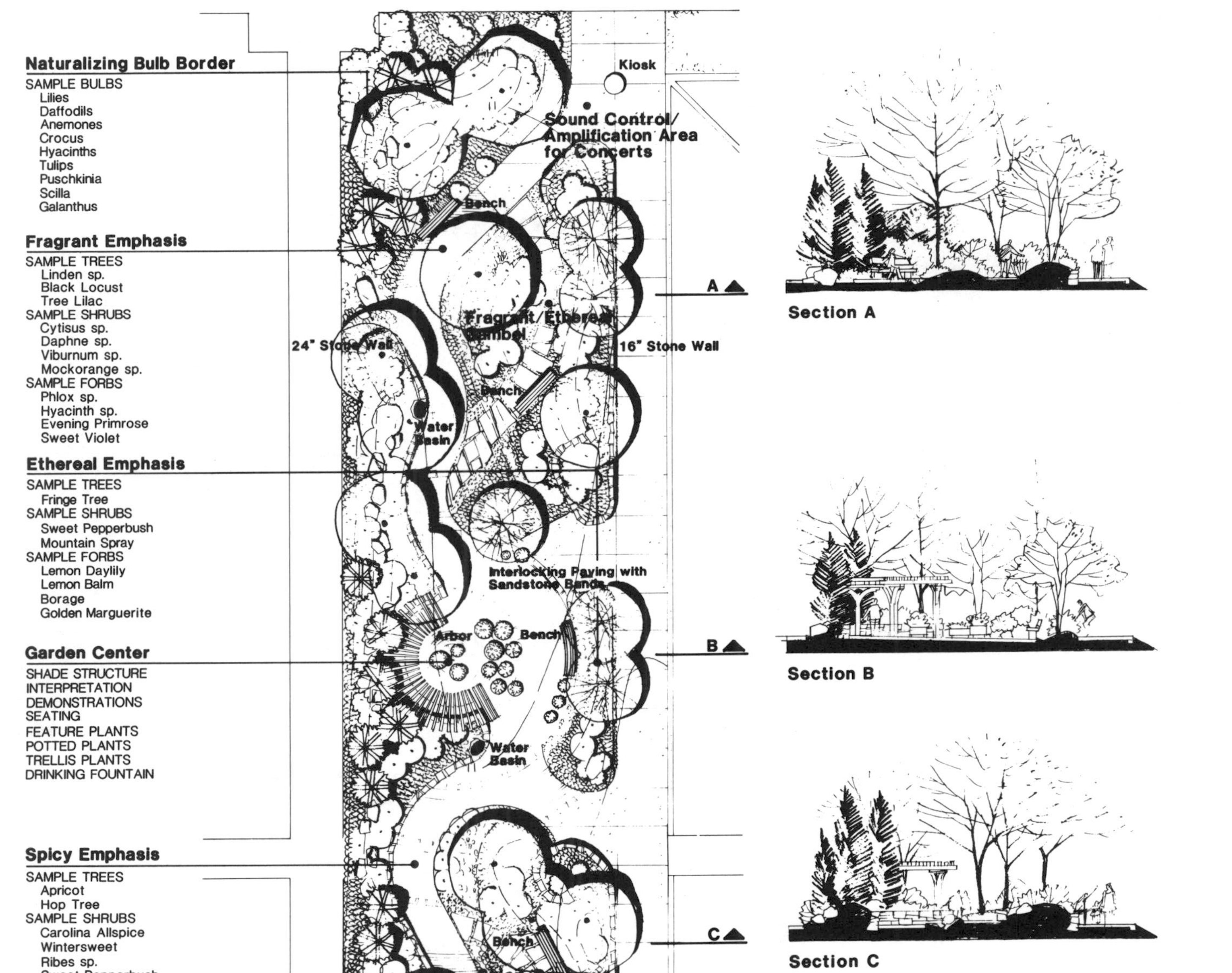

Master Plan

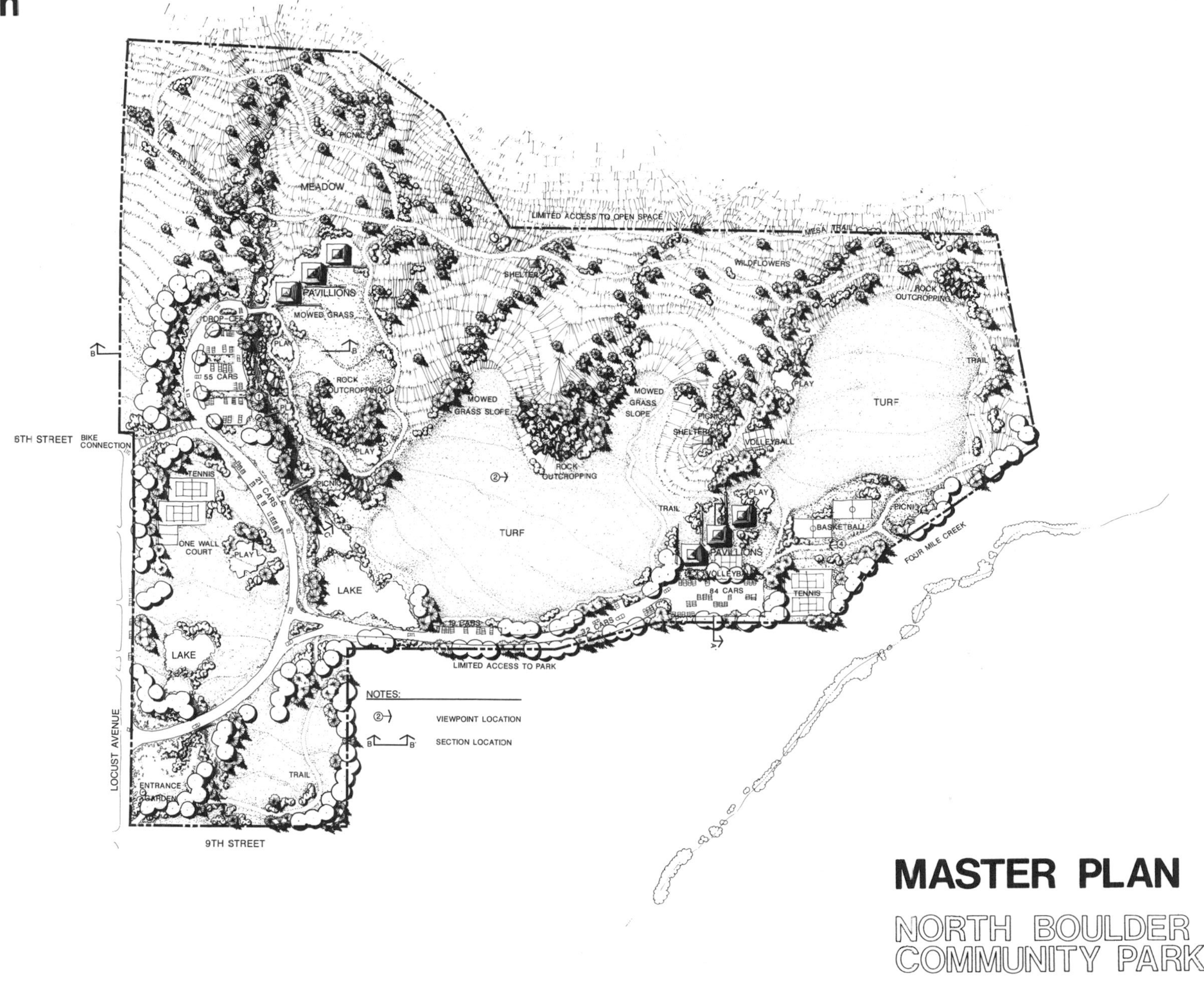

MASTER PLAN

NORTH BOULDER COMMUNITY PARK

CITY OF BOULDER PARKS AND RECREATION DEPARTMENT
BOULDER, COLORADO

WINSTON ASSOCIATES
1426 PEARL STREET MALL
BOULDER COLORADO 80302
(303) 440 9200

SCALE: 1" 100'-00"
DATE: JULY 10, 1986

CITY of BOULDER

Final Design

Content and Purpose

The landscape architect's final ideas, once they are approved by the client, need to be communicated to the people who will build the project. A series of construction **implementation documents** that contain working drawings must be produced for use by the various installation contractors. Along with detailed written instructions, called construction specifications, go a set of drawings that show exact sizes, shapes, quantities, types, and locations of all elements. Contractors use these documents initially to prepare prices and bids. A typical set of landscape working drawings may contain a site plan, grading plans, layout plans, irrigation plans, planting plans, and detail sheets.

Graphic Character and Media

Technical drafting is used to produce working drawings, although some freehand graphics are needed for lettering and organic symbols. The graphics must be complete, accurate, and very easy to read. Since multiple copies must be made of each finished drawing, the media used are pencil on vellum or ink on Mylar. Precision and good line quality are essential characteristics. Color is not necessary. For many kinds of projects, the computer generation of construction documents can save a significant amount of time.

Grading Plan

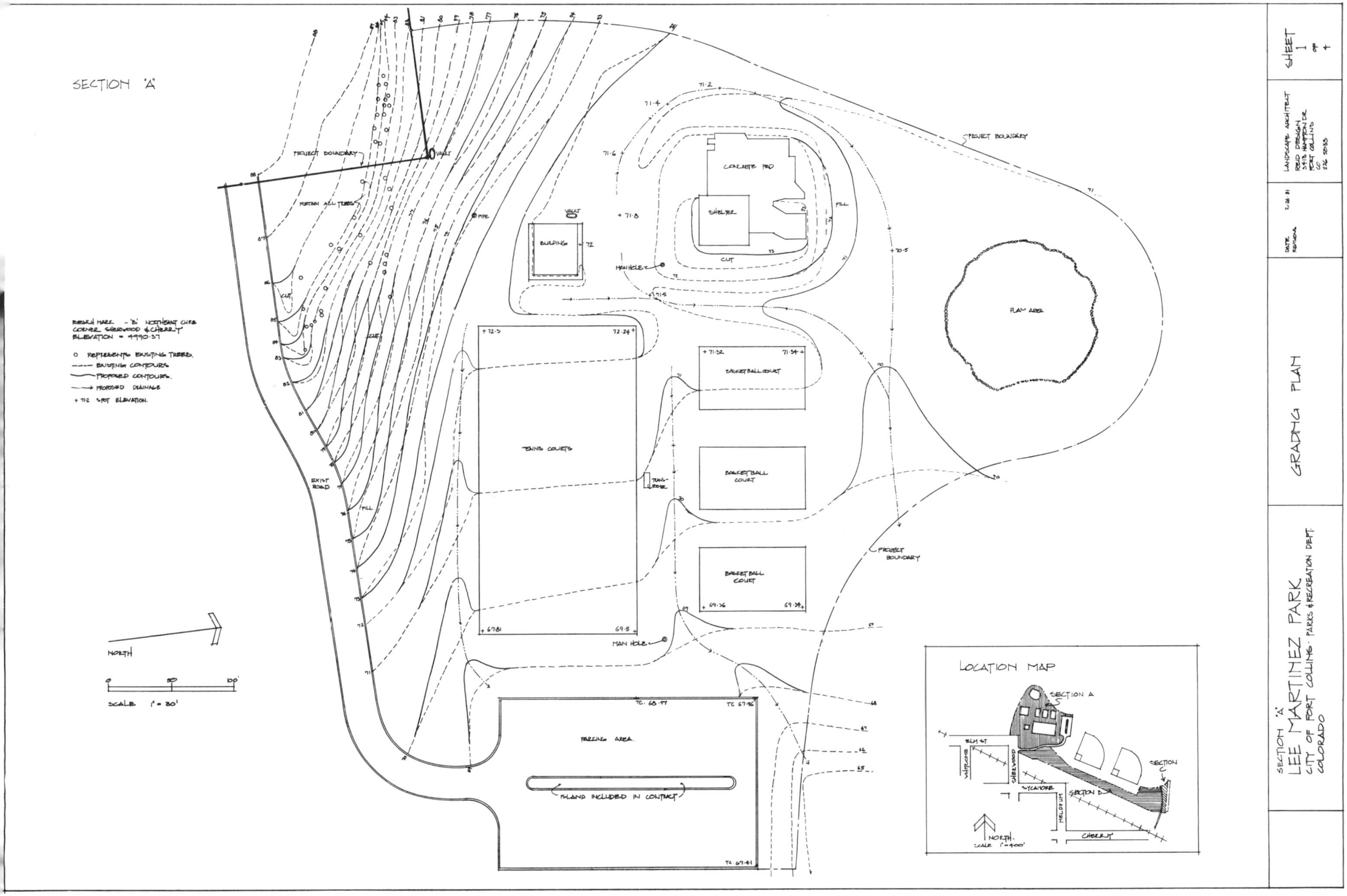

SECTION 'A'
BENCH MARK - 'B' NORTHEAST CURB CORNER SHERWOOD & CHERRY ELEVATION = 4990.37
o REPRESENTS EXISTING TREES.
EXISTING CONTOURS.
PROPOSED CONTOURS.
PROPOSED DRAINAGE
+ 71.2 SPOT ELEVATION.
NORTH
SCALE 1" = 30'
PROJECT BOUNDARY
RETAIN ALL TREES
VAULT
BUILDING
CONCRETE PAD
SHELTER
CUT
FILL
MANHOLE
TENNIS COURTS
BASKETBALL COURT
TRANS-FORMER
MAN HOLE
EXIT ROAD
PARKING AREA
ISLAND INCLUDED IN CONTRACT
PLAY AREA
LOCATION MAP
SECTION A
SECTION B
SECTION C
ELM ST
WHITCOMB
SHERWOOD
SYCAMORE
MELDRUM
CHERRY
SCALE 1" = 400'
SECTION 'A'
LEE MARTINEZ PARK
CITY OF FORT COLLINS · PARKS & RECREATION DEPT.
COLORADO
GRADING PLAN
DATE 2.26.81
LANDSCAPE ARCHITECT
REID DESIGN
3418 HAMPTON DR.
FORT COLLINS
CO
226 5085
SHEET 1 OF 4

Shows earth movement, drainage, and spot elevations of structures.

30% of actual size

Layout Plan

Shows location, size, shape, dimensions, and materials of structural elements.

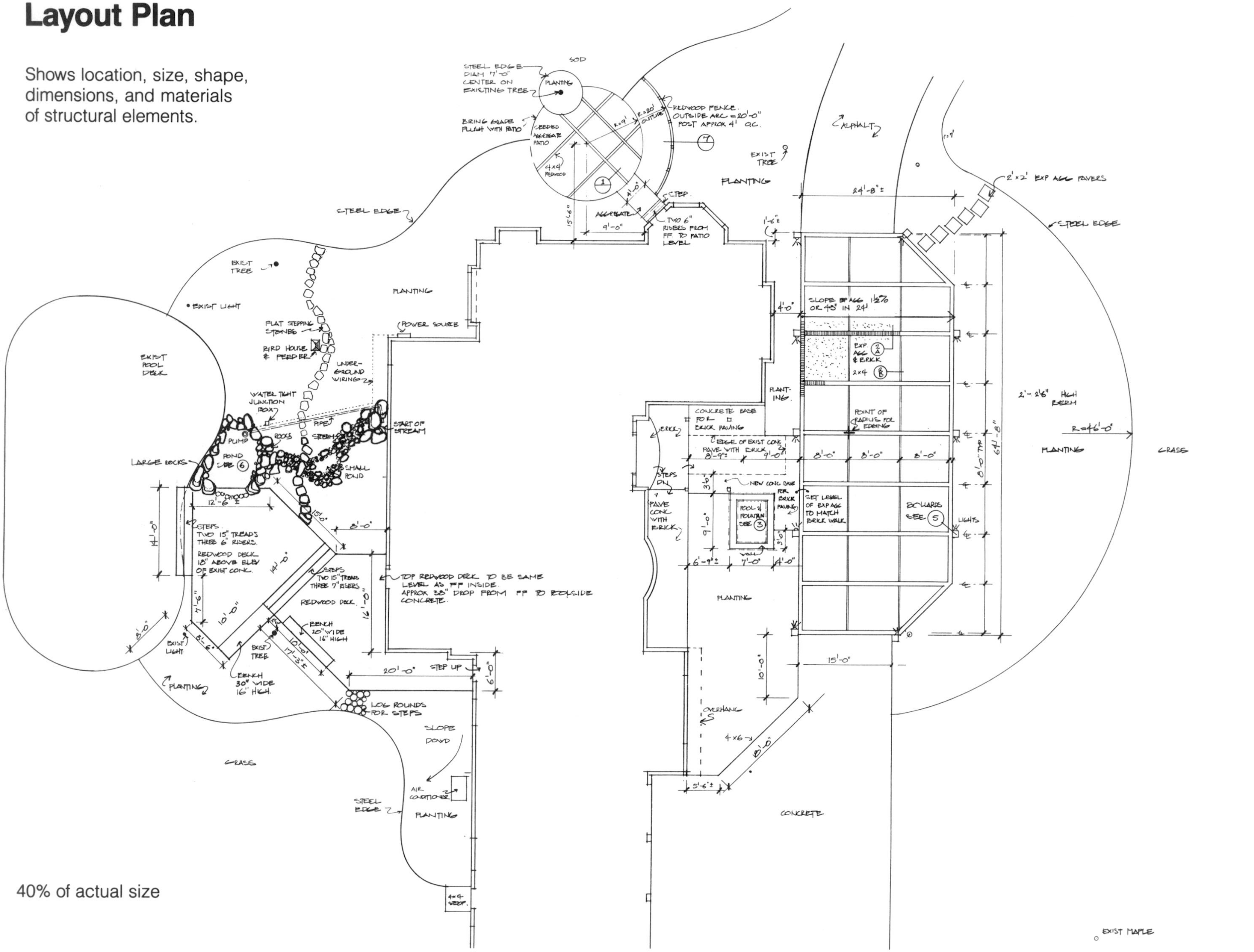

40% of actual size

Irrigation Plan

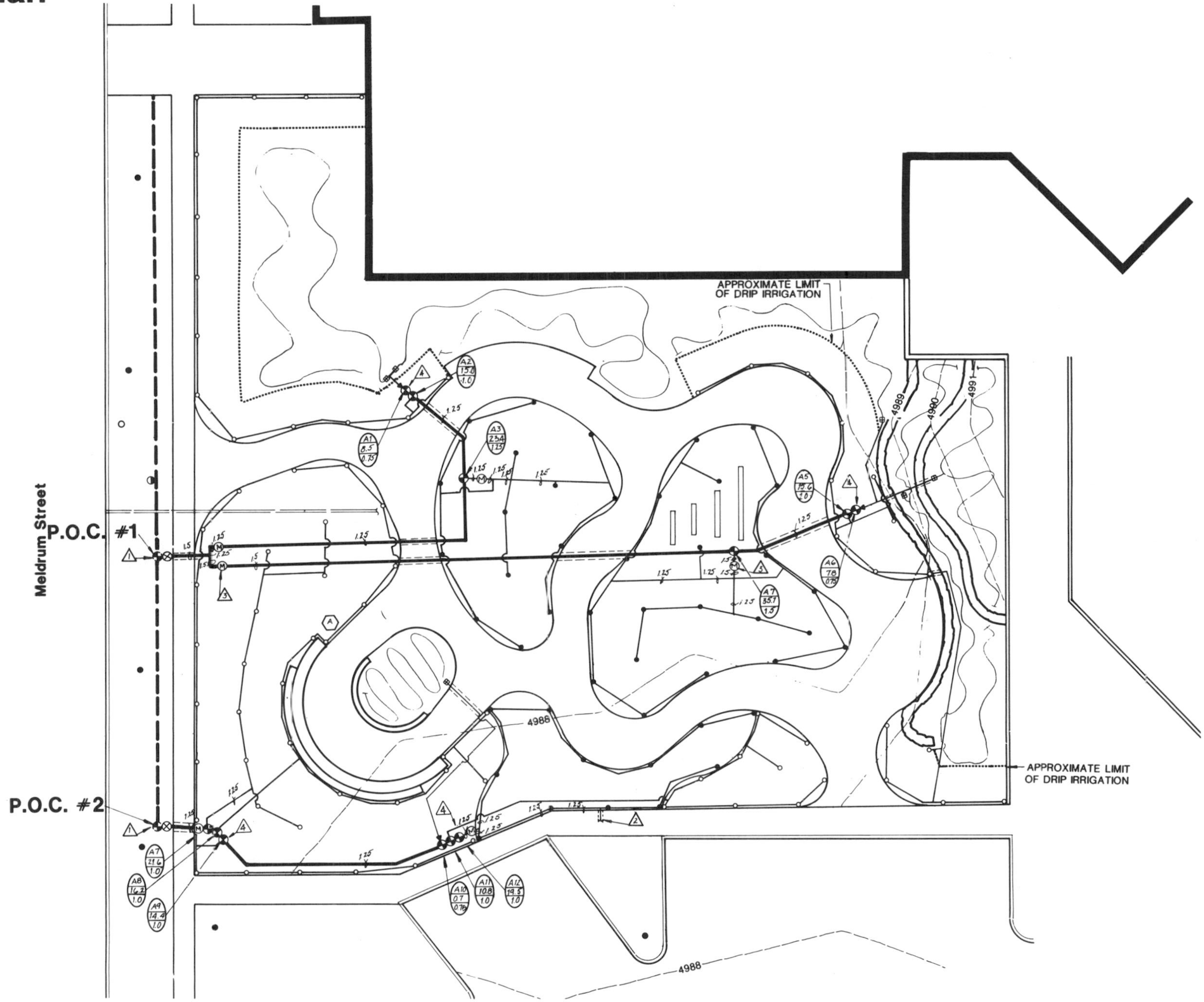

Meldrum Street
P.O.C. #1
P.O.C. #2
APPROXIMATE LIMIT OF DRIP IRRIGATION
APPROXIMATE LIMIT OF DRIP IRRIGATION
4988
4988
4989
4990
4991

Shows type, size, and location of conduit, heads, valves, sleeves, and other elements of the irrigation system.

40% of actual size

Preliminary Landscape Plans

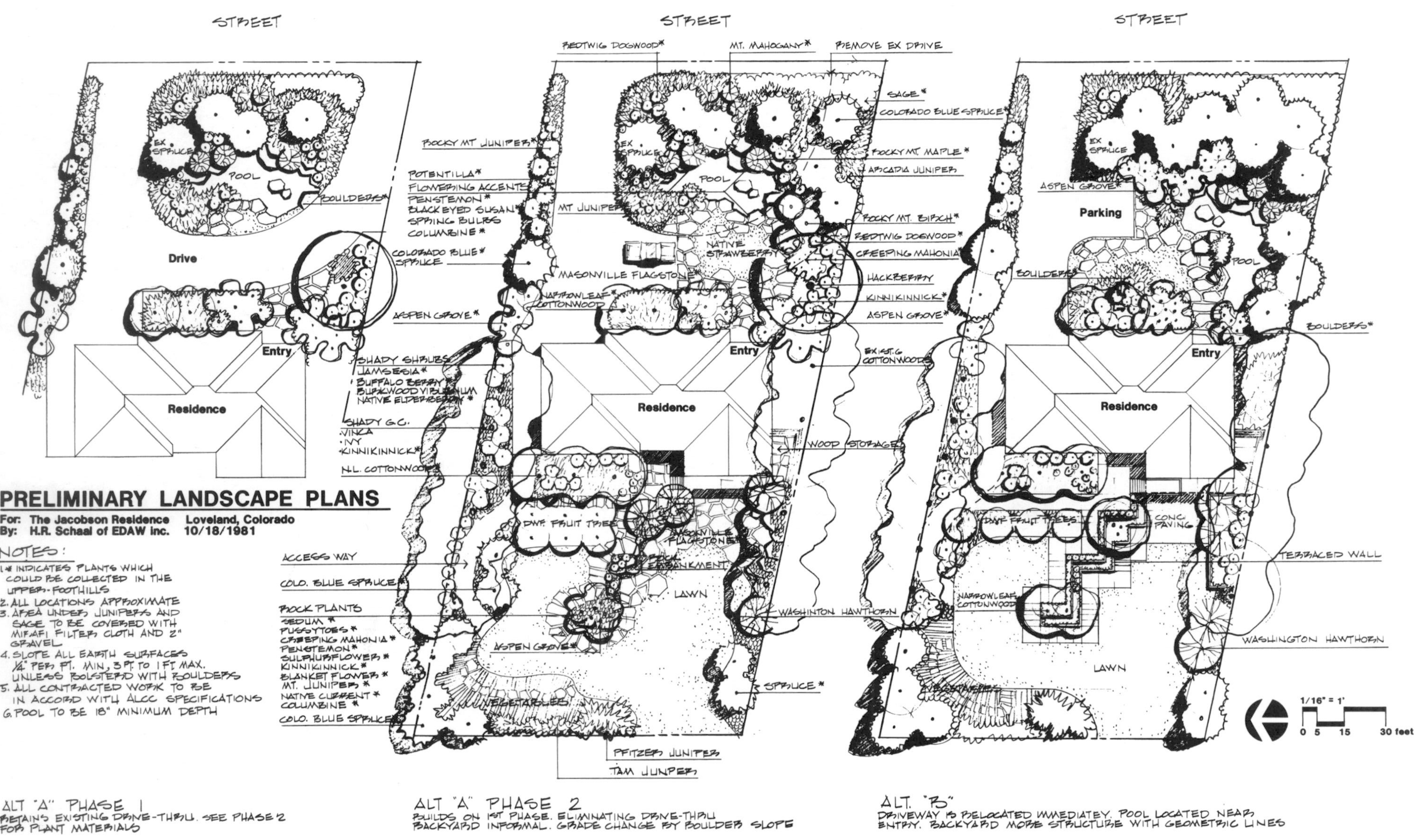

30% of actual size

Preliminary Planting Design Drawing

Rough freehand drawing that explores the optimum selection, location, and combination of plants.

A true planting plan for installation will be derived from this.

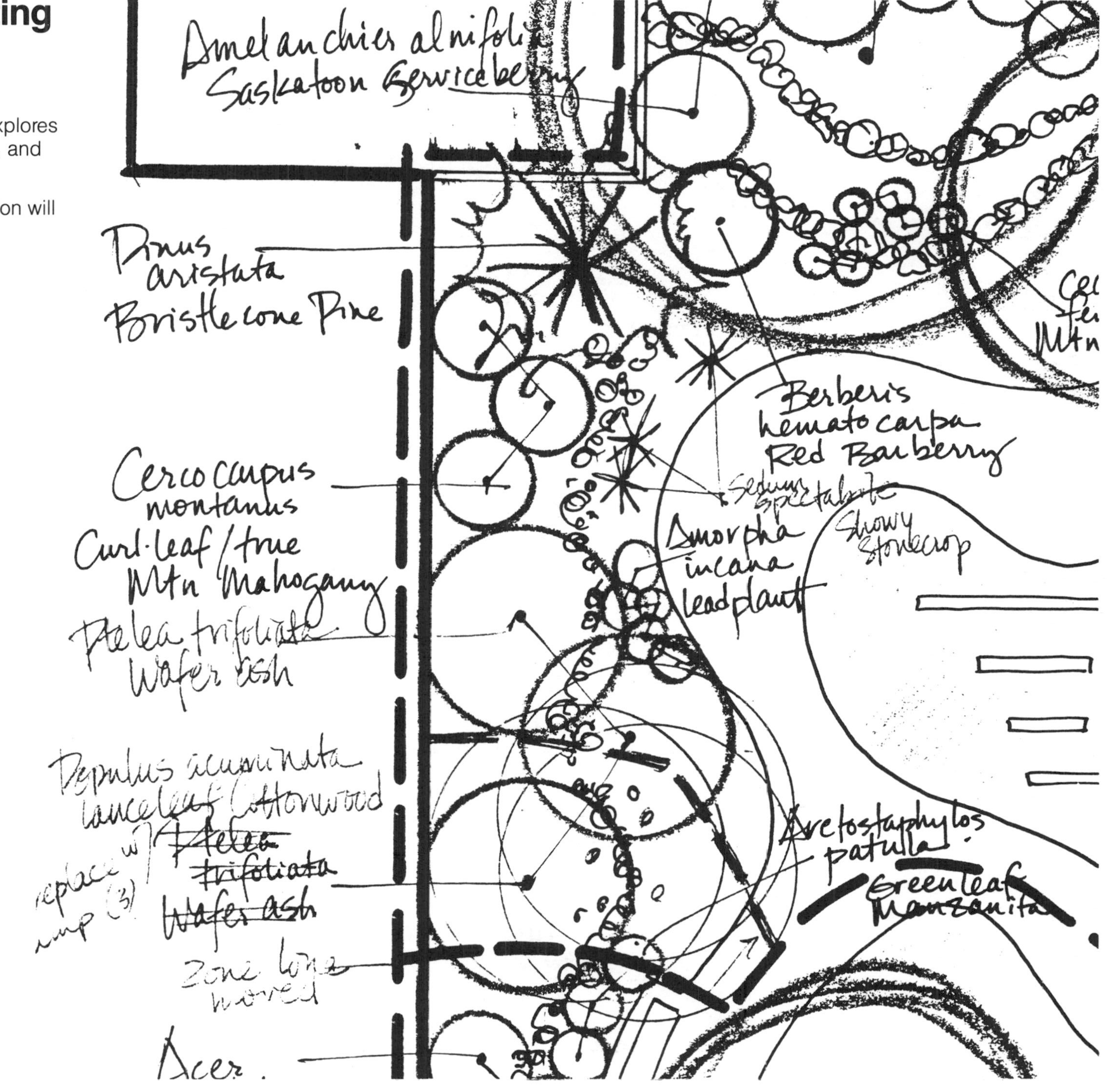

Detail shown actual size

Planting Plans

Final document used for installation of plant materials. Precise locations are shown.

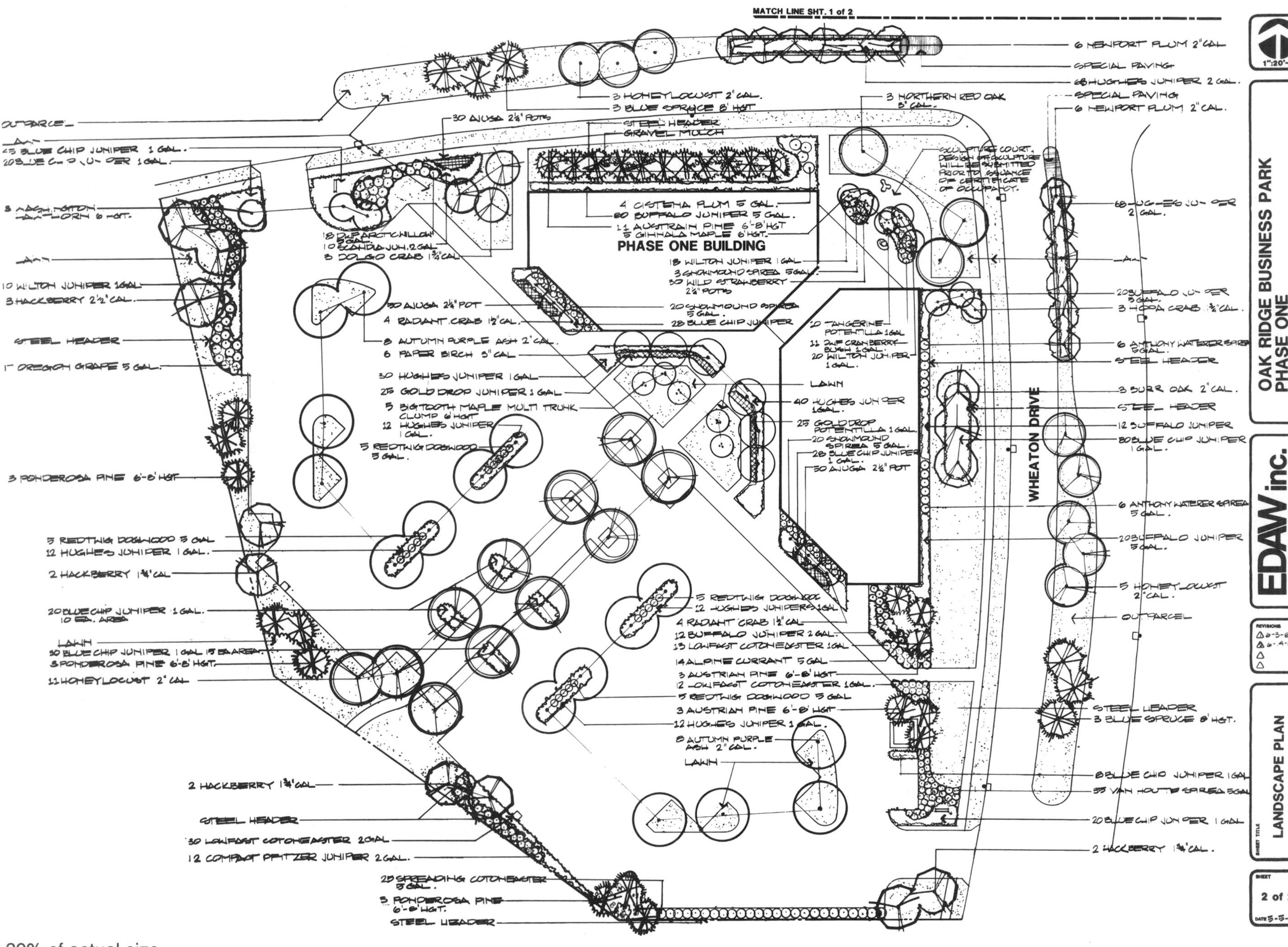

30% of actual size

Planting plans usually identify each plant by its common name and its botanical name. Sizes and quantities are also important.

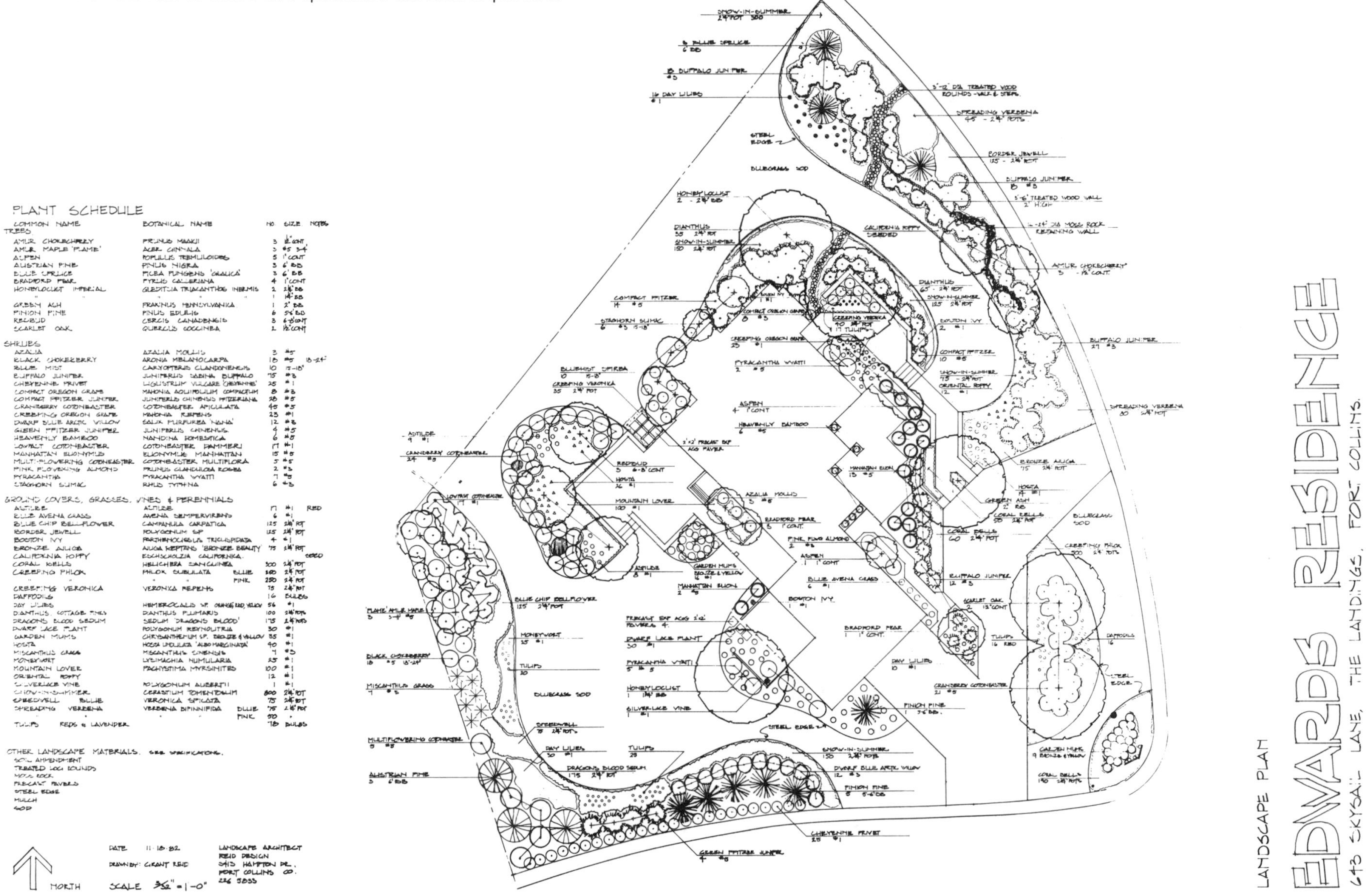

PLANT SCHEDULE

COMMON NAME	BOTANICAL NAME	NO.	SIZE	NOTES
TREES				
AMUR CHOKECHERRY	PRUNUS MAAKII	3	1" CONT	
AMUR MAPLE 'FLAME'	ACER GINNALA	3	#5 3-4'	
ASPEN	POPULUS TREMULOIDES	5	1" CONT	
AUSTRIAN PINE	PINUS NIGRA	3	6' BB	
BLUE SPRUCE	PICEA PUNGENS 'GLAUCA'	3	6' BB	
BRADFORD PEAR	PYRUS CALLERIANA	4	1" CONT	
HONEYLOCUST IMPERIAL	GLEDITSIA TRIACANTHOS INERMIS	2	2¼" BB	
" "	" " "	1	1¼" BB	
GREEN ASH	FRAXINUS PENNSYLVANICA	1	2" BB	
PINION PINE	PINUS EDULIS	6	5-6' BB	
REDBUD	CERCIS CANADENSIS	3	6-8' CONT	
SCARLET OAK	QUERCUS COCCINEA	2	1½" CONT	
SHRUBS				
AZALIA	AZALIA MOLLIS	3	#5	
BLACK CHOKEBERRY	ARONIA MELANOCARPA	18	#5	18-24"
BLUE MIST	CARYOPTERIS CLANDONENSIS	10	15-18"	
BUFFALO JUNIPER	JUNIPERUS SABINA BUFFALO	75	#3	
CHEYENNE PRIVET	LIGUSTRUM VULGARE 'CHEYENNE'	25	#1	
COMPACT OREGON GRAPE	MAHONIA AQUIFOLIUM COMPACTUM	8	#3	
COMPACT PFITZER JUNIPER	JUNIPERUS CHINENSIS PFITZERIANA	28	#5	
CRANBERRY COTONEASTER	COTONEASTER APICULATA	45	#5	
CREEPING OREGON GRAPE	MAHONIA REPENS	23	#1	
DWARF BLUE ARCTIC WILLOW	SALIX PURPUREA 'NANA'	12	#3	
GREEN PFITZER JUNIPER	JUNIPERUS CHINENSIS	4	#5	
HEAVENLY BAMBOO	NANDINA DOMESTICA	6	#5	
LOWFAST COTONEASTER	COTONEASTER DAMMERI	17	#1	
MANHATTAN EUONYMUS	EUONYMUS MANHATTAN	15	#5	
MULTI-FLOWERING COTONEASTER	COTONEASTER MULTIFLORA	5	#5	
PINK FLOWERING ALMOND	PRUNUS GLANDULOSA ROSEA	2	#3	
PYRACANTHA	PYRACANTHA WYATTI	7	#5	
STAGHORN SUMAC	RHUS TYPHINA	6	#3	
GROUND COVERS, GRASSES, VINES & PERENNIALS				
ASTILBE	ASTILBE	17	#1	RED
BLUE AVENA GRASS	AVENA SEMPERVIRENS	6	#1	
BLUE CHIP BELLFLOWER	CAMPANULA CARPATICA	125	2¼" POT	
BORDER JEWELL	POLYGONUM SP	125	2¼" POT	
BOSTON IVY	PARTHENOCISSUS TRICUSPIDATA	4	#1	
BRONZE AJUGA	AJUGA REPTANS 'BRONZE BEAUTY'	75	2¼" POT	
CALIFORNIA POPPY	ESCHSCHOLZIA CALIFORNICA			SEED
CORAL BELLS	HEUCHERA SANGUINEA	300	2¼" POT	
CREEPING PHLOX	PHLOX SUBULATA BLUE	180	2¼" POT	
" "	" " PINK	250	2¼" POT	
CREEPING VERONICA	VERONICA REPENS	75	2¼" POT	
DAFFODILS		16	BULBS	
DAY LILIES	HEMEROCALLIS SP. ORANGE, RED, YELLOW	56	#1	
DIANTHUS, COTTAGE PINKS	DIANTHUS PLUMARIS	100	2¼" POTS	
DRAGONS BLOOD SEDUM	SEDUM 'DRAGONS BLOOD'	175	2¼" POTS	
DWARF LACE PLANT	POLYGONUM REYNOUTRIA	30	#1	
GARDEN MUMS	CHRYSANTHEMUM SP. BRONZE & YELLOW	35	#1	
HOSTA	HOSTA UNDULATA 'ALBO MARGINATA'	40	#1	
MISCANTHUS GRASS	MISCANTHUS SINENSIS	7	#5	
MONEYWORT	LYSIMACHIA NUMULARIA	25	#1	
MOUNTAIN LOVER	PACHYSTIMA MYRSINITES	100	#1	
ORIENTAL POPPY		12	#1	
SILVERLACE VINE	POLYGONUM AUBERTII	1	#1	
SNOW-IN-SUMMER	CERASTIUM TOMENTOSUM	800	2¼" POT	
SPEEDWELL BLUE	VERONICA SPICATA	75	2¼" POT	
SPREADING VERBENA	VERBENA BIPINNIFIDA BLUE	75	2¼" POT	
" "	" " PINK	50	"	
TULIPS REDS & LAVENDER		78	BULBS	

OTHER LANDSCAPE MATERIALS. SEE SPECIFICATIONS.
- SOIL AMMENDMENT
- TREATED LOG ROUNDS
- MOSS ROCK
- PRECAST PAVERS
- STEEL EDGE
- MULCH
- SOD

NORTH

DATE 11-18-82
DRAWN BY: GRANT REID
SCALE 3/32" = 1'-0"

LANDSCAPE ARCHITECT
REID DESIGN
3413 HAMPTON DR.
FORT COLLINS CO.
226 5833

LANDSCAPE PLAN

EDWARDS RESIDENCE

643 SKYSAIL LANE, THE LANDINGS, FORT COLLINS

30% of actual size

Planting Plan

Portion of a planting plan.
Letter symbols are keyed to plant names.

Actual size

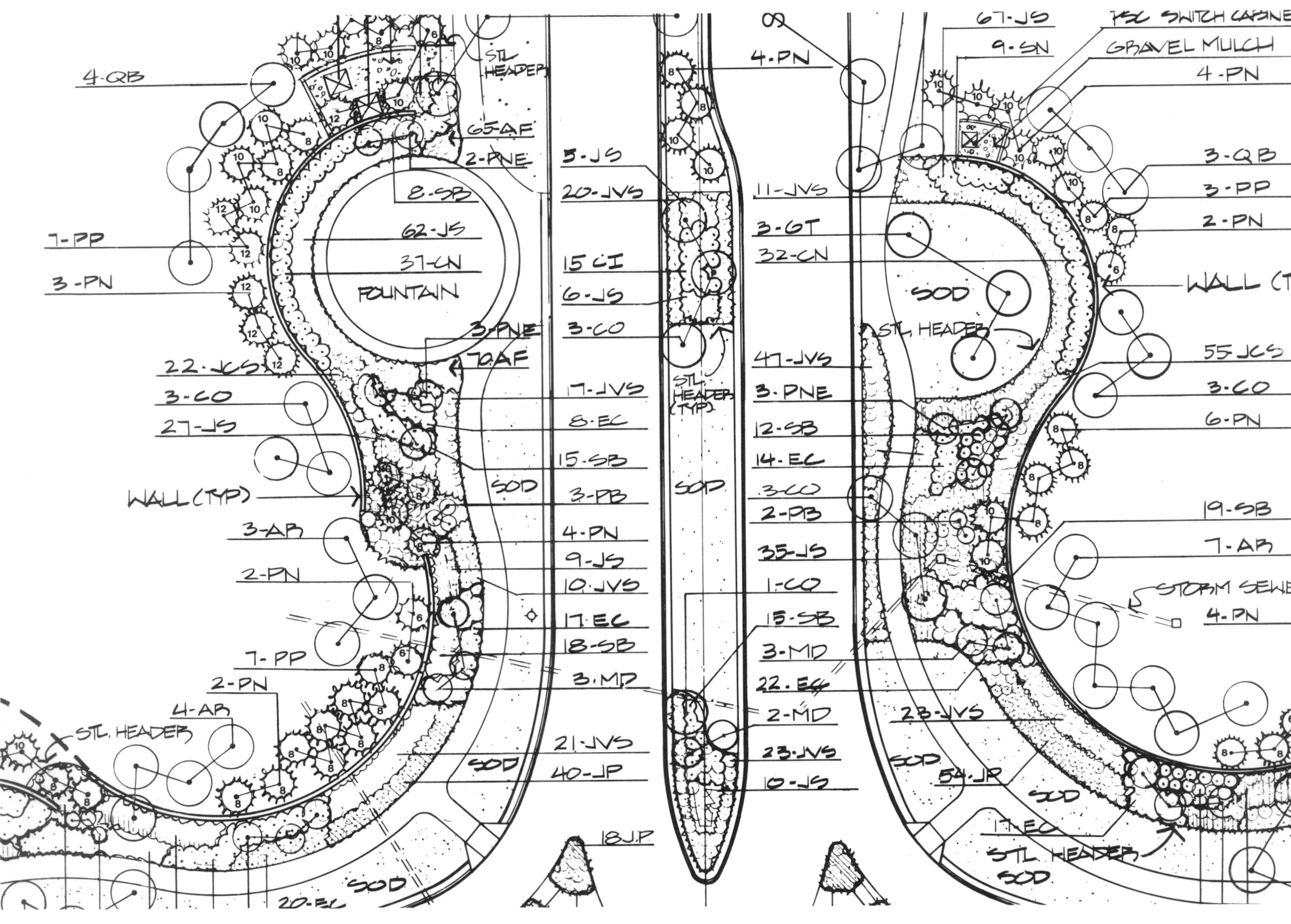

Construction Details

Usually expanded sections and plans, this kind of working drawing shows the detailed components of structures, including internal elements, and how they go together.

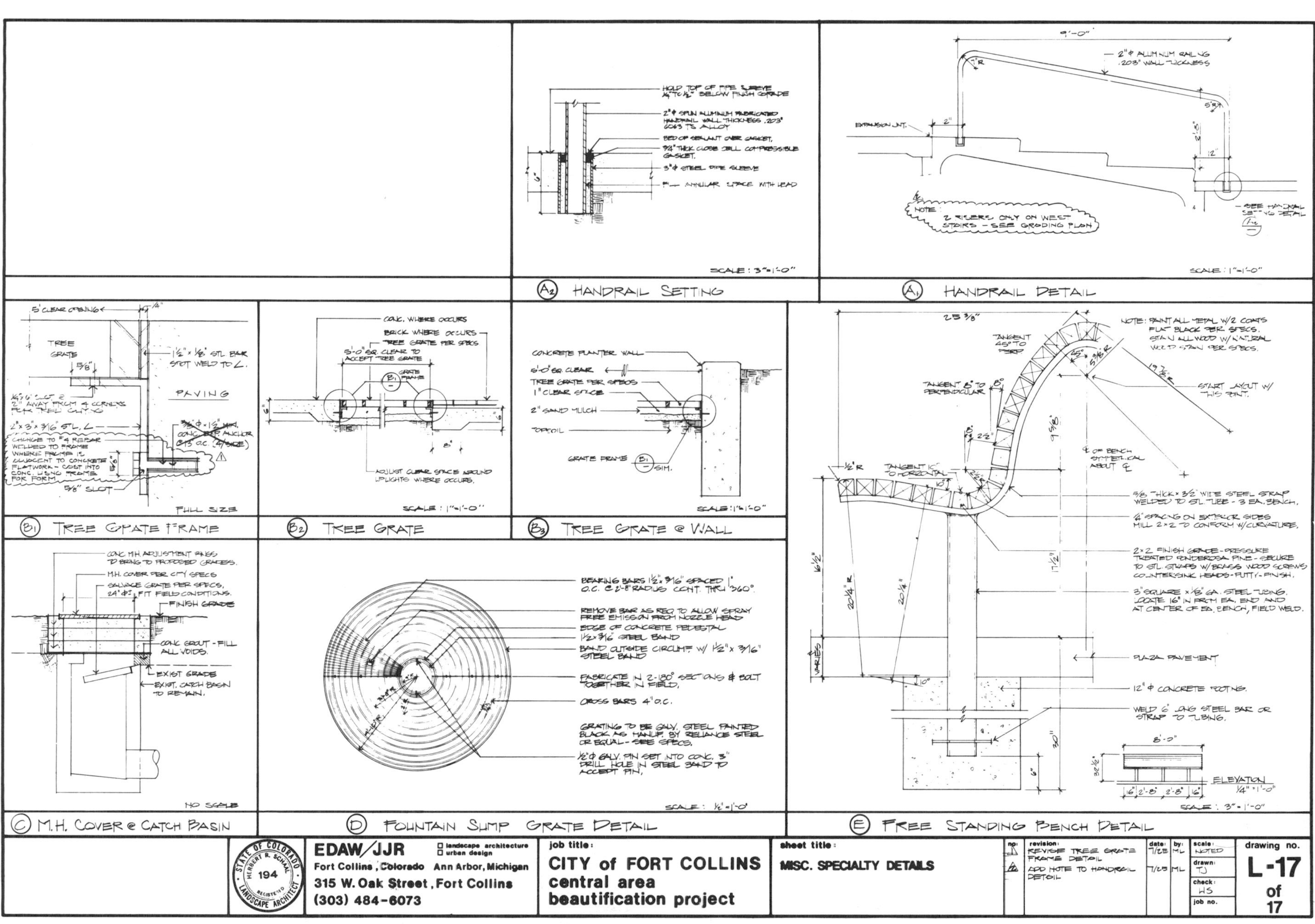

33% of actual size

2 Freehand Drawing

The very first graphic ideas in the design process are best expressed with freehand drawings. Concept drawings, thumbnail sketches, and preliminary plan ideas are all open, honest, free-flowing drawings that use few, if any, drafting aids or techniques. A more accurate label for freehand drawings would be "free arm drawings," because it is the fluid coordination of all arm joints (including the elbow and shoulder joints) that come into play more so than the finger and hand joints.

Exercises 1 through 9 in Appendix IV are useful for getting loosened up with freehand techniques.

Tools and Materials

Choose the drawing tools that allow smooth, easy, gliding strokes with expressive line character. These are soft graphite-based tools, felt tip pens, and sketch fountain pens.

Soft graphite smudges easily, but allows a variety of very dark and very light lines. The ordinary 4B or 6B lead pencil sharpened to a point gives a fine line and, chiseled down, gives a wide line.

Lead holders are available for large diameter (3 mm) sketch leads, which are very good for bold preliminary work.

Graphite sticks get a little messy but are excellent for drawing fast, wide lines and for toning larger areas. The larger stick has a 1.35 cm width and the smaller stick has a 7 mm width.

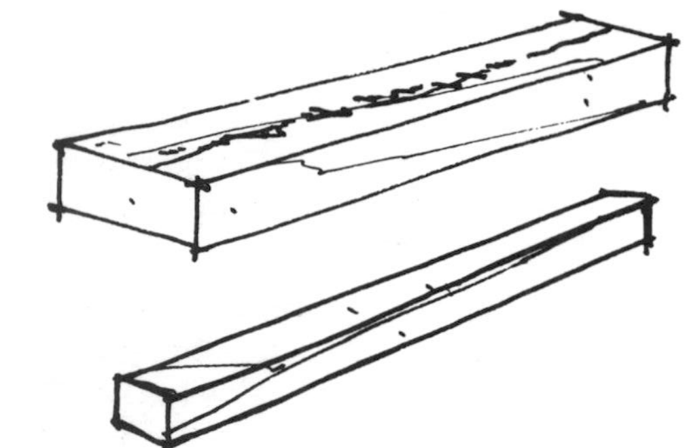

The flat sketch pencil, or carpenter's pencil, has a rectangular cross section in the lead which allows very broad strokes.

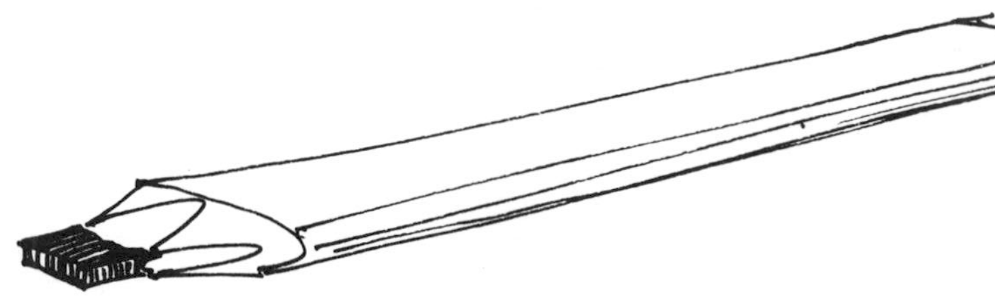

More stable sketching media that will not smear or smudge include the following:

Soft color rendering pencil

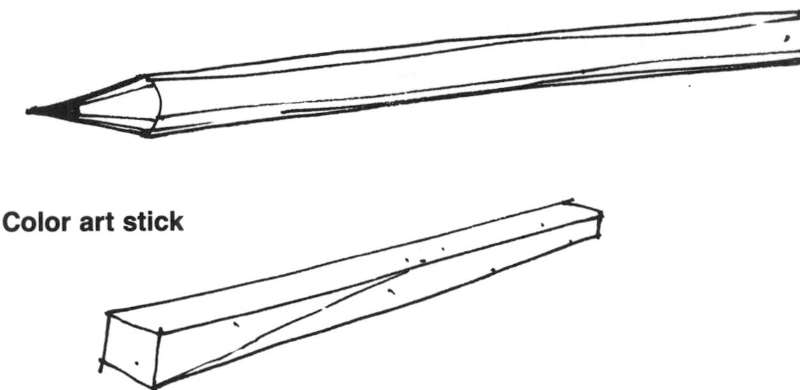

Color art stick

Harder and more waxy than graphite, this product works well for sketching on Mylar.

Felt tip pens are available in an almost unlimited variety of shapes and sizes. It is handy to have a range of point sizes, as shown in the small number of examples below.

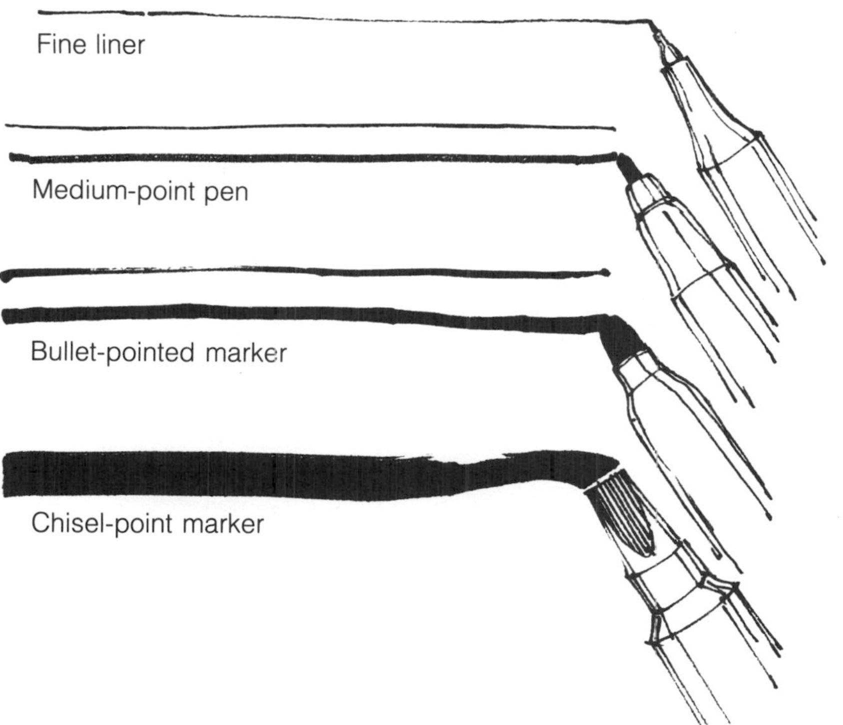

Ink fountain sketch pens give strong black lines. Pressure variation yields interesting changes in line weight. A smooth surface is needed for good results.

Sketching surfaces, such as lightweight tracing paper ("flimsy" or "bum wad"), comes in rolls of various widths. The common colors are white, yellow, or buff (canary paper). This is used for freehand design development drawings, refinement overlays, and quick sketches. It is inexpensive and yet transparent enough to print, although it is not recommenced for finished drawings because it is easily ripped. Best results are obtained with a felt tip pen or a soft pencil. A backing sheet is needed for use with markers.

Sketch paper in many different brands is available in varying weights, surfaces, finishes, and transparencies. Select a surface which suits the type of sketching tool and the effect desired. Smooth, dense surfaces are good for detailed, fine line drawings. Coarser papers provide textured interest for pencil toning. Special dense, smooth papers are available for ink sketching. For reproducible work, use the more stable transparent sketch papers.

Bleed-proof marker papers are specially treated to prevent marker fluid from bleeding through. Some lateral bleeding should be expected, but this varies significantly from one brand to another. For some drawings, lateral bleeding and blending is desirable; for others, crisper lines and detail are needed.

Some marker papers have high-contrast, dense white surfaces and are not meant for reproduction. Others have a degree of transparency that allows for printing. Select the brand to suit the purpose.

Butcher paper or freezer paper can be bought in large rolls and is excellent for outsized conceptual or preliminary drawings done with markers, though not for reproduction.

Drafting film, such as Mylar, is traditionally used with ink for technical drawings, but it is also a versatile surface for pencil sketching. A wide range of tone densities can be easily and quickly drawn on the finely toothed surface. The best sketch tools for Mylar are the sharp 2B pencil, the flat sketch pencil, the graphite block, or the more waxy art sticks.

Techniques

Keep the pencil or pen at a low angle and hold with a relaxed grip. Practice sketching. Coordinate all of the arm and hand joints together. Note how different joints come into play when sketching the five types of lines discussed here.

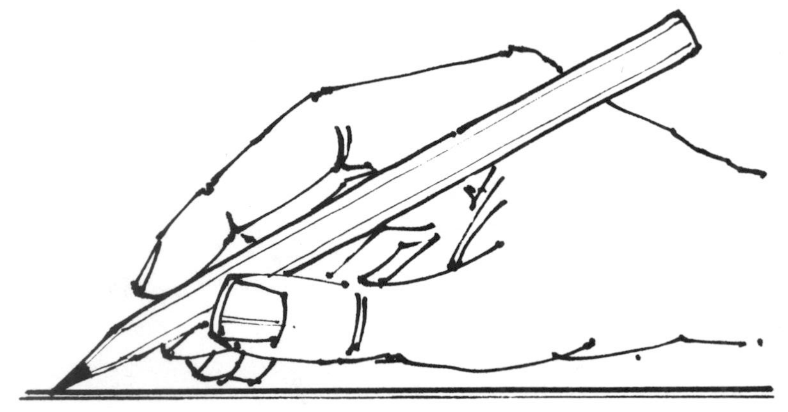

Free-flowing lines
In drawing curved, interconnected lines over a relatively large surface area or sheet, the forearm is not supported and the wrist is held rigid. All movement comes from the elbow and shoulder with the small fingers gliding across the surface for stability. There is no finger or wrist movement.

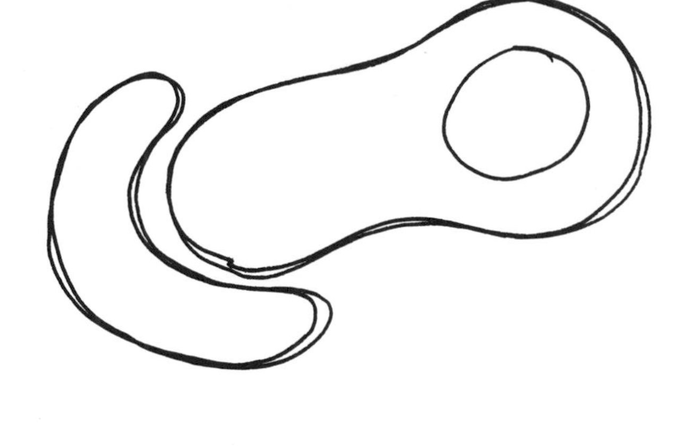

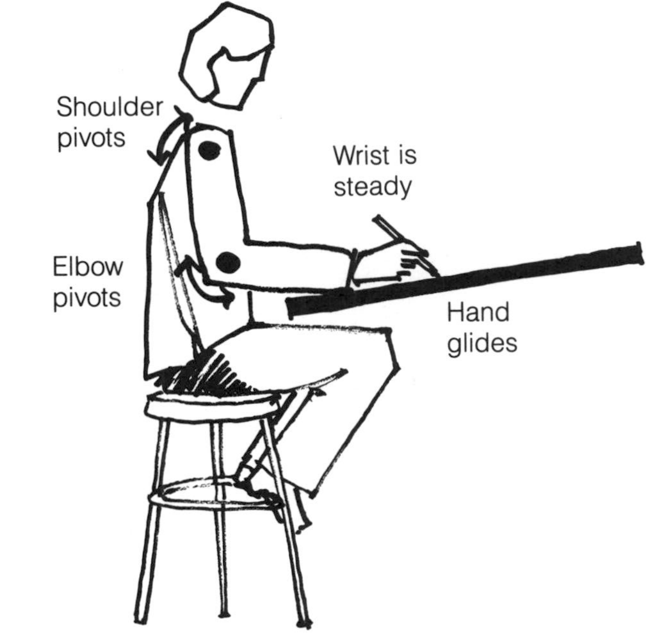

Freeform shapes with one line should have a clean connection, or match, with a slight gap. Multiple lines are also quick and effective.

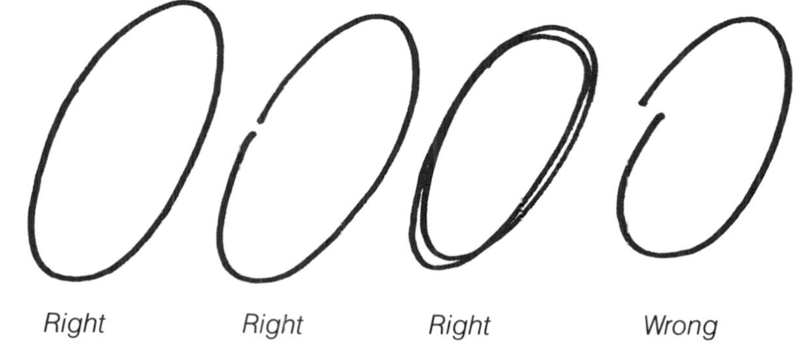

Long Straight Lines

These are easier to control by resting the elbow and using it as a pivot, keeping the wrist and fingers immobile. Horizontal lines are easiest. Stop and start if necessary, readjusting the elbow to draw very long lines.

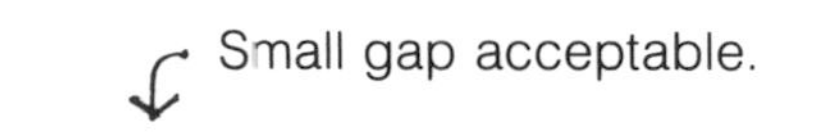

For diagonal or vertical lines, adjust body position or the paper to maintain the elbow as a pivot.

When joining two points with a straight line, start at one point, look at the other, then draw the pencil quickly toward it.

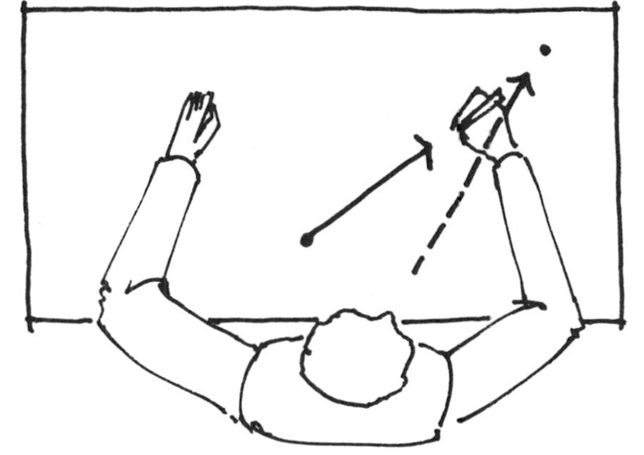

Shorter Straight Lines

These are done the same way as long straight lines, again with no wrist movement.

Draw each line with confidence and speed. Make definite endings by using a pressure start and a pressure stop. Let the line in between develop a tonal character.

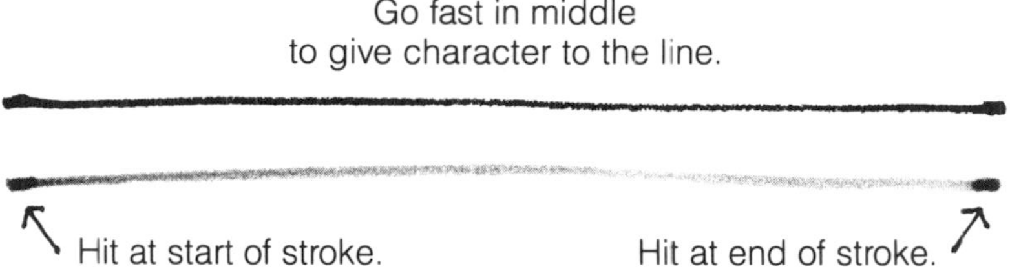

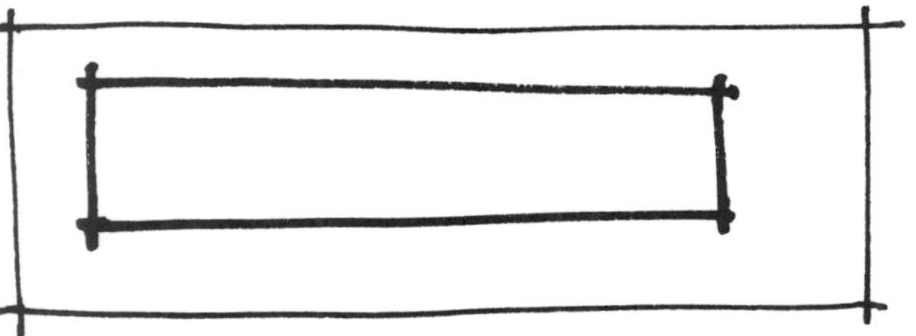

Correct: Fast, confident lines, with strong ends and positive connections from slight crossing.

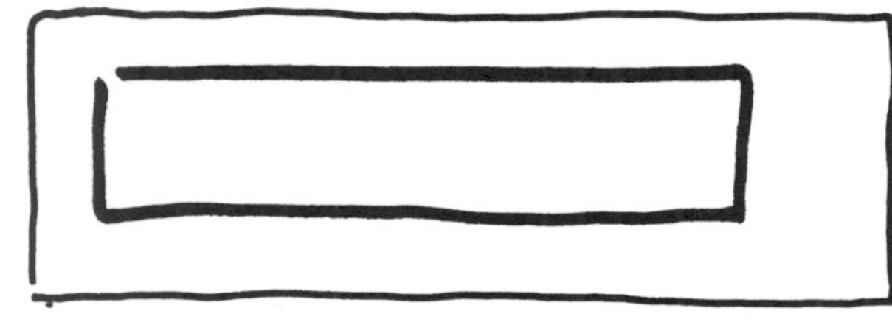

Wrong: Slow, deliberate, heavy pressure lines with weak corners.

Wrong: Hesitant hatch lines and scratch lines. Lack confidence and character.

Detail Lines

Very short hatch lines or smaller curved lines are drawn with the wrist and fingers working in harmony. The hand should rest on the side.

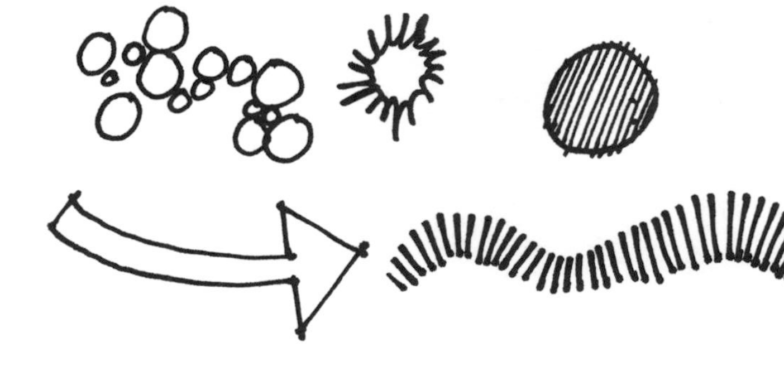

Hatching or Toning Lines

Keep lines parallel and try to connect each line to the outline. A slight overlap is acceptable.

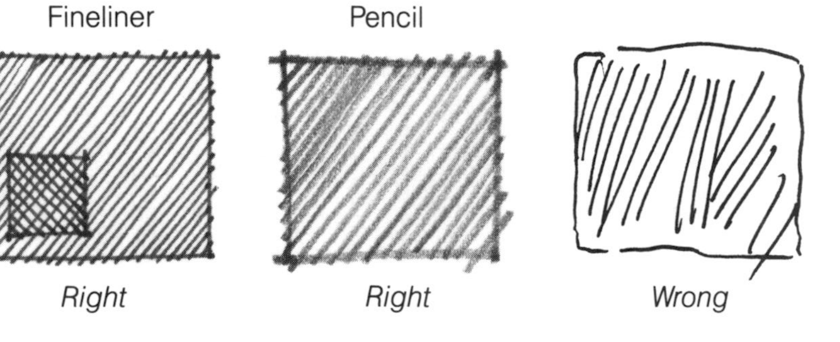

Marker Lettering

Wide-tipped color markers are versatile tools for quick, functional diagrams, freehand title lettering, and color rendering. It is appropriate at this point to learn how to use them properly. Before beginning, put a backing sheet of tracing paper under the drawing surface. Markers will bleed through many papers and can permanently stain the drafting table surface. Keep markers tightly capped when not in use.

Marker Grip

A light touch is all that is needed. Even mocerate pressure will destroy the tip. Wide-tip markers with a rectangular end need to be held so that this end touches the paper along the entire edge.

Side view

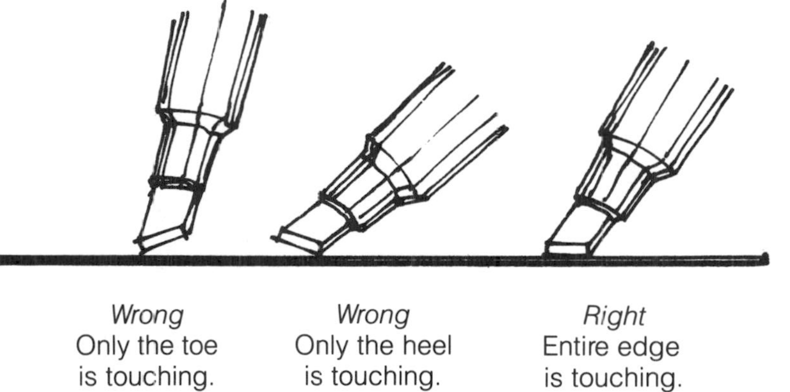

Wrong
Only the toe is touching.

Wrong
Only the heel is touching.

Right
Entire edge is touching.

Top view

Horizontal stroke provides a wide line.

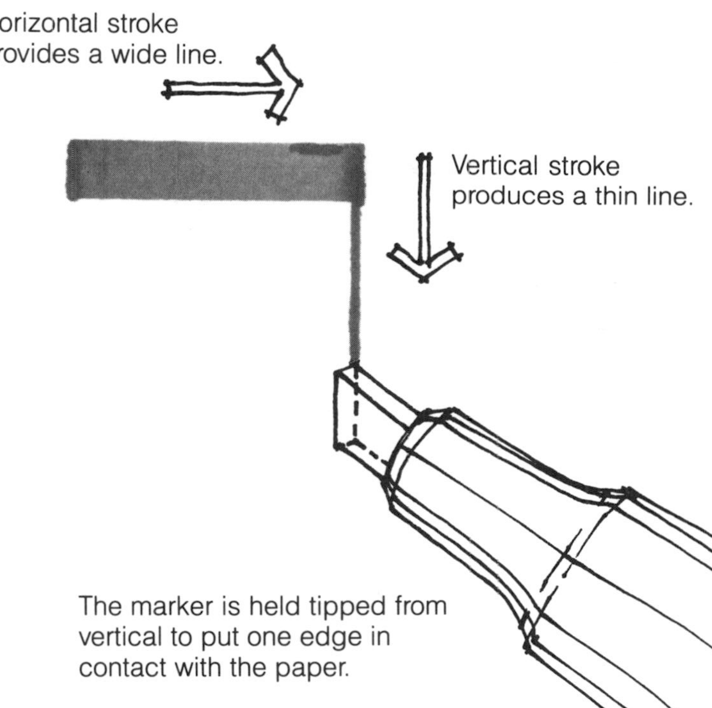

Vertical stroke produces a thin line.

The marker is held tipped from vertical to put one edge in contact with the paper.

Freehand Lettering

Freehand titles and subtitles requiring larger letters can be accomplished with markers and felt tip pens. This technique is good for schematic and preliminary drawings on marker paper, but the freehand outlining techniques shown can be adapted to other media.

Begin with guidelines about 1½ inches apart.

Hold the marker gently. Make some letters, checking these pointers as you go:

- The entire tip edge touches the paper.
- The edge is aligned vertically all the time for vertical, diagonal, and circular strokes.
- The marker is not rotated with the fingers, which would tip the marking surface onto its point or the heel.
- Neither arm nor body are rotated.
- The letters are made with a light touch, letting the edge of the marker create line width changes.
- The toe and heel do not extend over horizontal guidelines.
- Vertical strokes are consistently vertical. Use light vertical guidelines if necessary.
- Smaller letters use the small edge at the tip of the marker.

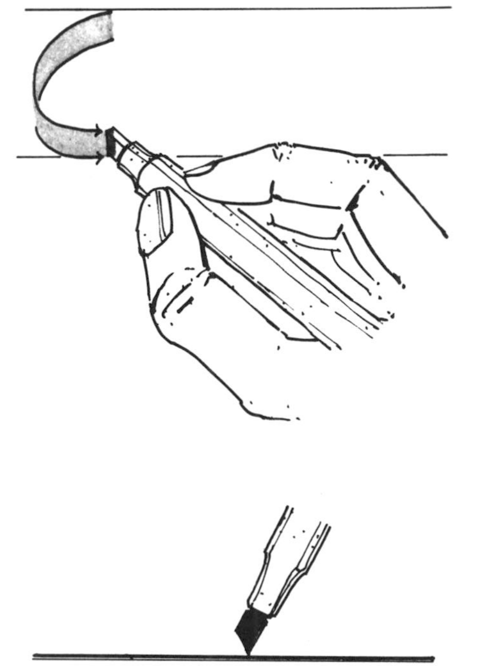

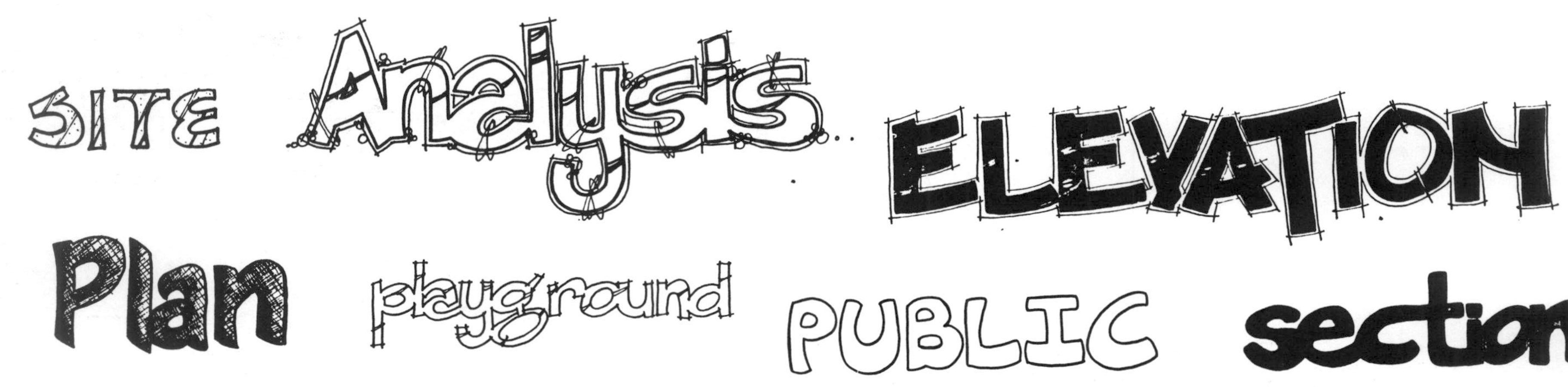

Try exercises 15 and 16. But first check Chapter 5 for correct letter shapes.

Outlining

Marker letters by themselves are weak and need the crispness obtained by outlining. One can either outline the colored shapes directly on the marker paper, or overlay the presentation sheet on the shapes for outline tracing.

Start with a bold outline. Do all the verticals, then all the horizontals, then the curved shapes. Allow the lines to form definite corners, even overlapping slightly.

Follow up with a fine line outside the bold line, keeping an even white space between.

Move the paper or your arm to permit comfortable, confident strokes.

Other dots and lines may be added for character and interest.

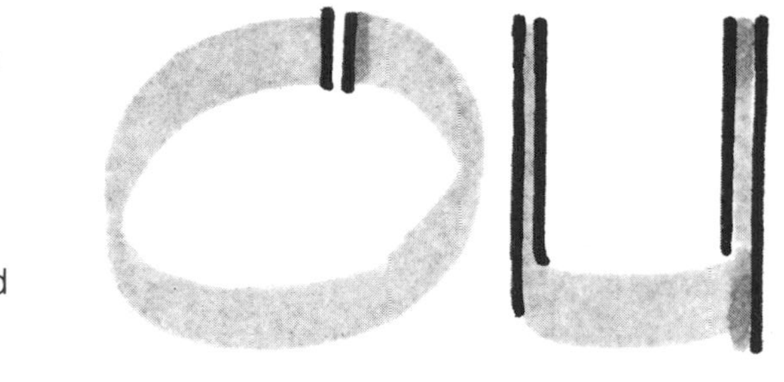
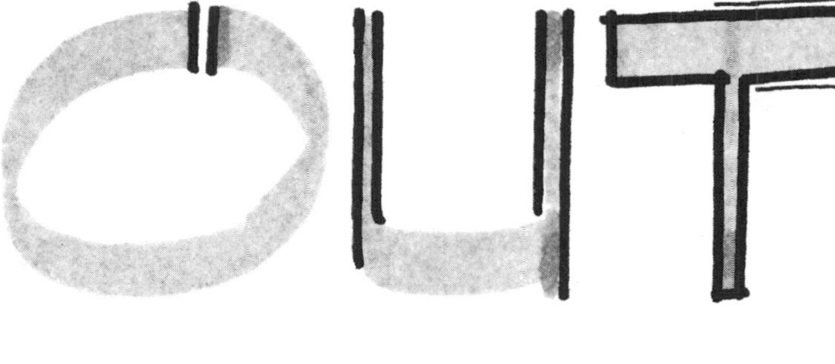

Concept Drawings

Conceptual drawings are loose and free in character. There are no conventional symbols that are right or wrong. However, most of the graphics at this beginning design stage are very abstract and are not meant to convey exact shapes, textures, or forms. They primarily express functions, activities, spaces, and their relationships. For example, use areas may be shown simply as bubbles or blobs, and movement corridors as arrows. At this stage, there is no attempt to show exact forms or edges of materials.

Conceptual Diagram

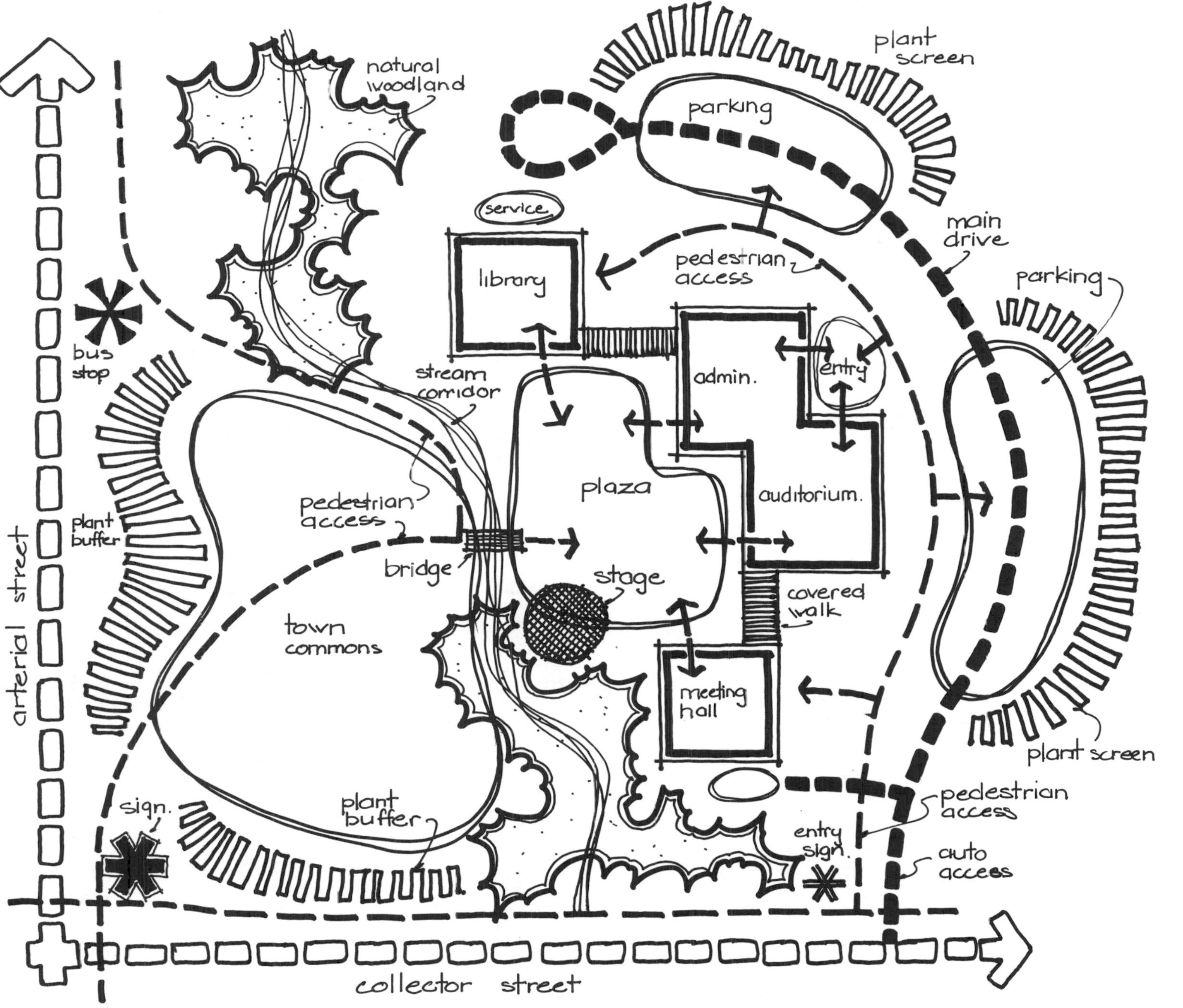

Some Symbols for Practice

Concept diagrams can be done with any freeflowing media, such as a 6B pencil, felt tip pens, or colored markers. Using the marker suggestions given in the previous chapter, try reproducing these various graphic symbols. Remember to put down a backing sheet.

For toning areas, first define with a narrower felt tip pen, then fill in with even, parallel strokes of a wide-tip marker. You may need to trim out the edges if a precise infill is desired.

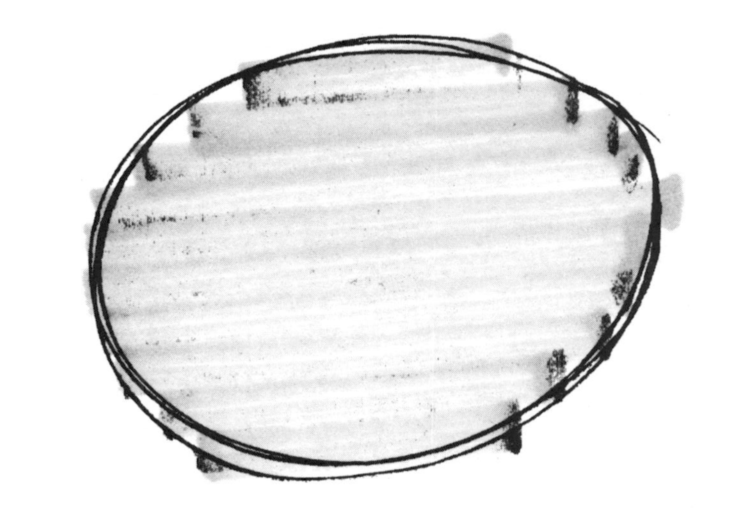

For directional signatures, start with wide, broken strokes of a colored marker, then outline with thick and thin felt tip pens using a technique similar to that for title lettering (see page 43).

For narrower lines, change the marker grip to place the narrow edge on the paper.

Try vertical and horizontal strokes joined in a continuous movement—with no change of grip. You may need to change your body position to get a smooth curving symbol.

Parallel or radiating strokes of consistent width are effective symbols for landscape barriers.

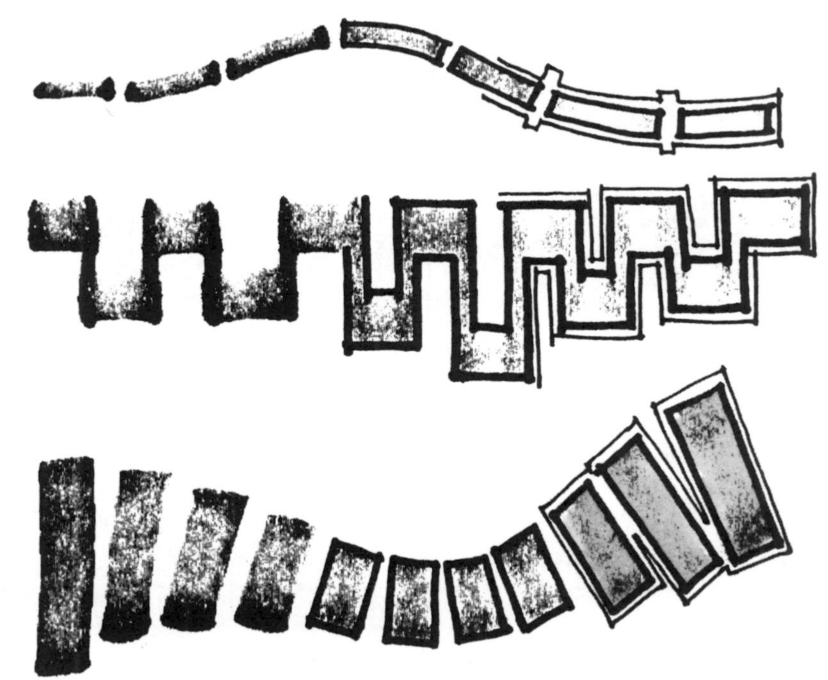

On the following pages are just a few of the many abstract graphic language elements which have meaning for conceptual design. Using any of these symbols, try exercise 17.

Non-lineal Symbols

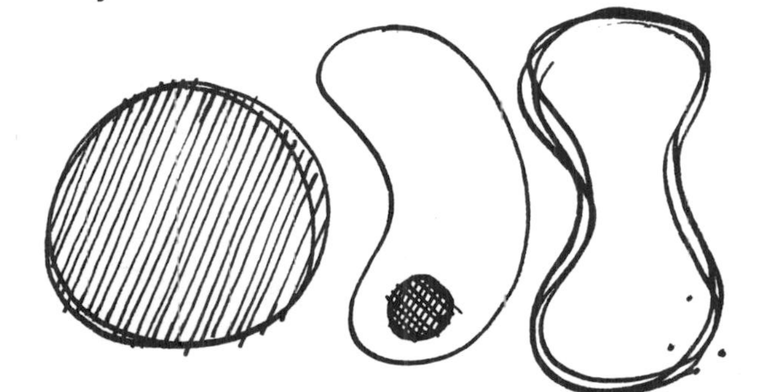

Activity areas, use zones, functional spaces

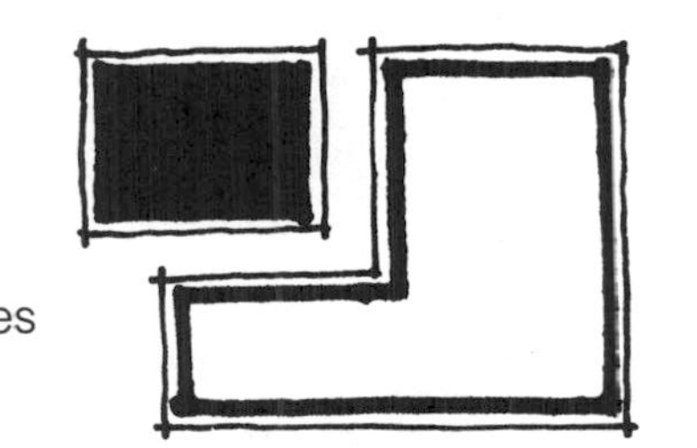

Buildings and structures

Focal areas, points of interest, conflict zones

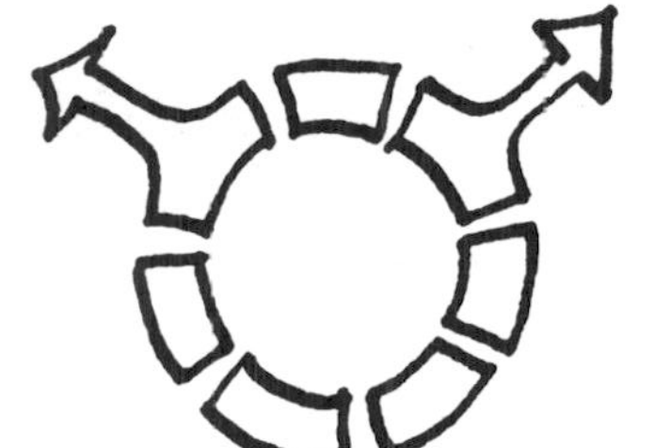

Activity or
circulation nodes

Static Lineal Symbols

Functional edges:
Barriers, screens, walls

Noise zones

Ecological edges:
Forested areas
Cliff area

Active Lineal Symbols

Automobile circulation
Pedestrian circulation
Access points
View direction
Wind direction
Ecological processes
Movement of anything

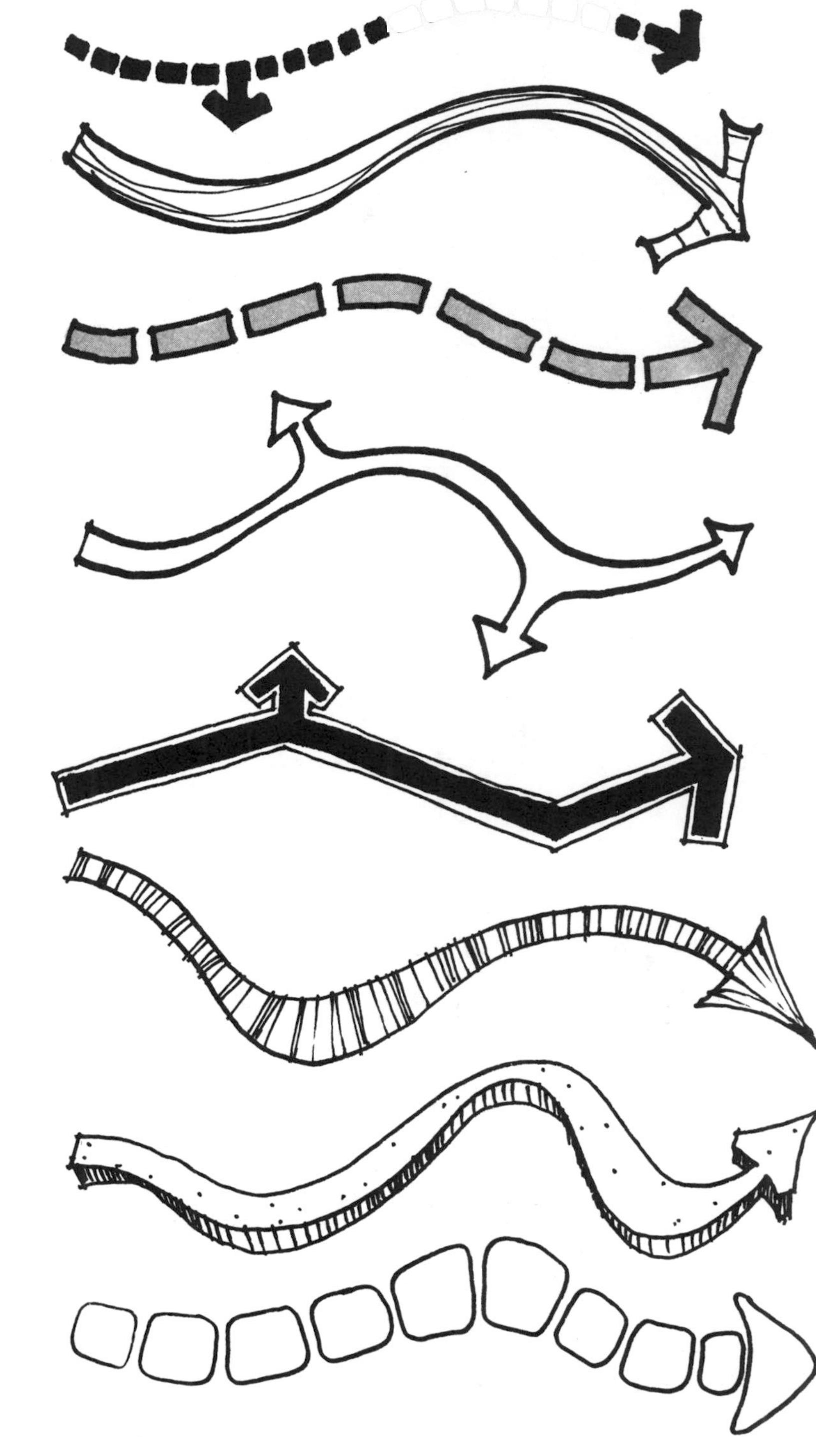

Conceptual Diagram

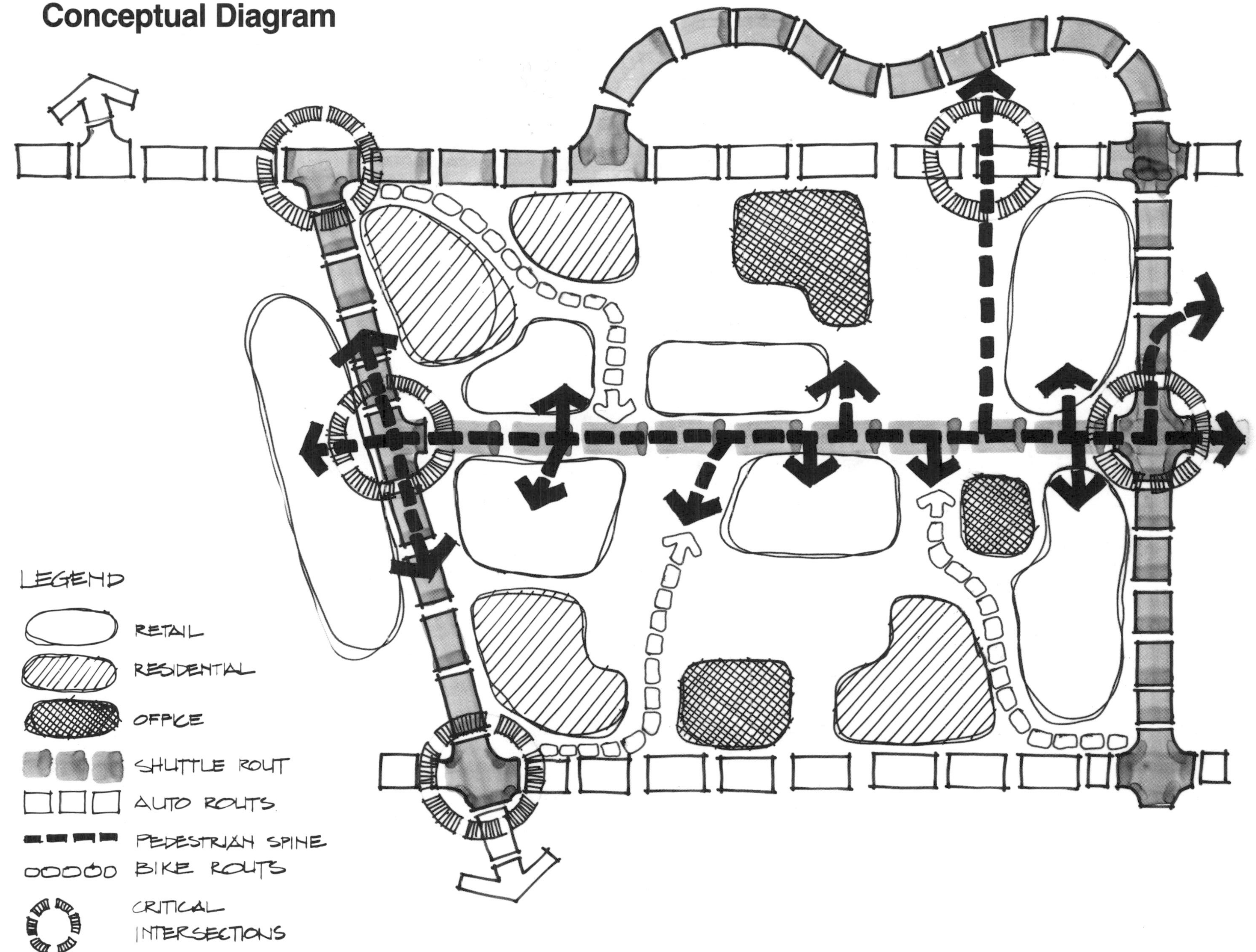

Concept Plan

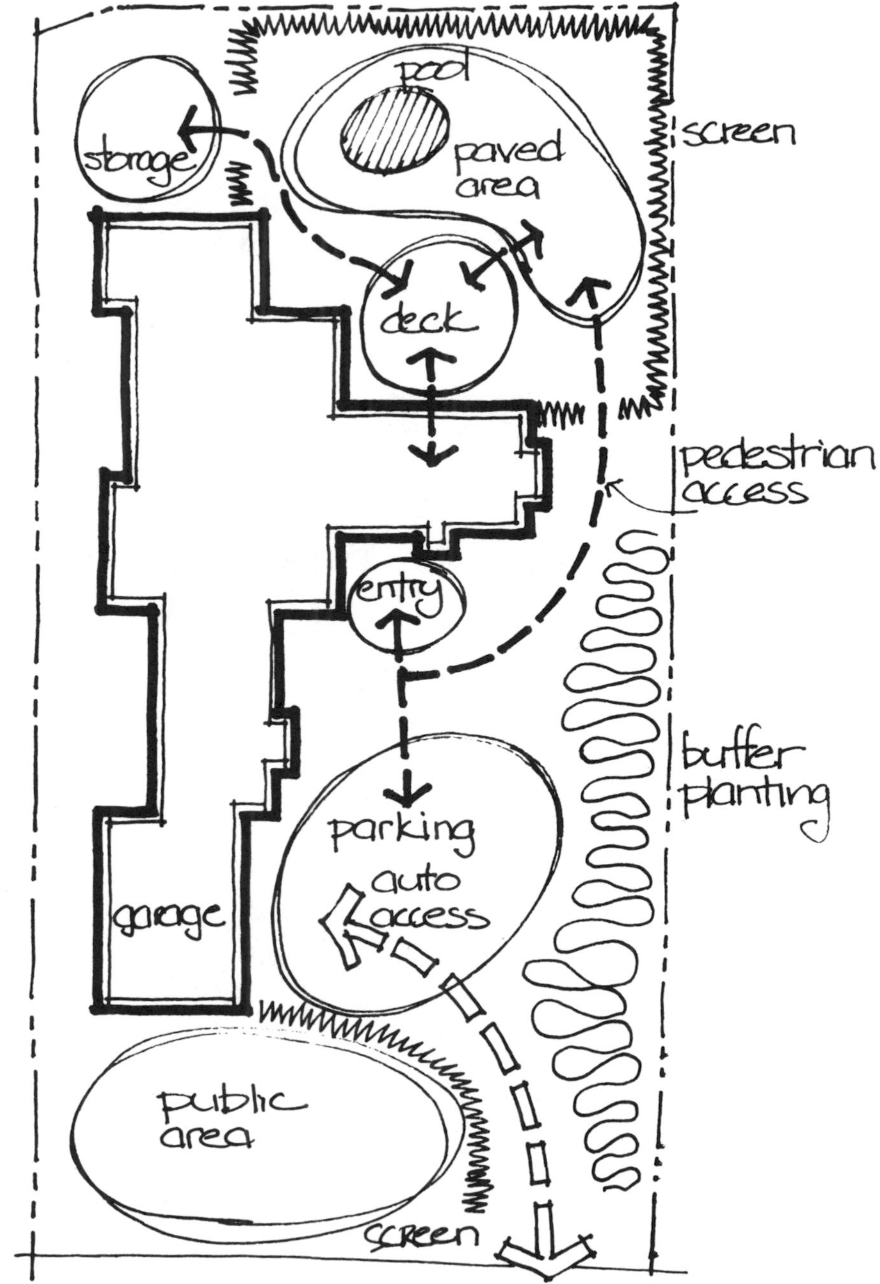

Conceptual Diagram

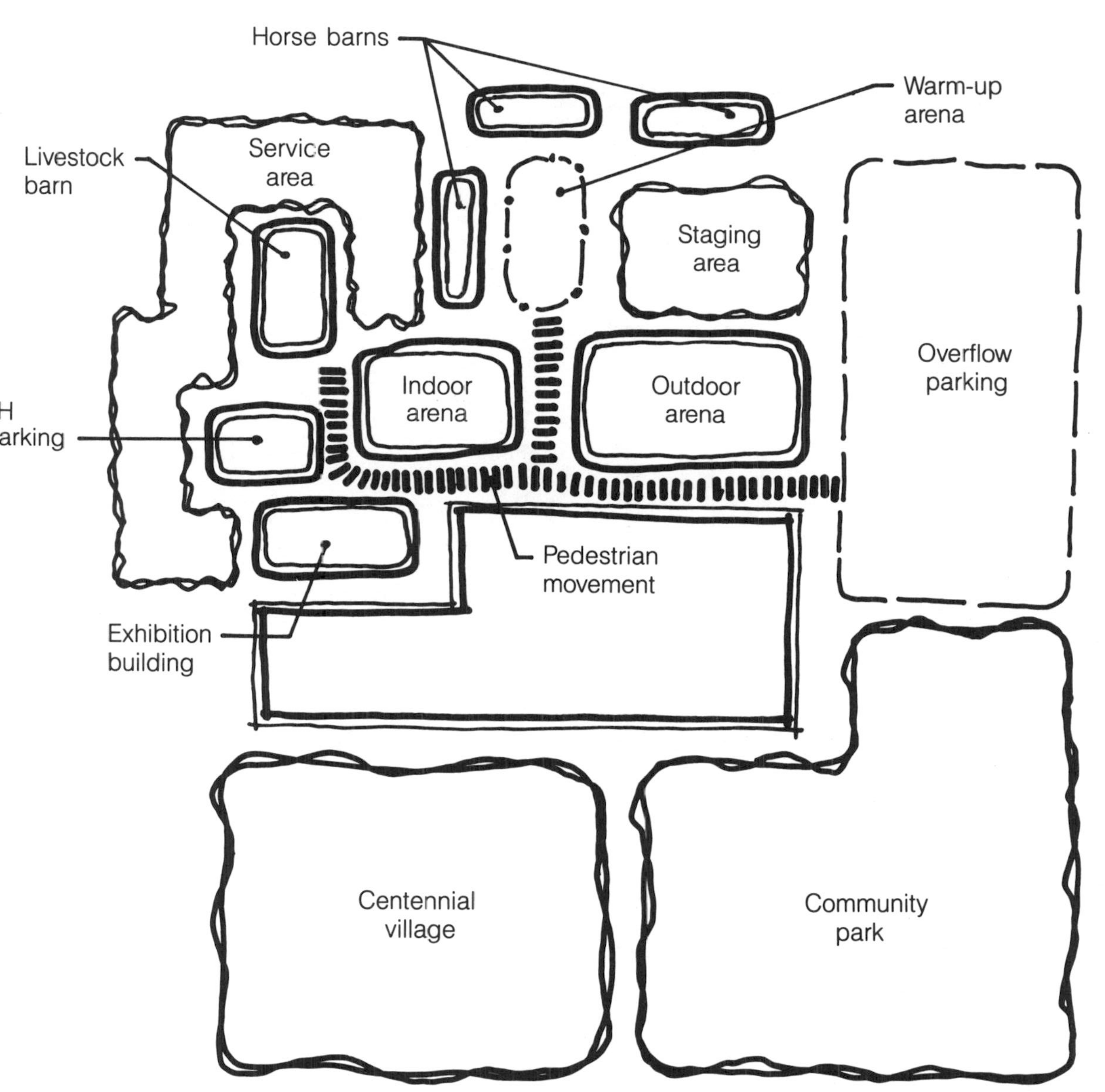

4 Drafting

The production of precisely drafted construction documents comes near the end of the design process, as discussed in Chapter 1. However, drafting is introduced here because all phases of landscape graphics require some knowledge of drafting equipment and media. Also, many of the basic drafting skills are used in the very early stages of design, such as lettering, and in the refinement of preliminary freehand drawings. The two most common manual drafting media are pencil on vellum and ink on drafting film or Mylar.

Plan

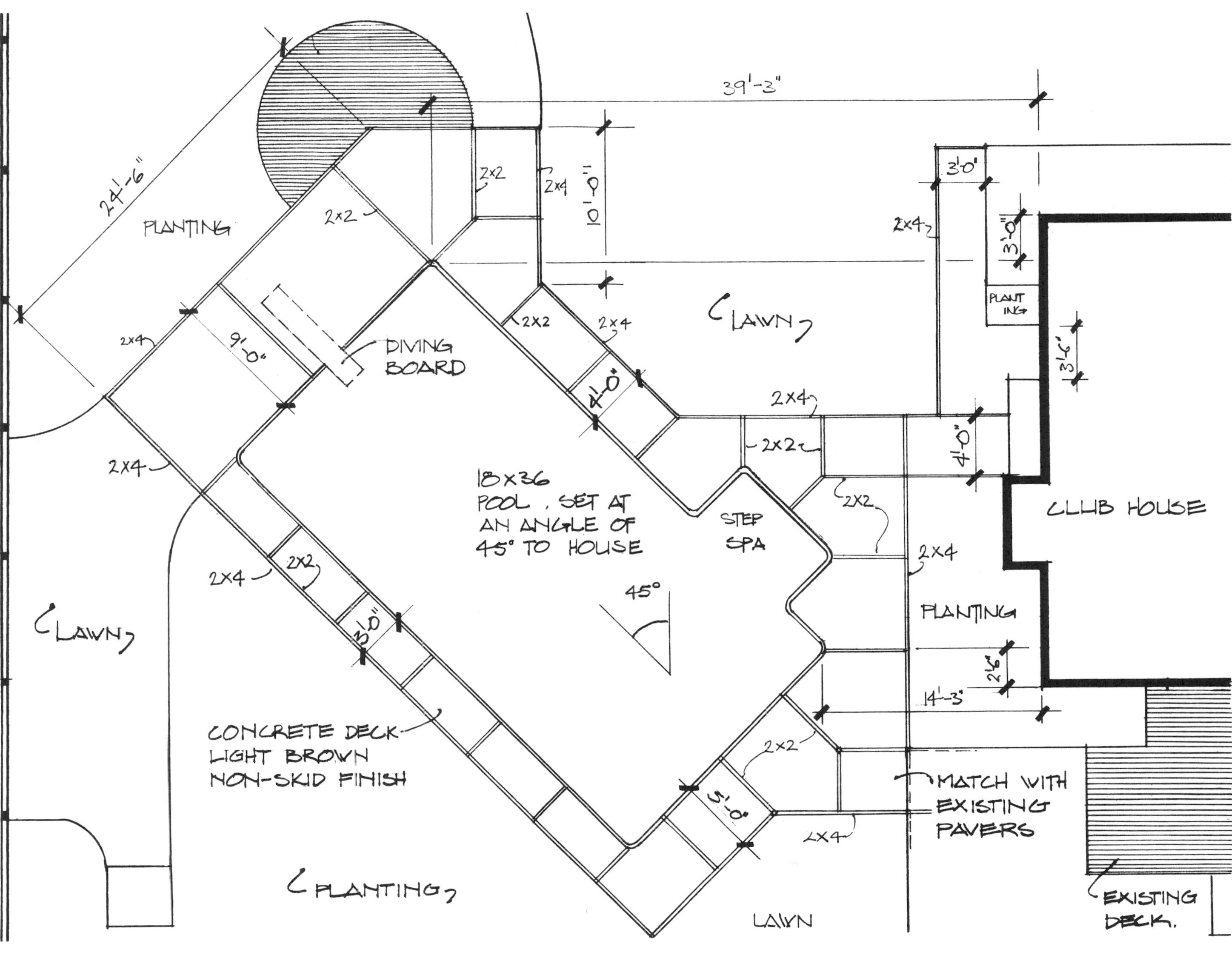

24'-6"
PLANTING
39'-3"
2x2
2x4
10'-0"
3'-0"
3'-0"
PLANT ING
3'-6"
9'-0"
DIVING BOARD
2x2
2x4
LAWN
4'-0"
2x4
2x2
4'-0"
CLUB HOUSE
18x36
POOL, SET AT
AN ANGLE OF
45° TO HOUSE
STEP
SPA
2x2
2x4
2x4
2x2
45°
PLANTING
LAWN
3'-0"
2'-6"
14'-3"
CONCRETE DECK
LIGHT BROWN
NON-SKID FINISH
2x2
5'-0"
MATCH WITH
EXISTING
PAVERS
2x4
PLANTING
LAWN
EXISTING
DECK.

Pencil Drafting

Pencil is still a favorite medium for many designers and drafters because it is easy to manipulate its line width and density. It is also easy to erase and modify. The major disadvantage—compared to ink on Mylar—is that pencil drawings are less permanent and less durable. They have a tendency to smudge, and they produce a weaker blueprint.

Equipment and Materials

Mechanical pencil or lead holder
This is the main tool for pencil drafting. There are many different brands available.

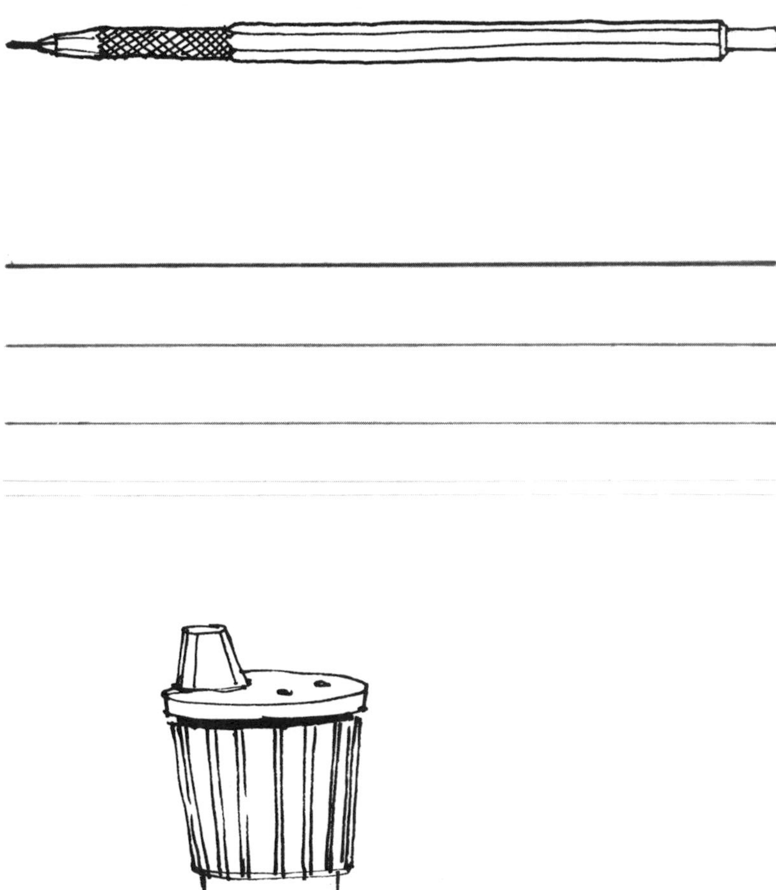

Leads
Available in a variety of hardnesses, the most common leads used are:

HB soft. For wider, dark infill lines or texturing. Smudges easily but also erases easily.

H medium. Good all-purpose drafting lead. Ideal for lettering on vellum. Prints well.

2H medium to hard. Good for layout lines and precision work. More difficult to erase but will not smudge as easily.

4H hard. For guidelines and light layout lines. Use with a very sharp point and a light touch. Will not print well.

Softer leads, ranging from the extremely soft 7B to soft B, are available but are more suited to sketching than to drafting. Harder leads, up to the extremely hard 9H, are also available but are seldom used.

Nonphoto blue is used for drawing guidelines because it does not reproduce when photocopied.

Pencil Pointer
A pointer is for sharpening lead. Empty the bowl before putting it away.

T Square and Parallel Rule
These are for drawing parallel lines and guiding other drafting tools, such as triangles. The recommended length for a T square is 24 inches.

For larger work, use a parallel rule, which attaches to the table with wires and brackets. It rolls over the drafting surface, maintaining a precise parallel relationship. Recommended lengths are 36, 42, and 48 inches.

A drafting arm is a more expensive, adjustable straightedge.

Triangle
Combined with parallel rules, triangles are used to draft straight lines in a variety of directions. Adjustable triangles save time and allow precise angles to be drawn. If made of plastic, do not use as a cutting edge. Also, do not use them with markers, and avoid damage to edges.

Compass
For drawing larger circles a compass is necessary. Buy a good one. The cheaper ones tend to be inaccurate and difficult to use. For very large arcs, a beam compass is used.

Template
The template most commonly used by landscape architects is the simple circle template. Get one with very large circles and another with medium to small circles. Many other template shapes are available as well.

Dry Cleaning Pad
Filled with powdered rubber, it is used to prepare a surface for drafting and to reduce smudging. Use sparingly.

Eraser
Everyone makes changes. The kneaded eraser is good for initially removing graphite with no smudging. Follow-up erasing can be done with any of the softer pencil erasers.

Erasing Shield
For use with erasers to mask areas that should remain, a shield is very necessary when using an electric eraser.

Drafting Brush
Available in various sizes, it is used to sweep drafting surfaces clean.

Flexible Curve
Many brands are available. An excellent aid for drafting freeform, flowing lines and better than French curves for landscape work. Get one which can be used with both pencil and ink.

Scales
Architect's scales and engineer's scales are more used in the United States than elsewhere. Metric scales of various types are used by landscape architects in most other countries. Do not use scales as a straight edge.

Sandpaper Block
For putting a wedge or chisel point on the lead, a block is used when lettering and for sharpening the compass lead. Store the block in a sealed envelope with one end slit open.

Drafting Tape
Supplied in rolls or as strips of "dots," it is used to secure the paper to the drafting surface. The best brands hold well, yet peel off easily without ripping the paper.

Drafting Paper
Vellum is a fairly stable paper suitable for pencil drafting. Some brands include Clearprint 1000-H and K & E Albanene. These are 16 to 20 pound, 100 percent rag papers. Not recommended for ink work.

Drawing Board Cover
A vinyl covering is recommended because it is durable and resists small holes. Attach to the board with double-sided tape along the top and bottom. To avoid buckling, keep out of direct sunlight and avoid close proximity to hot objects.

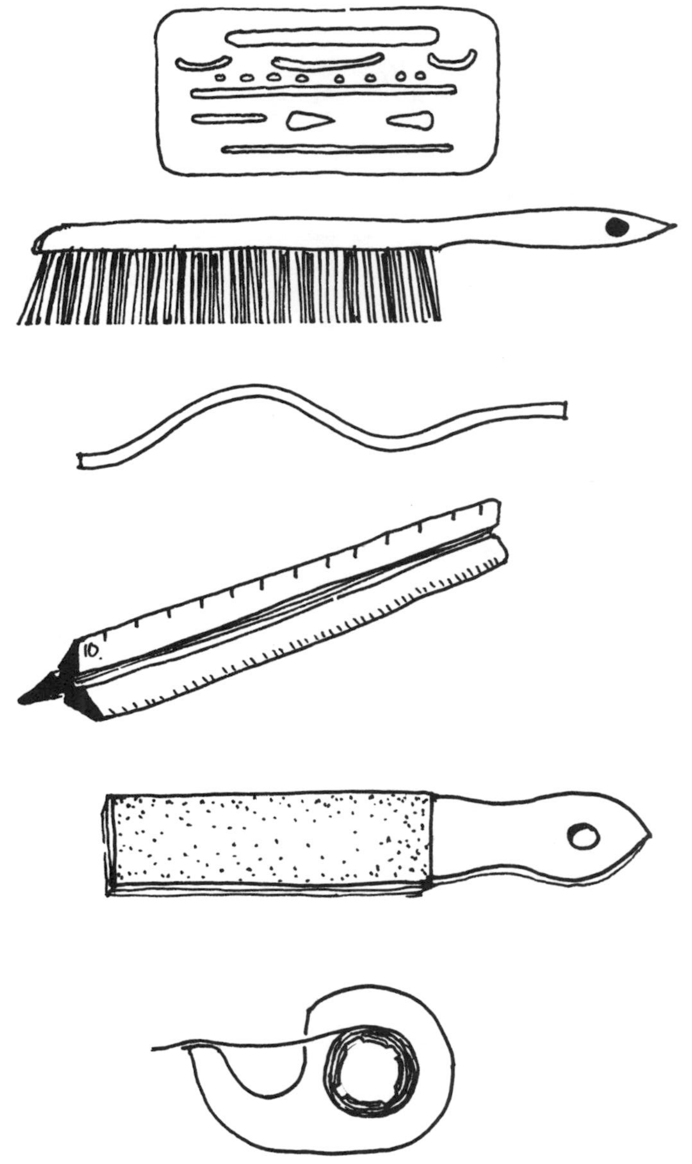

Techniques

Pencil drafting is mainly used on finished working drawings or base maps, where accuracy and precision are important. The advantages of pencil over ink are that there is no waiting period (ink needs to dry), erasing is easier, and pencil is generally faster. Ink has several advantages over pencil. (See Ink Drafting on page 64.)

Line Quality
The three important line characteristics of pencil drafting are: (1) the density or value of the line, (2) the width of the line, and (3) the consistency of the lines. The ideal line is dense, has sharp edges and ends, and maintains a consistent width along its entire length.

The density or darkness of a line depends on the lead and the paper used (rougher paper needs harder leads) and the pressure applied to the pencil.

Set up the sheet of vellum by lining up the top edge with the upper side of your T square or parallel rule. Apply a light sprinkling of dry cleaning powder.

Select the appropriate lead and sharpen to a point in the pencil pointer.

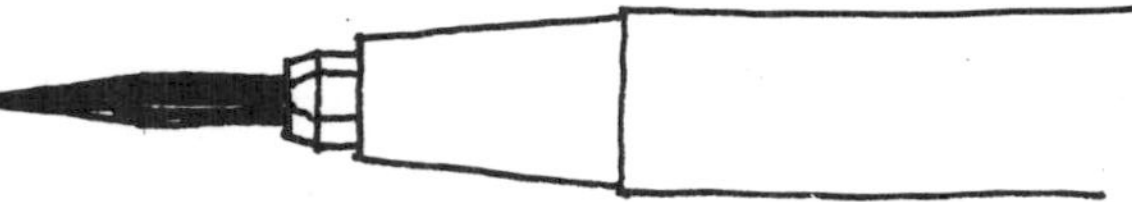

Now pop the very end off by tapping gently on a scrap piece of paper.

Next, round the corners of the lead by quickly doodling on the scrap sheet. The end should still be fairly sharp but not needle-like.

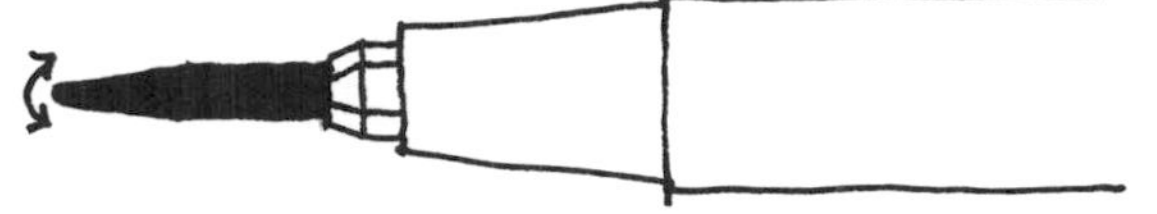

Hold the pencil firmly (but not too tightly), so that you roll it slowly as you pull it along the straightedge.

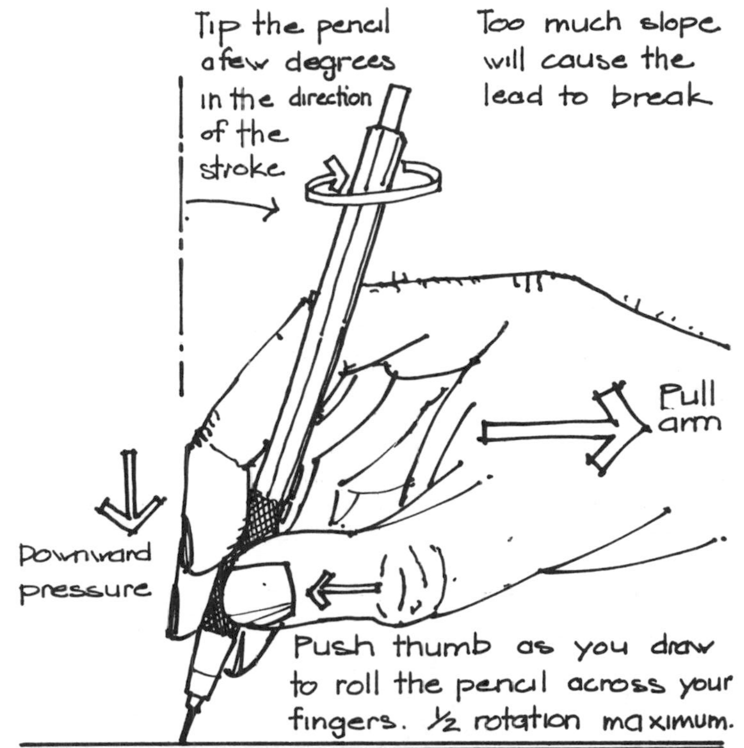

Use of Straightedge Tools

With your non-drawing hand, make sure the head of the T square is firmly against the edge of the board and hold the triangle firmly against the top edge.

For the next line, slide the triangle with very light pressure or lift and then move it to avoid smudging. If you use felt tip pens, be sure to clean the straightedge with cleaner or rubbing alcohol.

The parallel rule is used in much the same manner, except that it is held in a parallel position with wires and is not meant to be removed from the table. Adjust the wires to put a little tension on the spring.

Arcs and Circles

When using the compass, sharpen the lead to a steep angle with the sandpaper block. Test the point on a piece of scrap paper, then scribe the circle, always keeping an even pressure throughout the arc.

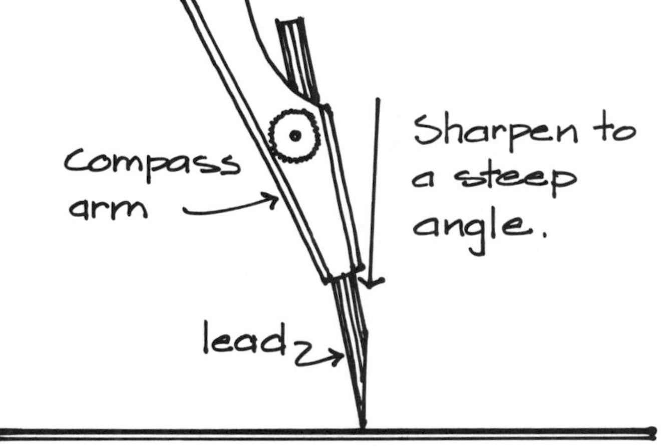

Connections

Make sure that all corners have positive connections.

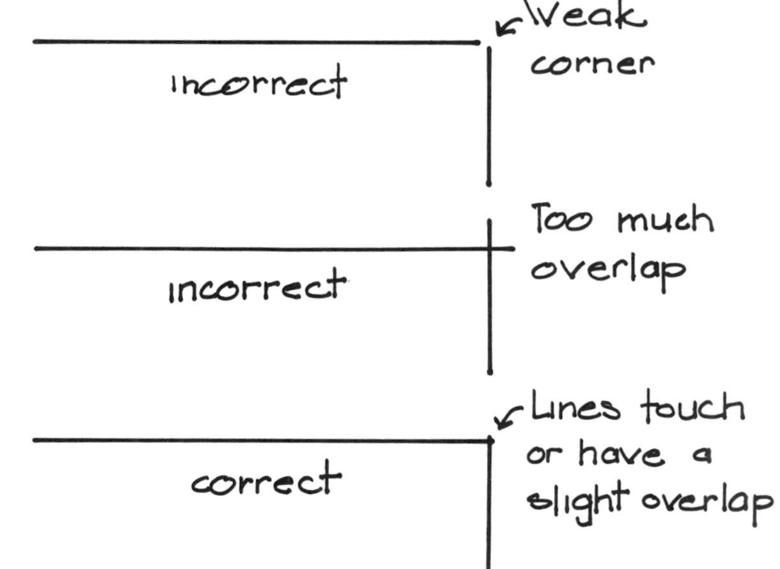

Pencil Drafting Sequence

1. Lightly dust your drafting surface.
2. Lay out shapes with very light, sharp lines drawn with needle-pointed 2H or 4H leads. (If tracing a preliminary drawing, this step may be omitted.)
3. Draw arcs.

4. Draft all major lines with F, H, or 2H leads. Work from top to bottom and from left to right.

5. Add thinner dimension lines.
6. Add lettering.
7. Last, add textural or tonal shading with HB or H leads to work around lettering and avoid smudging.
8. When finished, check the back side of the sheet and remove any graphite that may have been picked up from the work surface or from tracing.

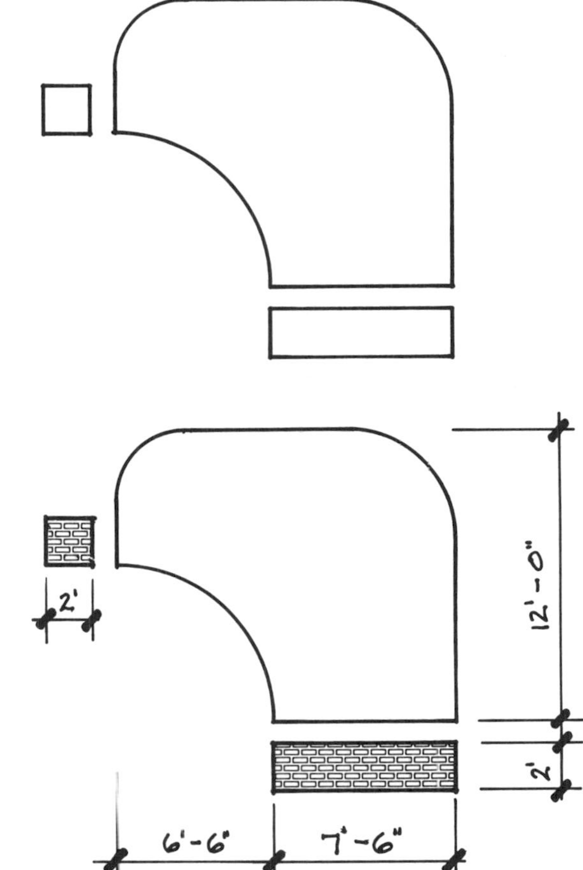

Conventional Symbols and Line Weights for Landscape Working Drawings

Line Symbols (construction plans)

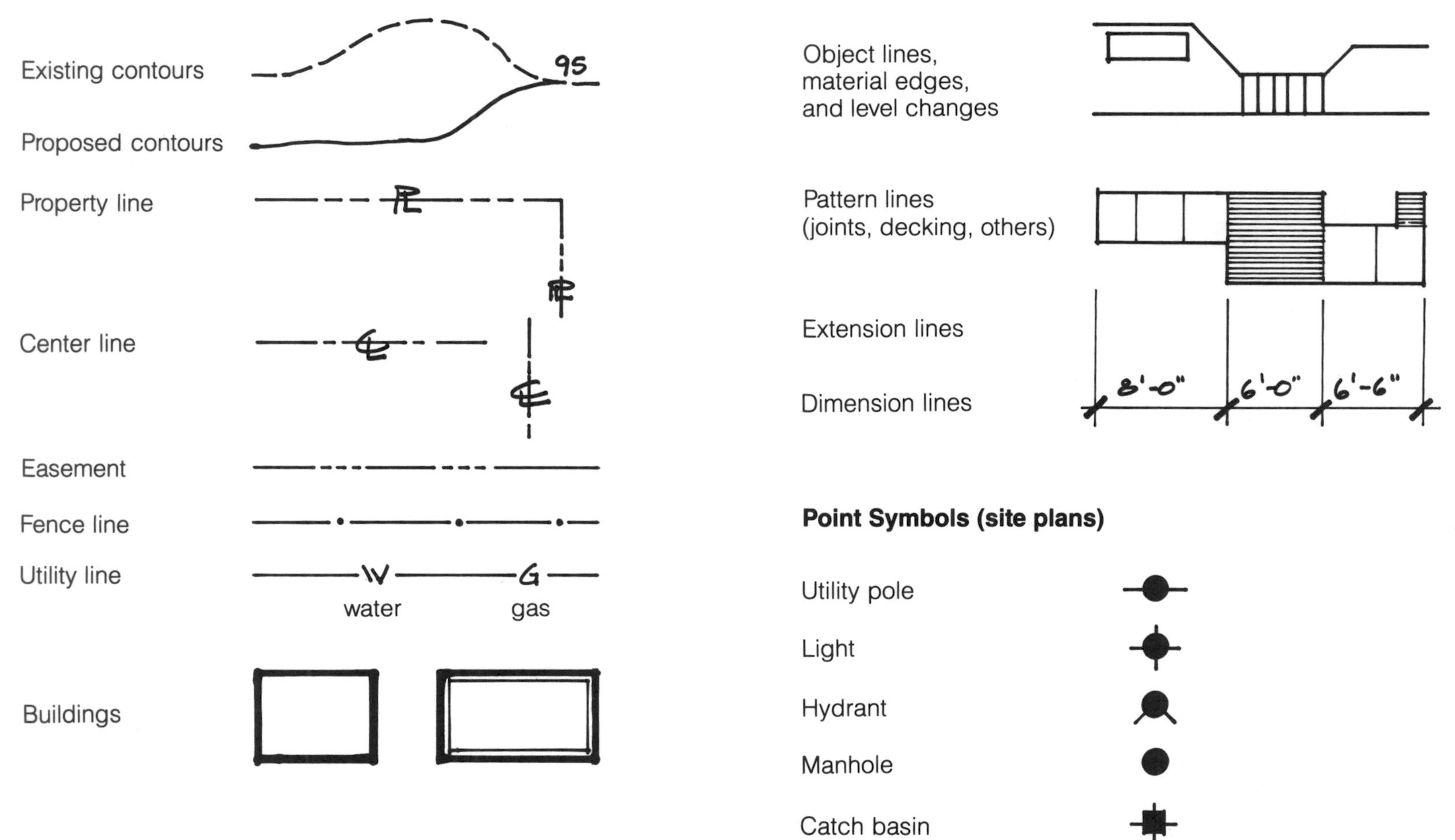

Material Symbols (construction details)

Concrete

Sand

Gravel or crushed stone

Rocks and stones

Wood mulch

Wood timbers

Soil

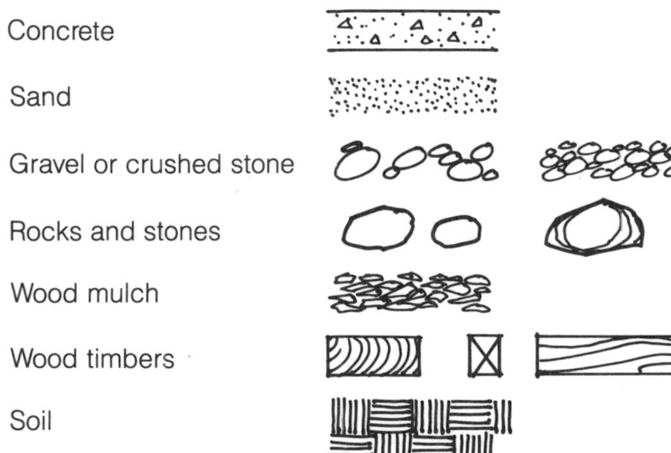

Note: These are mostly freehand.

Stone, brick

Bituminous paving

Filter mat

Steel

Re-bar

Bolts and rod

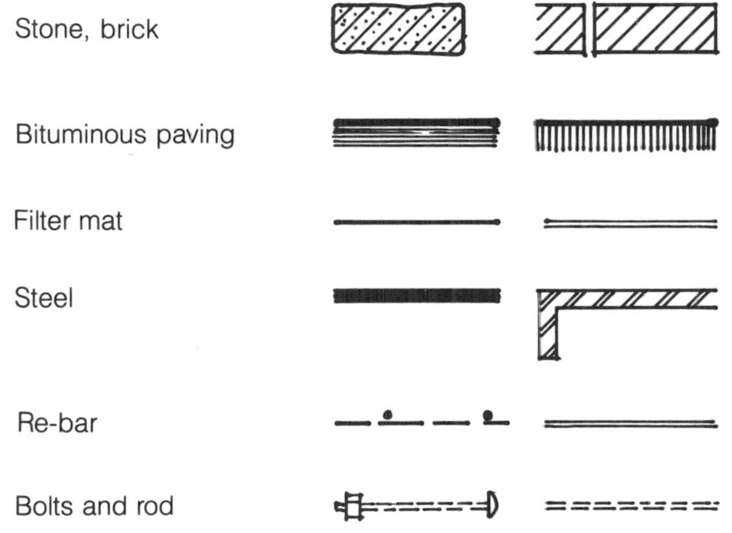

Note: These are mostly drafted.

Check your pencil drafting quality against these criteria.

1. Blackness. All lines should be dense and black enough to produce a high-quality print when submitted to the printing process.
2. Consistent line weight. Each line should have an even thickness, or weight, throughout its length with no narrowing or widening and no fuzzy edges.
3. Accuracy. Lines should meet, line up with precision, and have definite ends.
4. Hierarchy of lines. The various descriptive lines must be easy to distinguish from their width or pattern.
5. Tonal quality. Infill toning and texturing is used only to clarify the message. No unnecessary toning should clutter the work.
6. Sheet appearance. Overall, the sheet is clean and free of smudges, stains, and tears.

Ink Drafting

Ink on film has several advantages over pencil on vellum. Ink drafting makes precise, consistent line widths possible, with lines that are denser and that produce much clearer prints. Film is more resistant to damage than paper and is more stable. It will not shrink or stretch with variations in humidity.

Equipment and Materials

Technical Pens

These are precision drafting tools designed to be used on film.

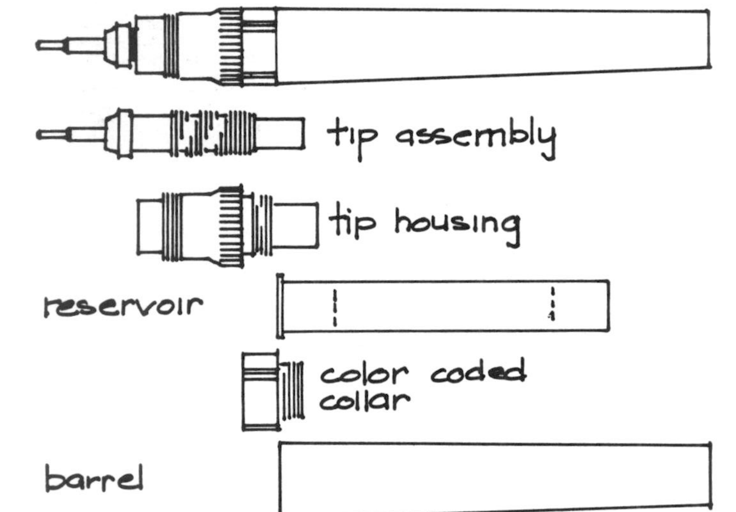

Pens come in a variety of set sizes and brands. The best sets have jewel tips, but these are expensive. Tungsten tips are less expensive and quite durable. Stainless steel tips are the least expensive. A good starting set would have a mix of four point sizes.

2 × 0 or 0.2 mm—fine
1 or 0.4 mm—medium
2 or 0.6 mm—medium broad
4 or 1.0 mm—broad

Point sizes as fine as 5 × 0 and as broad as 6 are available. To fill, remove only the barrel, the color-coded collar, and the reservoir. Add ink (¼ to ½ inch), then reassemble.

Do not take the pen apart any more than shown here. The wire needle inside the tip assembly is delicate and easily damaged if removed.

Pen Care

Handle carefully and avoid shocks or jarring.

Keep caps on and store with points up or secured in their own set containers.

Empty and rinse with warm water periodically throughout the year and always before storing when they are not going to be in use for a month or so.

Stubborn, "frozen" pens should be soaked in warm soapwater or immersed in a special sonic bath for technical pens.

Inking Triangles and Templates

If working with both ink and pencil, purchase inking triangles and templates. These have a recessed or beveled edge to prevent ink from running beneath the guide.

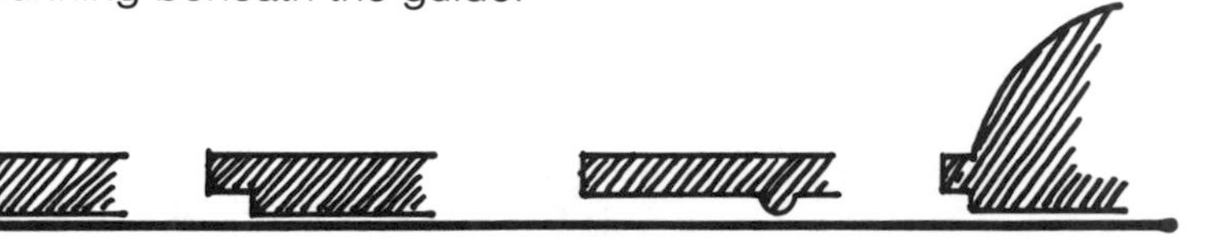

Ink Eraser

These are impregnated with erasing fluid especially designed for erasing ink lines from drafting films.

Ink

Usually ink comes with a set of pens, but it can be bought separately. Look for brands which give true, intense blackness, are free-flowing, fast-drying, and have good adhesion to drafting film.

Drafting Film

Use polyester film which is 3 to 4 mil thick. The most common film is Mylar, which has a roughened surface, called matt, on one or both sides. Do not draft on the smooth side. Look for film that has a high degree of transparency.

Other tools are similar to those shown under pencil drafting materials (pages 57, 58).

Techniques

Tape the film down, but before starting, clean the surface with rubbing alcohol to remove possible fingerprints or stains. Gently shake the pen in a vertical position to activate the flow of ink. Test on a scrap piece of vellum. Unlike the pencil, the pen must be held vertical to the drafting surface in all directions. Do not tilt the pen in the direction of movement or point it into the straightedge.

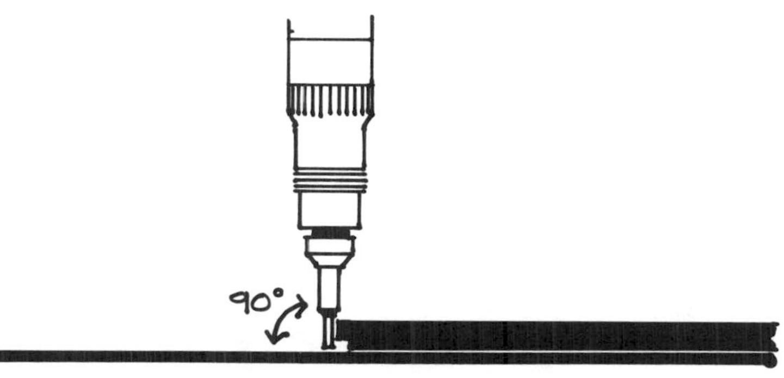

Use a very light touch; do not press down. Move slowly and evenly across the film. (Fast strokes will disrupt the even line quality.) Wait until the ink dries before moving tools across the film. Lifting templates between strokes may be necessary. Erase with ink eraser or moistened eraser soon after the ink has dried. Old inked drawings can be erased with rubbing alcohol.

To obtain sharp corners on large areas of solid black, begin by outlining with a narrow pen size, such as a 0, and then infill with a wider pen size, such as a 3 or a 4.

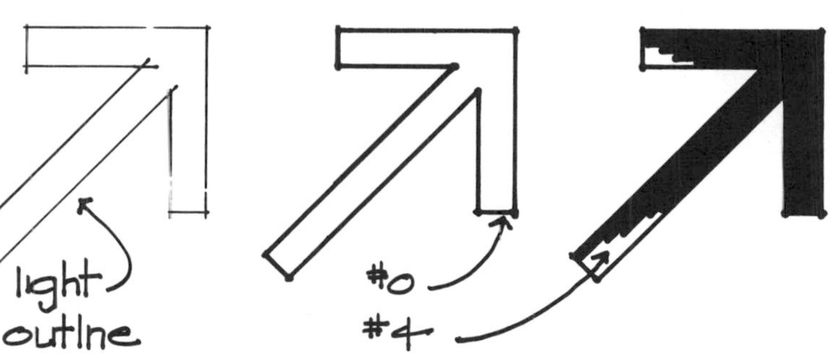

North Indication and Scale

Both north indication and scale must be drawn onto all landscape plans. Often they are integrated into a combined graphic element.

North indications should:

1. Be simple, unobtrusive, yet easy to find.
2. Have a prominent, straight shaft portion.
3. Point straight up, if possible, and always at some angle above horizontal.
4. Never point down.

The north indication is usually placed close to the scale and sometimes integrated with a graphic scale. It is usually placed near the bottom or the right side of the sheet and often in the title block area.

Graphic scales
The value of a graphic scale is that it retains its true relationship to the drawing in the event the drawings are reduced or enlarged.

0 20 40 60 100

0 5 10 20 30 N

0 5 10 15

ONE ACRE

0 20 40 60 80

0 100 200 300

North indicators

Written Scale Conventions

The left side of the written scale equation tells the size of a unit on the plan, whereas the right side tells the size of this same unit on the actual site.

For example, ¼″ = 1′-0″ would mean that one quarter of an inch on the drawing equals one foot on the site.

Architects' scales are written with fractions of an inch on the left side and a unit of one foot on the right side.

For example, 1″ = 1′-0″, ¾″ = 1′, and ½″ = 1′-0″ are used for expanded details such as those for deck construction or steps. Smaller units, such as ¼″ = 1′-0″, ⅛″ = 1′-0″, and ¹⁄₁₆″ = 1′-0″, are used for detailed site work such as the landscaping close to a building.

Engineer's scales are written with a unit of one inch on the left side and increments of ten feet or one hundred feet on the right side. Thus one inch on the scale equals ten or twenty feet on the actual site. For overall site plans, it is common to use scales of 1″ = 10′, 1″ = 20′, 1″ = 30′, and 1″ = 50′. For large urban or regional projects, it is common to use scales of 1″ = 100′, 1″ = 200′, and 1″ = 500′.

Do not mix the architect's scale convention with the engineer's scale convention. It is incorrect to use 1″ = 4′-0″, or ½″ = 20′.

The metric system of measurement uses the metric scale and a simple ratio to show the scale relationship: 1:50, 1:100, 1:200, 1:500, and 1:1000.

Reading Scales

Architect's Scale

Engineer's Scale

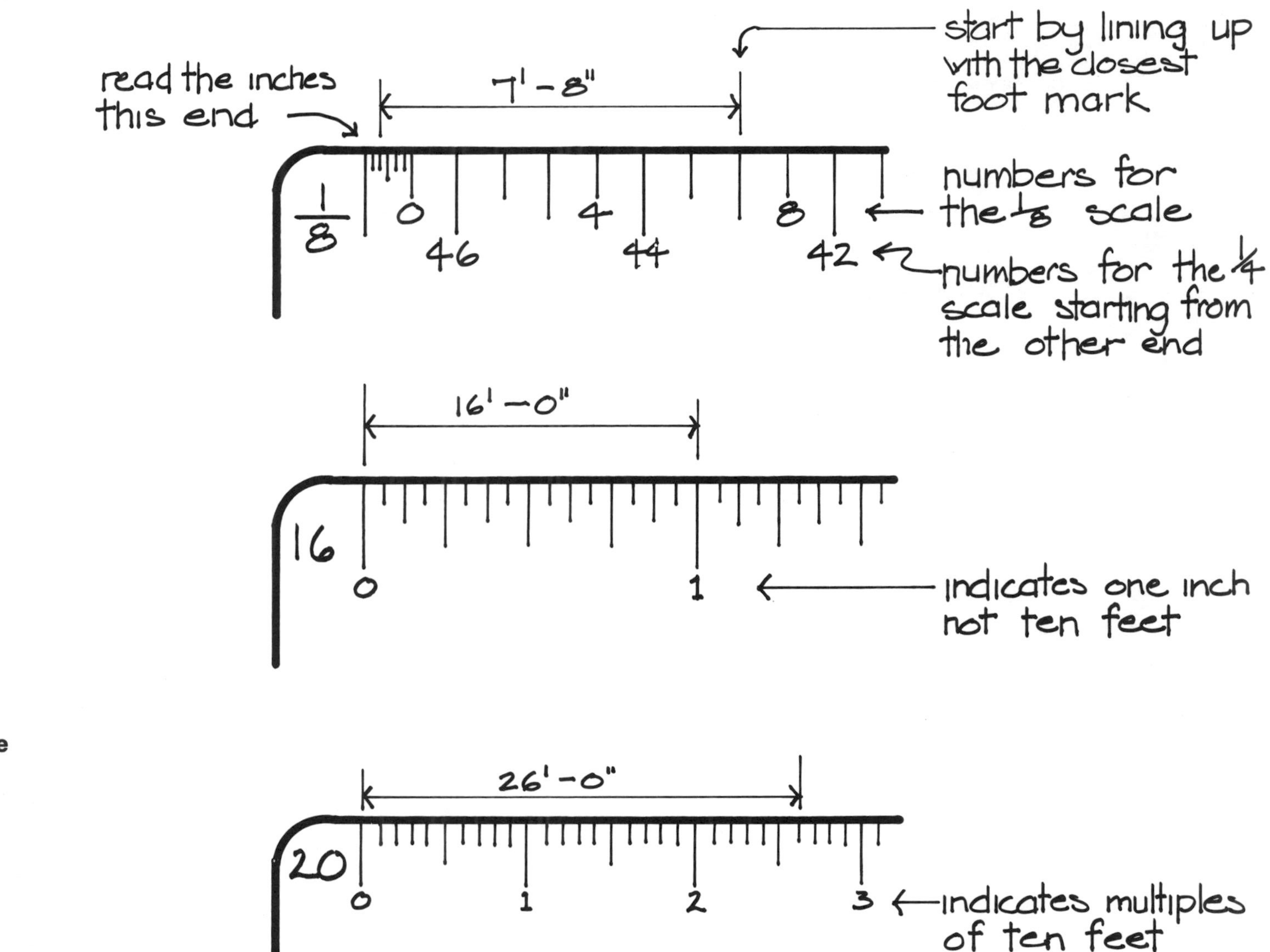

Title Blocks

All plan view working drawings must have a well-organized title block, usually along the lower edge or right-hand side of the sheet. They include several essential elements.

Elements	Examples
Title of sheet content	Planting Plan
Name of project	Shores East Townhomes
Address of project or developer's name	618 Front Street
Sheet number	4 of 6
Design company (with logo and address)	Gordon Associates
Spaces for check signatures	Checked Date
Revisions and dates	Revised Date
Scale	
North indication	

Many companies have standard pre-printed Mylar base sheets with the gaps and company logo laid out to save redrafting time for these repetitive elements.

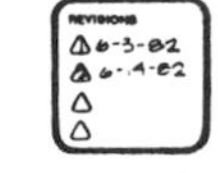

Conceptual Site Plan
Wind Creek Bay (south)
Map 10

Legend

Existing Trees
New Tree Plantings
Open Area
Steep Slope
Cliffs
Trail
Campsite
Developed Playfield
Rail Fence
Wire Fence
One Way Traffic
Note: 2' Contour Interval

Key Map

Site
Wind Creek Bay
Mule Creek Bay
Little Keyhole Lake

0 100 200 300 feet north

Keyhole State Park Master Plan

Wyoming Recreation Commission

EDAW inc.

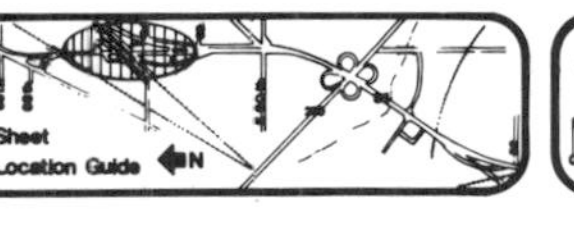

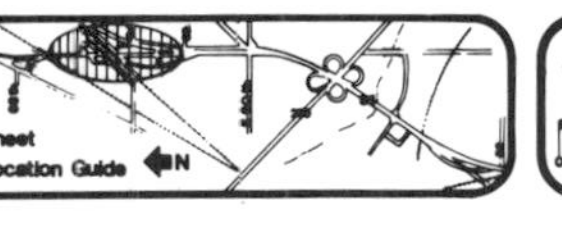

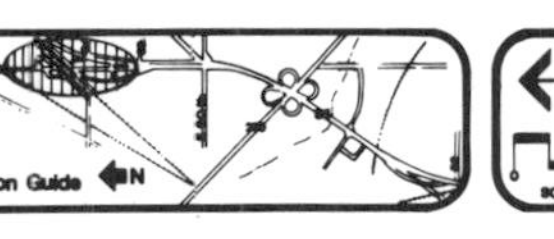

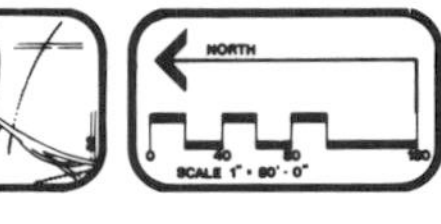

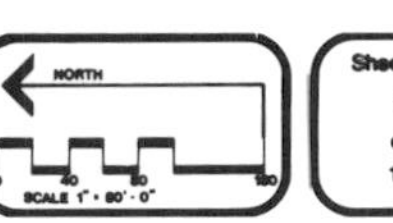

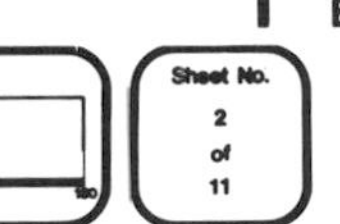

Lettering

Lettering on a drawing fulfills an important requirement. Information that cannot be revealed by graphic shapes and lines alone must be included in the form of notes, titles, labels, dimensions, and identification. The lettering can either enhance the drawing by making it easy to interpret and pleasant to look at, or it can ruin an otherwise good drawing by making it difficult to read and unsightly to look at. Legible lettering should be planned as part of the overall graphic composition of the drawings on which they appear.

MOST LANDSCAPE ARCHITECTS USE A SIMPLE UPPER CASE (CAPITALS) STYLE WITH NO SERIFS AS SHOWN HERE. KEEP LETTERS VERTICAL AND CONSISTENT IN SHAPE. THIS UNIFORM STYLE IS EASY TO READ.

A B C D E F G H I J K L M M M N O P Q R S S T U V W
W X Y Z. 1 2 3 4 5 6 7 7 8 9 0

lower case letters are less formal and are suited for use on concept plans, preliminary sketches and plant lists.

a a b c d e f g g h i j k l m n o p q r s t u v w x y z

Pencil Lettering

Shape and Spacing

Most letters should fit within a slightly narrowed square. Spacing between words should be the equivalent of the letter N.

TOO NARROW TOO WIDE

ABOUT RIGHT

Size

Always use guidelines to obtain correct size and uniformity. The Ames Lettering Guide, shown here, will help. It has a rotating disc which allows quick set-up of guidelines of any size.

Running through the center of the disc is a row of evenly spaced holes. At the end of this row is the number ten. Rotate the disc so that the ten lines up with the frame index mark near the base of the frame. Insert a needle-sharp 4H pencil into the top hole. Move the pencil lightly across the paper, keeping a slight pressure toward the straightedge. Shift the pencil down to the next hole and repeat the back-and-forth motion until there are enough lines for the purpose. If you want closer lines, rotate the disc to a lower number.

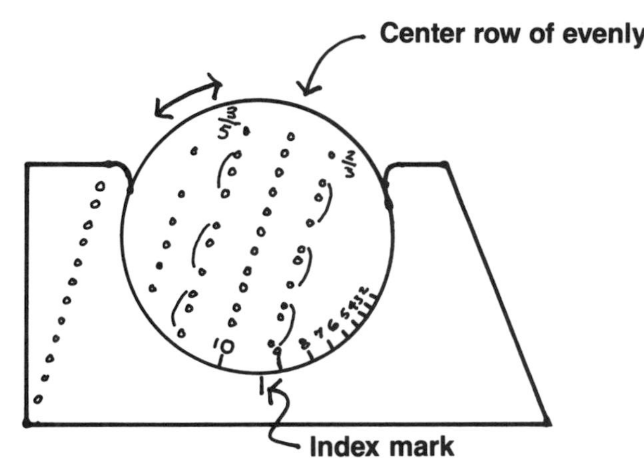

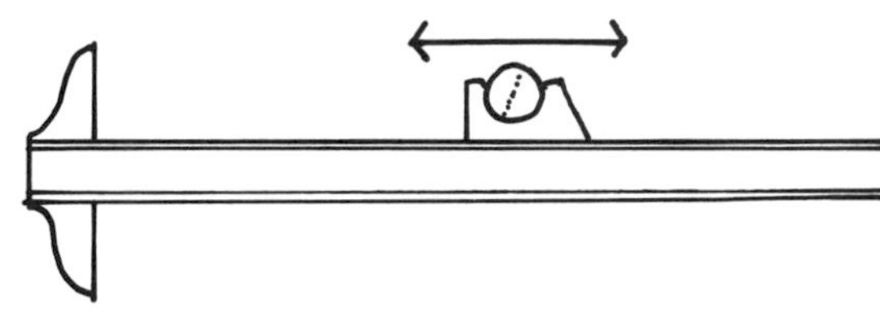

SETTING 10 CENTER ROW
GIVES LINES WITH EQUAL
SPACING AT THIS SIZE

The rows of holes on either side of the center row produce sets of three lines (between the brackets) which have the middle guideline slightly above center. A middle guideline is helpful to obtain consistency of shape for upper case letters such as B, E, F, H, and P. This is particularly true for larger letters (3/16-inch or more).

Several different lettering sizes and their applications are shown on the next page.

LEFT OF THE CENTER ROW
IS THE 2/3 ROW WHICH GIVES
A SLIGHTLY RAISED MIDDLE
GUIDELINE

Letter Sizes and Applications

HEIGHT	LETTER GUIDE SETTING	EXAMPLE
1/16"	CENTER ROW SETTING 4	TOO SMALL FOR HAND LETTERING
3/32	CENTER ROW SETTING 6	GOOD FOR SMALL LABELS & BLOCKS OF LETTERING. CAN WRITE A LOT IN A SMALL SPACE ALWAYS LEAVE A GAP BETWEEN LINES OF LETTERING
1/8"	CENTER ROW SETTING 8	A VERY COMFORTABLE SIZE FOR MOST LABELLING
3/16"	3/5 ROW SETTING 6	GOOD FOR SUB TITLES. USE A CENTER GUIDE LINE.
1/4"	3/5 ROW SETTING 8	UPPER LIMIT FOR PENCIL LETTERING.

Technique

After setting up guidelines and lightly dusting the surface with the dry cleaning pad, begin with a small triangle on the lower side of the parallel rule.

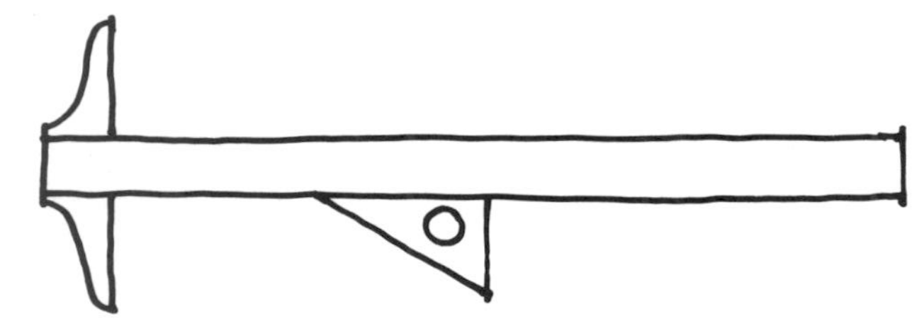
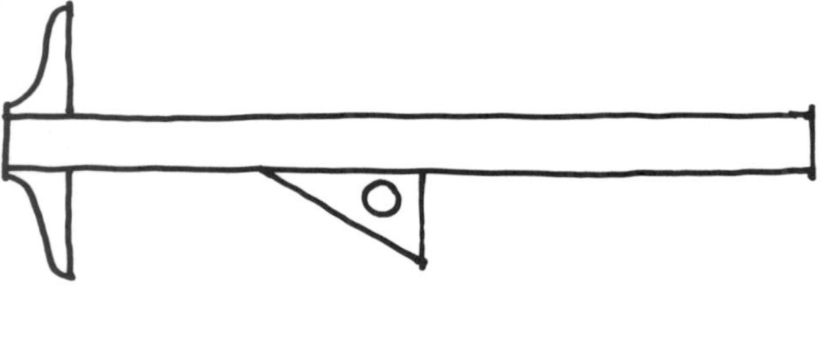

A 0.5 mm pencil with H or HB lead is ideal because you never have to sharpen it. Regular lead holders are better for large letters (3⁄16-inch) but the lead must be periodically sharpened. For Mylar, use a harder lead (2H) or plastic leads.

The Lettering Grip

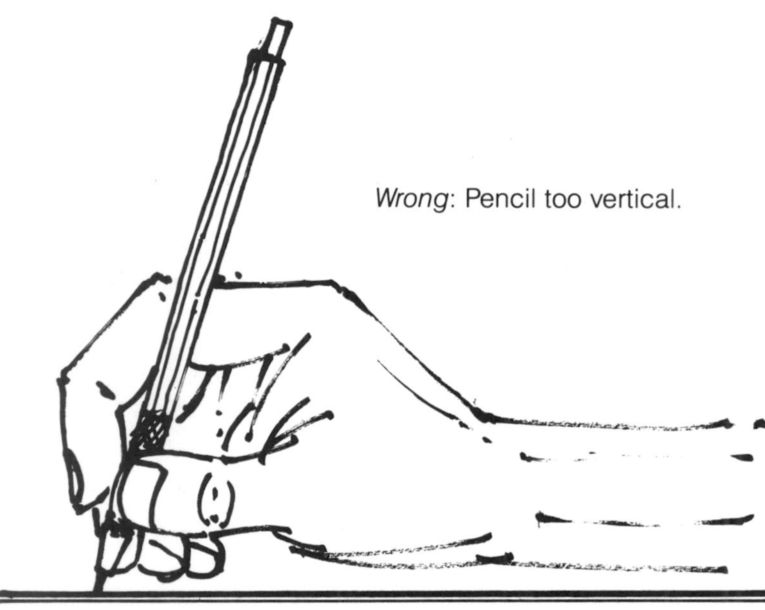

Wrong: Pencil too vertical.

Right: Pencil held at a low angle.

Flatten the end of the lead on a scrap sheet or with a sandpaper block.

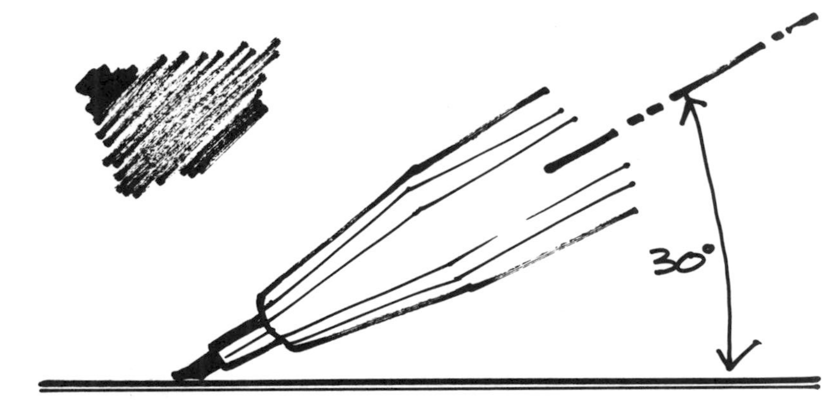

Rotate the pencil slightly, so that the flattened edge is against the vertical guide.

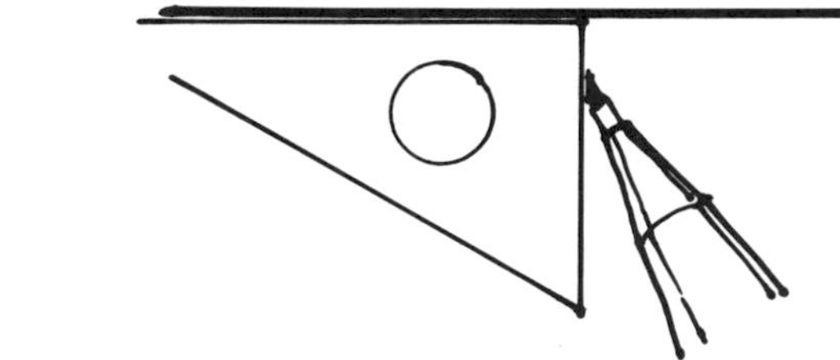

Draw verticals as thin lines with strong, dark ends.

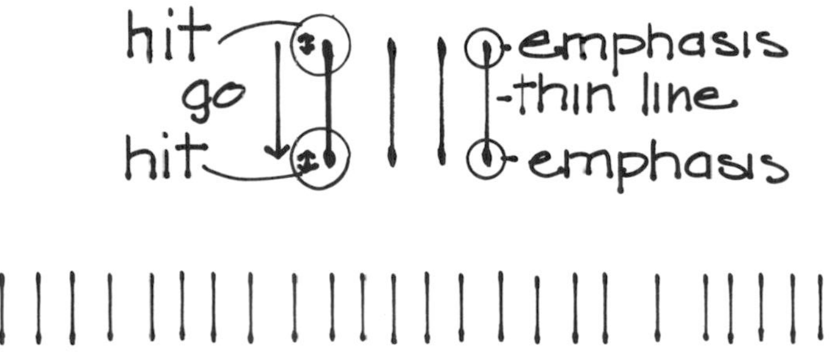

Watch the guidelines, keeping the verticals a consistent size.

The horizontals should be drawn as thicker, darker lines. Maintain a firm pressure throughout. Avoid brushing off the ends. A slight upward slope is acceptable.

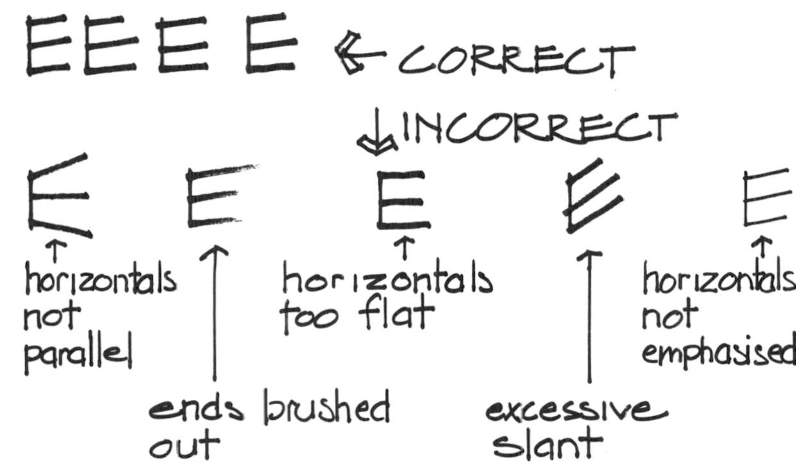

Do not move the fingers. Pivot on the palm or forearm muscle and let the fingers slide and steady the hand.

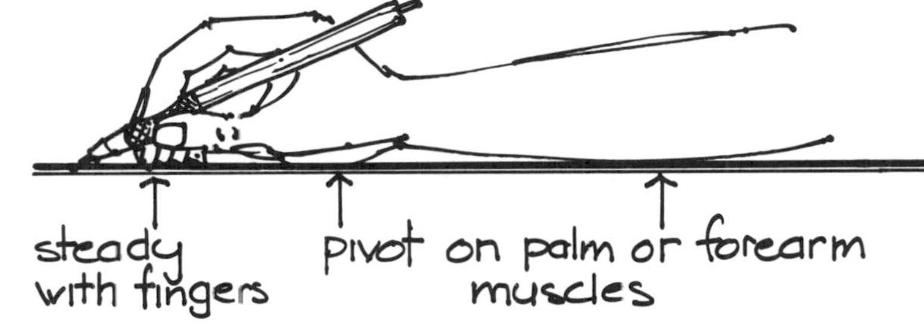

A small wrist movement may be necessary for horizontals. Remember: Make thin verticals with strong ends and thick, dark horizontals. As the lead wears down, simply rotate the pencil slightly to place the new chiseled side against the vertical guide and thus maintain the narrow verticals.

E F H I L T

Diagonal strokes and circular strokes are done with an even pressure. Some variations of line width will occur as a result of direction change. Do not move wrist or arm position. Move the vertical guide away and use quick, confident strokes with adequate pressure.

A K M N V W X Y Z

B C D O P Q R R S S

More Hints for Better Lettering

- Letter a drawing last to avoid smudges and overlapping with other areas of the drawing. This will enable you to space out your lettering and to avoid lettering through important details.
- Don't try to develop speed at first. Make each stroke quickly, but take your time between letters and between strokes until you have mastered each letter. Then gradually increase your speed. You will soon be able to letter almost as fast as you can write script.
- Organize lettering in logical blocks. Wherever possible, align notes down a vertical guideline. Place notes where they will not obscure other messages.
- Relate the size of the lettering to the importance of the labeling.
- Choose a style of lettering that is compatible with the character of the presentation and maintain that style consistently.
- Make letters bold and distinctive. Avoid a delicate, fine touch. Try emphasizing the beginnings and ends of strokes.
- Form the habit of lettering whenever possible—as you take notes, address envelopes, write letters, and compose memos.

Lettering Evaluation Guidelines

Check your pencil lettering against these criteria:

- All letters are dark with no fuzzy gray lines. (Test by running a blueline print.)
- The shapes are similar to the example alphabet and are consistent throughout.
- There is a uniformity of size, with all letters meeting the guidelines.
- The verticals are thin, dark lines with strong ends.
- The horizontals have a slight upward slant and are thick, dark, and parallel.
- The sheet has a neat, clean appearance with no smudges.

Prepared Letters

A variety of prepared lettering systems is available. These are usually used instead of freehand lettering when a more finished appearance is required.

Dry Transfer Letters

Also called rub down letters, these are available in many different font styles. Helvetica medium is a neutral style favored by many landscape architects. Dry transfer letters come in a variety of brand names, such as Chartpak and Letraset.

Advantages

- A wide variety of font styles is available.
- Many point sizes are available.
- Dry transfer letters give a professional, finished appearance.

Disadvantages

- They are expensive, especially in the larger sizes.
- They are time-consuming, especially when working with smaller sizes.

It is a good practice to cover dry transfer letters with clear tape to prevent their being dislodged during printing or filing. Burnish well to remove air bubbles.

A quick touch with clear tape is a good way to remove transfer letters.

Kroy Lettering System

Kroy is a brand name for a mechanical process whereby letters are punched out onto an adhesive strip. After removing the backing, the strip is applied to the drawing.

Advantages

- Gives fast, uniform, and professional-looking titles.
- A variety of styles is available.

Disadvantages

- The equipment and discs are expensive.
- Current machines have size limits.

Sticky Back Transfers

When large blocks of notes or plant lists are required on a drawing, it is faster to use the typewriter and an adhesive-backed clear sheet. Simply type or copy the notes onto the transfer sheet. Remove the protective backing, and apply the sheet adhesive to the drawings.

Advantages

- The method permits fast and uniform letters.

Disadvantages

- When printed, a ghosting effect sometimes appears due to the extra thickness and the adhesive material.
- It cannot substitute for the character of handlettering.

Try exercises 26, 27, and 28.

Presentation Plans

Presentation plans need to combine both straightedge and freehand techniques. They should be looser in style than working drawings, but more realistic than concept plans.

The most commonly used projection in the landscape design process at the design development stage is the plan view. There are some good reasons for this. In a plan view, it is easy to manipulate and show the horizontal relationships between objects and spaces. Furthermore, these elements can be accurately drawn to scale.

Picture the plan view as a diagram of the site as seen looking straight down from a hot air balloon. The graphic symbols represent the real objects and materials which are to be part of the design. Of course, this is an abstraction of reality and the symbols chosen can create a fairly realistic message or a rather abstract message. Abstract symbols are simple and fast to create but are not as convincing as the more realistic drawing. The graphic artist must choose the correct balance between time and realism to suit the message, the budget, and the time available.

The symbols and signatures shown in this chapter have been developed to produce the most convincing message of reality with economy of time in mind. Only black-and-white techniques are shown here. After mastering these methods, adapt them to color media and replace some with faster, more vivid color rendering techniques. Keep in mind that a black-and-white rendering is less expensive to reproduce than is a color rendering.

Understand the objects you are representing. Know something about their shape, texture, and reflective qualities. Choose line tone and textural symbols that match these qualities. Practice plan graphics by copying ideas from the following pages, developing your own symbols and style along with proficiency.

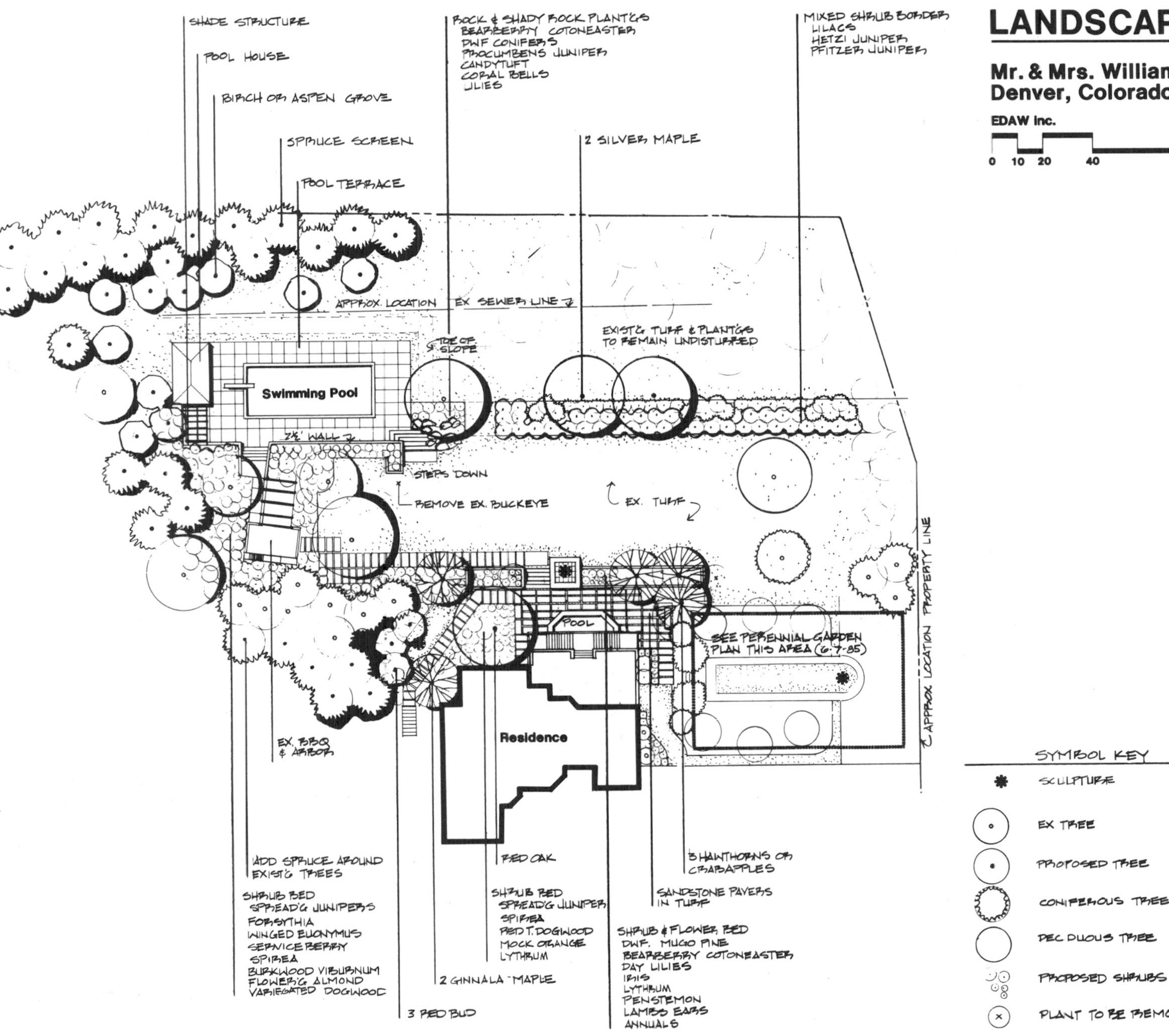

30% of actual size
Medium: Pencil on Mylar

Quick Trees

Very fast template and freehand outline symbols

Trees should be drawn at about two-thirds to three-fourths of their mature, ultimate spread. This gives a fair representation of the impact of the planting design in the near future, rather than in twenty or thirty years.

Always use a light guideline and show the center of the tree.

Simple single circle template outline

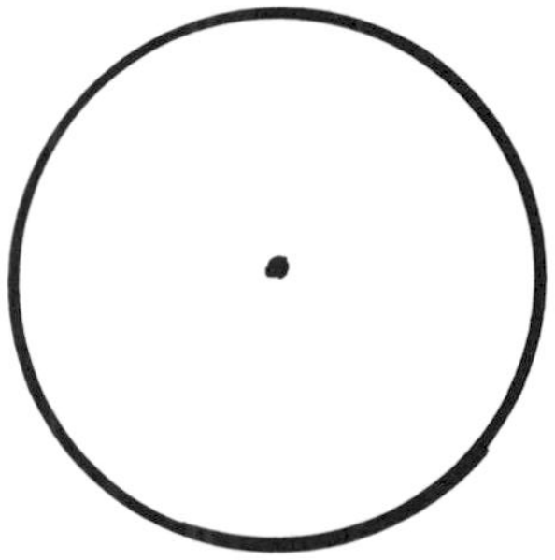

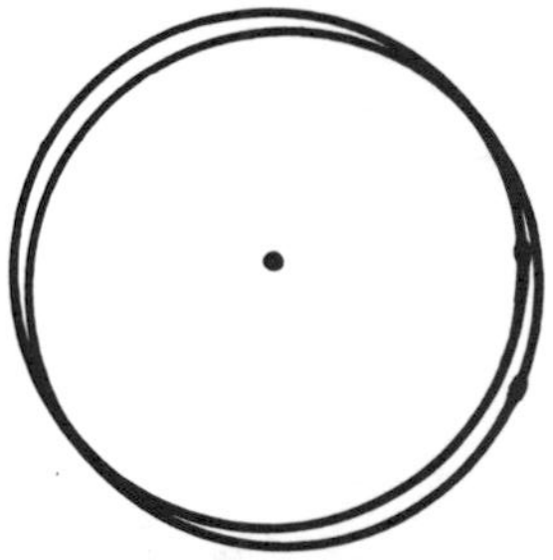

Double circle template outline, offset

Freehand double outline around a light guideline circle

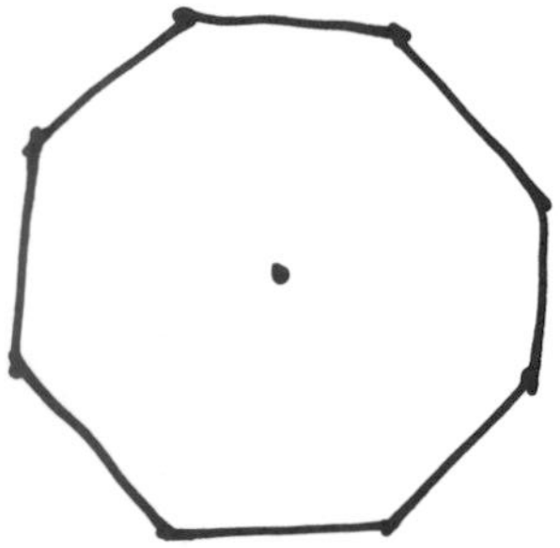

Angular outline

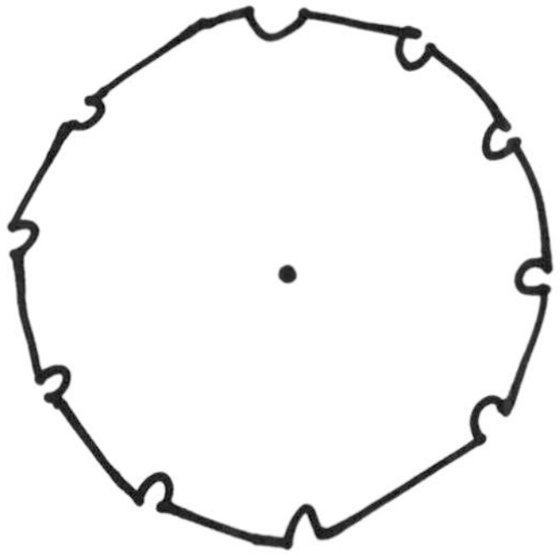

Angular outline with half-circles at the corners

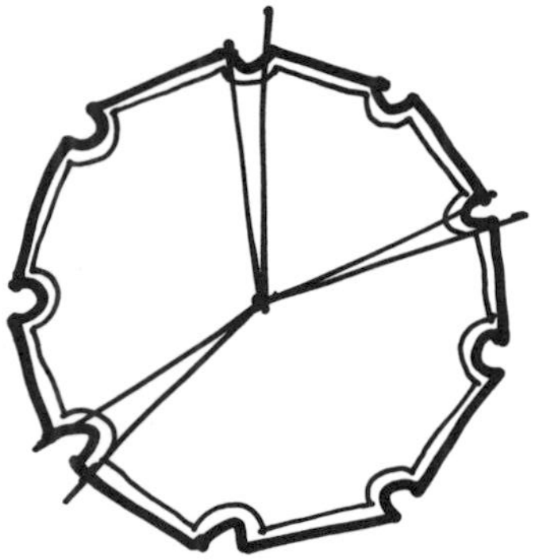

Thick and thin double outline with quick branching

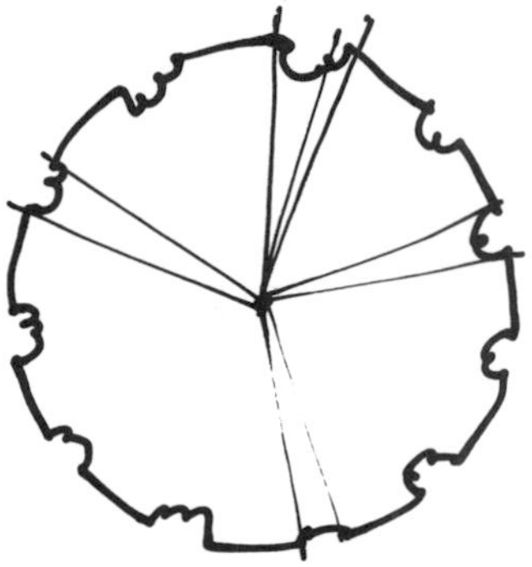

Circular outline with small Ws removed

Double wavy line

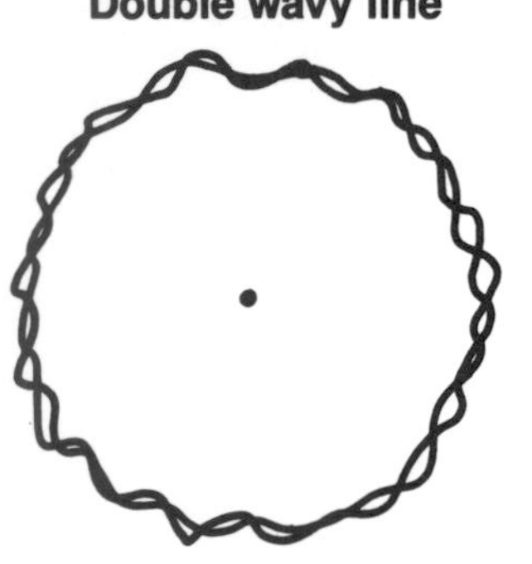

Irregular puffy edge

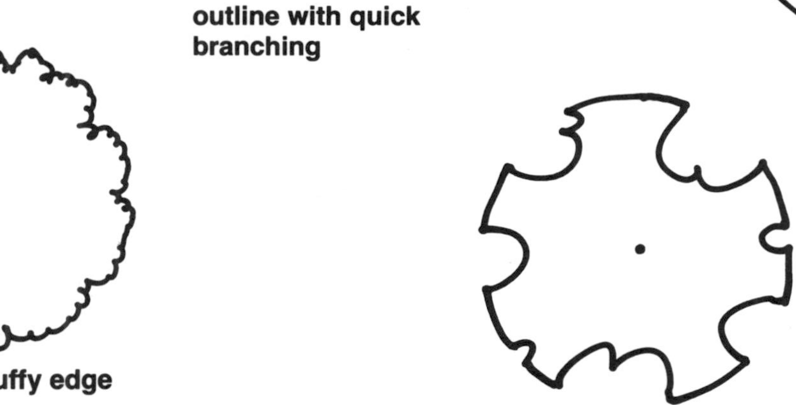

Bites out of the cookie

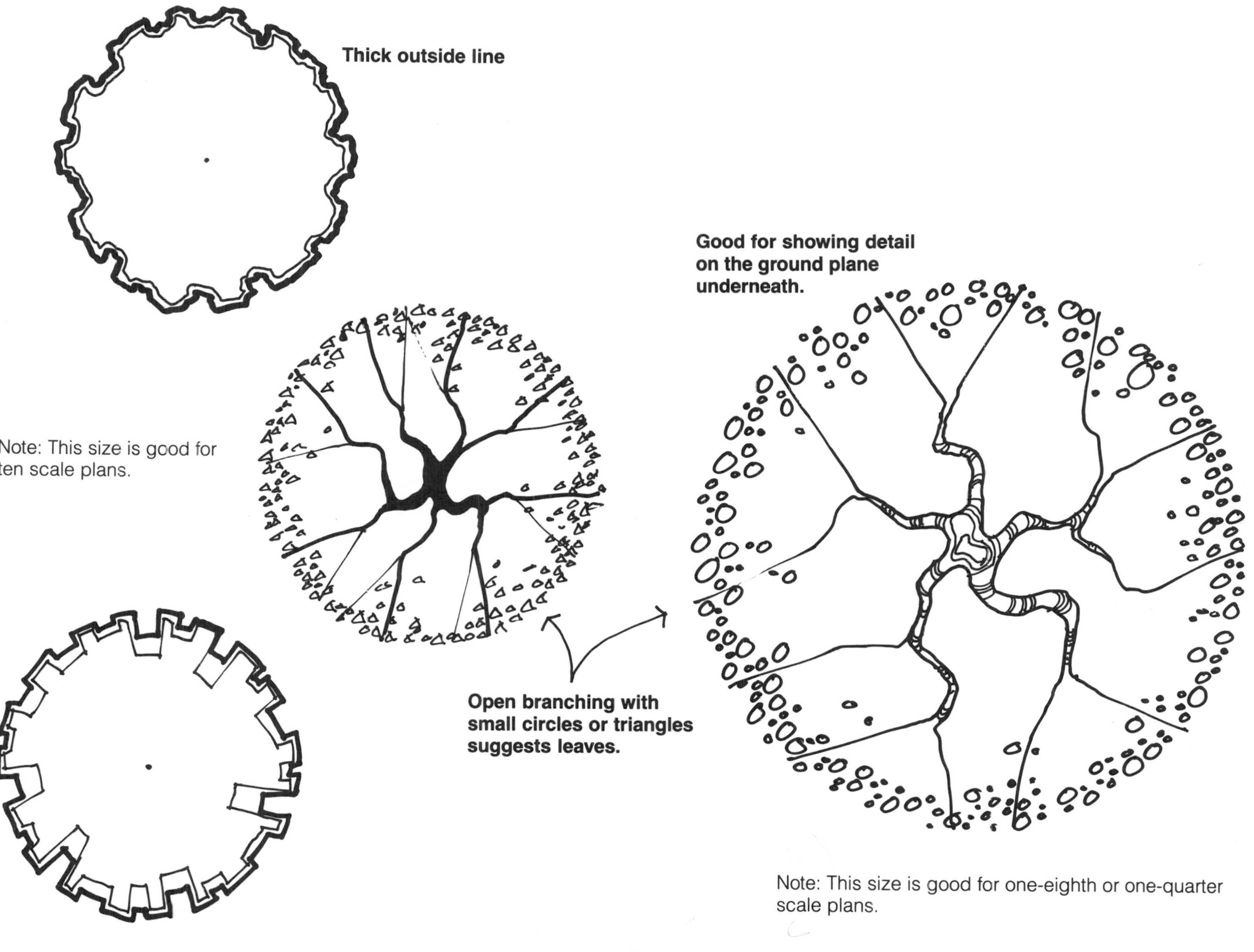
Thick outside line
Note: This size is good for ten scale plans.
Open branching with small circles or triangles suggests leaves.
Good for showing detail on the ground plane underneath.
Note: This size is good for one-eighth or one-quarter scale plans.

Trees with Foliage Texture

A simple shape is repeated around the edge and piled up on the shaded side to give an appearance of roundness.

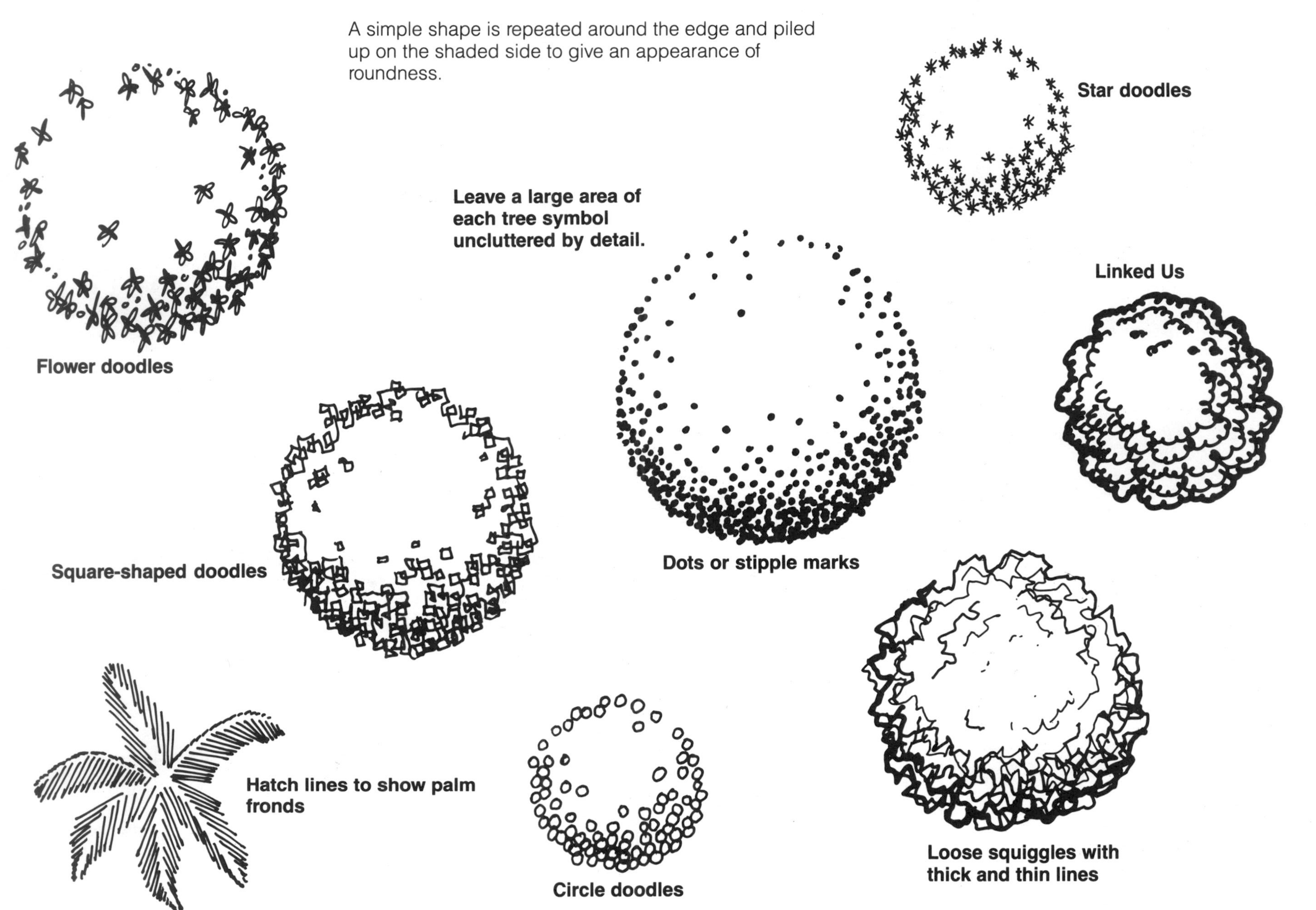

Trees with Branch Patterns

Good for showing winter effects or layering other symbols underneath, this kind of symbol is also easy to color.

Five main branch spokes looks most natural. Make sure that any thickened center becomes gradually thinner toward the edge.

Simple straight lines

Many lines toward the outside defines the edge.

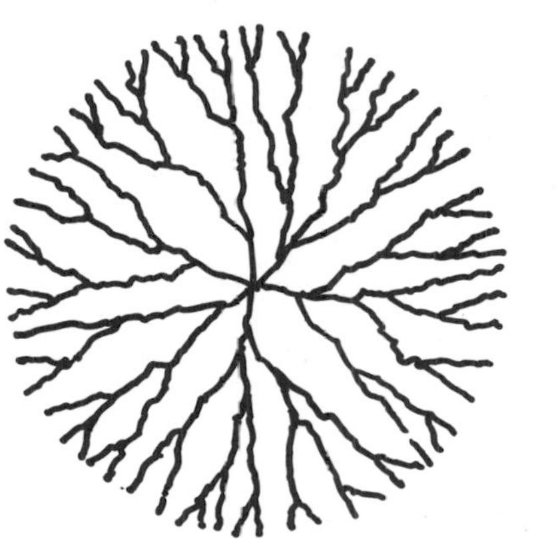

Irregular bumpy lines

Angular lines

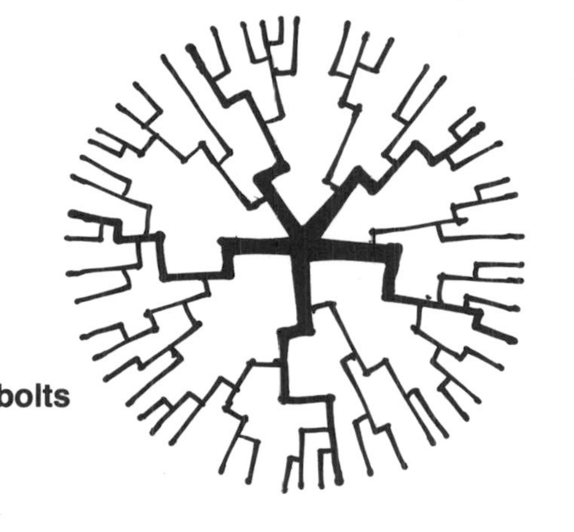

Lightning bolts

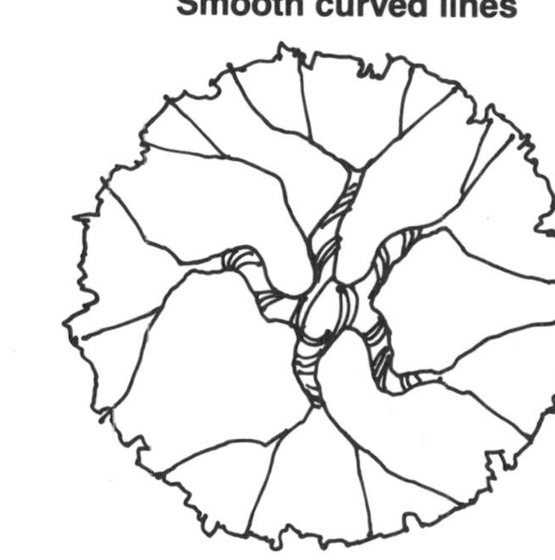

Smooth curved lines

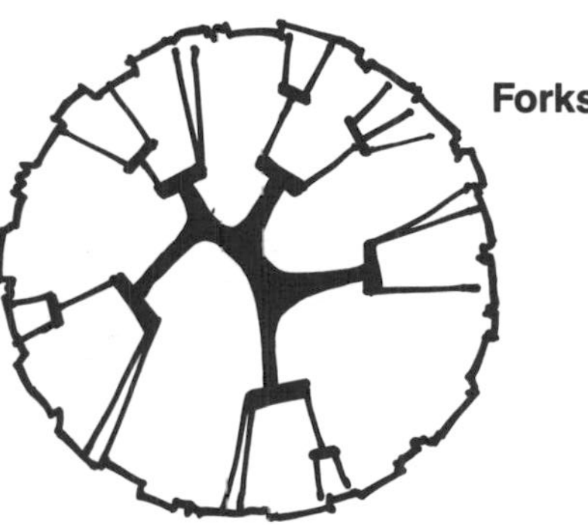

Forks

When only a few branches are shown the outside of the symbol may need some edge definition.

Sequence for Drawing Branched Trees

1. Start with a light guideline circle and locate the center.
2. Draw in the main branch structure. Solid branches should taper from thick near the center to thin near the outside.
3. Add a few more secondary branches, each one touching the outer circle guideline.
4. Add many small branches to emphasize the edge.

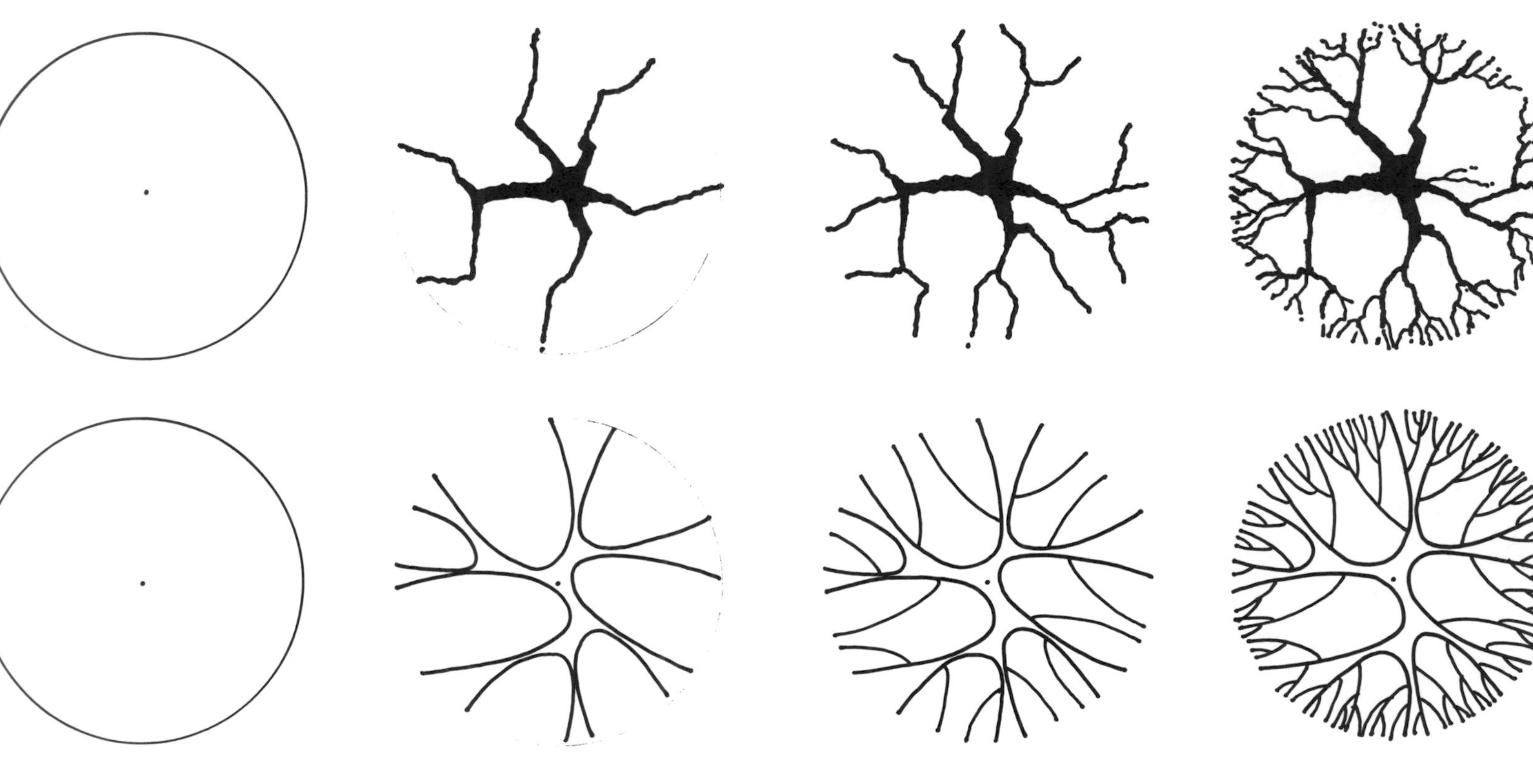

Coniferous Trees

Drafted lines

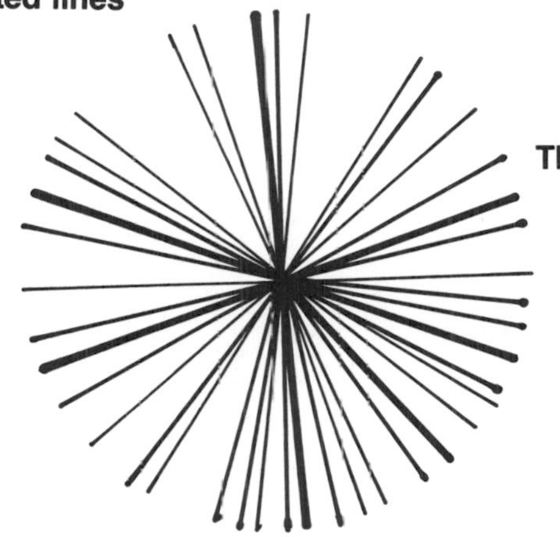

Thick and thin lines

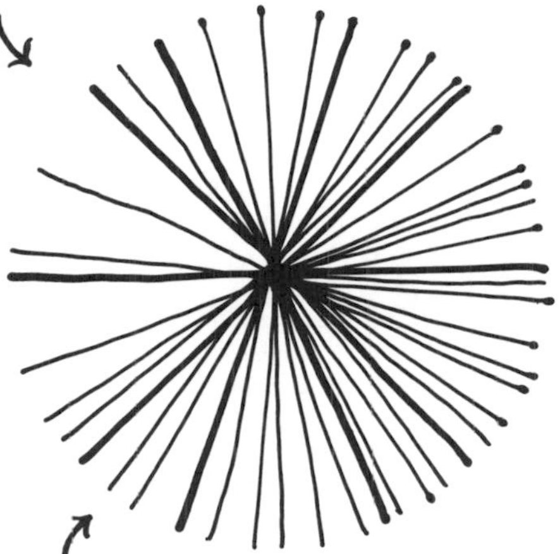

Freehand lines

All lines the same

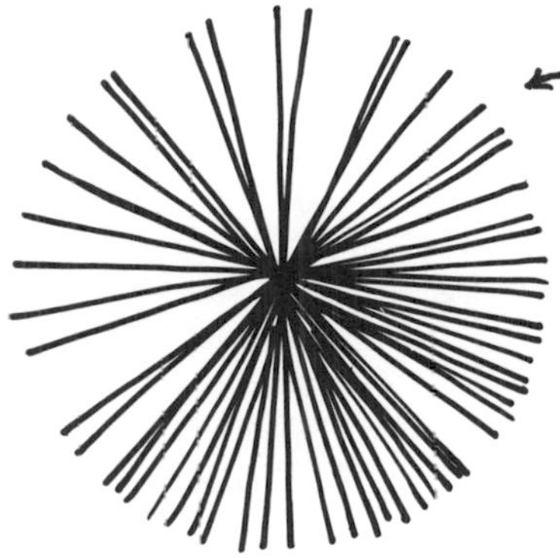

The addition of more lines on one side gives an added depth.

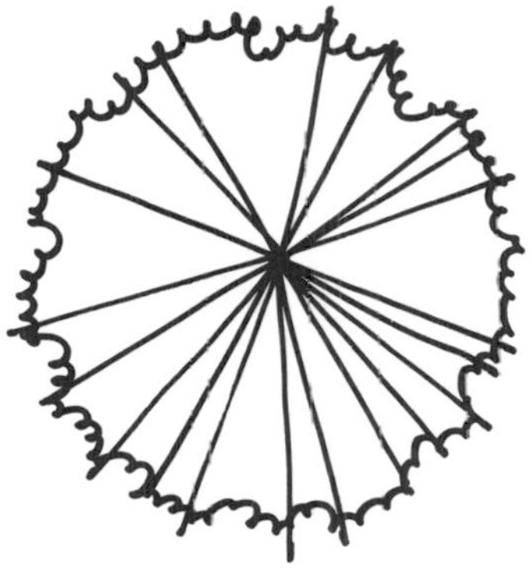

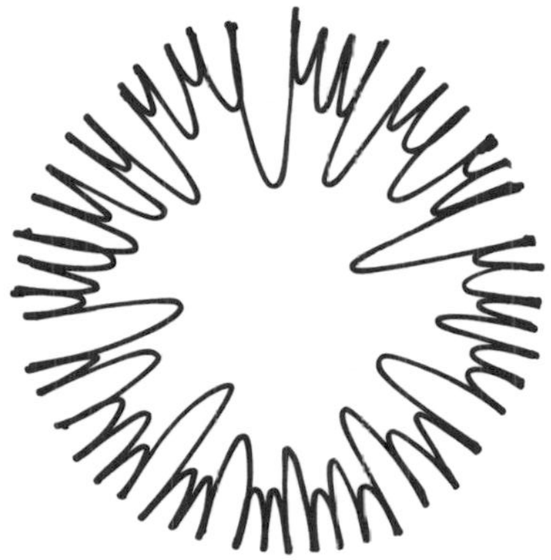

Deep and shallow U shapes

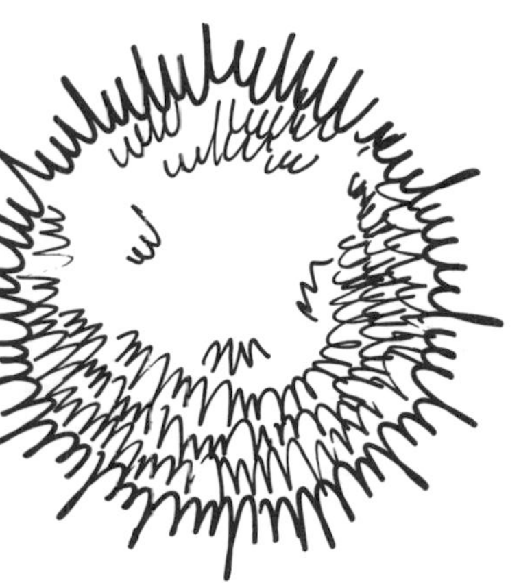

Sequence for Radial Line Symbols

1. Set up guide circle.
2. Place a larger circle template around it.
3. For drafted symbols, draw lines with the triangle on top of the circle template.
4. For freehand symbols, place the smaller template over the larger one and draw lines from one side to the other.
5. Make sure that all lines cross in the center.

Plant Groups

The symbols shown here and on the next three pages can be used to represent forests and groves of trees at larger scales or groups of shrubs at smaller scales.

Begin with a series of circles as light guidelines. Vary their size a little.

A simple, heavy outline is the fastest method.

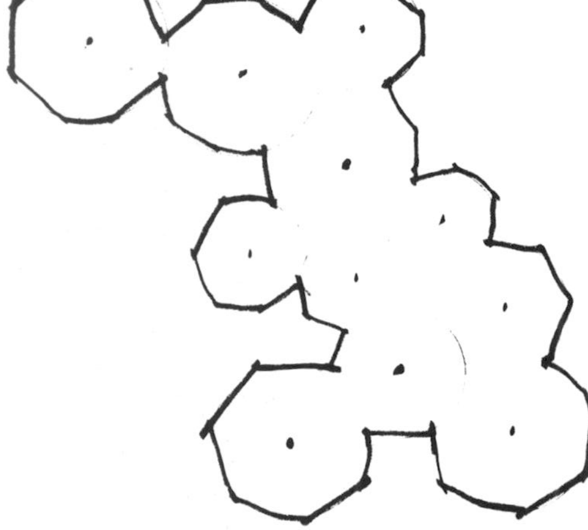

Angular lines, like a stop sign, are used for outlines.

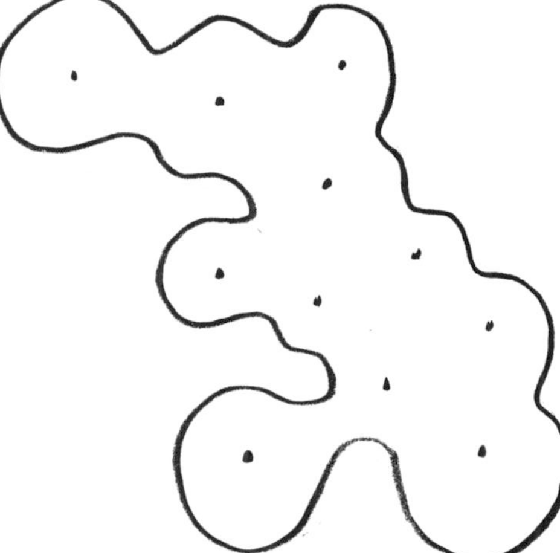

Centers may or may not be located.

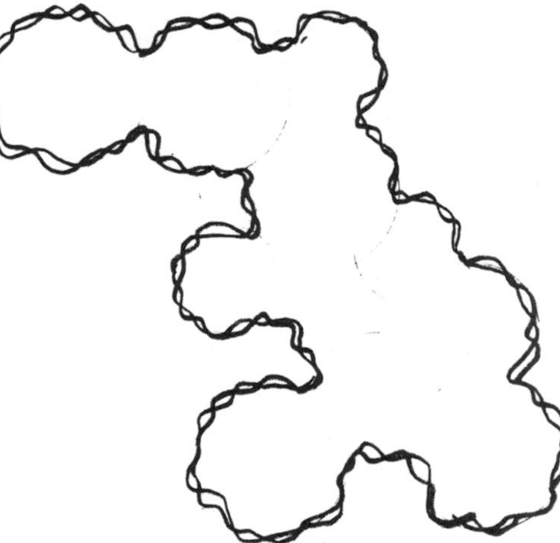

Loose wavy lines, double or single, are used for outlines.

Tropical Plants

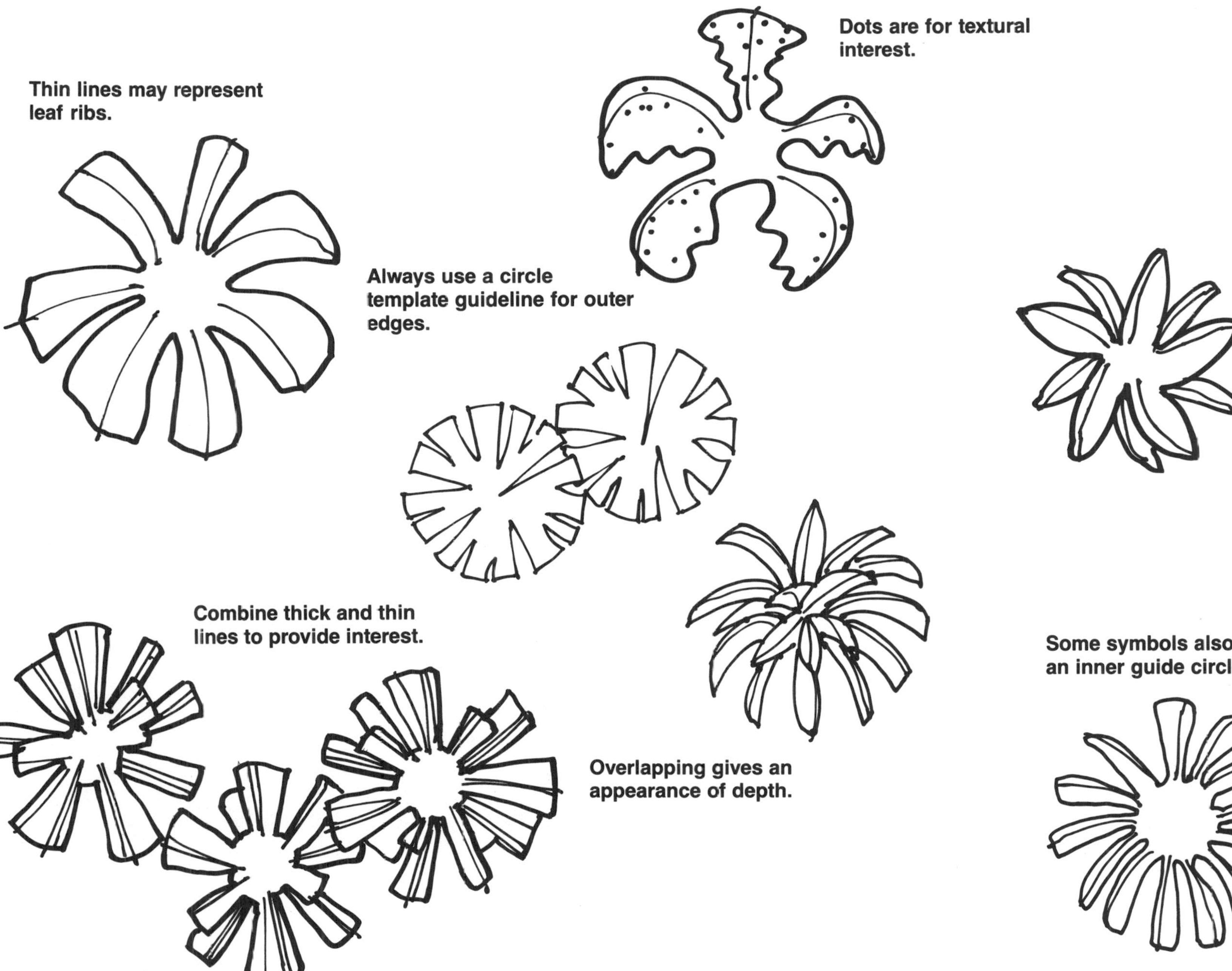

More Deciduous Shrubs or Tree Groups

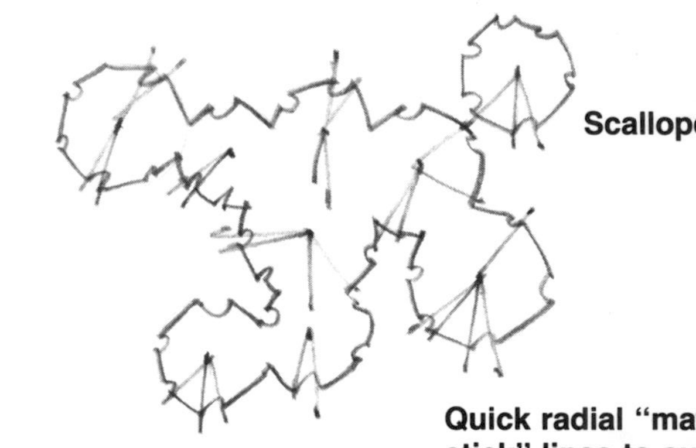

Scalloped edges

Quick radial "match-stick" lines to suggest branching

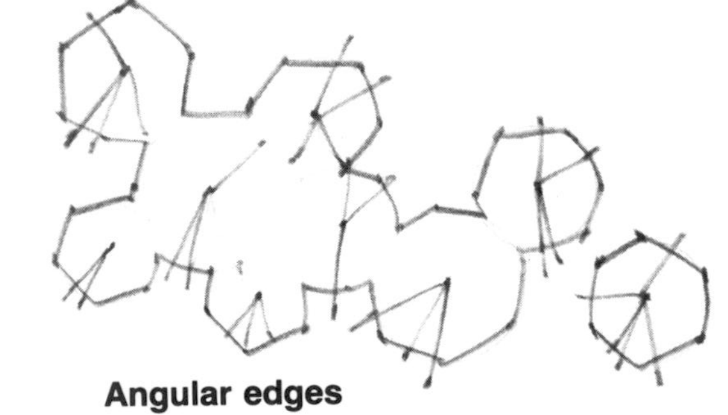

Angular edges

Double outline

Double stop sign, thick and thin

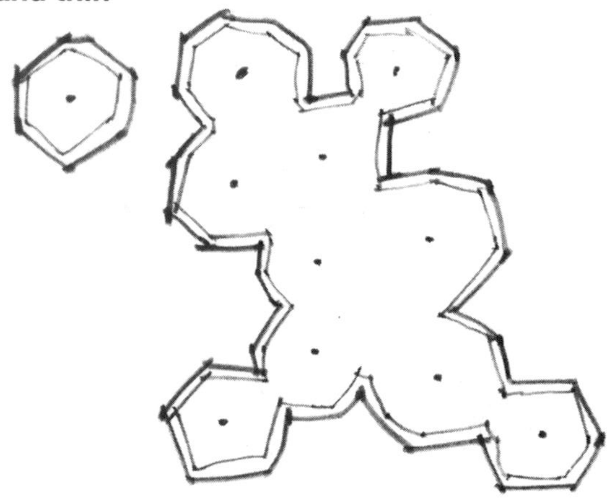

Puffy outline with some pencil hatching on one side to show roundness

Irregular outline with some dots

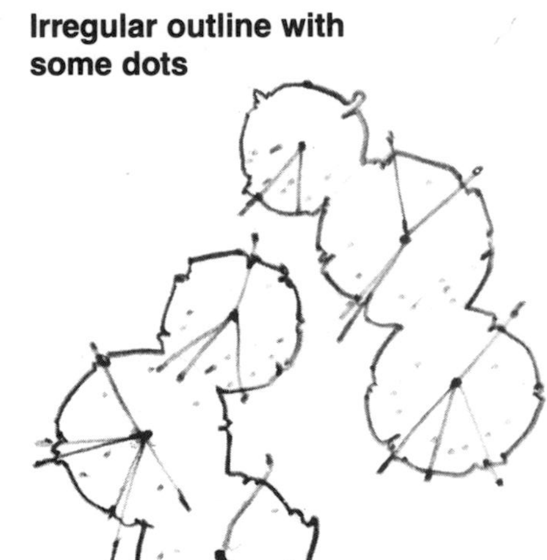

Fine-textured Shrubs

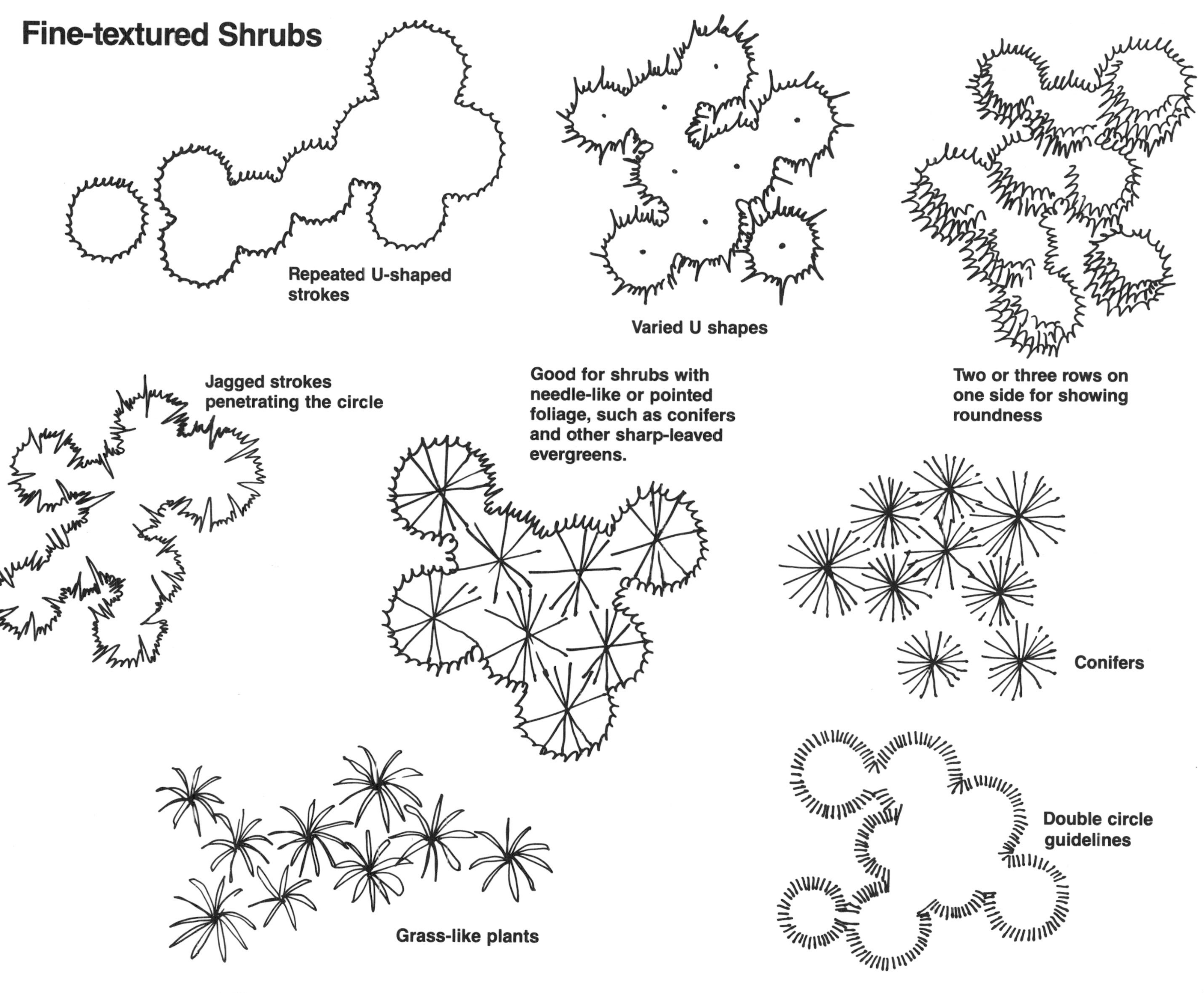

Hedges or Rows

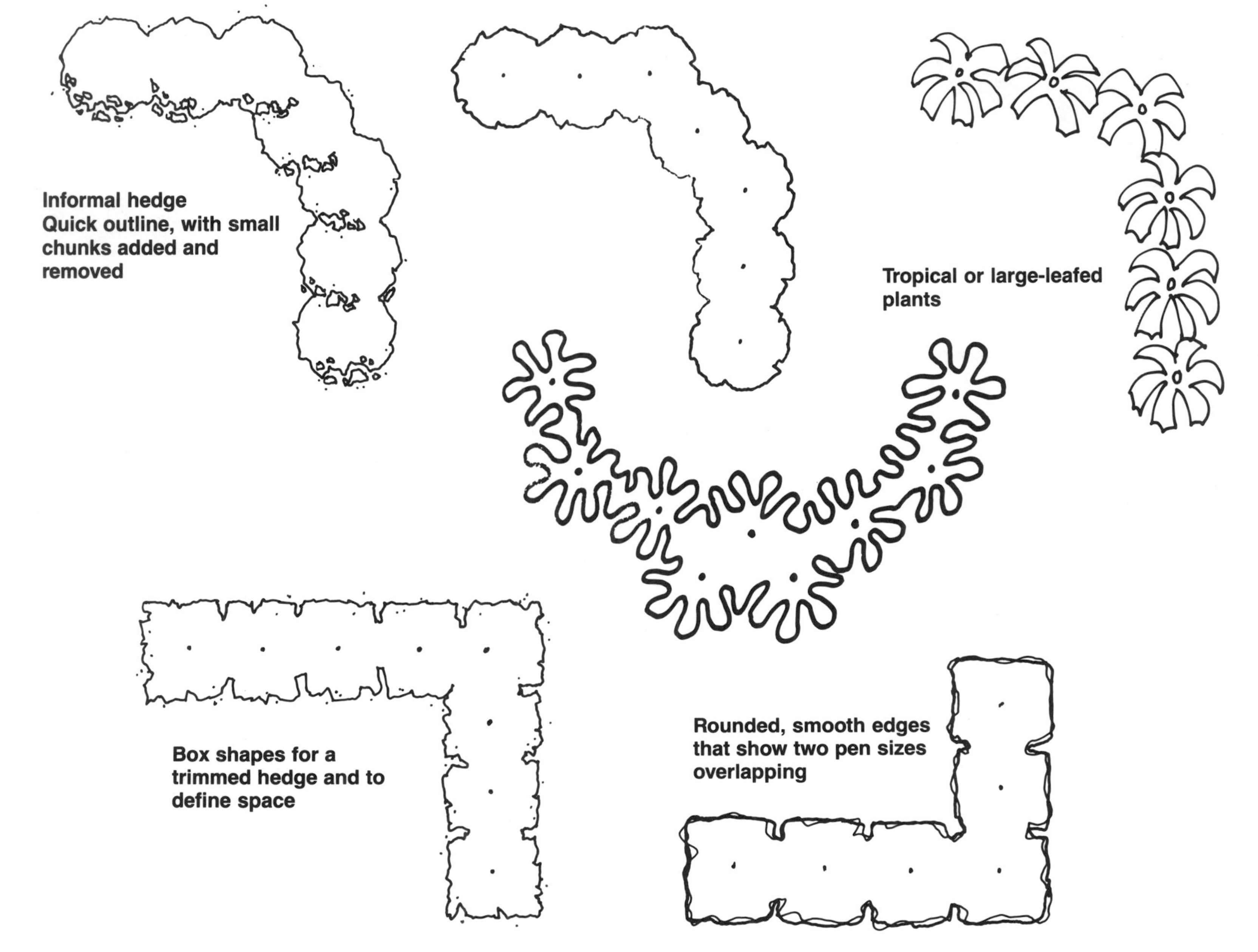

Informal hedge
Quick outline, with small chunks added and removed

Tropical or large-leafed plants

Box shapes for a trimmed hedge and to define space

Rounded, smooth edges that show two pen sizes overlapping

Ground Covers

Large areas of grass may be left untextured or shown with a stipple pattern of dots near the edges. For smaller areas where a denser tone is desired, the patterns shown here may work.

A fast method to obtain consistent rows is to tape two triangles together, leaving a small gap of ⅛-inch to ¼-inch. Choose a doodle and quickly stroke between the triangles.

Best results are obtained by keeping rows horizontal and parallel. Make sure that successive rows touch or overlap slightly.

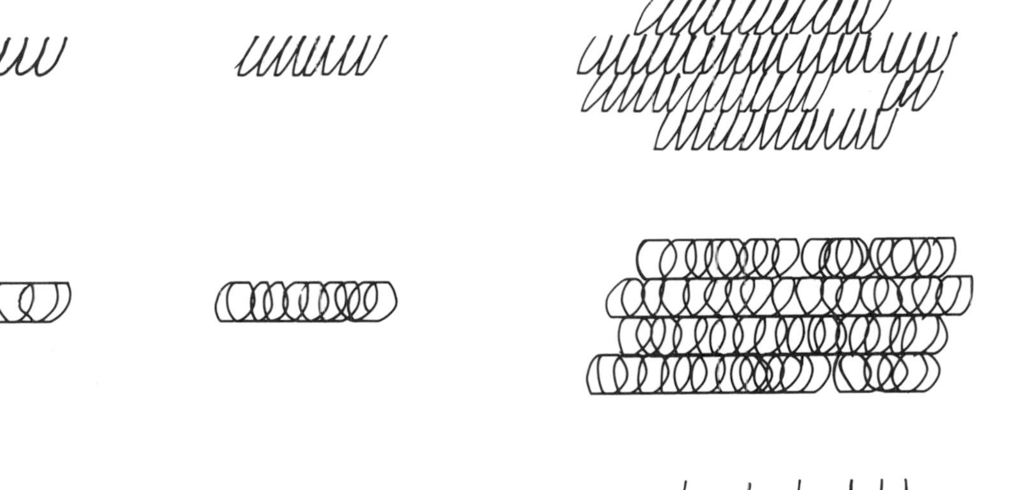

More Ground Covers

The basic line shape shown on the left is repeated to form a build-up of pattern as shown on the right.

These shapes can be drawn freehand with no horizontal guides.

Connected squares

Downward arches

Upward arches

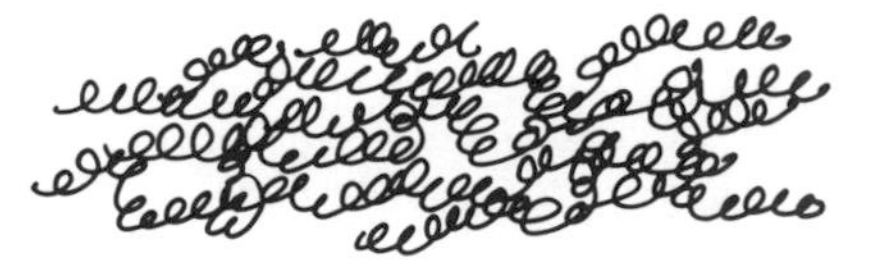

Connected loops

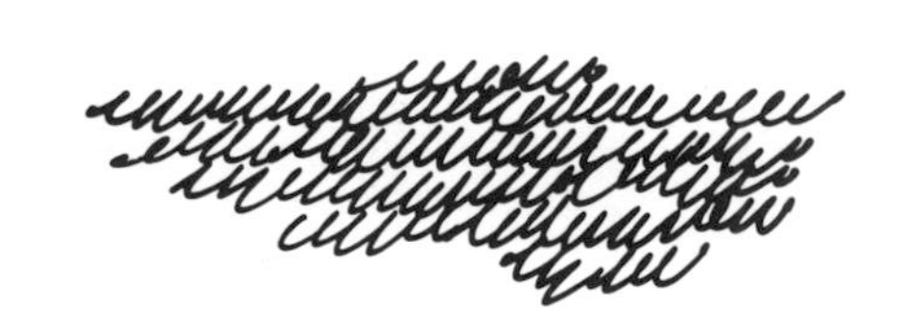

Diagonal Ws

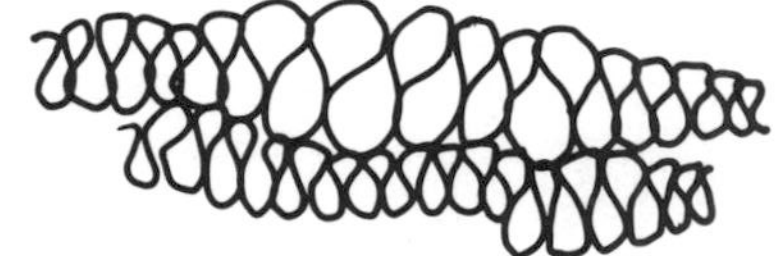

Snake loops

Tone Contrast and Balance

These techniques are time-consuming and should only be used when the plan must read well without color.

Large area of untextured surface may be needed to balance areas of dense tone.

When ground covers are heavily toned, the shrub groups can be left white for contrast.

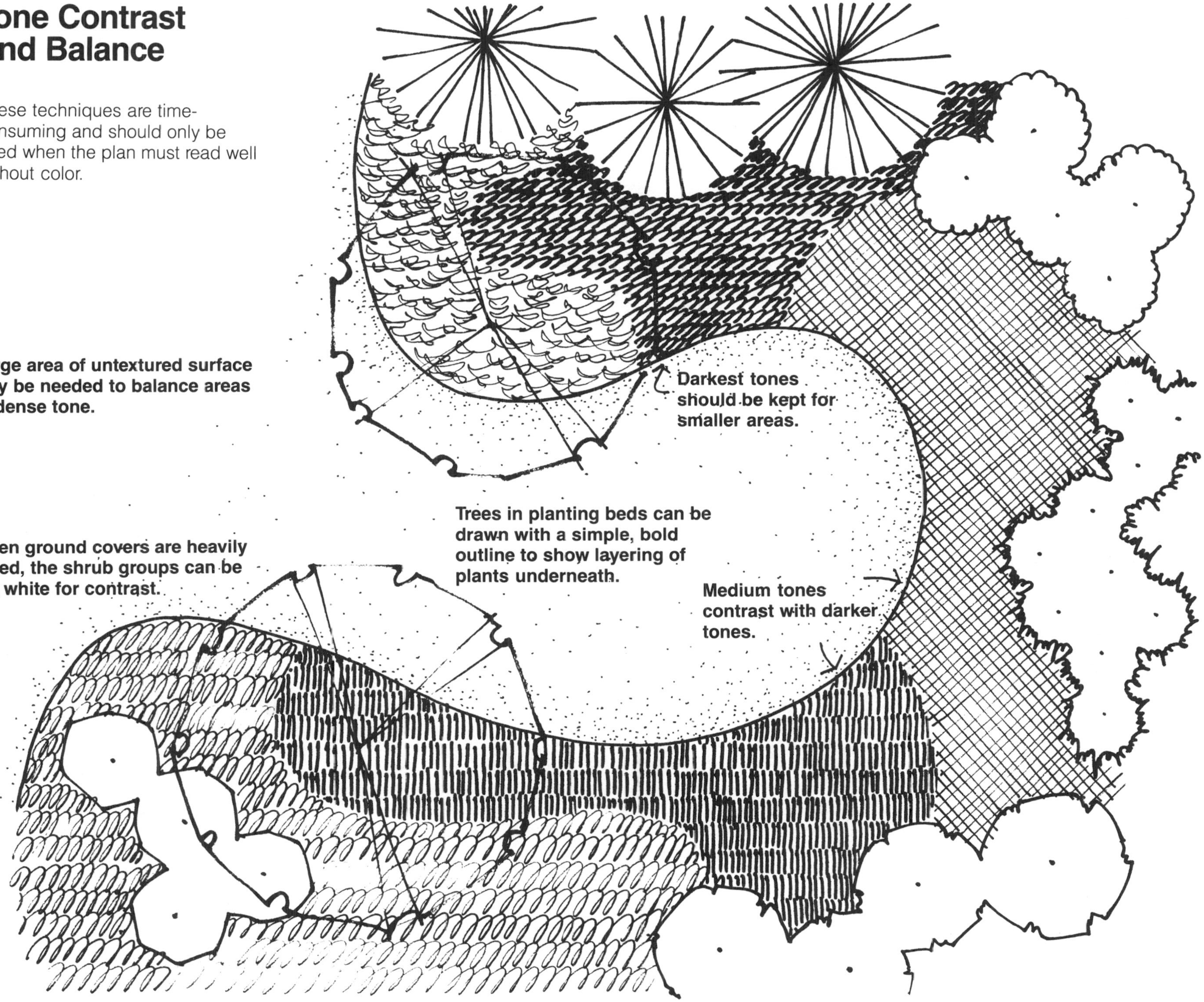

Darkest tones should be kept for smaller areas.

Trees in planting beds can be drawn with a simple, bold outline to show layering of plants underneath.

Medium tones contrast with darker tones.

Layering

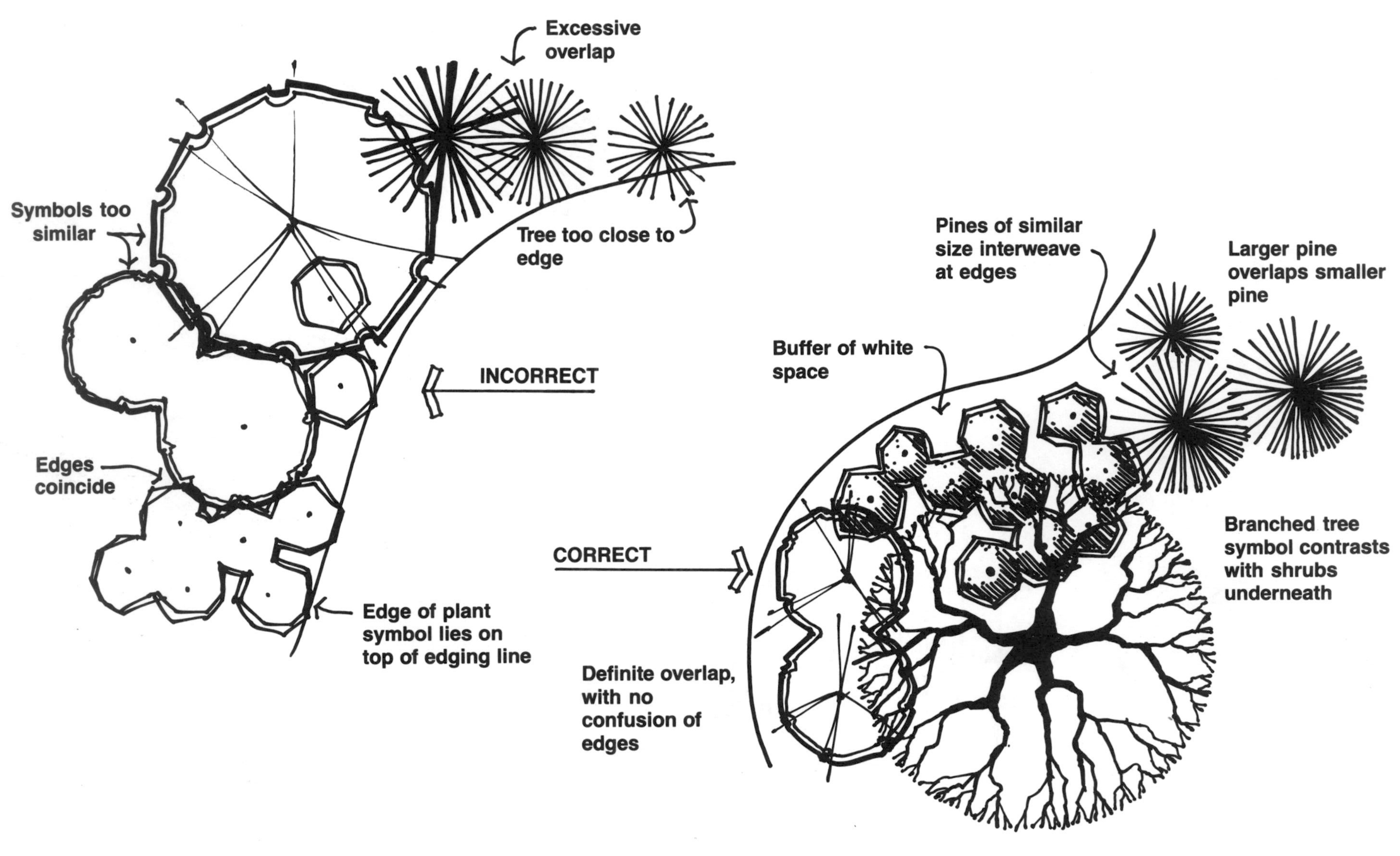

Excessive overlap
Symbols too similar
Tree too close to edge
Edges coincide
INCORRECT
Edge of plant symbol lies on top of edging line
Pines of similar size interweave at edges
Larger pine overlaps smaller pine
Buffer of white space
CORRECT
Branched tree symbol contrasts with shrubs underneath
Definite overlap, with no confusion of edges

Landform

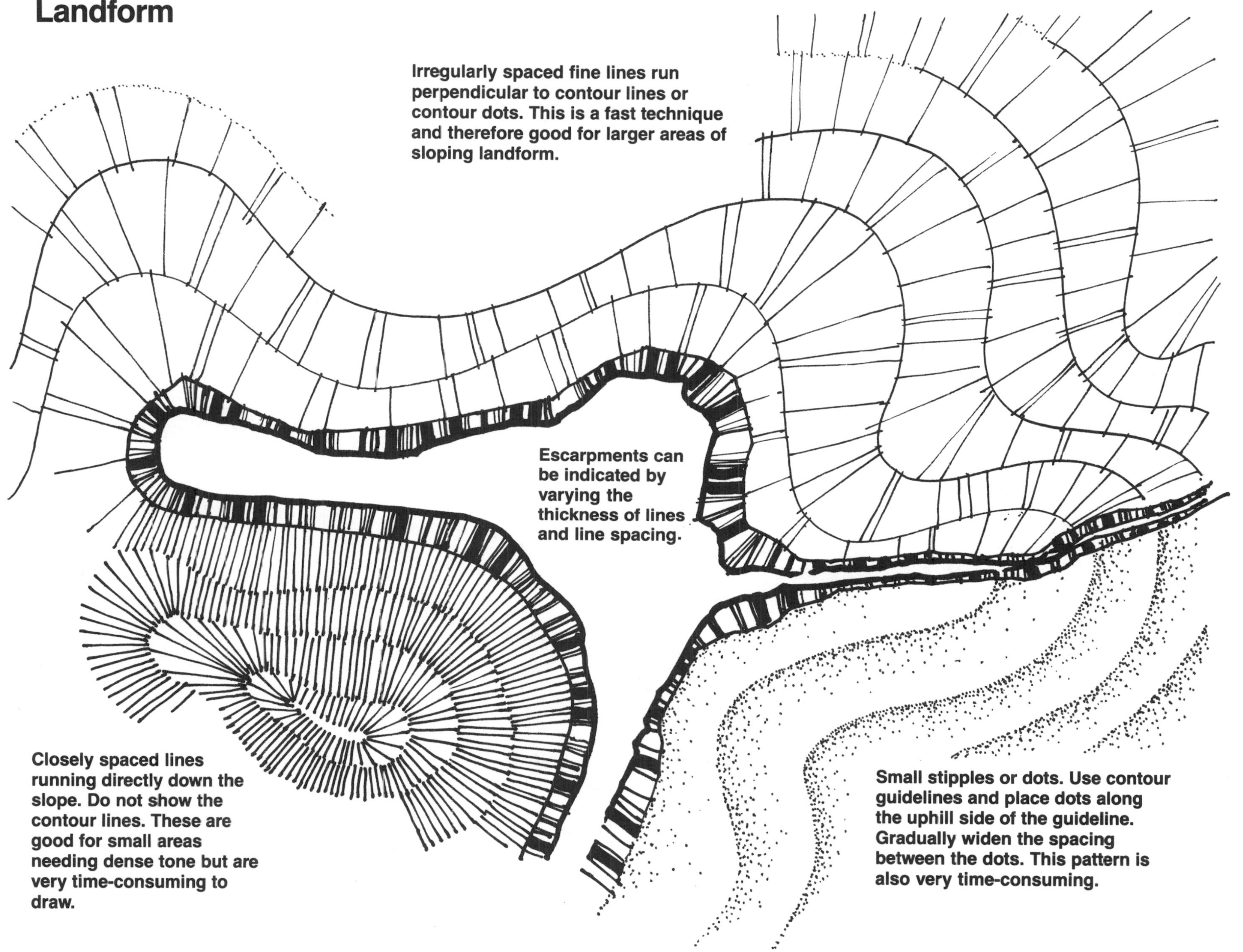
Irregularly spaced fine lines run perpendicular to contour lines or contour dots. This is a fast technique and therefore good for larger areas of sloping landform.
Escarpments can be indicated by varying the thickness of lines and line spacing.
Closely spaced lines running directly down the slope. Do not show the contour lines. These are good for small areas needing dense tone but are very time-consuming to draw.
Small stipples or dots. Use contour guidelines and place dots along the uphill side of the guideline. Gradually widen the spacing between the dots. This pattern is also very time-consuming.

Rocks

Angular rocks. Vary the sizes. Use thick and thin lines.

Rounded boulders. Draw with smooth thick and thin lines. Offset the loops.

Flat, layered rocks. Show overlapping. Pile up lines along the edges. Keep lines directional to show stratification.

Water

Natural waterways, such as ponds, lakes, and streams can be left white. The addition of smooth, flowing lines near the edges give a hint of motion.

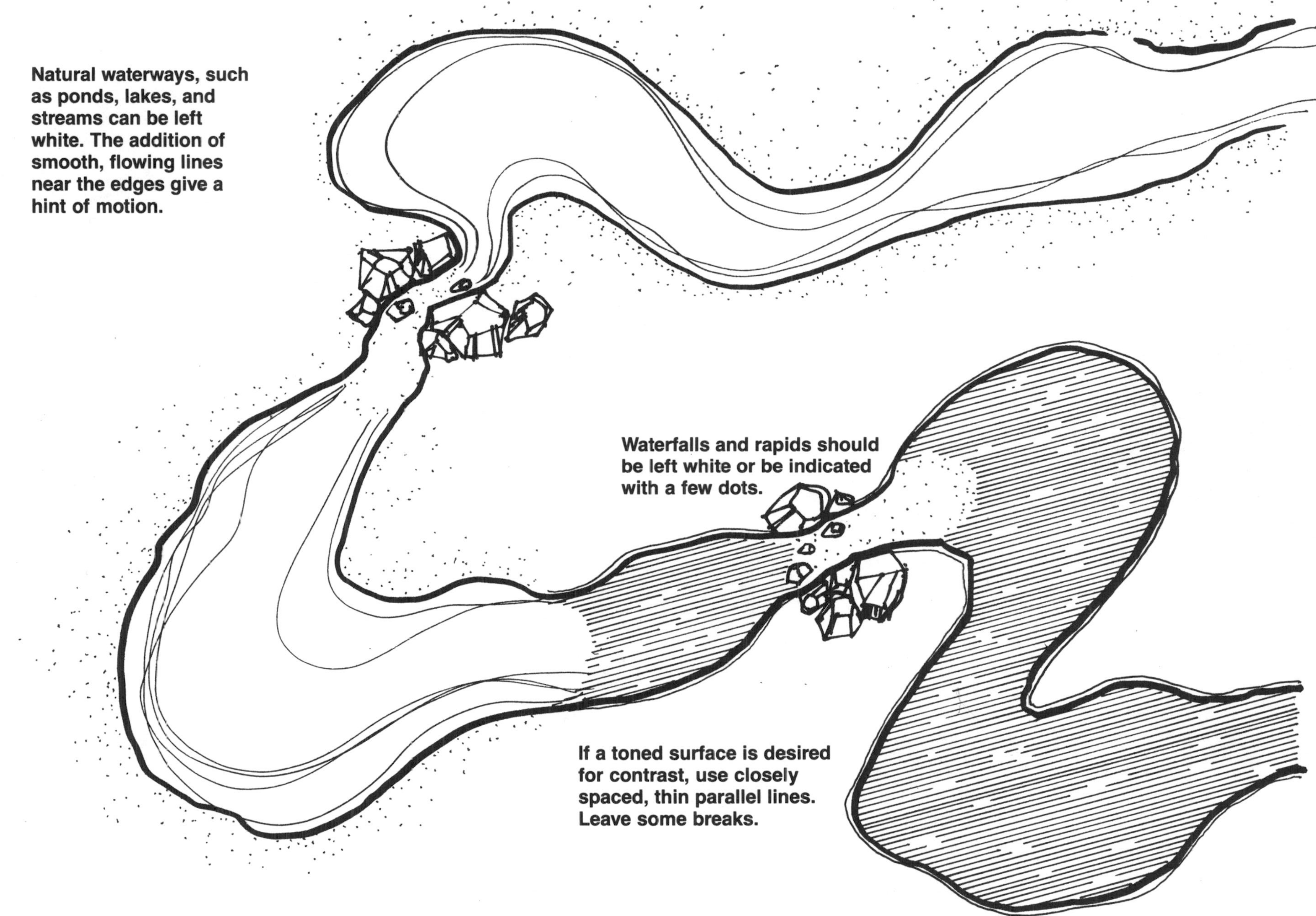

Waterfalls and rapids should be left white or be indicated with a few dots.

If a toned surface is desired for contrast, use closely spaced, thin parallel lines. Leave some breaks.

Pools and Fountains

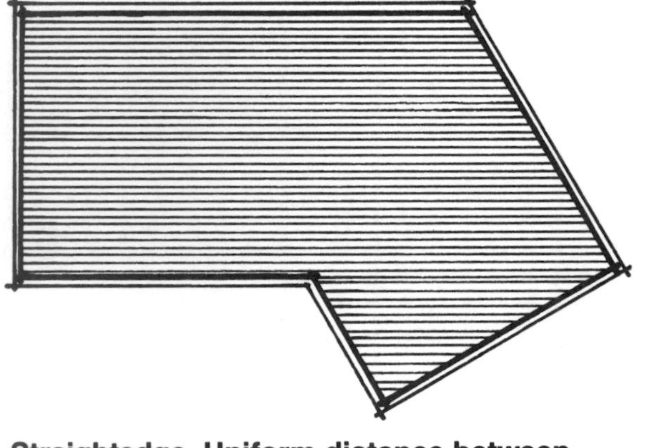

Straightedge. Uniform distance between lines.

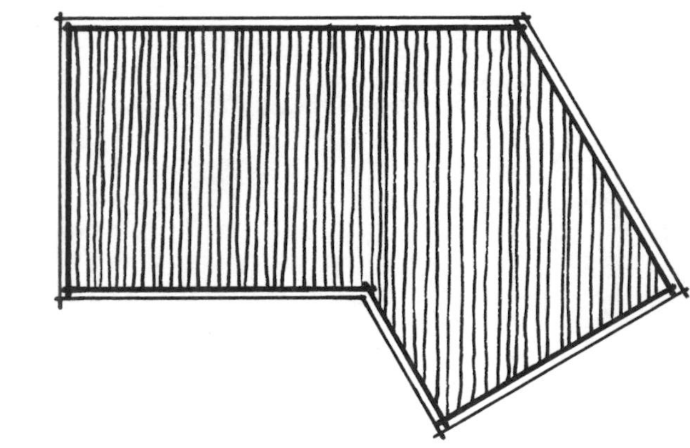

Freehand lines. Some variation in spacing.

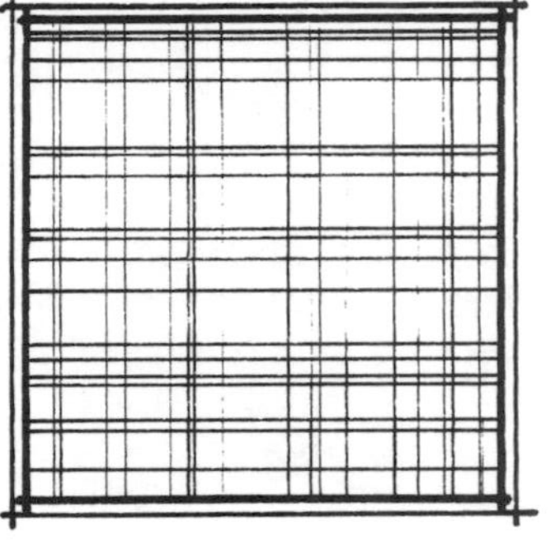

Reflecting pool. Lightly ruled cross lines. Allow pen to skip.

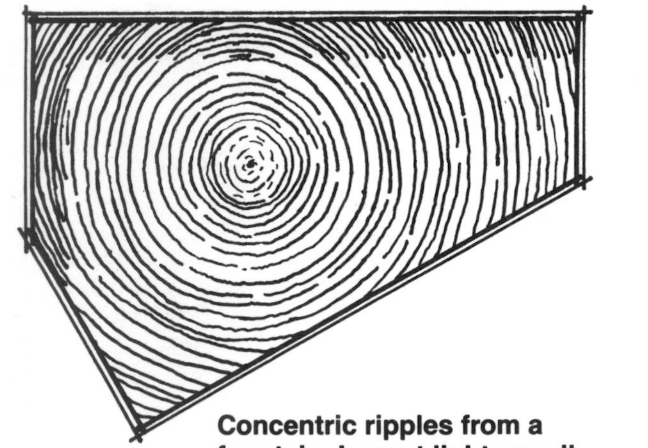

Concentric ripples from a fountain. Layout light pencil guidelines. Freehand circles.

Implies movement. Time-consuming.

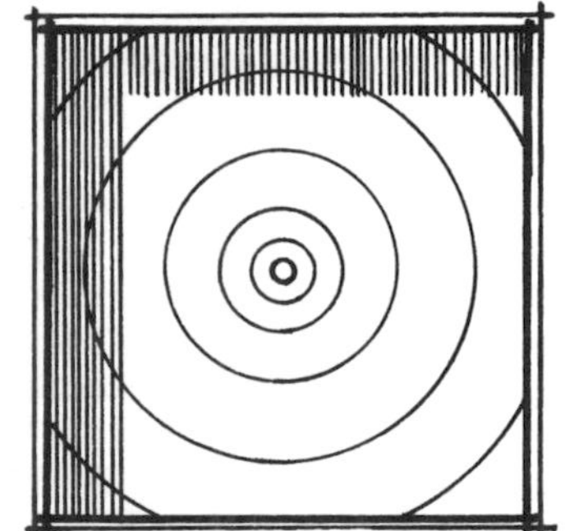

Concentric circles drawn with template. Shadow lines added. Fast.

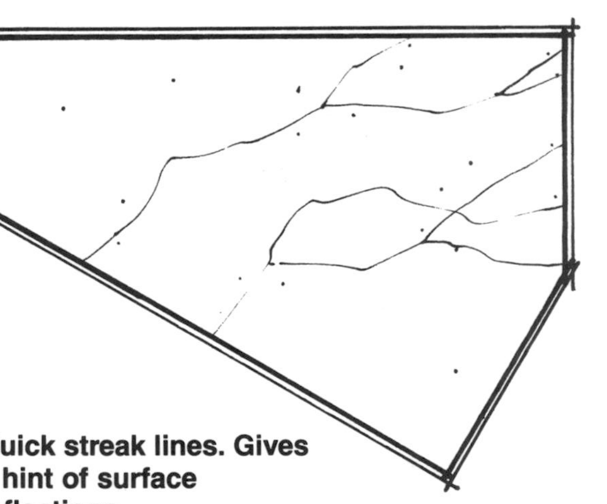

Quick streak lines. Gives a hint of surface reflections.

Water Surface Texture

Place a textured material such as plywood, pressboard, or sandpaper, under drawing. The same techniques can be used with colored art sticks.

Rub surface with a graphite stick. This technique produces a rippled effect.

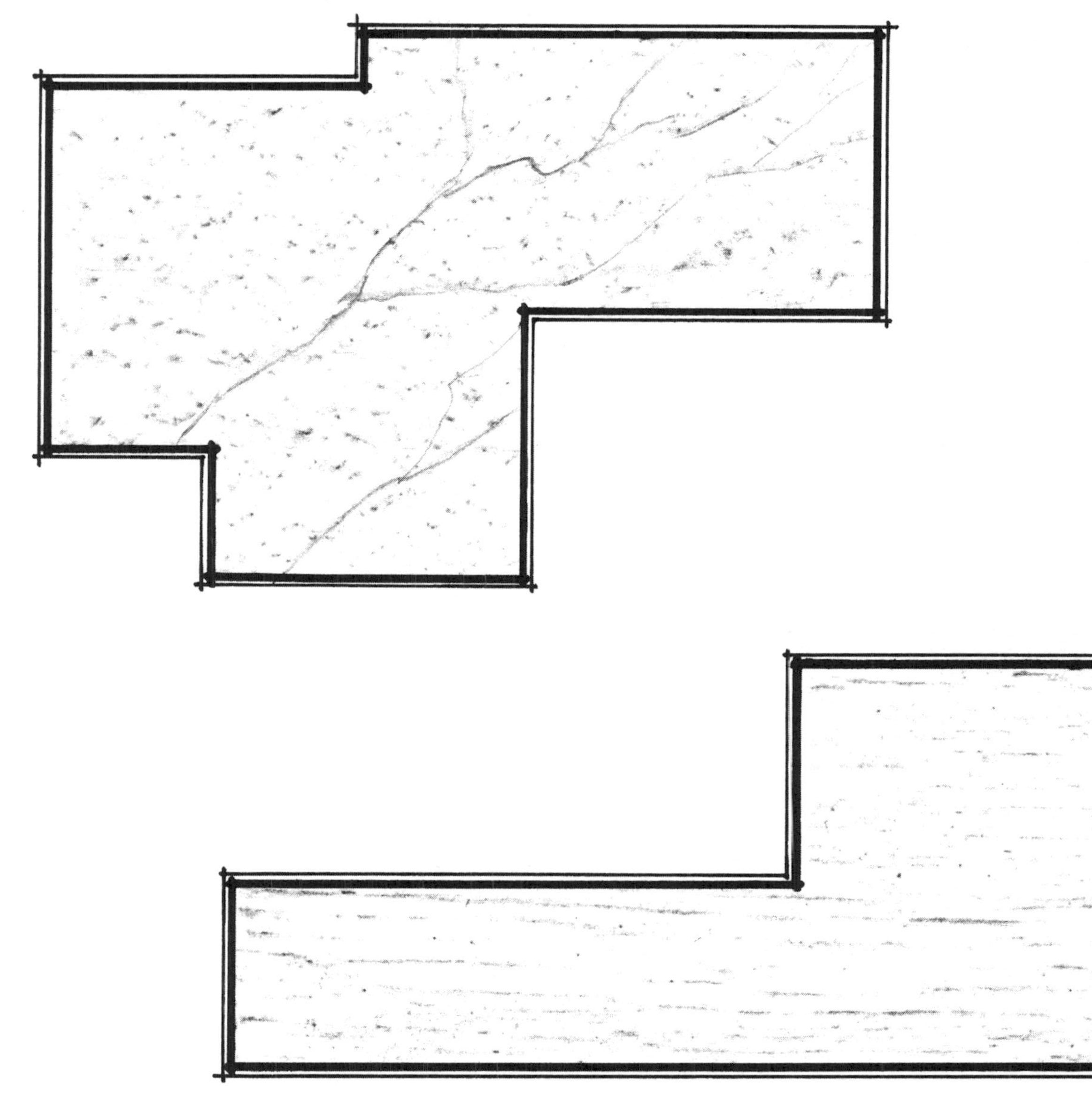

Paving

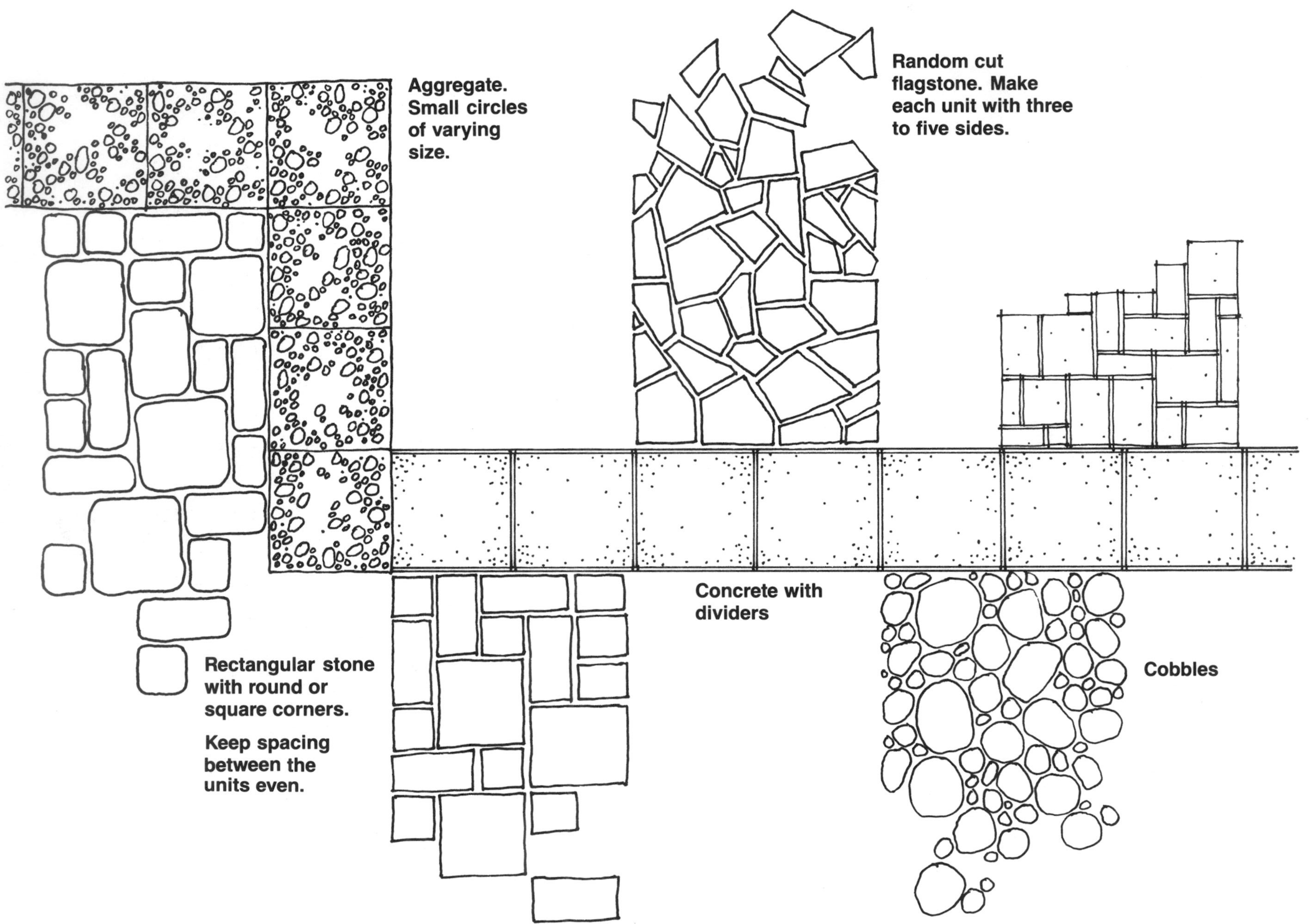

All paving types on this page are freehand examples.

Prepared Hardscape Patterns

Many pattern shapes are available with adhesive backing. They are trimmed to fit the desired form. They are expensive, but fast and precise and are useful if fine detail is needed.

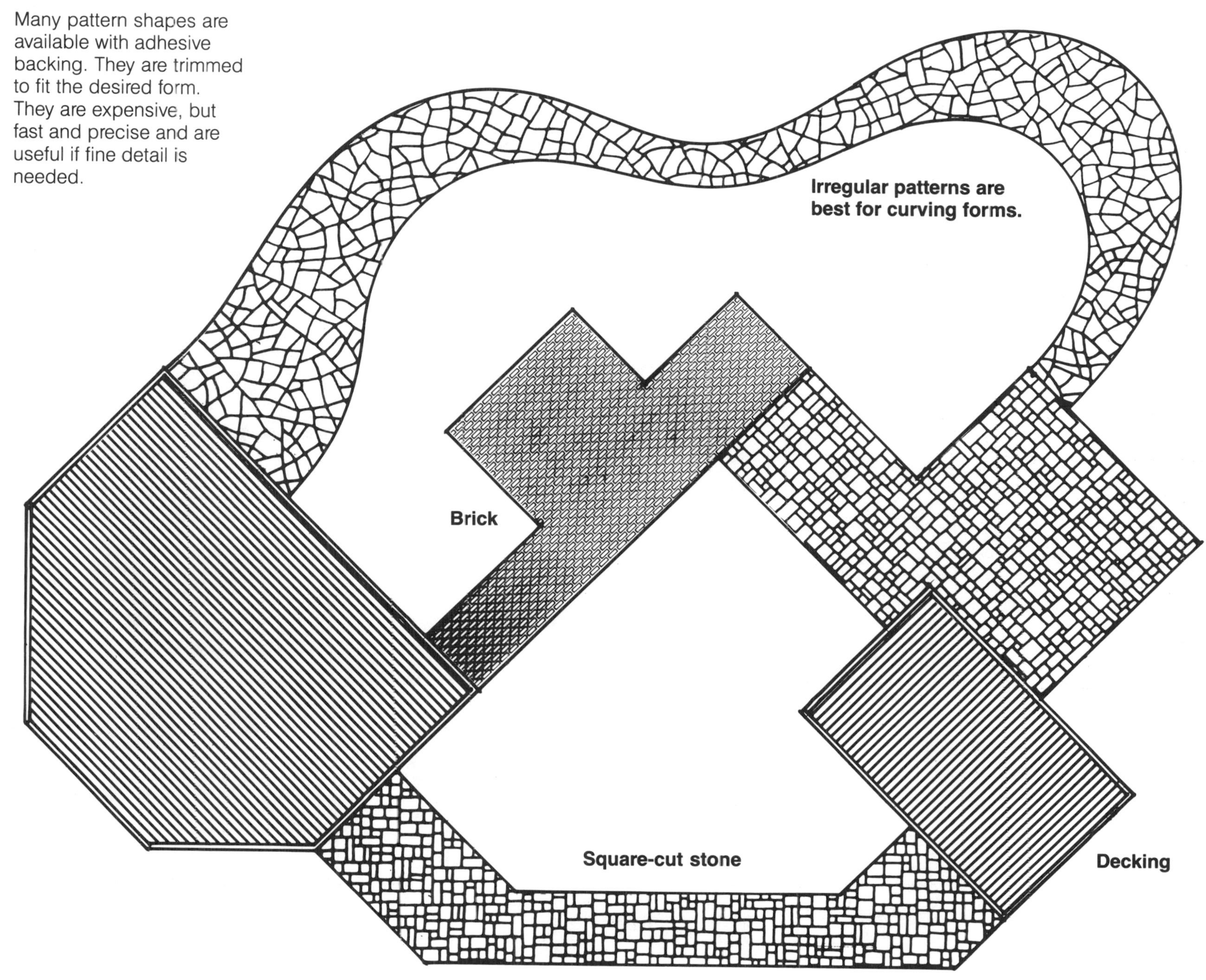

Buildings

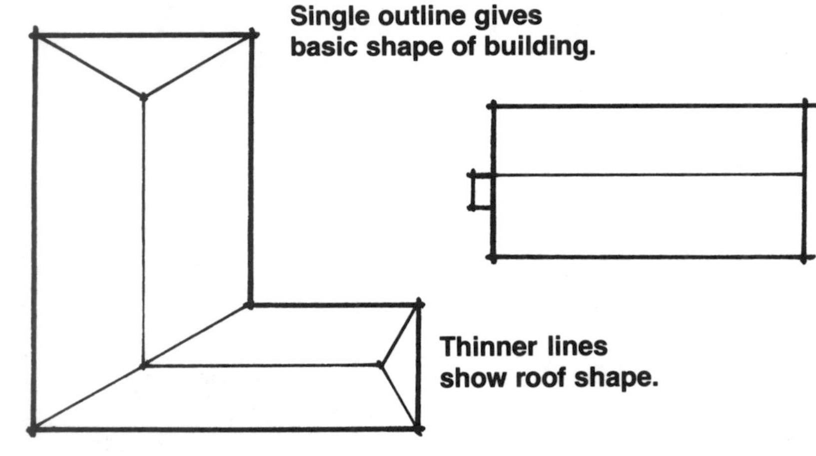

Single outline gives basic shape of building.

Thinner lines show roof shape.

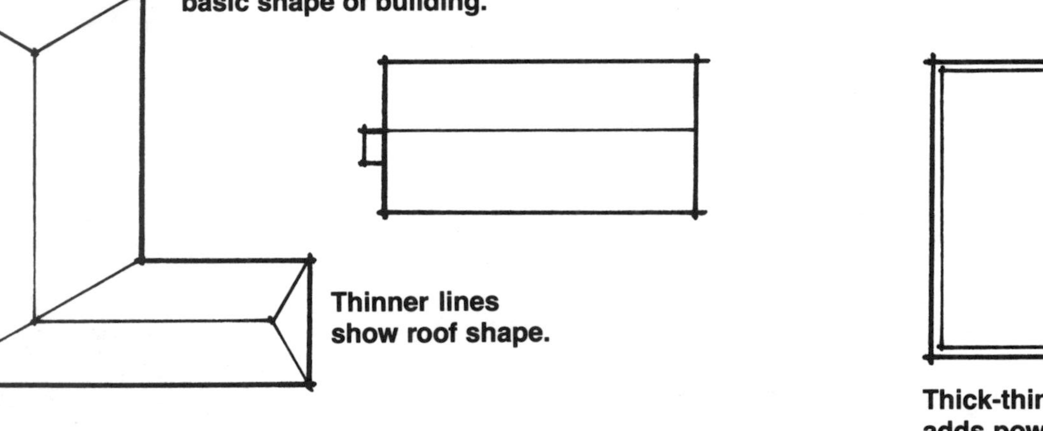

Thick-thin double outline adds power to the structure.

Positive connections are important.

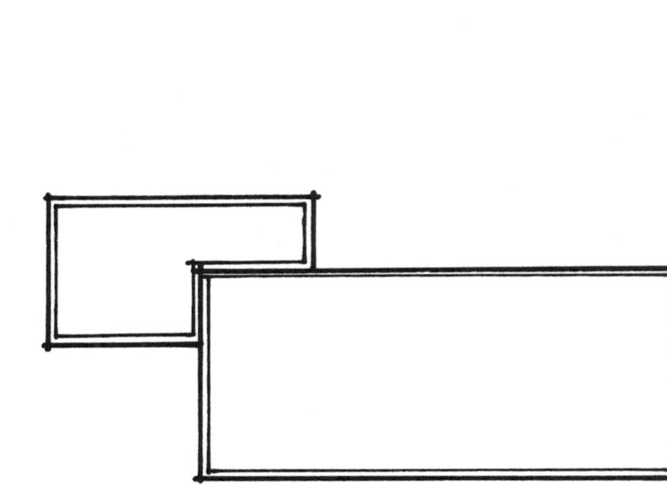

Freehand Buildings

Quicker than drafted buildings, freehand structures are permissible if accuracy is not critical.

Roof shading is effective on larger-scale plans where ground details are less important. Leave buildings simple on small-scale plans. Use guidelines or graph paper.

Avoid roof patterns if large overhangs exist.

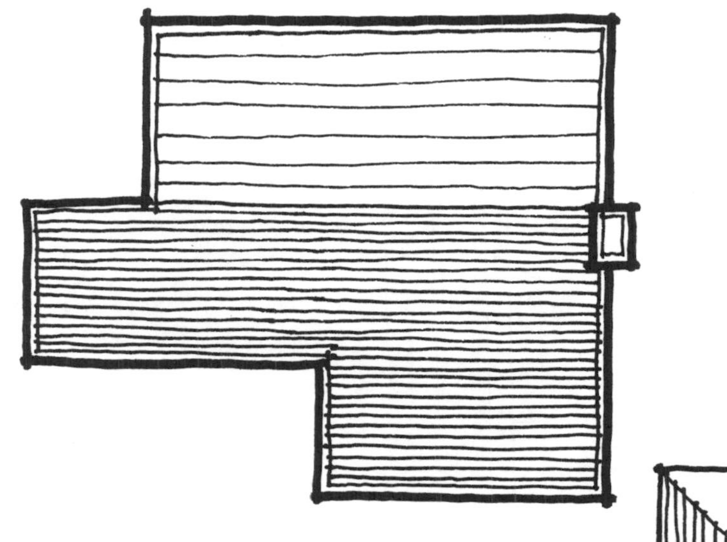

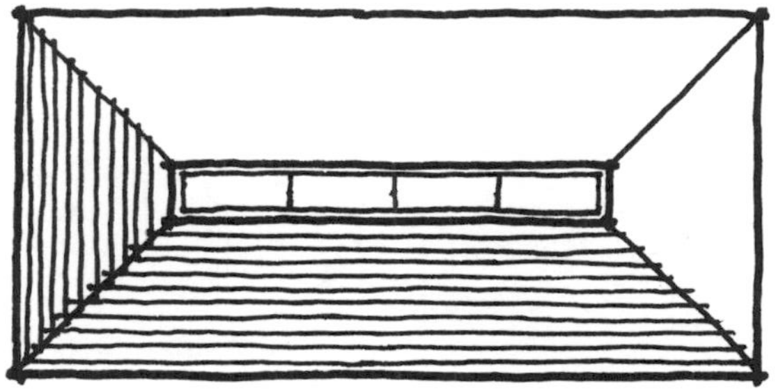

Roof shading adds a three-dimensional quality and indicates light direction.

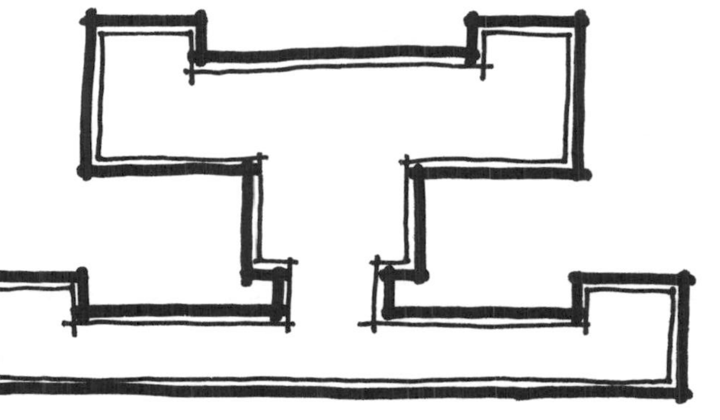

Roads and Sidewalks

Cars and people show activity and function.

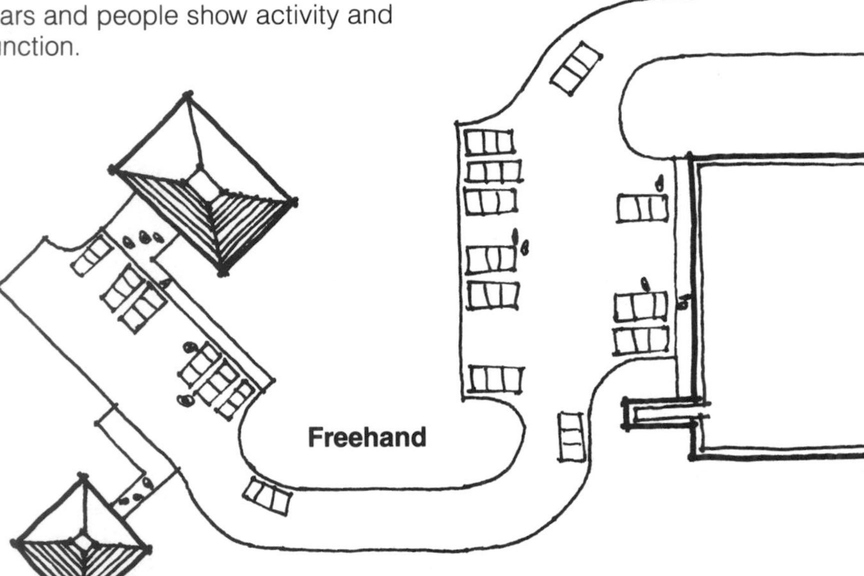

Cars and Trucks

A help in showing scale and function, cars and trucks are best done freehand. Keep shapes simple.

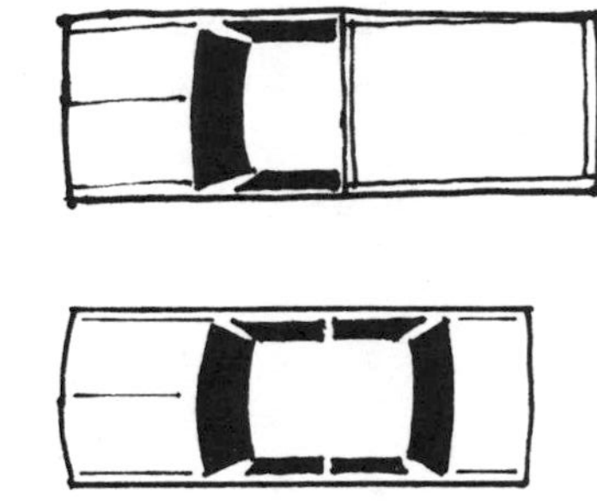

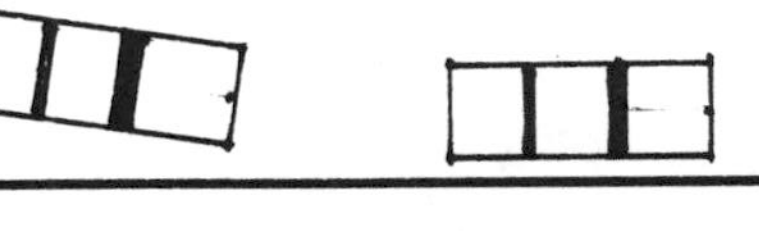

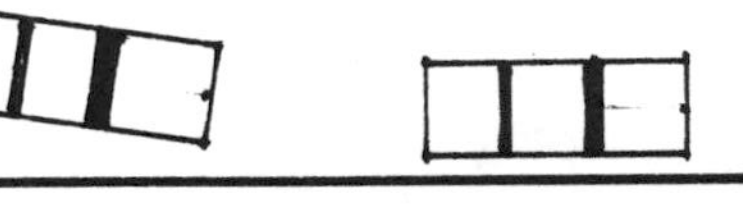

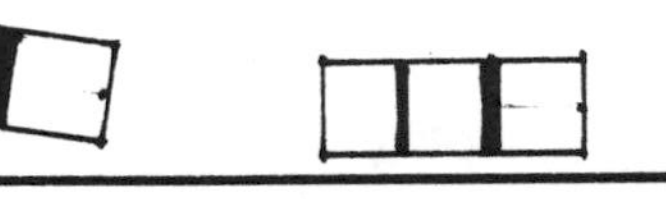

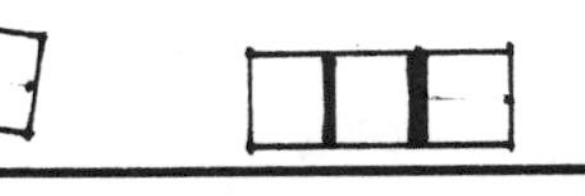

People

Oval with a black dot for the head

Abstract shadow

Hint of feet possible on larger people

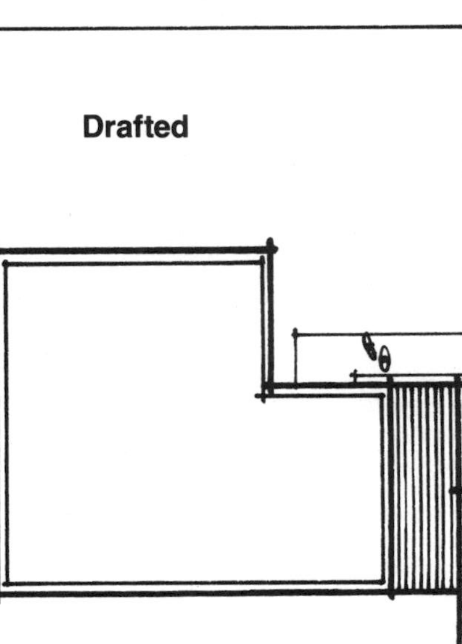

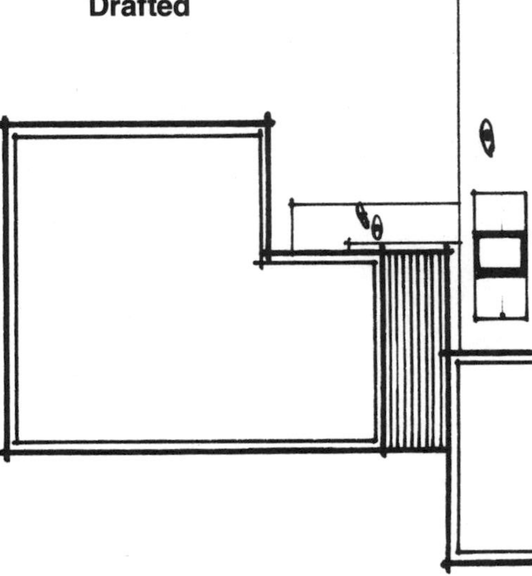

Shadows

Shadows bring depth to a plan by indicating relative heights of objects.

If the north arrow points up on the plan, the most realistic direction for shadows in the northern hemisphere is above the symbols. When the shadow pattern is critical (e.g., solar studies), use this direction.

A more powerful three-dimensional effect is obtained by placing shadows on the lower side to the left or right. This is because our eyes are used to having light come from above.

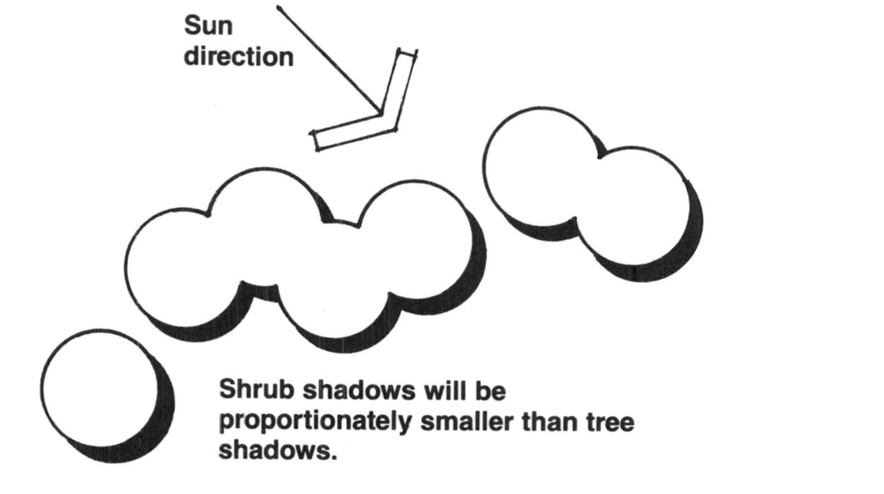

Shrub shadows will be proportionately smaller than tree shadows.

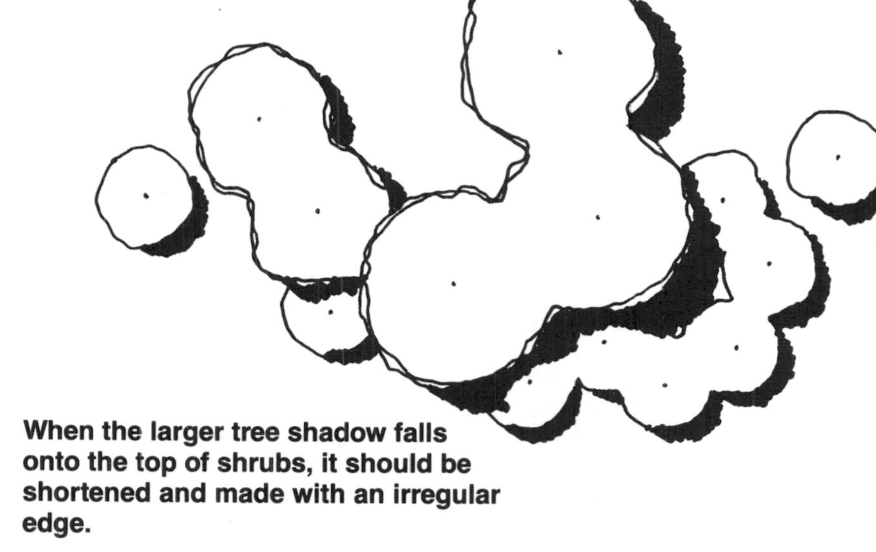

When the larger tree shadow falls onto the top of shrubs, it should be shortened and made with an irregular edge.

Sequence for Drawing Shade Tree Shadows

1. Start with the circular tree symbol. Assume a sun direction.
2. Move the template in the sun direction and draw a light guideline.
3. Fill the void.

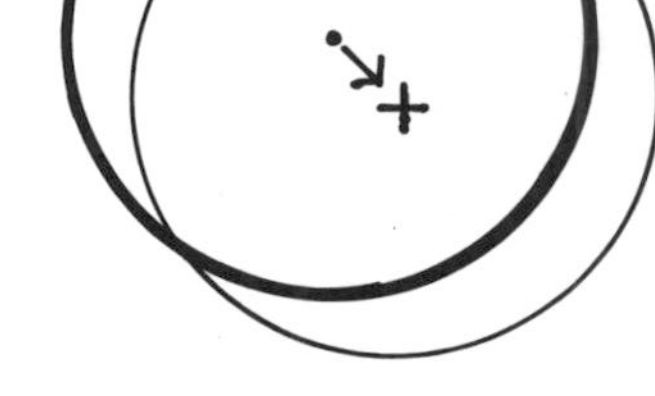
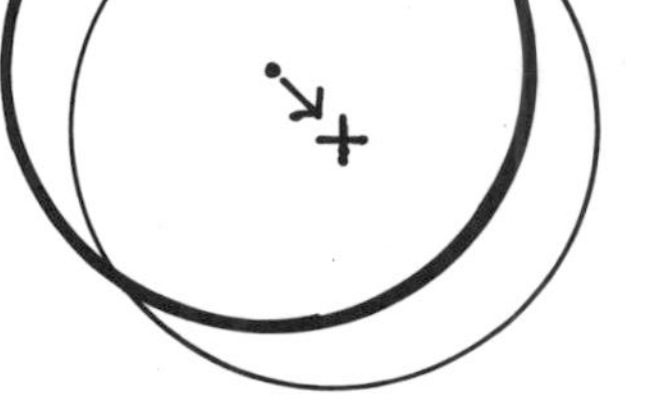
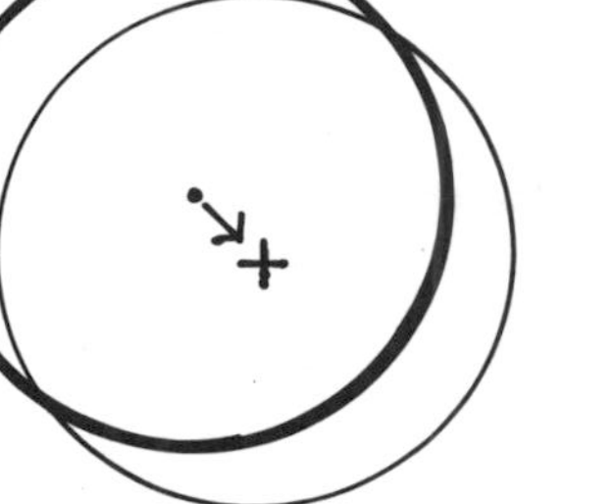

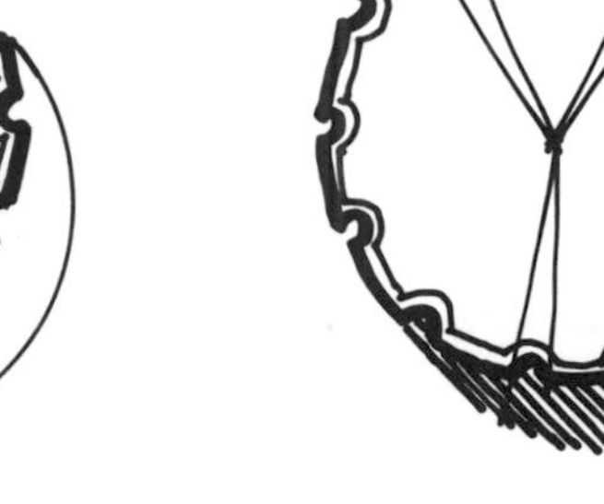
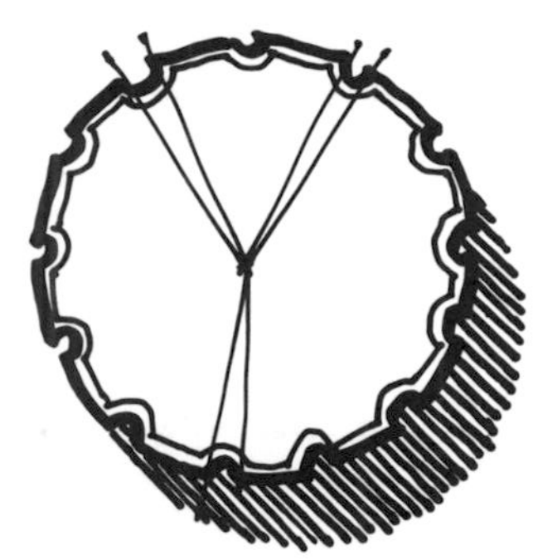

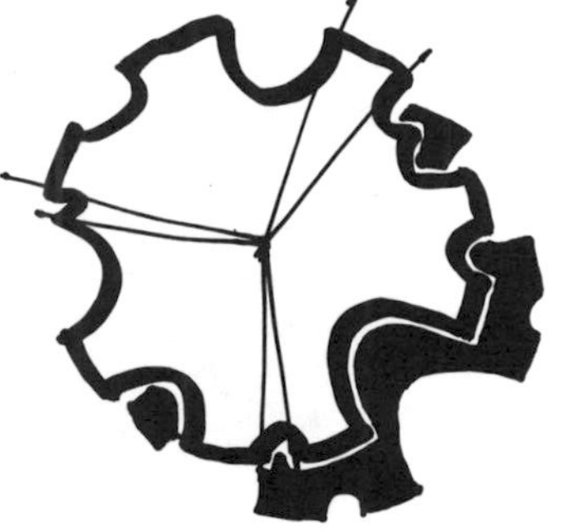

Black shadows are best, but a toned shadow can be made by drawing a series of parallel lines which follow the sun direction.

For complex outlines, repeat the symbol shape around the shadow guide circle.

Leave a thin white space to define the edge of the symbol.

Sequence for Drawing Coniferous Tree Shadows

1. Start with the circular tree symbol and assume a sun direction.
2. Offset circle guideline.
3. Fill the space.

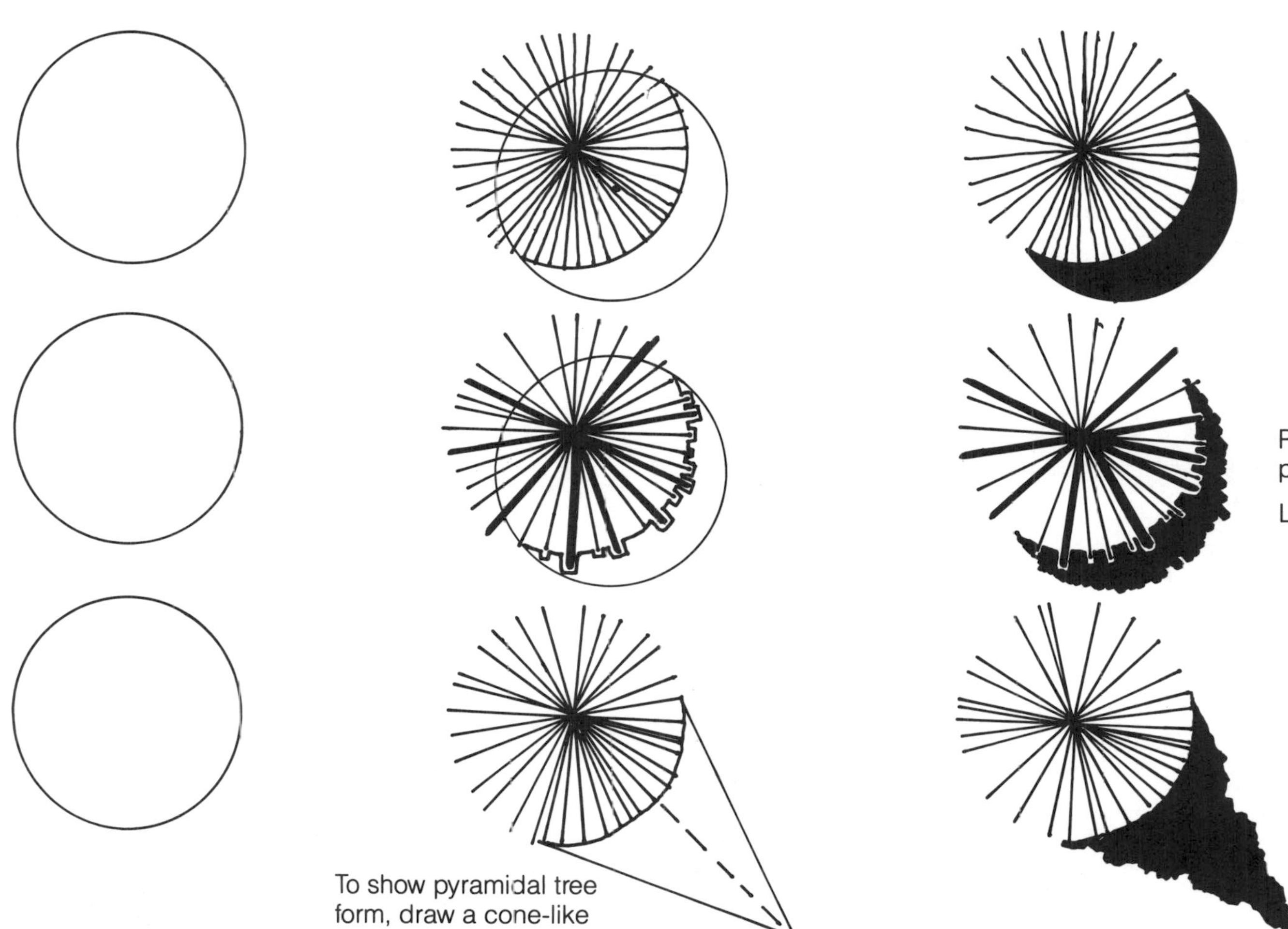

To show pyramidal tree form, draw a cone-like guideline.

The centerline follows the sun direction.

Parallel strokes with a thick pen give a textured edge.

Leave white space.

Draw a loose shadow edge.

Sequence for Drawing Building Shadows

1. Start with basic outline and assume a sun angle.

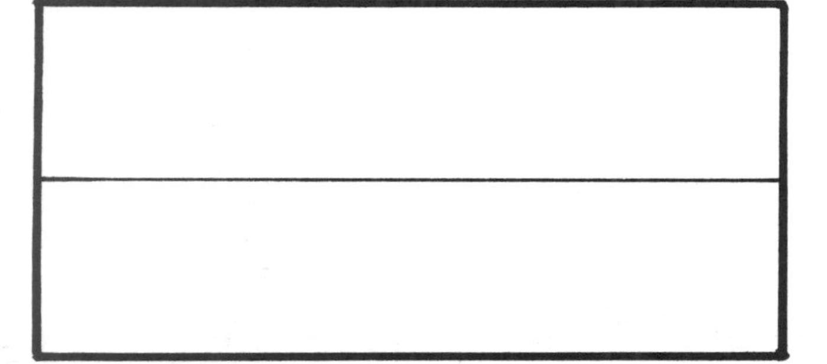

2. Draw parallel lines from each corner. For peaked roofs, the line should be longer. Connect the corners.

3. Add any additional details. Note how the shadow is longer on the shaded side of the roof due to the roof slope.

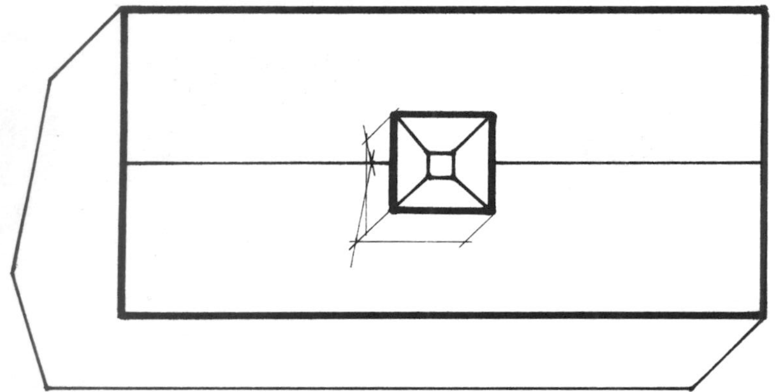

4. Add texture to the shaded side of the roof to help accentuate the feeling of depth.

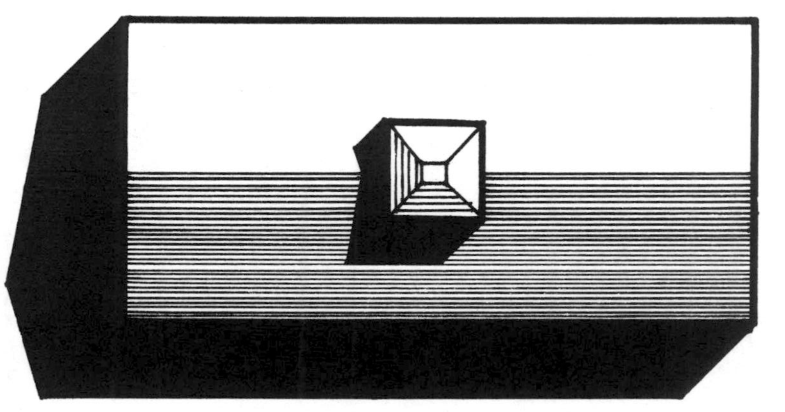

Shadow Proportions

Once the initial shadow length of an object has been selected, all other shadows must be proportionately longer or shorter, depending on the relative heights of the objects.

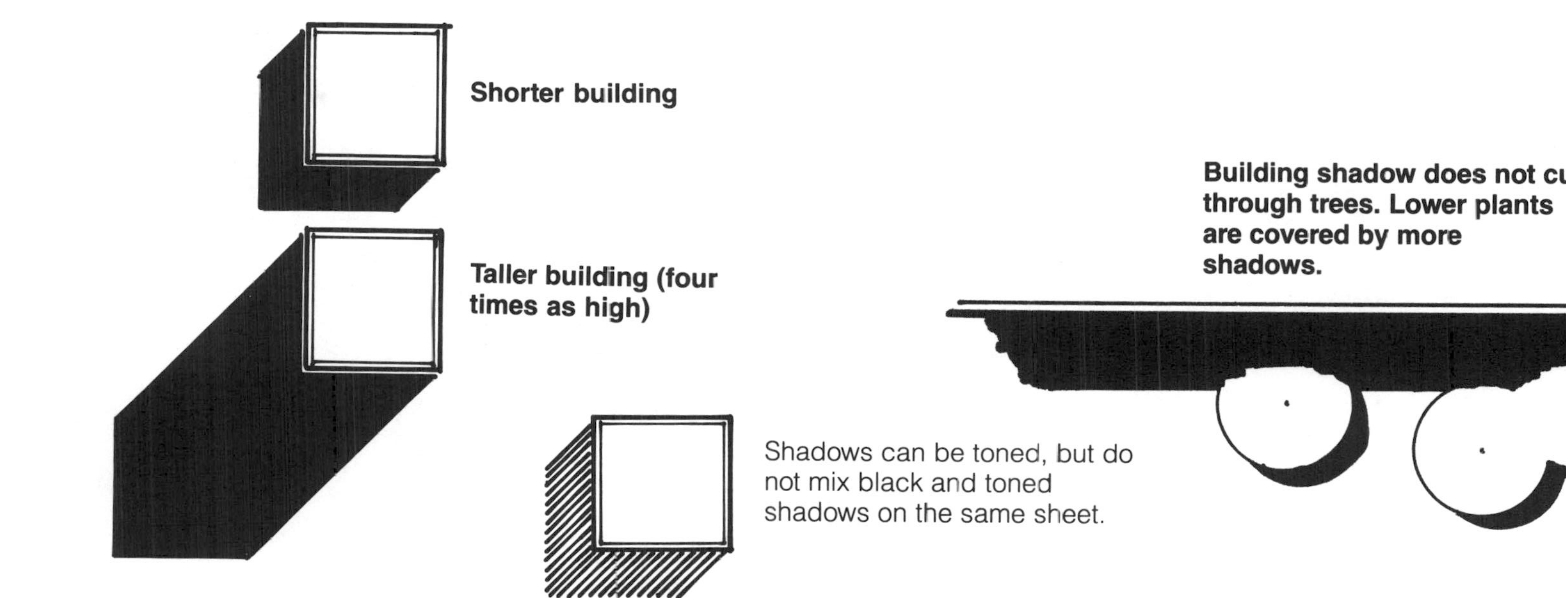

Building shadow does not cut through trees. Lower plants are covered by more shadows.

Shadows can be toned, but do not mix black and toned shadows on the same sheet.

Shadows also indicate slopes and level changes on the ground plane.

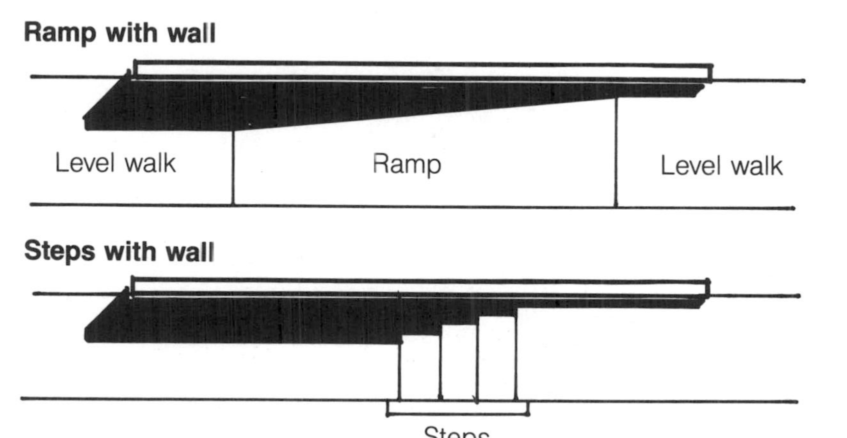

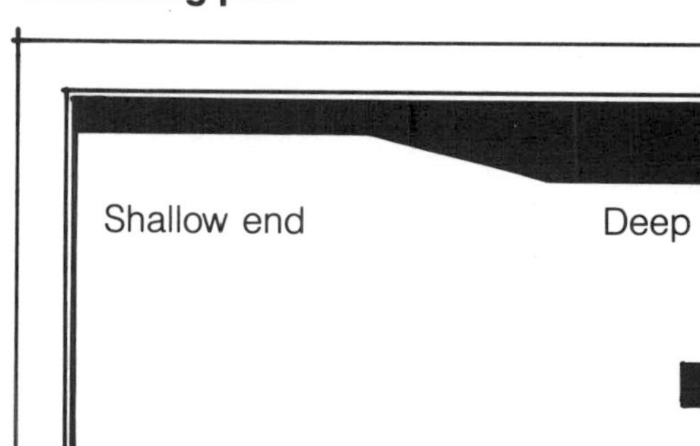

Fast Shadows

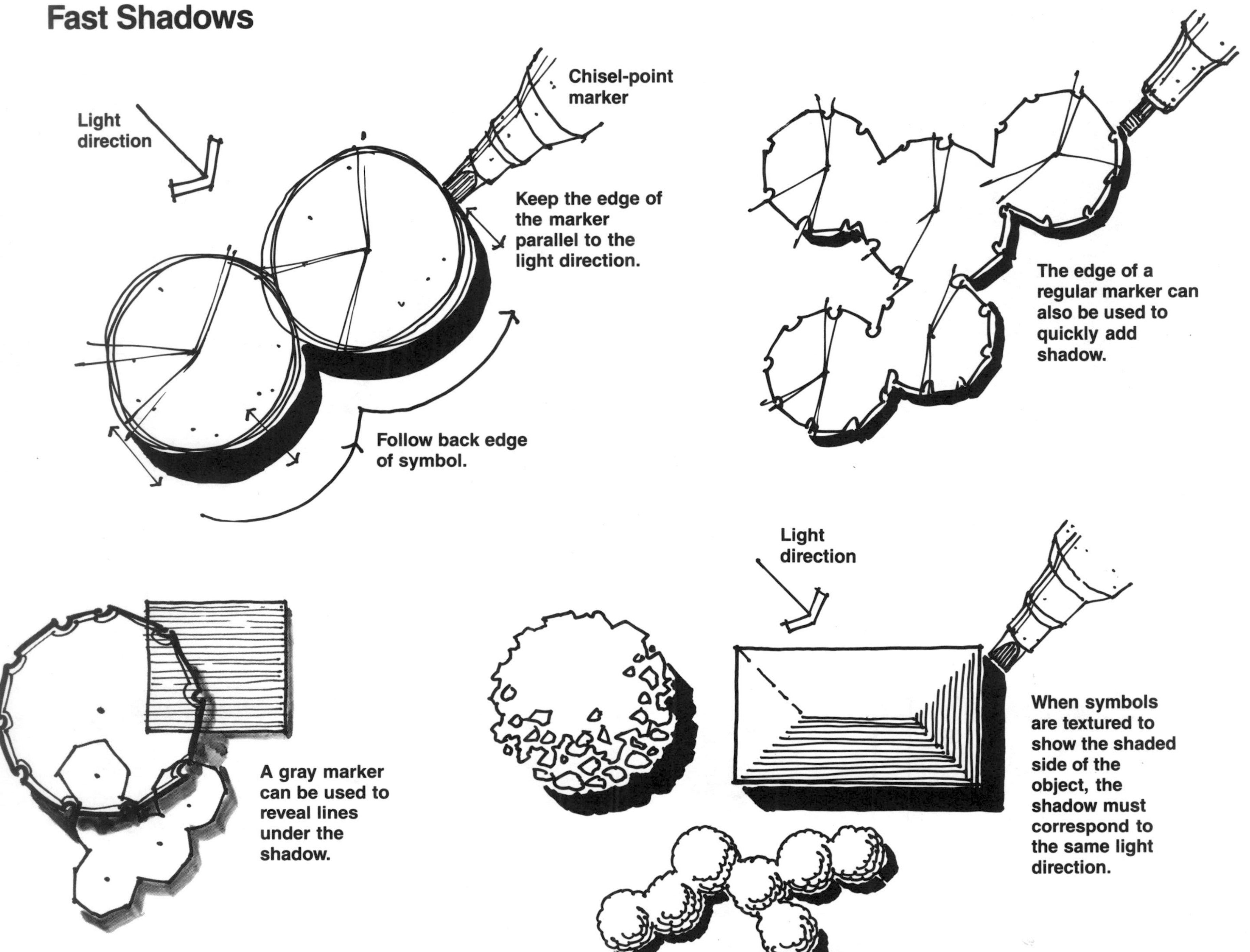

Composite Shadows

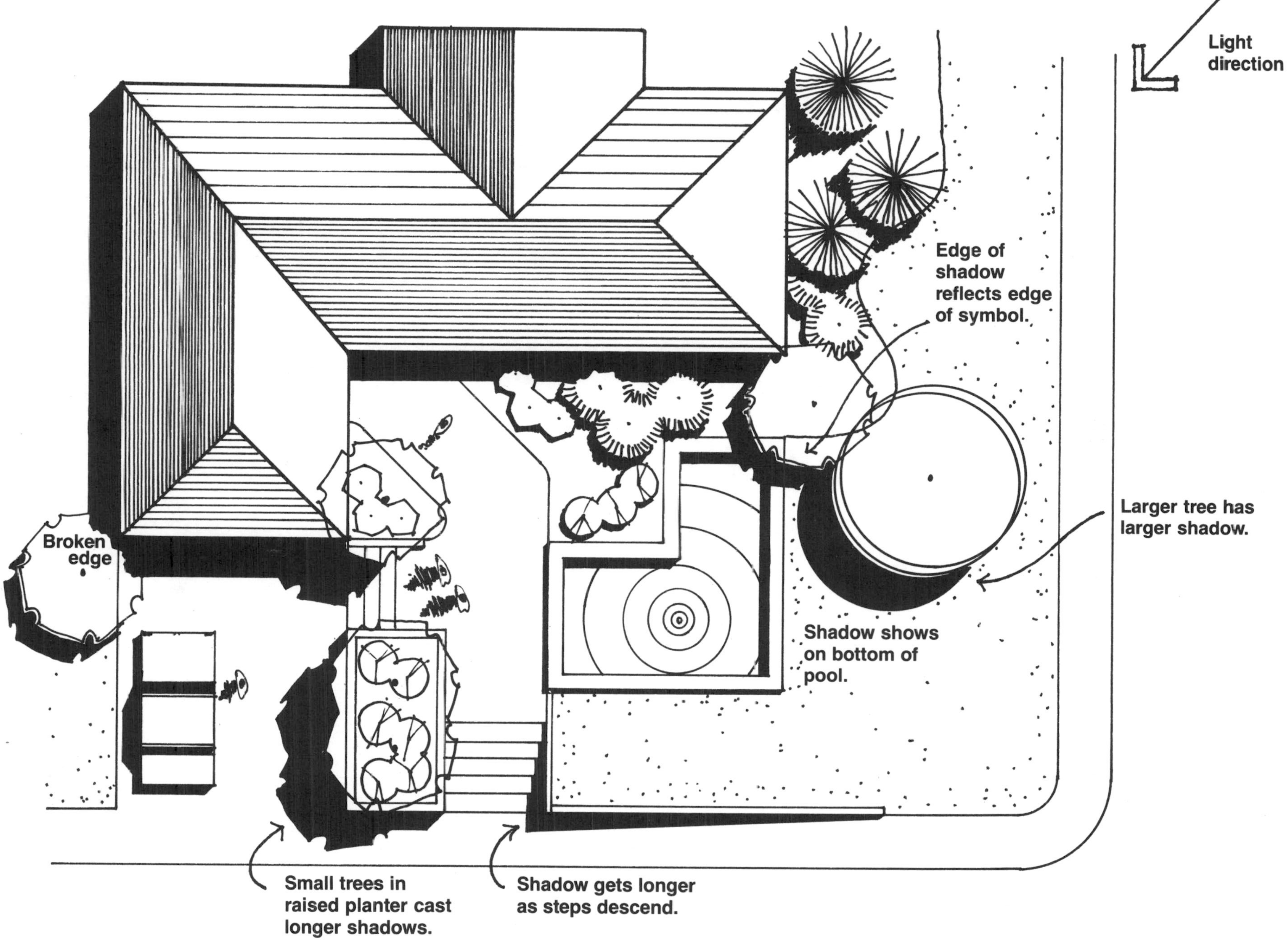

Section-elevations

It is usually necessary to communicate more about a design idea than can be shown on plans. Despite the use of shadowing and layering in plan views, it is not possible to show the detail of vertical elements and how they relate to the horizontal shapes. Section-elevations are an excellent tool for this.

section - elevation

Section-elevations

The relationship of a section-elevation to a landscape plan is demonstrated here by slicing a landform vertically with a large cleaver. When the pieces are pulled apart, a cross section is revealed.

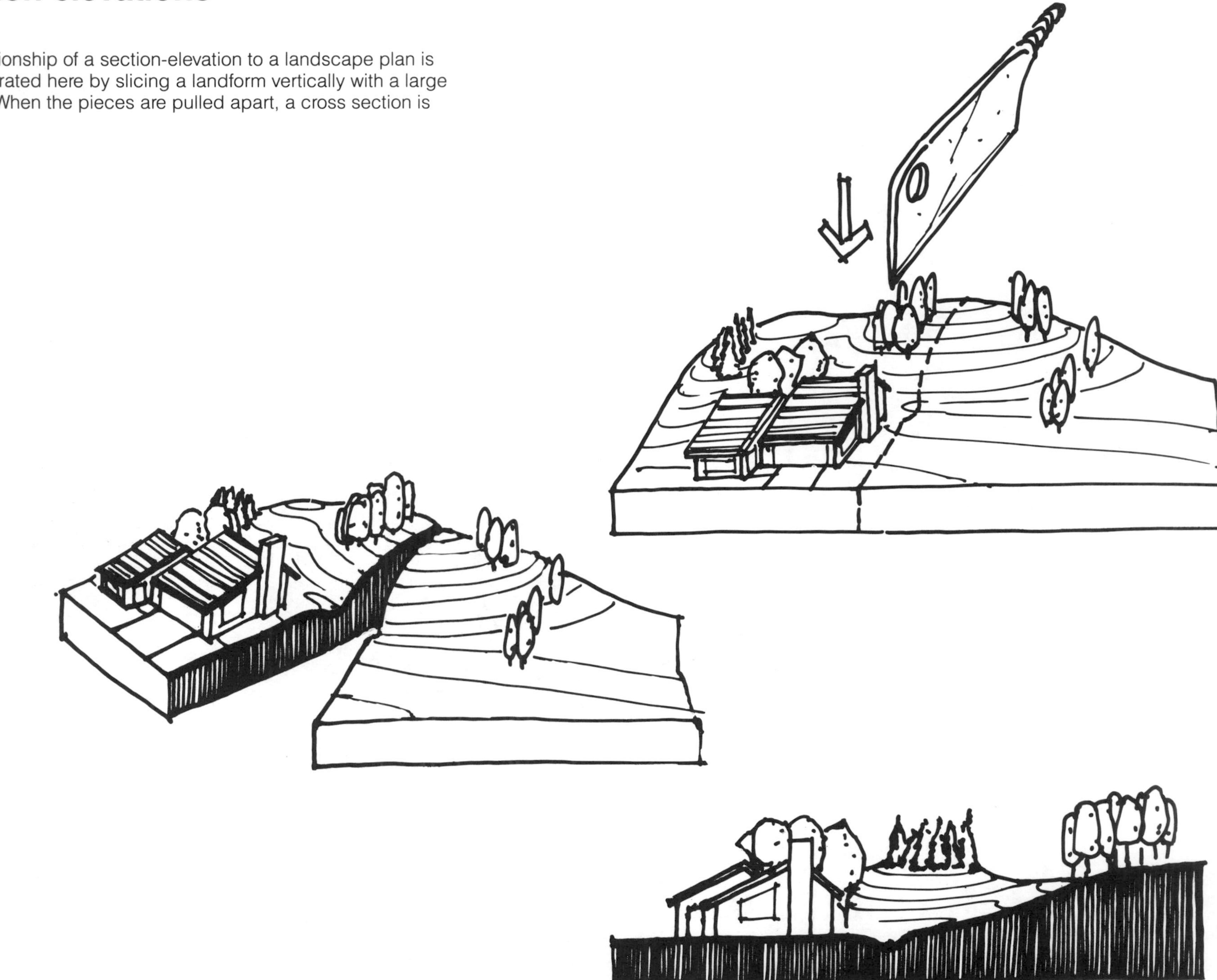

The vertical surface made by the knife cut is a true **section.** Nothing in front of or behind this surface is shown.

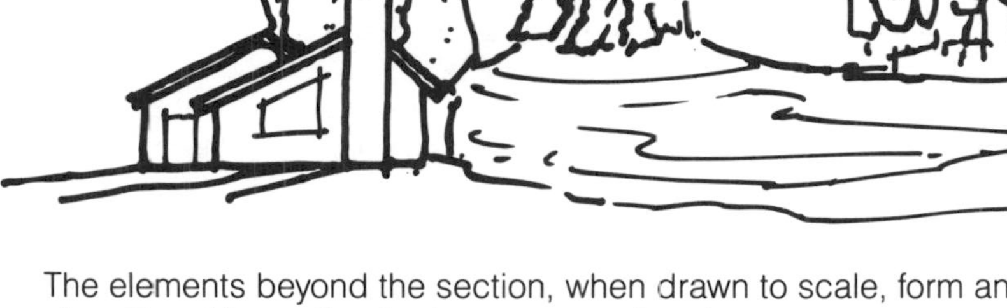

The elements beyond the section, when drawn to scale, form an **elevation.** No cut line is shown on an elevation.

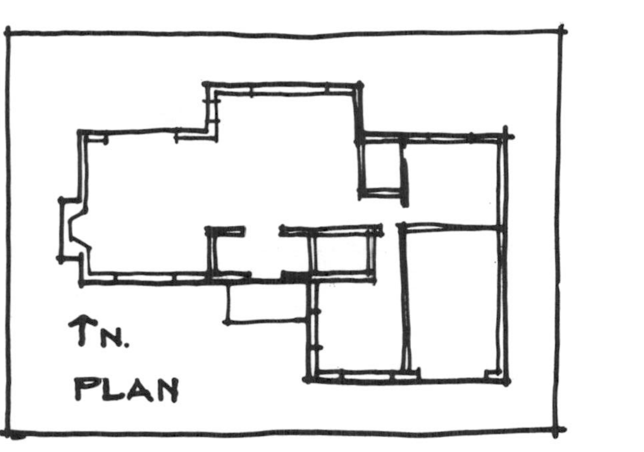

Elevations are more common on architectural drawings than landscape architectural drawings. They are an effective way to show surface detail on the facades of buildings. Often they relate to a plan view of the same set of drawings.

For landscape architects, the combined **section-elevation** is the most useful tool. These usually have the shorter title of "sections". In practice, the terms are interchangeable.

Section-elevation Characteristics

The **section-elevation** shows the cut surface and/or the profile line plus true-to-scale elements a selected distance beyond the profile line. It is up to the graphic artist to decide how much to show beyond, but normally the closer objects have bolder lines with ample detail and distant objects, if shown at all, rendered as lighter outline shapes. This can be accomplished by using ink for closer elements and pencil for middleground and distant elements, especially if making diazo prints from the finished drawing.

The two essential characteristics of a landscape section are:

1. A bold, prominent profile line.
2. All vertical features drawn at the same scale, no matter how far they are from this profile line.

This makes the section very easy to draw. It can be related to a corresponding plan view by labeling on the section (e.g., section through fishing pier) or a cut line showing view direction on the plan.

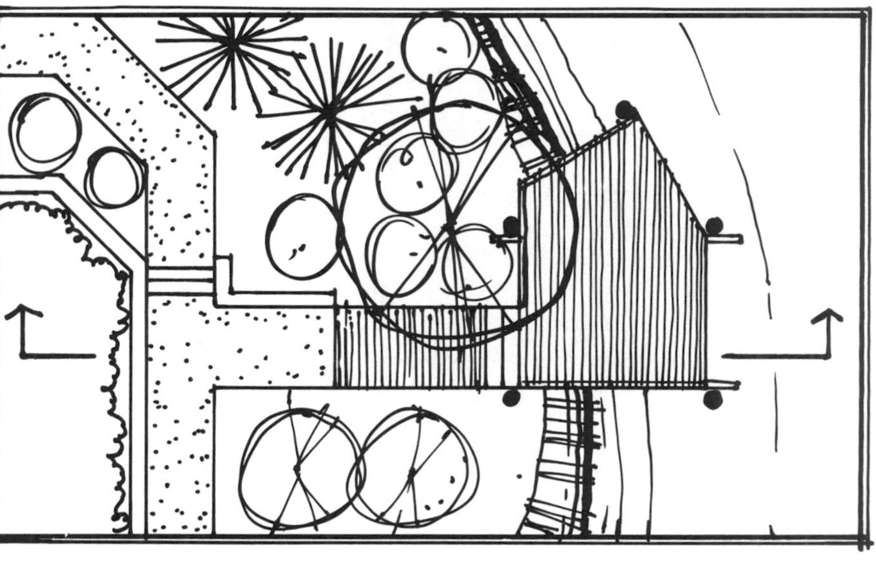

Drawing a Section from a Plan

1. On an overlay, draw a cut line (AA) through the area to be shown in section. Using known vertical information, place marks on the line corresponding to each vertical elevation. In this case, each contour line represents five more feet above the pond level.

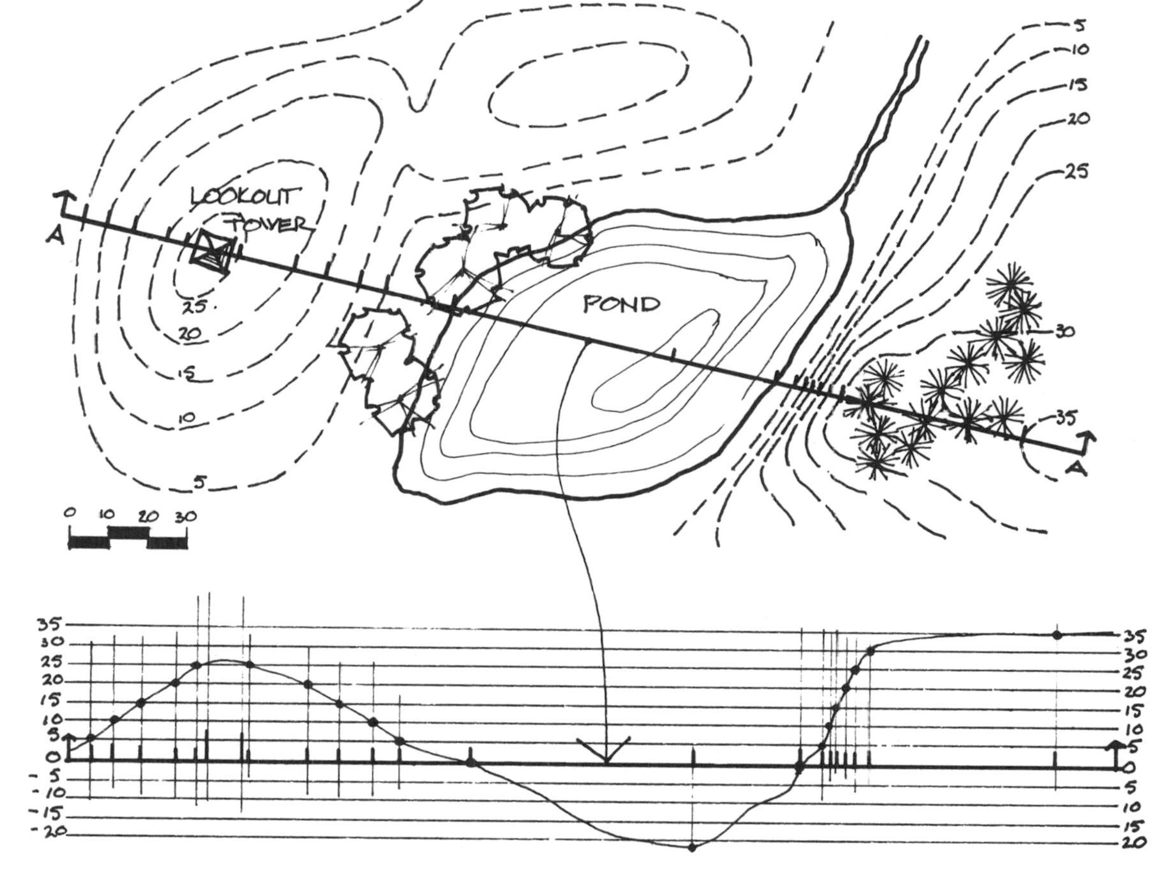

2. Remove the overlay and construct a series of horizontal lines above (and below) to represent even increments of vertical change. You may use the same scale or one which multiplies the horizontal scale by 1.5 or 2 for exaggeration. At each mark on the base line, draw a vertical guideline and mark with a dot where it intersects the correct elevation. Join the dots.

3. On another overlay, sketch the appropriate landscape features at their correct heights. Make the section line bold.

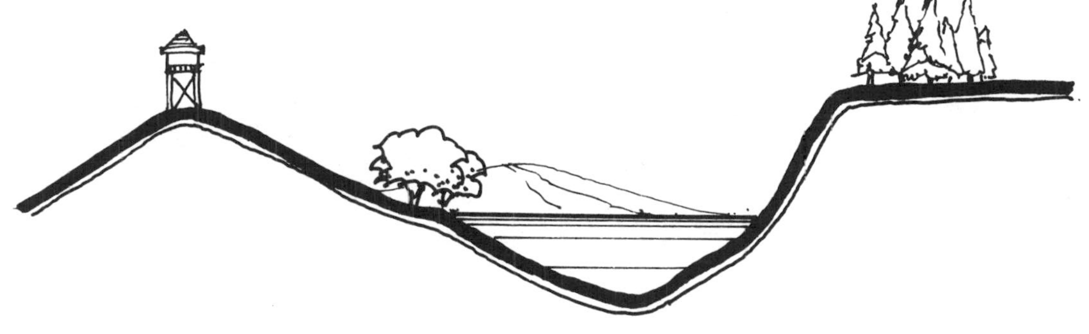

Uses of Landscape Sections

The examples shown on this and the following nine pages give some of the main purposes for and values in drawing landscape section-elevations.

1. To emphasize the importance of vertical elements as they relate to activities and use.

For sections showing people, activities, uses, and the built environment, it is best to keep the vertical scale and the horizontal scale the same to avoid unrealistic distortions.

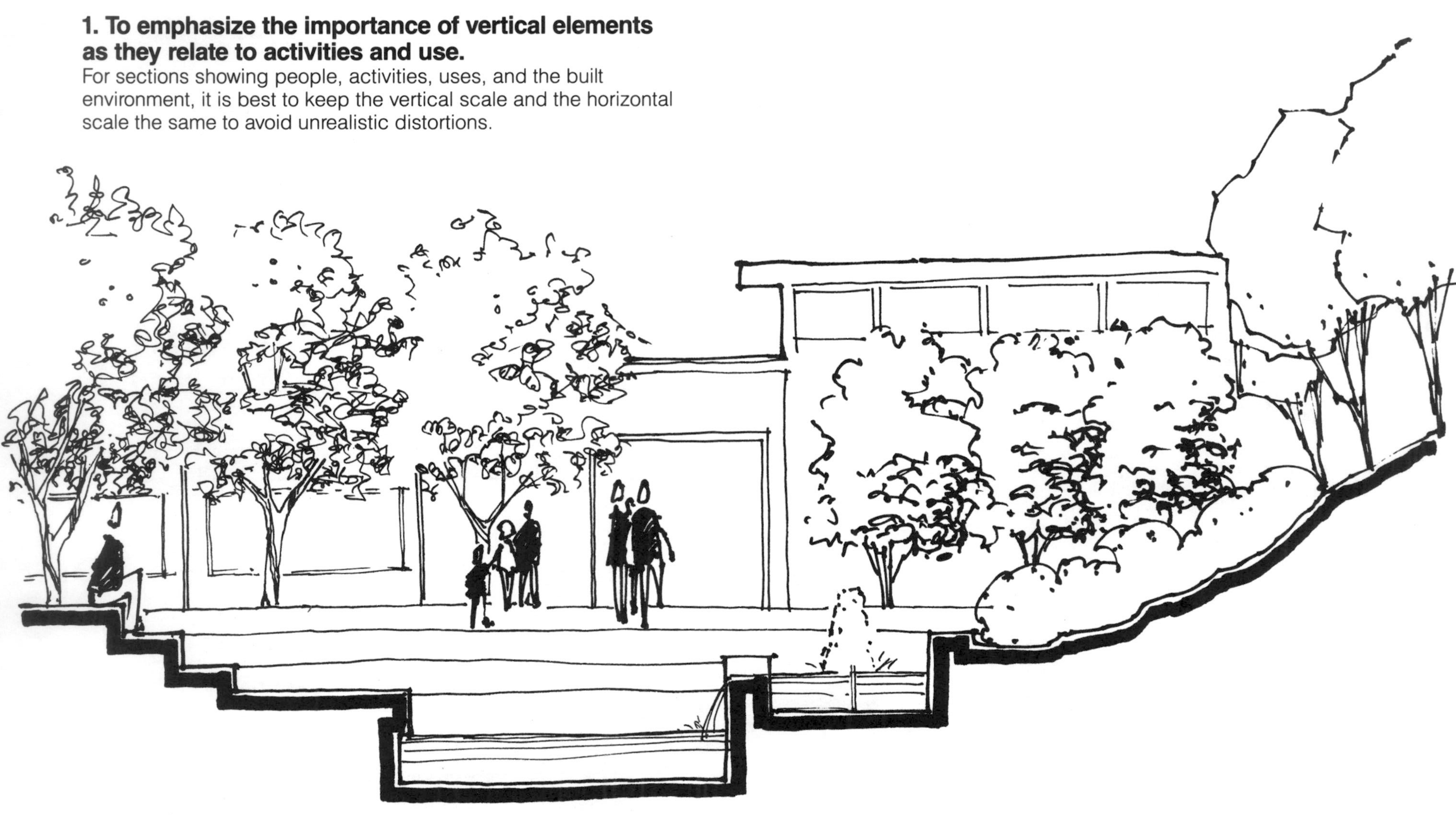

Section Sketch

Section Drawing

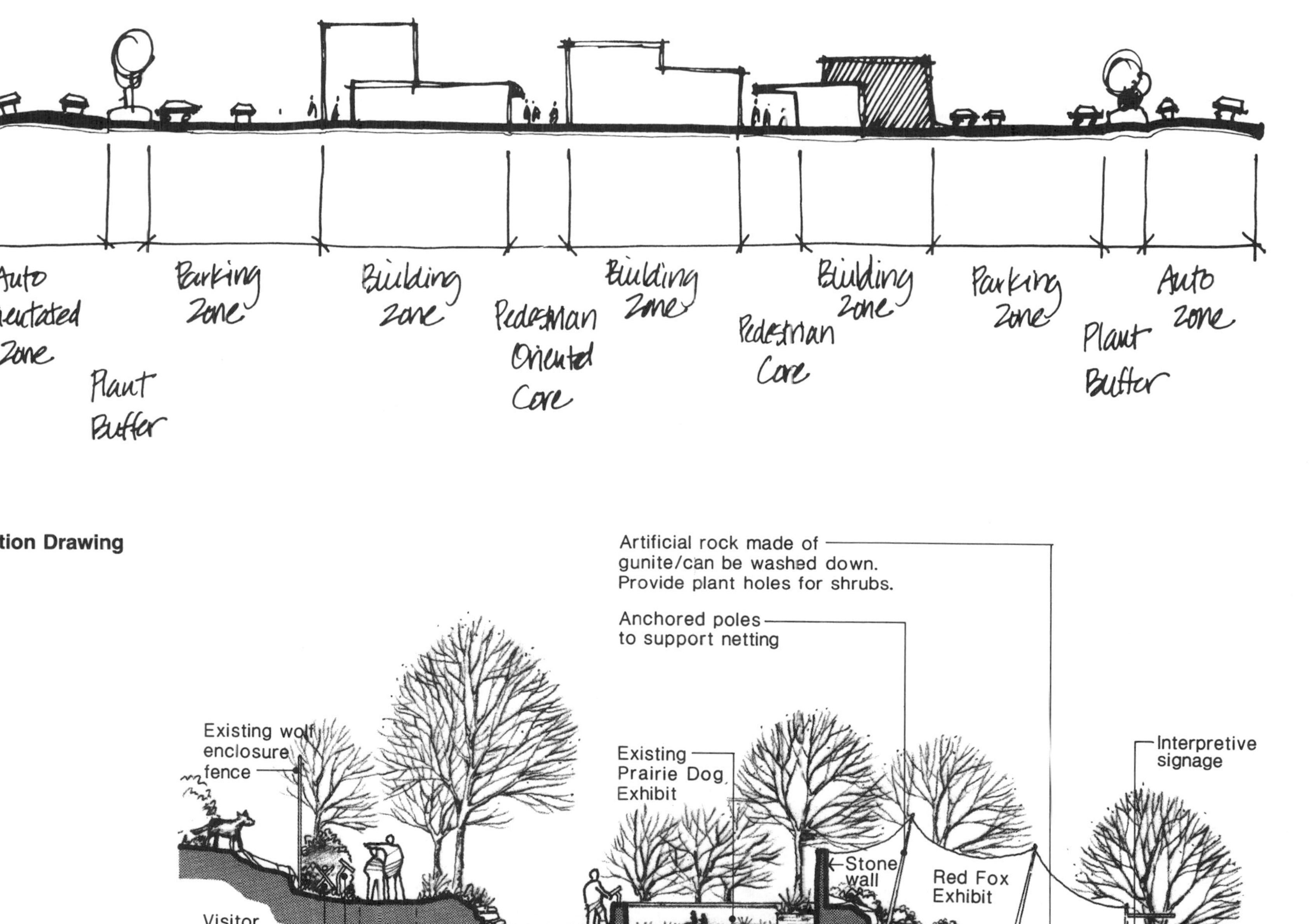

Section/Elevation
WOLF AND SMALL MAMMAL EXHIBITS

2. To communicate hidden elements in plan view.
Caves, overhangs, depths of water, and underground features are some of the elements that are impossible to show in plan view.

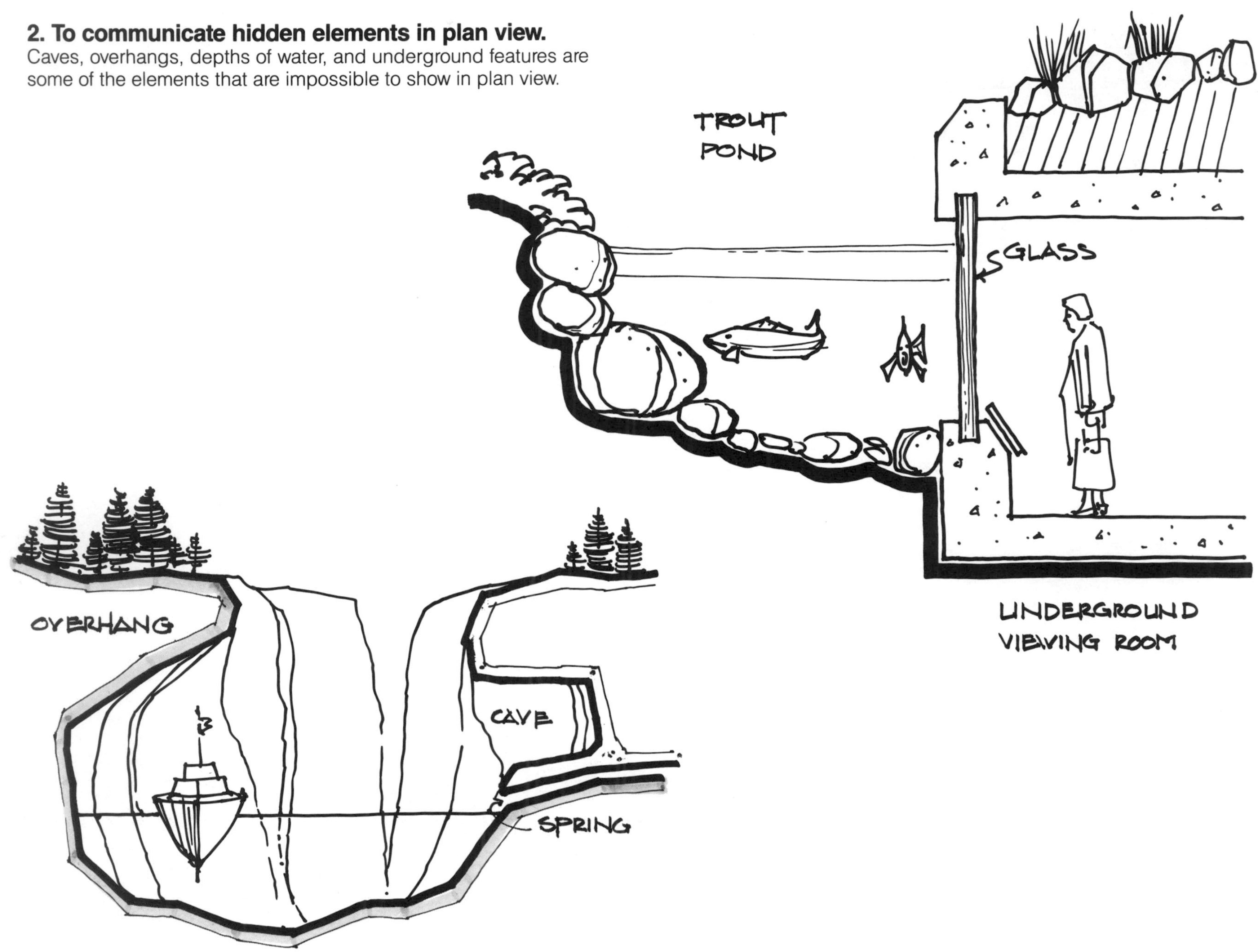

3. To analyze screening and views from specific vantage points.
These are called sightline studies.

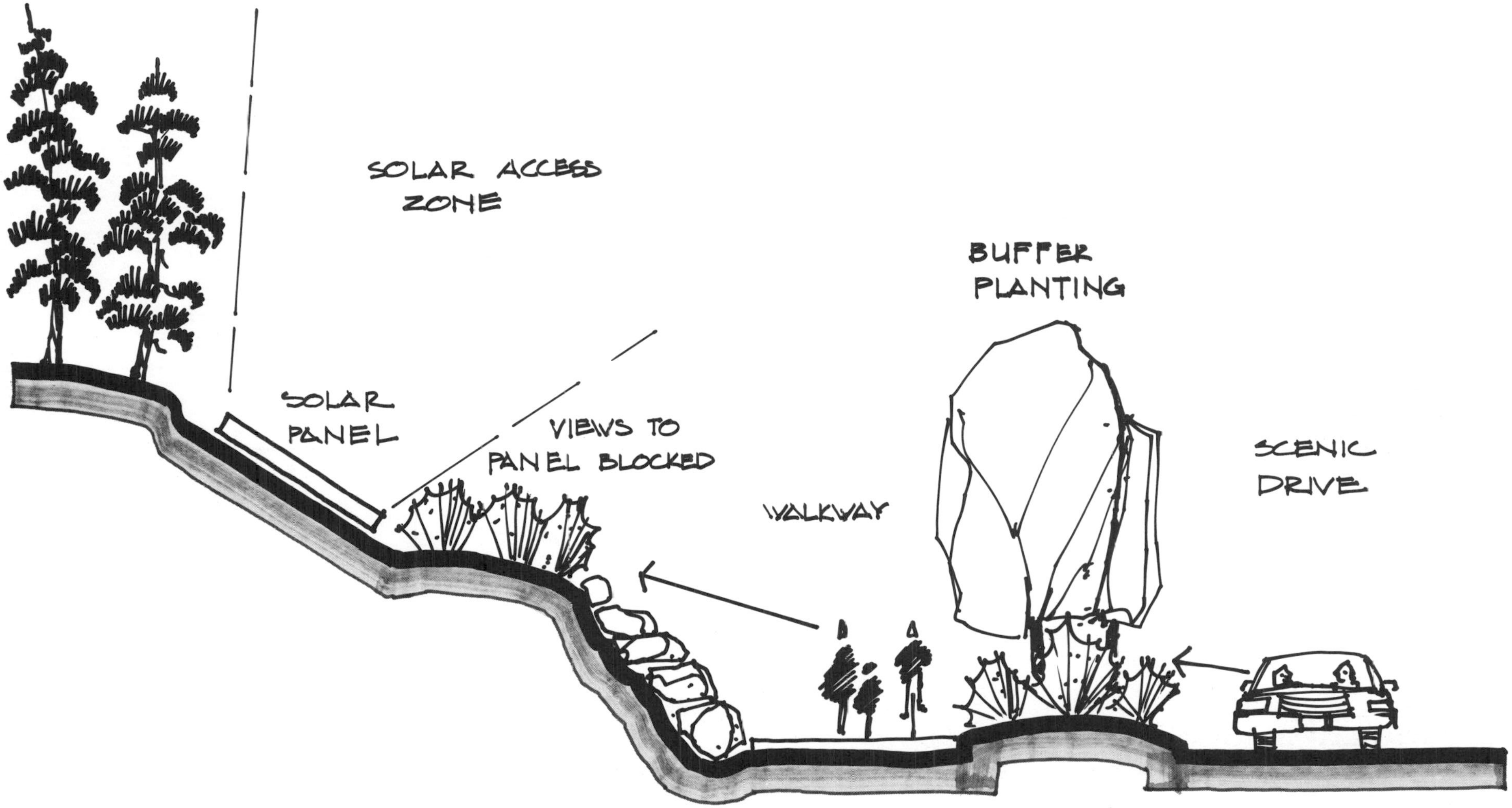

SOLAR ACCESS ZONE

SOLAR PANEL

VIEWS TO PANEL BLOCKED

WALKWAY

BUFFER PLANTING

SCENIC DRIVE

4. To study landform.

On larger-scale landscapes with subtle landforms, it is sometimes helpful to exaggerate the landform by enlarging the vertical scale by a factor one and a half or two times the horizontal scale.

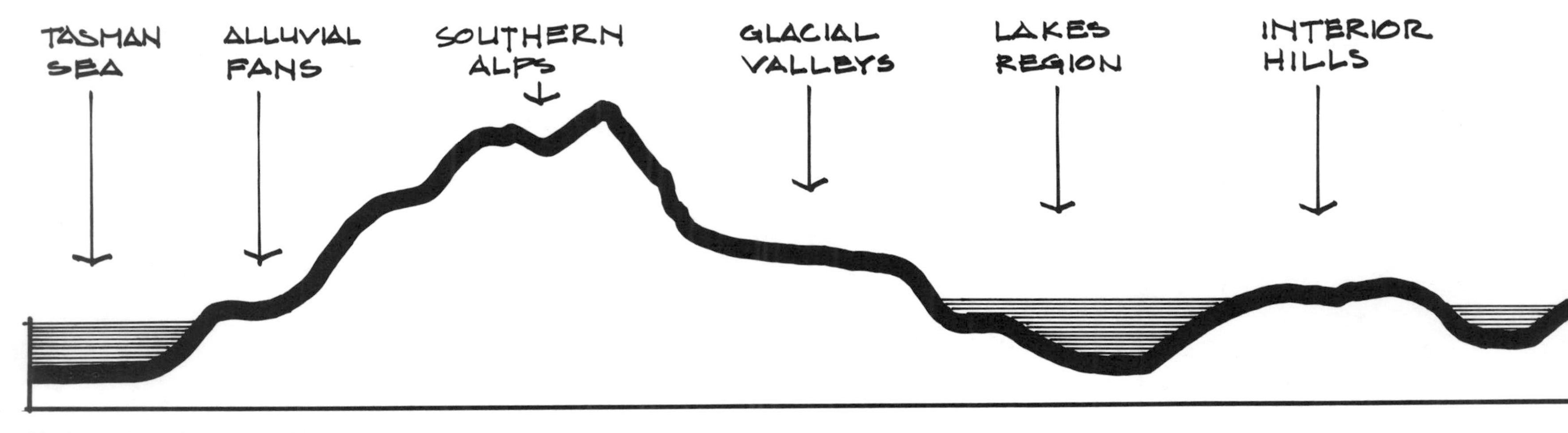

Horizontal scale: 1:100,000
Vertical scale: 1:50,000

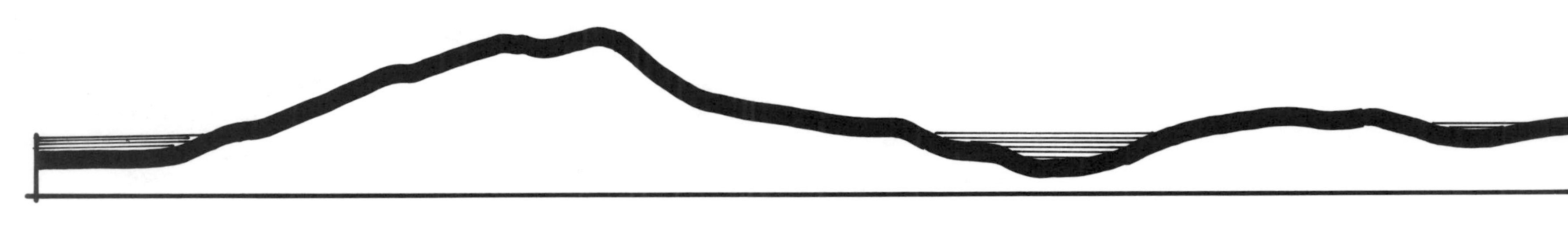

Horizontal and vertical scale: 1:100,000

5. To illustrate landscape processes.

6. To demonstrate the importance of climate and microclimate.

7. To use in lighting studies.

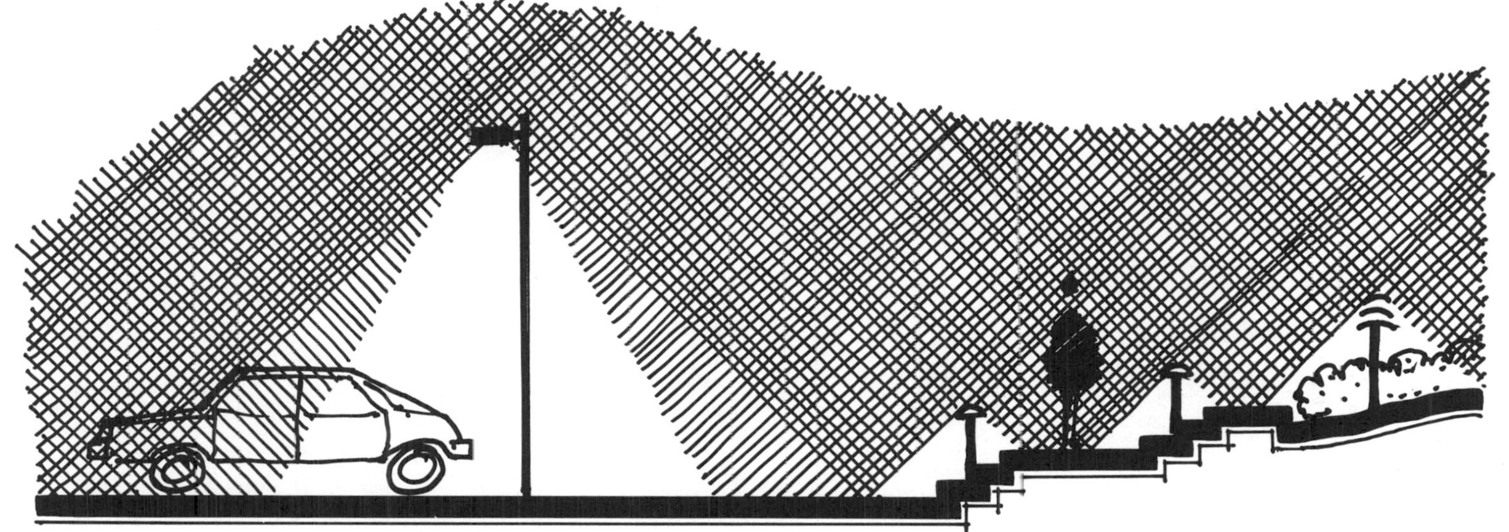

8. To show ecological relationships.

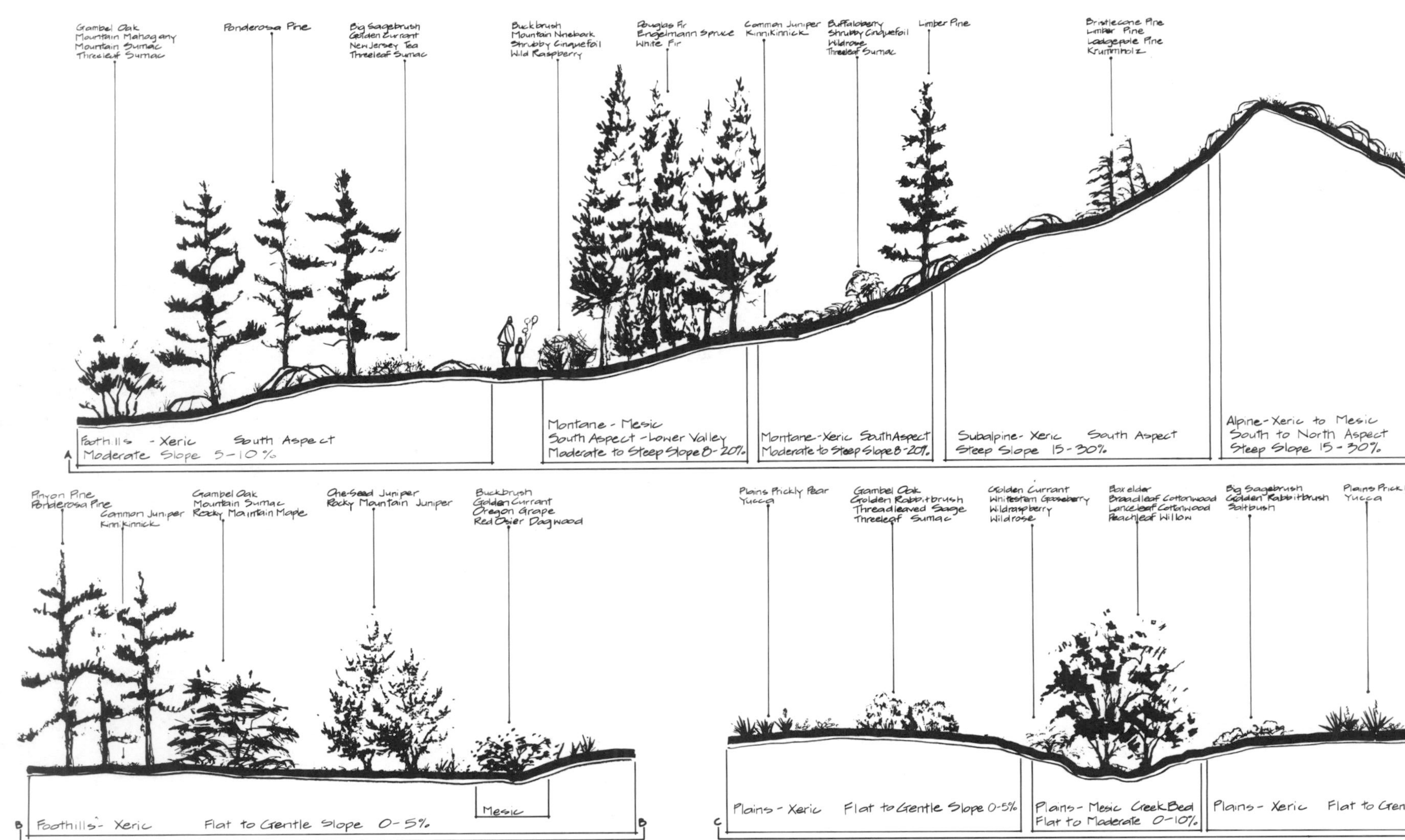

9. To show the internal structure of a built element.
These kinds of drawings are called construction sections or details. They usually form part of the working drawings and show in detail the components of a structure and how they fit together.

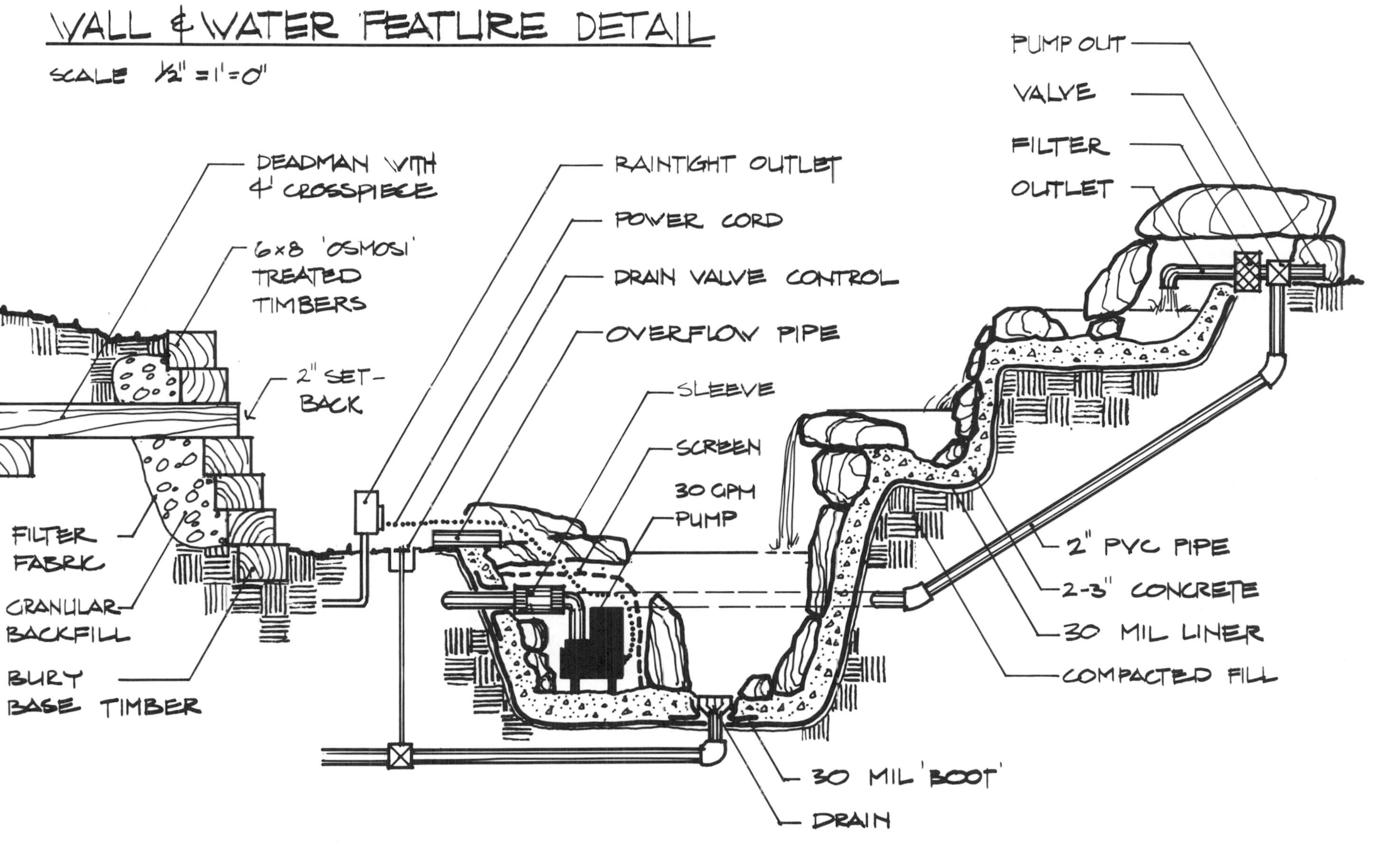

Graphic Symbol File

The file of drawings in this chapter show examples of graphic symbols commonly used in sections and perspectives.

- Trees
- Shrubs
- Foreground plants
- Foreground trees, rocks, and ground covers
- Water
- Vertical plane elements
- Ground plane elements
- Automobiles
- People

Most of these examples emphasize economy of time—using simple, fast techniques. Some can be applied to both sections and perspectives (vegetation, rocks, people). Others are applicable to perspective drawings only (water, vertical and ground plane elements, automobiles). See Chapter 9 for discussion of perspectives.

First try to copy the ideas, altering the size and shapes as necessary. If that proves too difficult, then trace them first to get the feel of their essential character. Very quickly, it should be possible to copy without tracing and also to inject a personal style.

When copying the symbols, be aware of their appropriate context. Select the correct graphic for the message and intent of the drawing. Also give thought to their combination and composition within the drawing. Some hints to guide selection and composition are included.

Be sure to explore the exciting realm of color with these examples. Not only can color be applied to prints of these symbols, but these black-and-white speed techniques can be adapted for direct color rendering.

Development Sketch

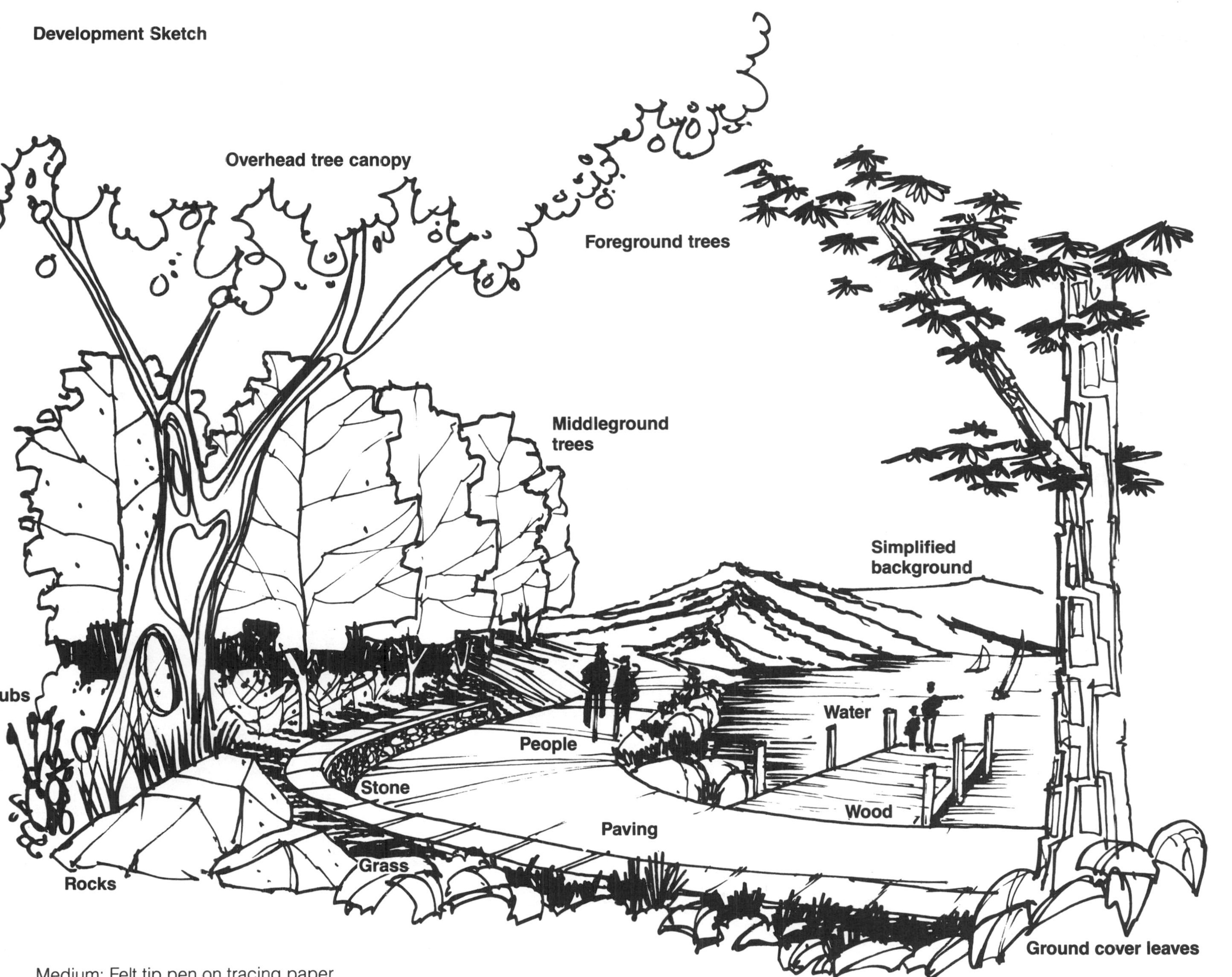

Medium: Felt tip pen on tracing paper

Outline Trees

With this very fast line technique, less than 30 seconds are needed.

Vary the line weight for interest; add some "why not?" dots.

Capture form and size only, not detail. Be abstract rather than realistic.

These outline trees are good for quick preliminary sketches or sections and for use as middleground elements.

Medium: Felt tip pen on marker paper

More Outline Trees

Medium: Felt tip pen on marker paper

Outline Trees with Branching

Also quick, this sketch technique takes one to two minutes per tree.

Use it to capture form and an abstraction of branches.

Place in middleground of preliminary sketches.

Medium: Felt tip pen on marker paper

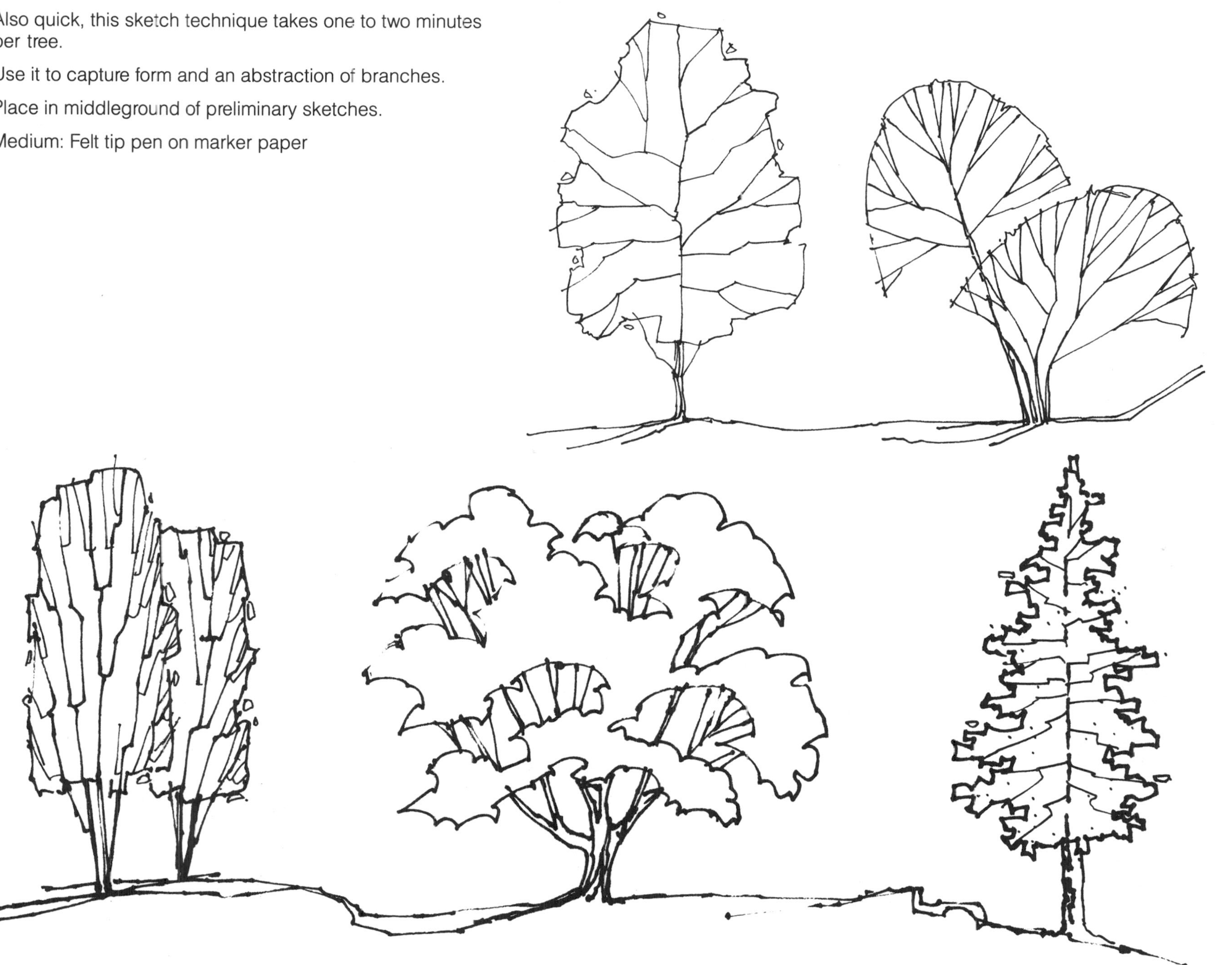

Branched Trees

Branched trees take more time than outline trees, but still less than two minutes. Capture the branching character: angular, knarled, drooping, upright, horizontal.

No outline should be visible, but a guideline is helpful.

Let the branching define the form. Lines are more numerous near the edges.

Branches give a sense of realism and can represent a winter effect.

They are good for revealing architectural features behind them.

Use as middleground elements.

Medium: Pencil on Mylar

Foliage Texture Trees

Follow this sequence showing texture build-up. Do the strokes rapidly. Takes a little more time than other techniques—two to three minutes depending on size.

Very realistic at capturing the textural expression of the foliage as well as the three-dimensional light qualities, these are suited to more refined sketches where other details are shown. Use in middleground or closer.

Medium: 2B pencil on smooth sketch paper

1. Lightly outline the form and assume a light direction.
2. Select a doodle and begin to shape the tree.
3. Build up a heavier pattern on the bottom and shaded side.

Conifer Texture Trees

Medium: 2B pencil on marker paper

Toned Trees

Use a fast shading and hatching technique to capture the form, the light quality, and an abstraction of the texture. These are quite fast—one to two minutes—and very versatile. They can be adapted to foreground, middleground, and background vegetation. Be sure to have some solid black and leave some open white.

Medium: 3B wide-tip sketch pencil on Mylar

Arching strokes

Stippled squares

Radiating strokes

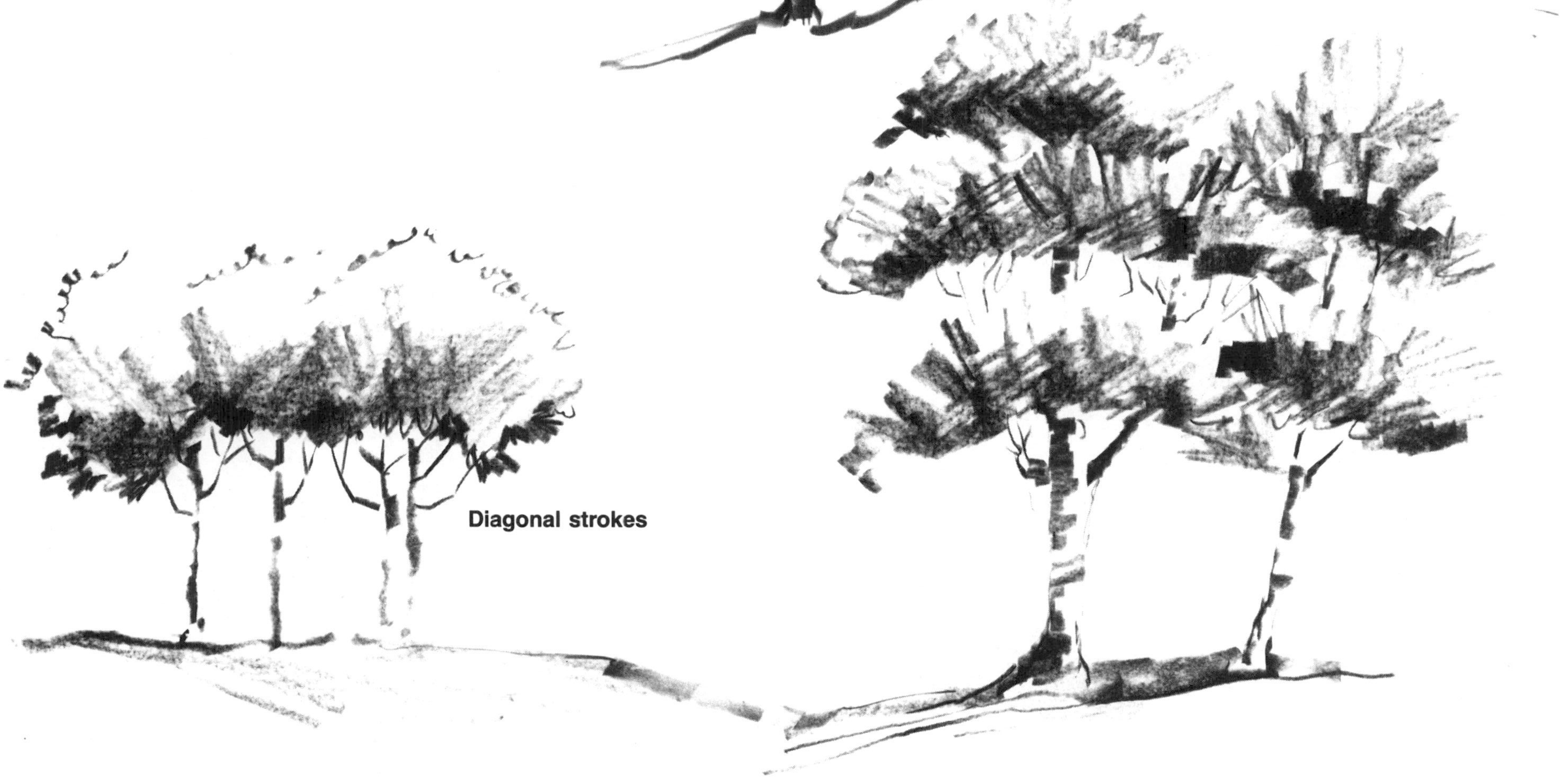

Diagonal strokes

Toned Evergreen Trees

The emphasis here is on form and light quality. Larger sketches can be drawn rapidly with a wider sketching tool. Try to abstract the overall foliage character without drawing individual leaves.

Medium: Graphite stick on Mylar

Tree Rubbings

Overlay the lightly outlined tree form on an embossed surface. Using a graphite stick and quick strokes, vary the pressure to show the light direction. Let the surface underneath express the texture. A very fast way to get textural interest: less than one minute.

There are many suitable surfaces. Those shown here are briefcase, suitcase, sandpaper, emery mesh.

Medium: Graphite stick on Mylar

Shrubs

Use similar techniques as shown for trees: quick outline, branched forms, and textured shapes to show foliage or berries. The more detailed elements should be placed in the foreground, the simpler shapes in the middleground.

Medium: Felt tip pen on smooth paper

Toned Shrubs

High-contrast toning emphasizes shape and overlapping and also distinguishes between different groups of plants. Use in foreground or middleground.

Medium: 2B pencil on Mylar

Tropical plants and grass-like foliage

Foreground Trees, Rocks, and Ground Covers

Because of their closeness to the viewer, detail becomes important. Individual leaves, branches, and bark texture can be shown.

Medium: 2B pencil on Mylar

These elements help to frame the composition as well as keeping the eye from wandering off the page. Only the lower portion of foreground trees needs to be shown.

Medium: Felt tip pen on marker paper

More Foreground Trees, Rocks, and Ground Covers

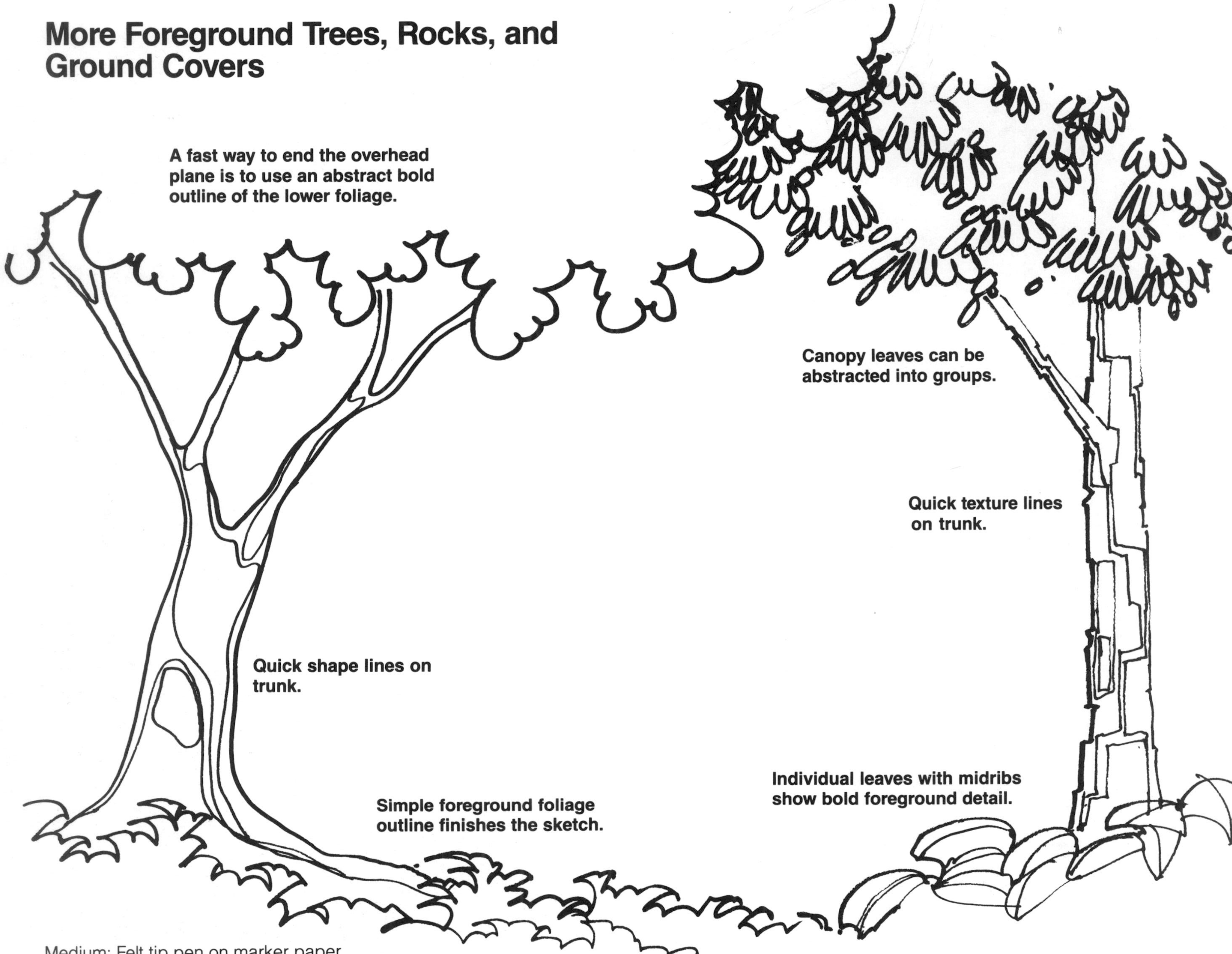

Medium: Felt tip pen on marker paper

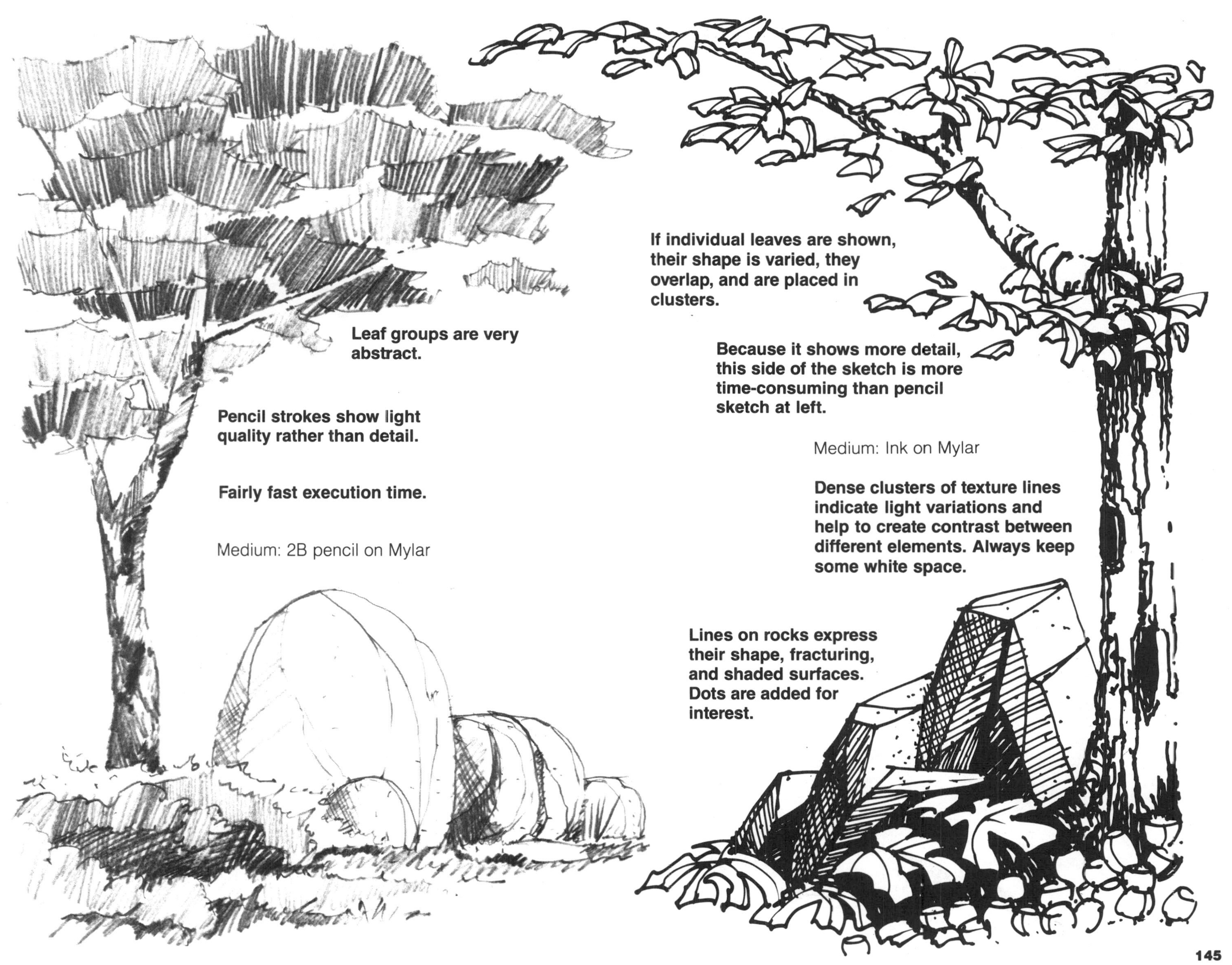

Leaf groups are very abstract.

Pencil strokes show light quality rather than detail.

Fairly fast execution time.

Medium: 2B pencil on Mylar

If individual leaves are shown, their shape is varied, they overlap, and are placed in clusters.

Because it shows more detail, this side of the sketch is more time-consuming than pencil sketch at left.

Medium: Ink on Mylar

Dense clusters of texture lines indicate light variations and help to create contrast between different elements. Always keep some white space.

Lines on rocks express their shape, fracturing, and shaded surfaces. Dots are added for interest.

Water

Architectural Context

Water can be toned with a series of textured horizontal lines to express a rough surface (left pool) or kept white with perhaps a reflection to show a calm, still surface (right pool). The center pools have a hint of ripple to define the surface. Hatching techniques can be used to show the bottom of a pool and light quality.

Fountains with air-filled water are best left white with a few splash dots and dashes.

Medium: Felt tip pen on marker paper

Natural Context
Still water can be left white to indicate reflected light, with the edges defined by shoreline toning. If the land edges are lighter in tone, a contrasting water surface tone can be appropriate.

Medium: HB pencil on Mylar

Moving water should be predominantly white. A few toned strokes can effectively show flow pattern.

Vertical Plane Elements

Lines express edges, cracks, joints, indentations, and light quality. Examples shown here are more appropriate for foregrounds. For middleground and background planes, the patterns should be simplified and abstracted.

Medium: HB pencil on Mylar

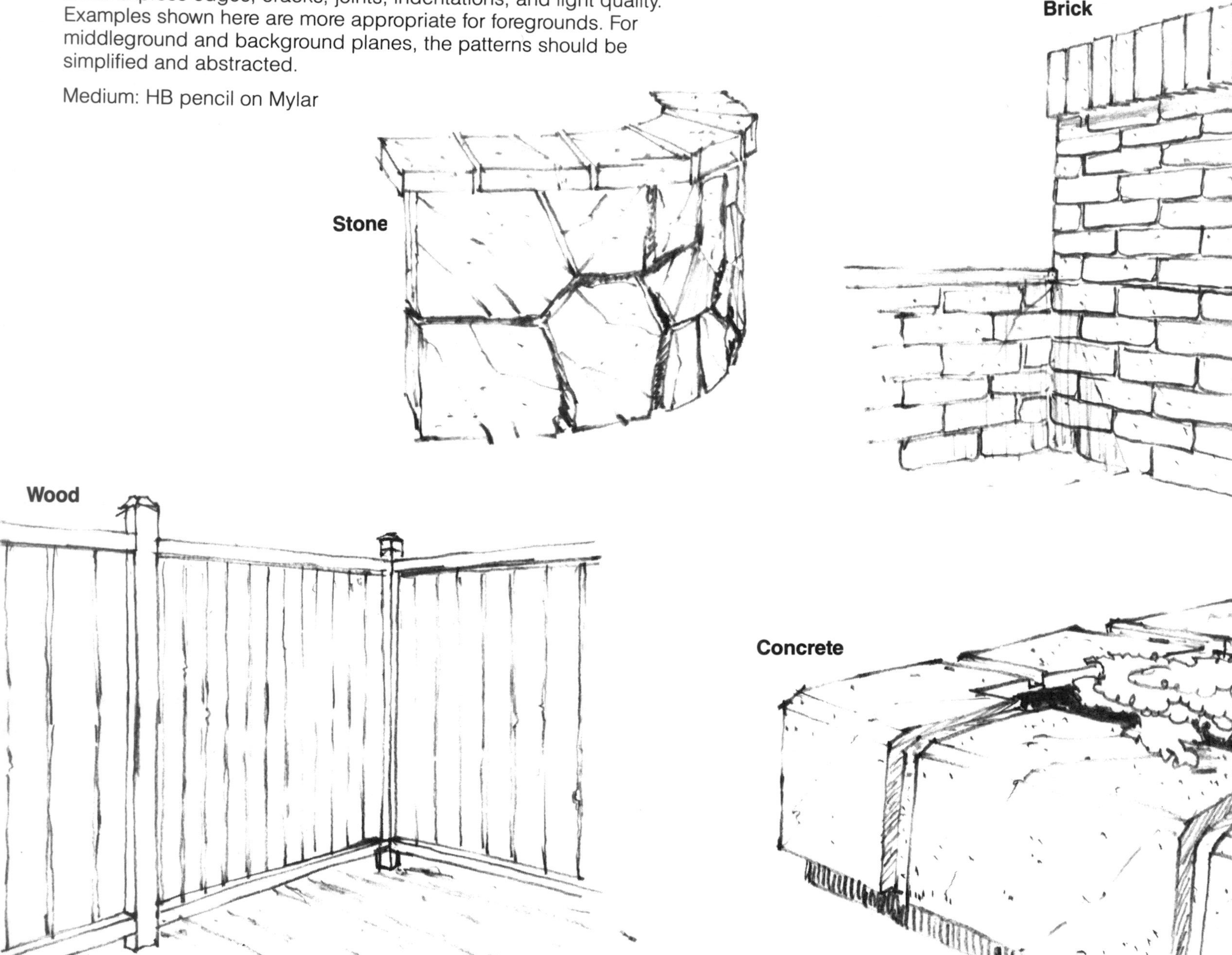

Ground Plane Elements

Make sure that shapes and lines become smaller, foreshortened, and compressed as they move into the background of the sketch. This creates textural perspective.

Medium: HB pencil on Mylar

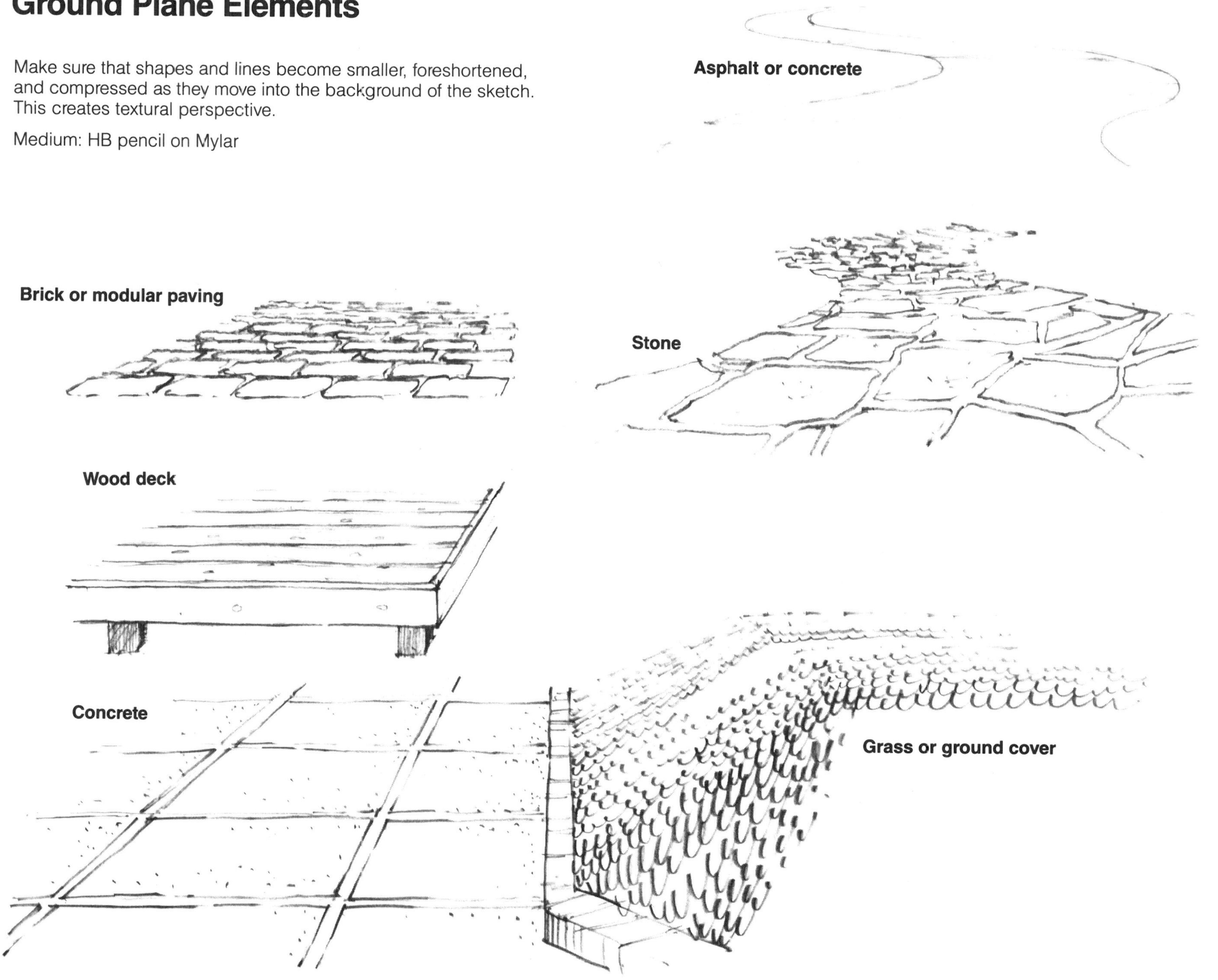

Automobiles

One very good way to draw automobiles is to trace them. Build up a file clipped from magazines and newspapers. Be sure to get various sizes and orientations. There are some disadvantages in this approach: You may not always have the correct auto perspective alignment in your file or you may be short of rear-angle views.

Here is a way to fit cars to any view. It uses the perspective charts as a base. (See Chapter 9 for an explanation of their use.) For a compact car, begin by blocking out the lower body of the car five feet wide, fifteen feet long, and three feet high. Put a one-foot high line for the bottom of the doors.

Now add a central cabin box four feet wide, six feet long, and four feet-six inches high six feet back from the front of the lower body. Add boxes for the grille zone and the wheel wells. Connect the corners of the central cabin box to the bases of the front and rear windows. Do the same with the grille zone box to form an overall streamlined shape. Add the finishing touches and shaping by sketching in doors, windows, lights, grille, wheels, interior, and other details.

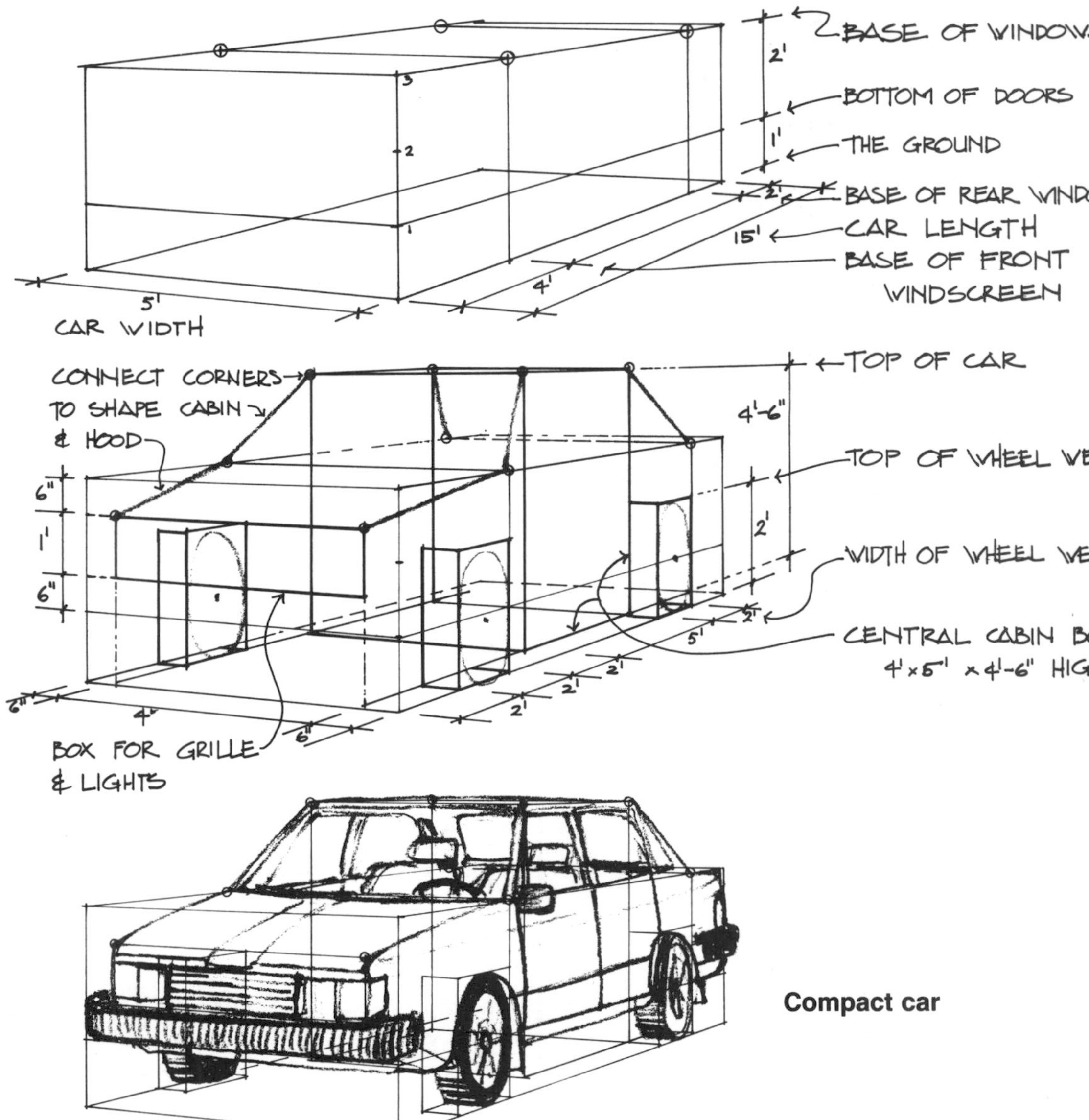

Compact car

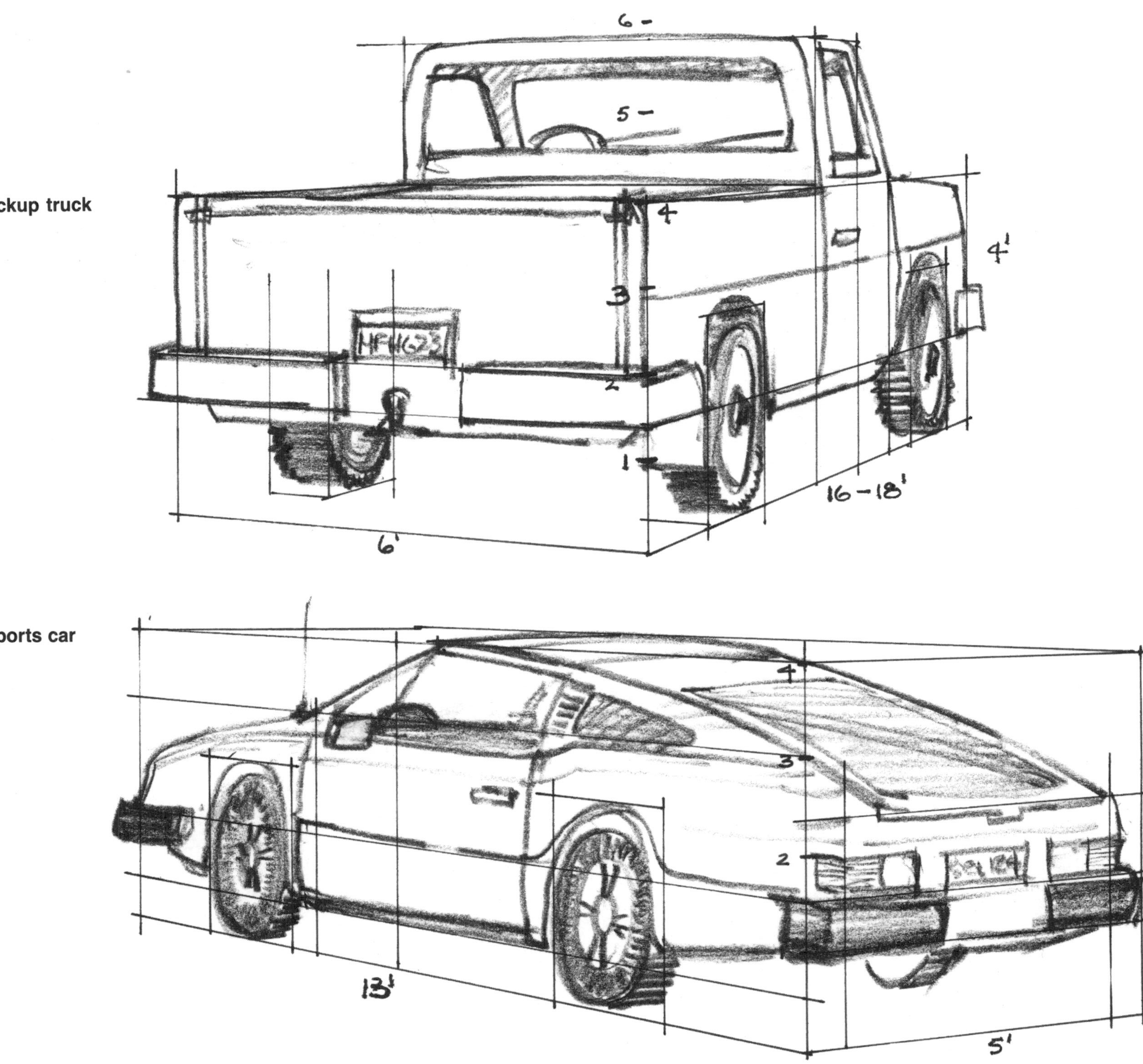

Pickup truck

Sports car

Fast People

A very simple method of drawing people is to begin with the head (1); add the angular trunk (2), leaving a gap for the neck. Then make quick strokes for the arms and legs (3).

Some other fast people are shown to the right of the sequence. A diagonal shading technique with stick legs gives a dark shape that is good for light backgrounds. Heads may be solid or open. Legs can be tapered or made as long rectangles.

These figures are ideal for quick preliminary sketches or for the back of the middleground in any style of sketch.

For more finished sketches, the middleground figures need to have a little more detail, as shown below. All adult eyes align on the horizon line—no matter how large the people are drawn.

Build up a file of people cut from magazines and trace them into your perspective drawings.

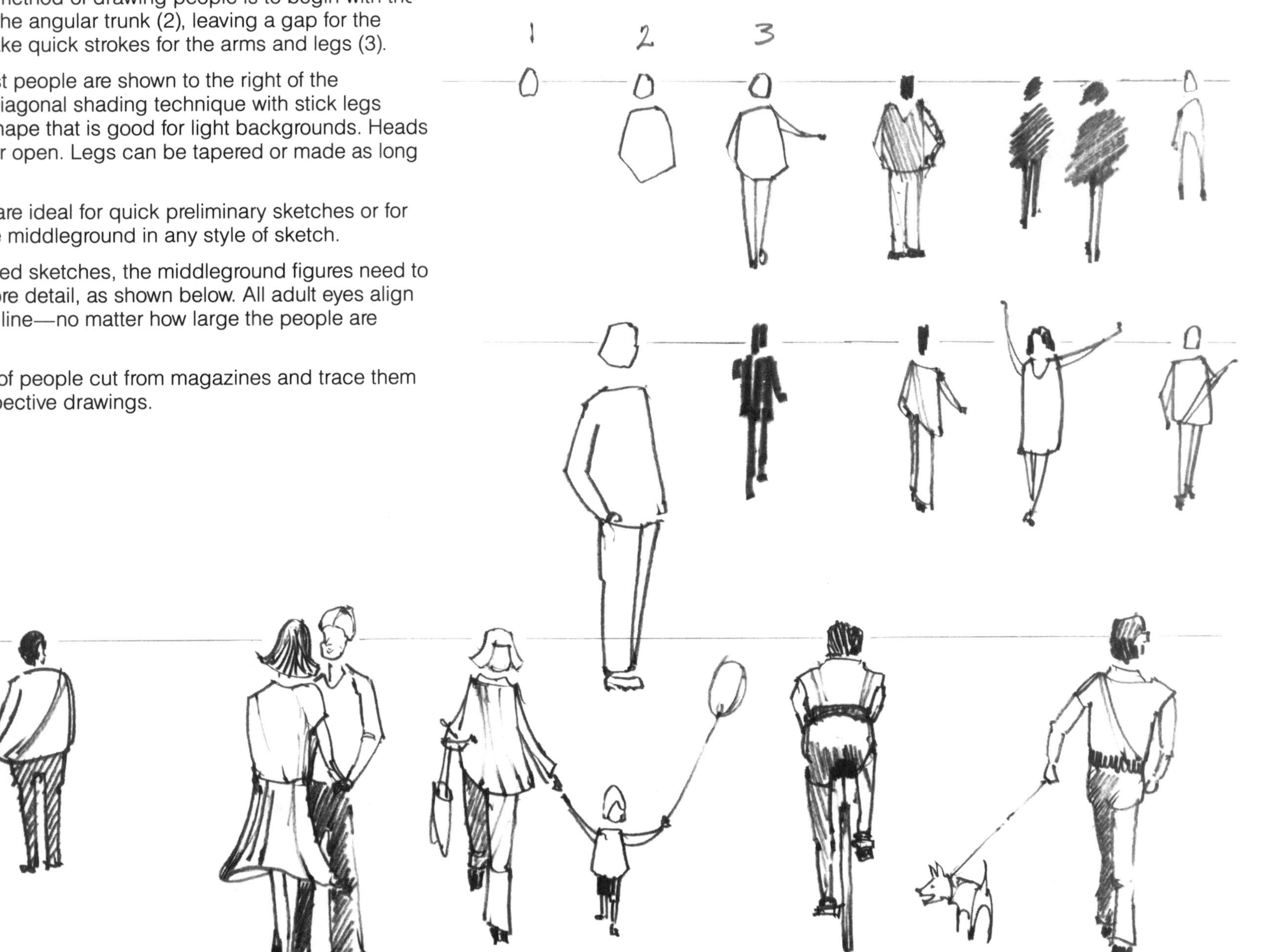

People

Placement and Composition
People bring a drawing to life and express the functional values of the space. In perspectives, they also emphasize depth, level change, and the scale of the environment.

Use these hints to guide the placement and choice of figure types.

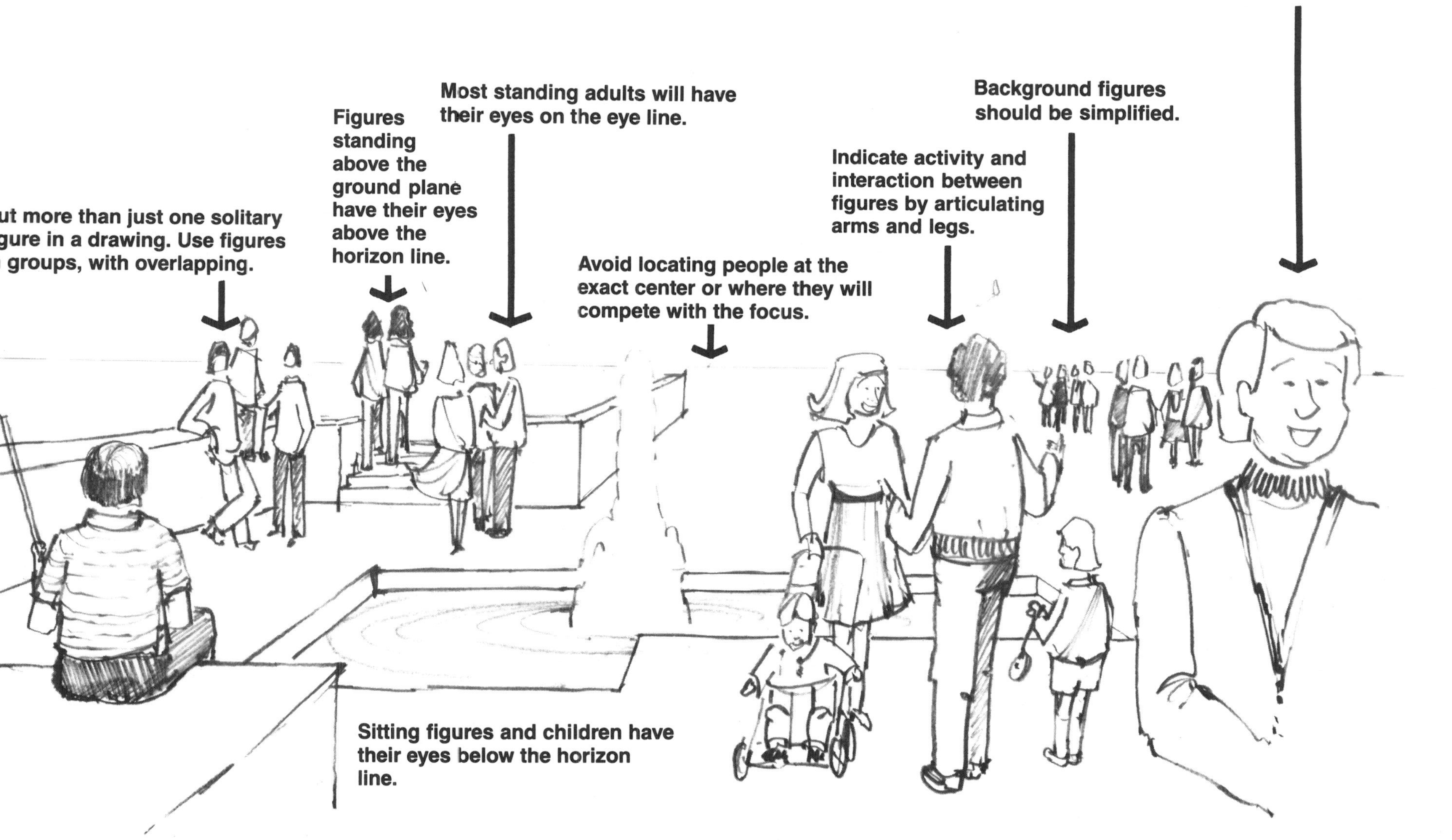

Quick Perspectives

A perspective drawing is a fairly realistic view of space and objects that shows some of their three-dimensional qualities. The plan and section drawings described in Chapters 6 and 7 are excellent for showing horizontal and vertical relationships which can be measured and evaluated in a quantitative manner. They do not, however, give a good feeling for the depth of space, and they are of limited value in describing the experience of moving toward, through, or around a space.

Perspectives, as perspective drawings are often called, do convey this feeling of depth. They can communicate qualities of enclosure, privacy, and openness; they can show relationships between space, time, and light. They can predict much of the visual interest available in a space, such as shadows, reflections, textures, tones, colors, and forms which are difficult to show on plans or sections. Thus they rarely need supporting labels, notes, or abstract symbols.

There are two main uses for perspectives. The first is as a design tool, where they may take the form of fairly fast, rough, and indefinite doodles and sketches. Designers who understand perspectives and use them as representative drawings in their own design process usually produce the best designs. The most valuable drawings for the design process are those that suggest more drawings, suggest improvements, or show where changes should be made.

The methods shown here for both one-point and two-point perspective focus on quick, easy techniques to give confidence and to encourage the use of perspective to externalize three-dimensional ideas early and frequently in the design process. Do not worry if initial perspectives look rough, bare, inaccurate, and are not what you had in mind. Accept them; then revise, change, and enhance them. The more you try these techniques the more comfortable it will feel. Before long, your perspective drawings will communicate more realism.

The second use of perspectives is as a sales tool. Sales perspectives are persuasive drawings done when the design is substantially complete. For smaller-scale, lower-budget design projects, the techniques shown in this chapter are very applicable. For larger-budget landscape architectural projects with corporate or public agency clients, you will need to develop accurate, polished, and colorful renderings. The techniques required for these renderings demand more time investment, but they are worth the effort.

Development Sketch

View from Prospect Street

Medium: Felt tip pen on tracing paper

One-point Perspective

The Basics

To understand the basic elements of perspective and what each represents, follow the steps shown on these two pages.

1. Start by doing exercise 39 in Appendix IV.
2. On a sheet of tracing paper draw a long horizontal line freehand. Label this the **horizon line** or eye line.

   Now draw fast people of different sizes—all with their eyes on the eye line. Assuming that all the people are in reality the same size, the people drawn smaller appear farther away. This demonstrates the fundamental principle of perspective: *"The apparent size of an object varies inversely with its distance from the viewer."*

   In this drawing, person number 2 is twice as far away as person number 1, and four times as far away as person number 3. Translated into actual distances, this means that an object forty feet from the viewer will appear half the size of an object twenty feet from the viewer because it is twice the distance away.
3. On another sheet, draw a horizon line and place a dot somewhere on it labeled VP, for **vanishing point**.

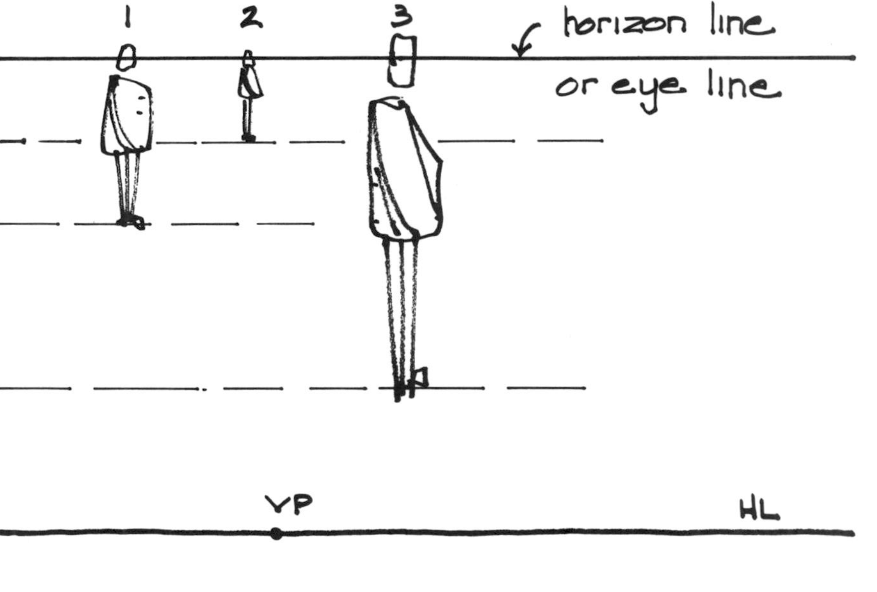

4. Now draw a large rectangle surrounding the vanishing point. Keep all lines horizontal and vertical as shown.

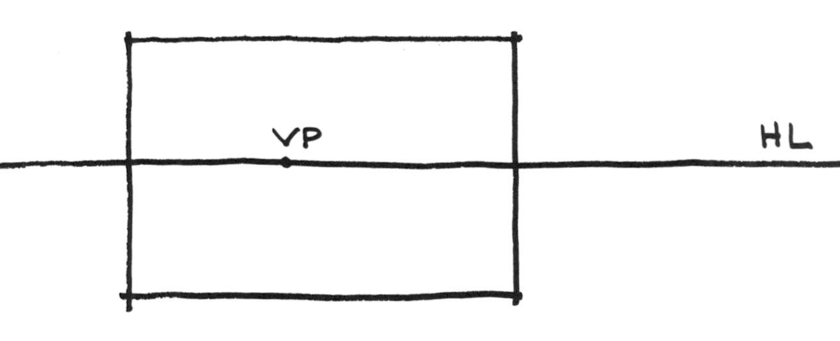

5. Connect the four corners of the rectangle to the vanishing point (VP). These **vanishing lines**, or converging lines, will form the edges of the space.

6. Place a smaller rectangle with vertical and horizontal sides inside the larger one so that the corners intersect with the vanishing lines. This shows the basic lines of a one-point perspective.

7. Add a large person with eyes on the horizon line at the vanishing point. Note the lines that represent **ground lines** on the **ground plane**.

A side view, or section, of this one-point perspective set-up would look like this. The **line of sight** is an imaginary line between the eyes of the viewer and the vanishing point on the horizon.

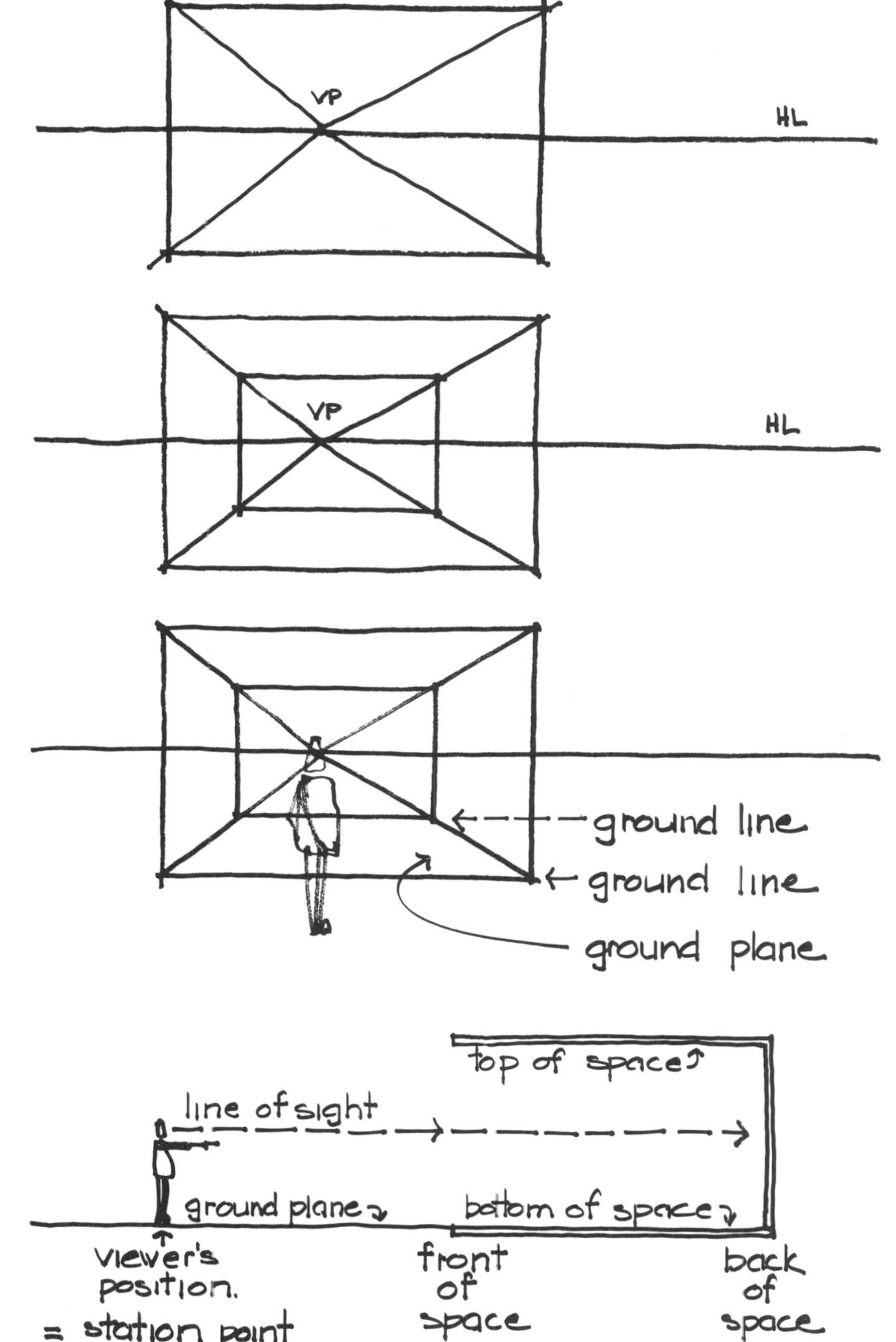

Note these key aspects of a one-point perspective:

1. All lines parallel to the line of site converge to one vanishing point on the horizon line.

2. All horizontal lines that are perpendicular to the line of site are drawn parallel to the horizon line.

3. All vertical lines in the space are drawn vertical in the perspective.

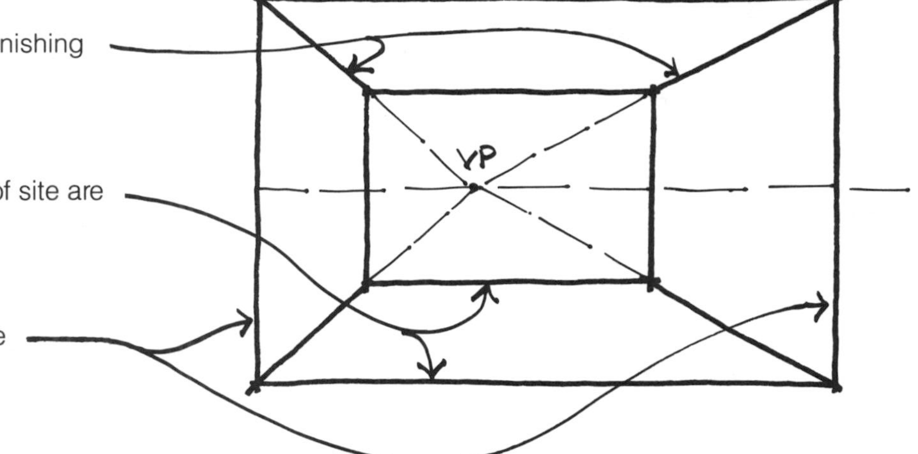

Now do exercise 40, Appendix IV.

Proportion Method for One-point Perspective

A perspective space is composed of the three dimensions: width, height, and depth (or distance from viewer). Each of these dimensions can be quickly estimated using multiples of a human figure to establish correct perspective proportions. For convenience, assume that the distance from ground to eyes is five feet.

To find width

Place people lying down feet to eyes in multiples of five feet to get desired width.

To find height

Stack people up—feet to eyes—in multiples of five feet to get desired height.

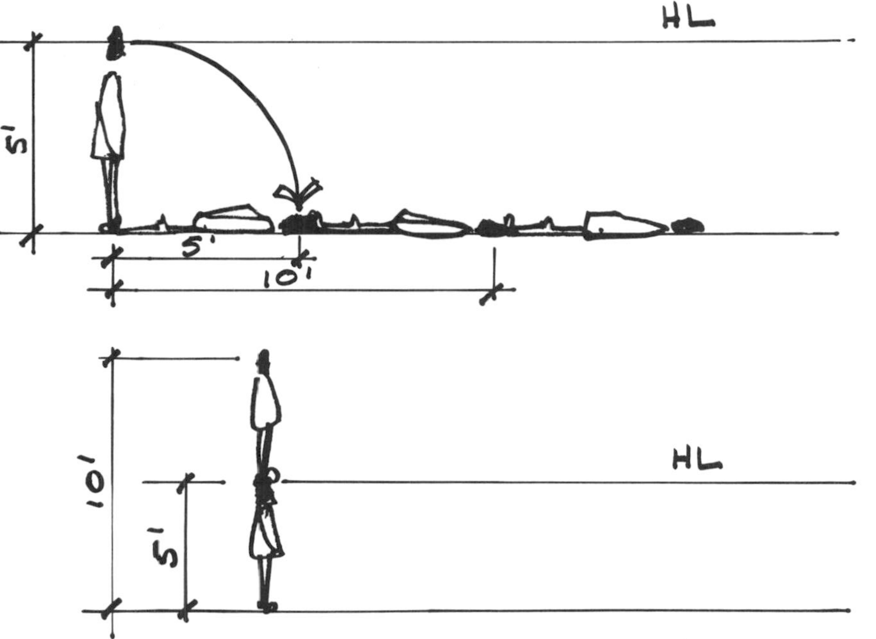

To find depth

Assume that the first figure you draw is located twenty feet away from the viewer. Then draw smaller figures that are a known fraction (e.g., one half) of that first figure. A horizontal line through their feet will give you known ground line distances.

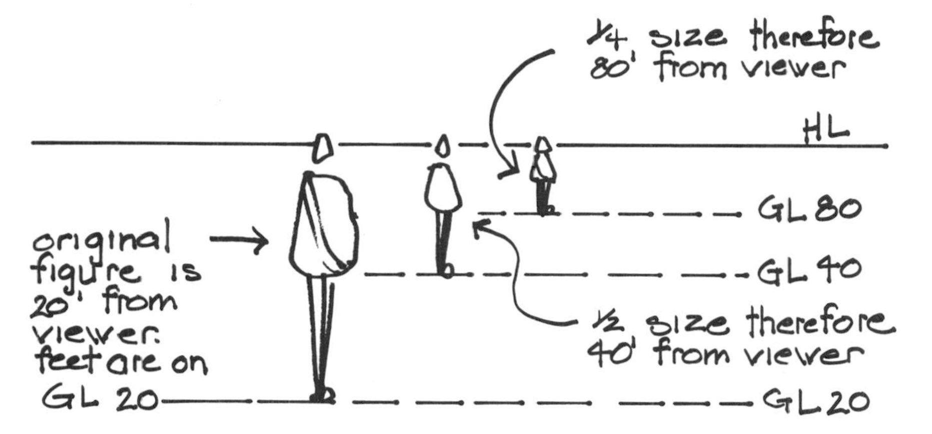

Set-up Sequence

Using proportional techniques, follow the thirteen steps on these two pages to draw an outdoor courtyard that is twenty feet wide, twenty feet deep, and surrounded on three sides by ten-foot-high walls. Do it all freehand with a soft pencil or a felt tip pen on tracing paper.

1. Draw a person.
   Make his or her size appropriate for both the size of the space and the size of your sheet. Place the person near the left side of your page with feet near the bottom of the page.

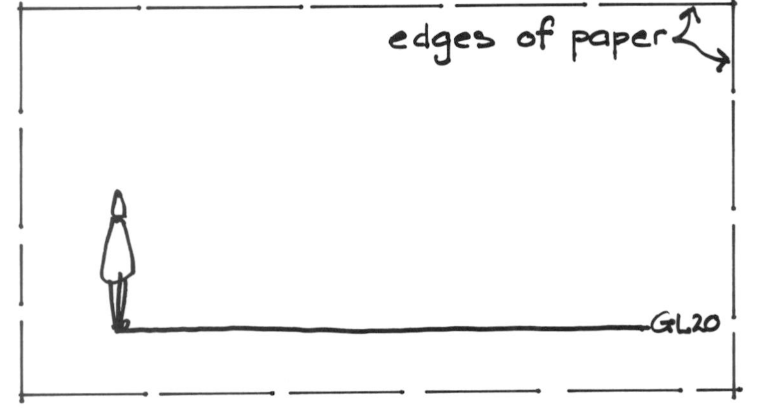

2. Draw the ground line (GL) 20.
   This horizontal line going through the feet assumes that the figure is twenty feet from the viewer.

3. Draw the horizon line (HL).
   Show a horizontal line going through the head.

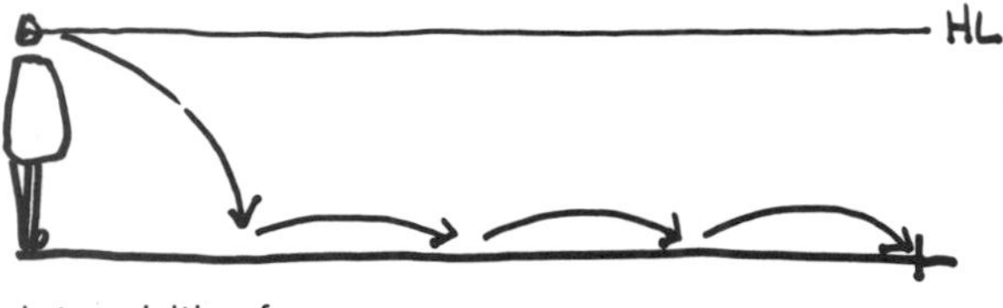

4. Calculate width of space.
   Lie the person down, adding increments of five feet until you have the correct width; e.g., four people lying down equals twenty feet wide.

5. Draw verticals.
   Vertical guidelines define the left and right edge of the space or the width.

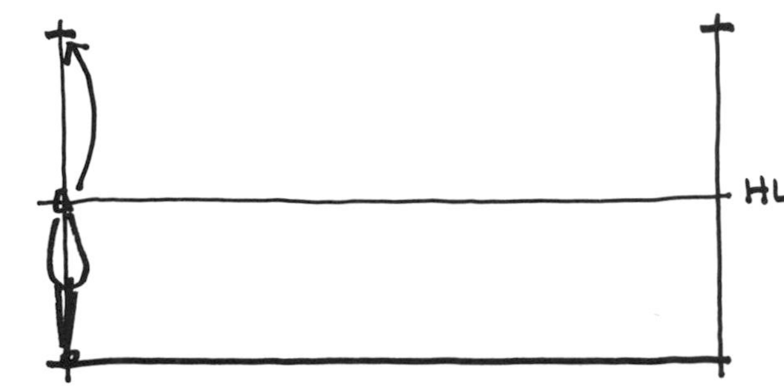

6. Calculate height of space.
   Place one person on top of another in five-foot increments to get the desired height. Mark the verticals on both sides.

7. Adjust size if necessary.
   If the resulting height and width are too large or too small for your paper, go back to step 1 and redraw your person at a different size.
   Redo steps 1 through 6.

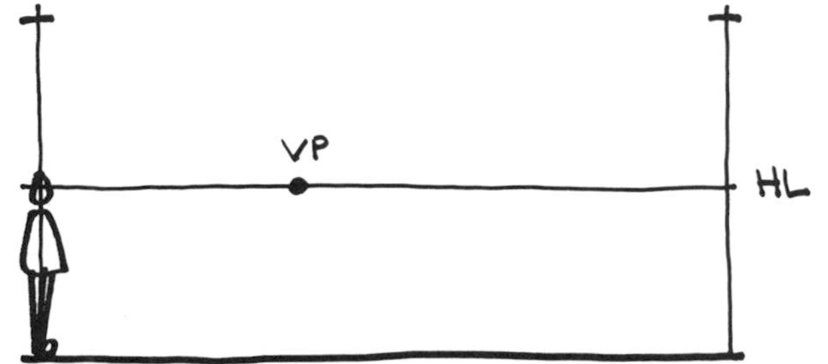

8. Select a vanishing point.
   Locate a dot on the horizon line slightly to the left or right of center.

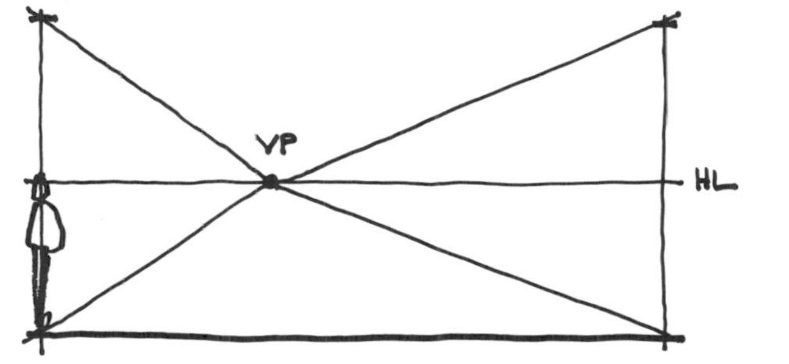

9. Draw vanishing lines.
Draw four lines which connect the vanishing point to the top and bottom of the left and right verticals.

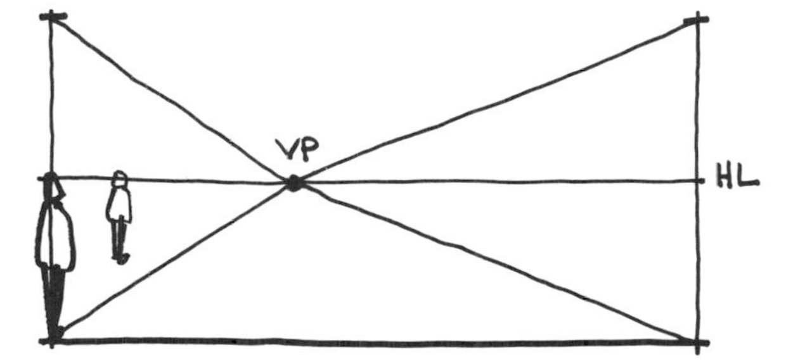

10. Find depth or distance lines.
Draw another person at the correct fraction (one-half, one-fourth, one-fifth) of the original person to simulate the back of the space. In this case, the back of the space is two times the distance from the viewer as the front of the space. Draw the person one-half the original size, keeping the head on the horizon line.

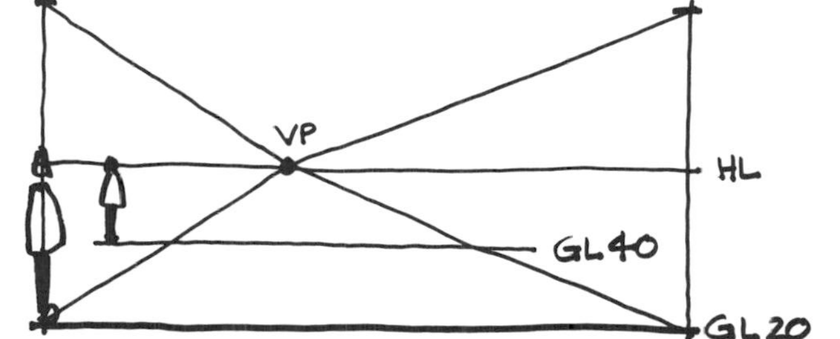

11. Put in the ground line at the back of the space by drawing a horizontal line at the feet of the person in back.
This is GL 40.

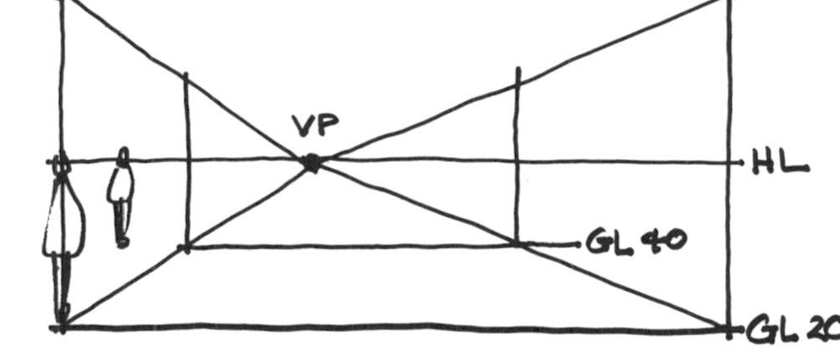

12. Draw the remaining back of the space.
Where the back ground line intersects with the vanishing lines, draw two more verticals to represent the back corners of the space.

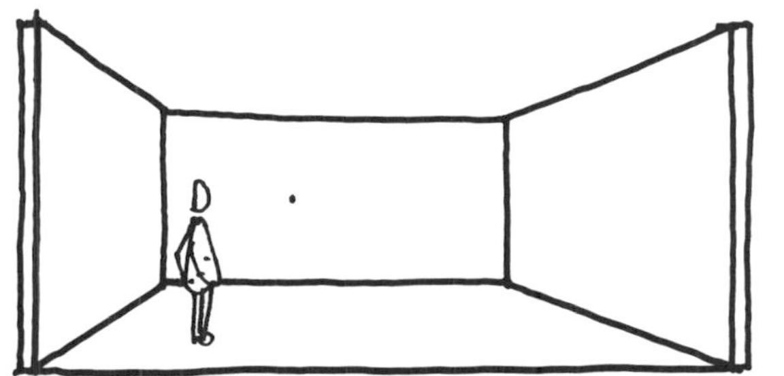

13. Redraw the space.
On an overlay, draw the essential edges of the space—omitting hidden lines and construction lines.

Once you have completed a very simple space like this, you can add complexities and entourage. Use fractions of a person to get smaller objects, such as benches, low walls and shrubs. Add to this space two fifteen-foot-high trees anywhere. Now add a box two-and-a-half feet high, five-feet wide, and any length, anywhere. Place these elements within the space by first visualizing a five-foot person standing at that location. The element will be a multiple or a fraction of that person. Redo exercise 39 and compare it with your first try.

Scale Method for One-point Perspective

Using proportional estimates to get depth is very approximate. A more accurate, and also fast, method is to use a scale.

Here is a section view of a space showing objects at various distances from the viewer.

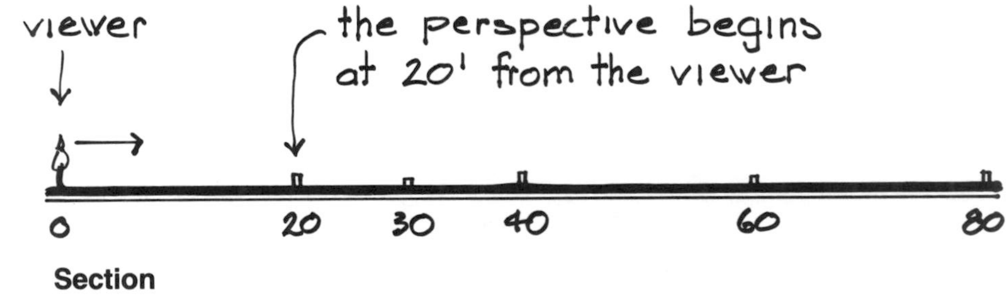

To find GL 30, GL 40, and any others, follow these steps:

1. Draw in the nearest ground line (here GL 20) near the base of the sheet.
2. Add the horizon line at a selected distance above GL 20.
3. Select one of the engineer's scales which seems to fit (see step 4) and place the zero on the horizon line.
4. Keeping the zero as a pivot, rotate the scale so that the desired ground line (e.g., number 30) lies on the GL 20. If it does not fit, select another scale.
5. Make a short horizontal mark next to the 20 on the scale.
6. Remove the scale and extend the mark to make the new horizontal depth ground line.
7. Rotate the scale, keeping the zero as a pivot, and set the new desired GL number right on the GL 20.
8. Repeat for any ground line depth, always marking the 20. For heights and widths, use the proportional method described on the previous pages.
9. Do exercise 41.

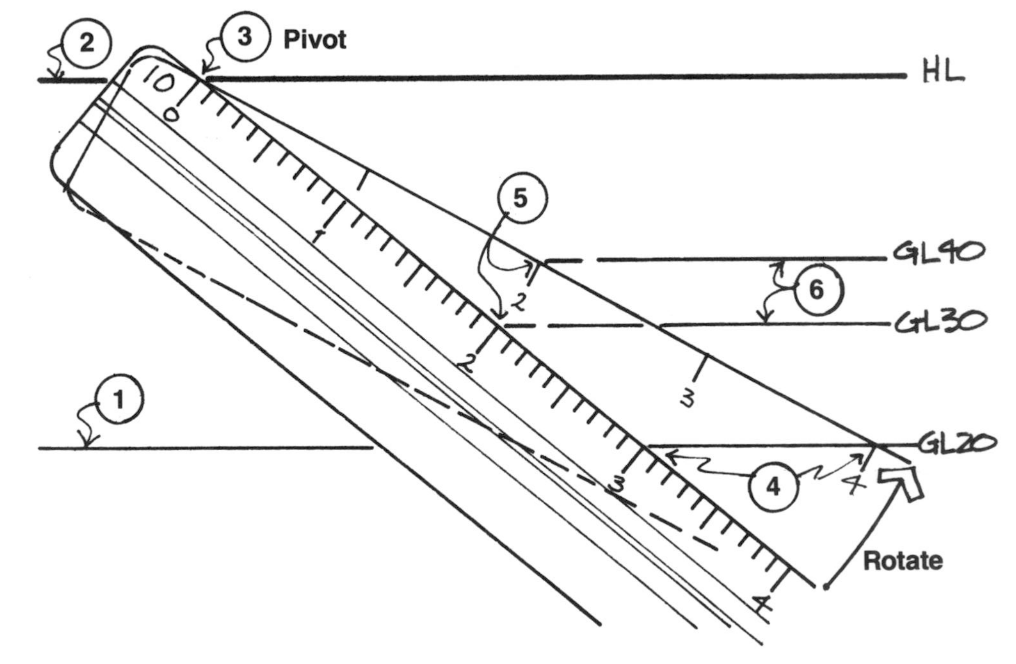

Diagonal Method for One-point Perspective

Another fast technique for obtaining depth lines uses a geometric principle of diagonals.

1. Begin with the GL 20 horizon line.
2. Draw a five-foot square which connects both (A B C D).
3. Place a diagonal line from top left corner to bottom right corner (A C).
4. Draw the first opposing diagonal between opposite corners (B D).
5. Where it intersects with A C, draw a horizontal line, which will be GL 40.
6. GL 40 will intersect A D at E.
7. Draw the second opposing diagonal B E. Where it intersects with A C, draw a horizontal line for GL 60.
8. It will intersect A D at F.
9. Connect B F. Where it intersects A C, draw a horizontal line for GL 80.
10. Continue this process to locate ground lines of twenty-foot increments.

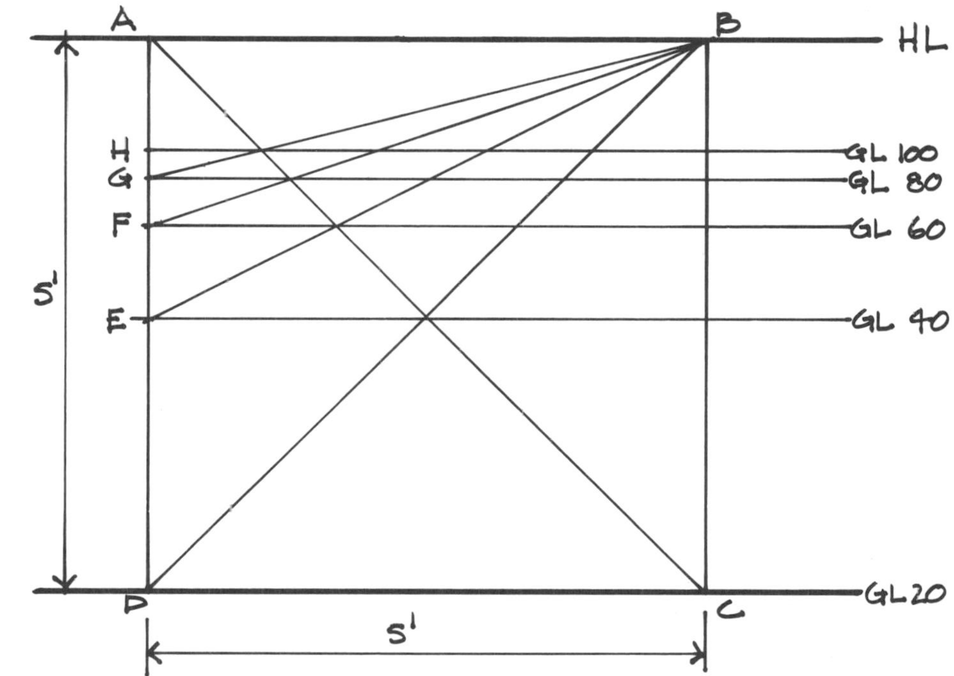

Perspective Charts for One-point Perspective

One of the best aids for doing perspectives is the prepared perspective chart. These are made by a number of companies and are available as packaged sets in places that sell other drafting materials and equipment. For purposes of discussion in this book, we refer to Lawson perspective charts, a package that offers a particularly wide range of options. Most of the discussion pertaining to Lawson charts is applicable to other brands as well.

The Lawson charts are identified by number. For example, chart number 8 is a one-point, or parallel, perspective chart with a five-foot horizon line.

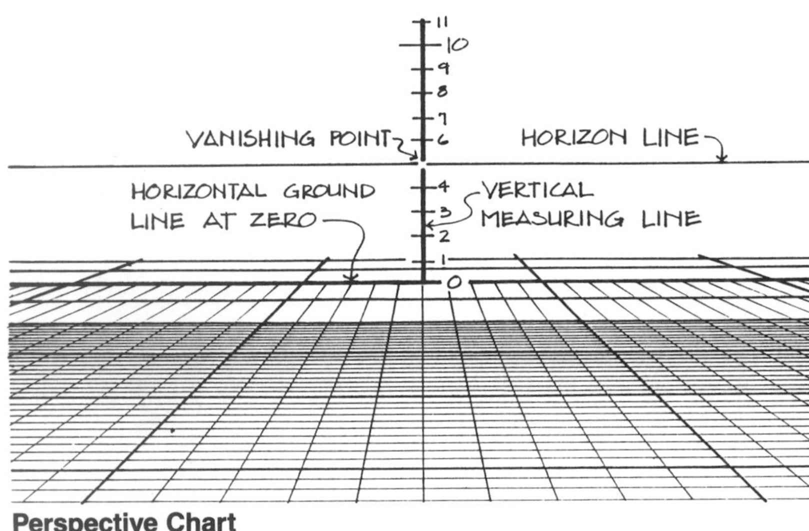

Perspective Chart

On the ground plane of this parallel perspective is a grid pattern which represents one-foot increments in both directions. This is what the square grid pattern of a plan view looks like when foreshortened into a perspective view. The lines get closer together as they get further away. Every tenth line is heavier and there is an extra thick horizontal ground line at the zero point of the vertical measuring line (VML) in the center. This line also intersects the horizon line at the vanishing point.

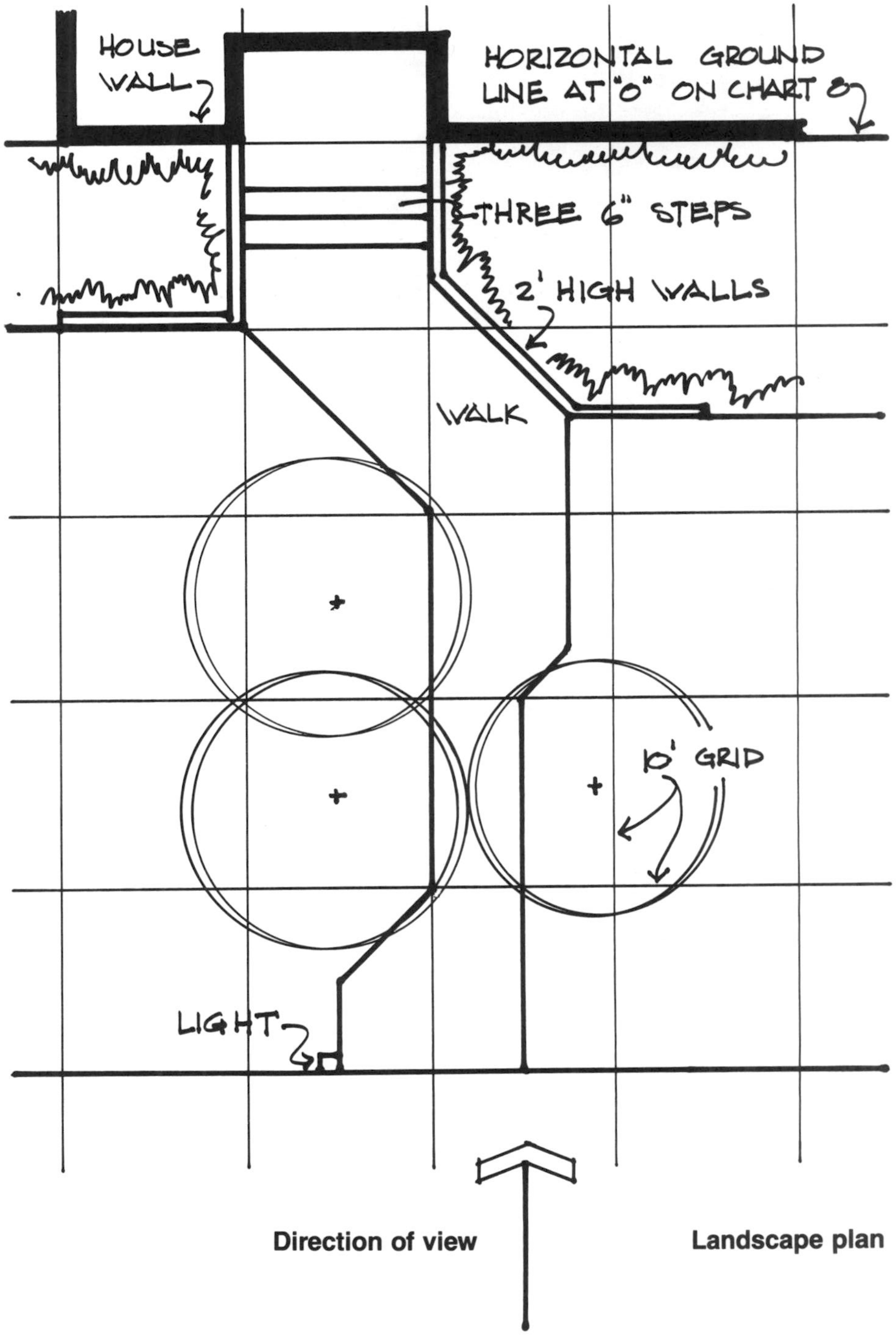

HOUSE WALL
HORIZONTAL GROUND LINE AT "0" ON CHART 8
THREE 6" STEPS
2' HIGH WALLS
WALK
10' GRID
LIGHT

Direction of view

Landscape plan

Suppose you have a preliminary plan idea for an entryway, as shown on the previous page, and you wish to test it out on the one-point perspective chart. Follow these steps.

1. Place a ten-foot grid on the plan with the grid lines parallel or perpendicular to the majority of the architectural lines.
2. Select the viewing direction and location. Draw one of the grid lines heavier to represent the horizontal ground line at the zero on the chart. The closer this line is to the point of view, the larger the final perspective sketch will be. Move the view point left or right on your plan to achieve the desired composition of the perspective view.

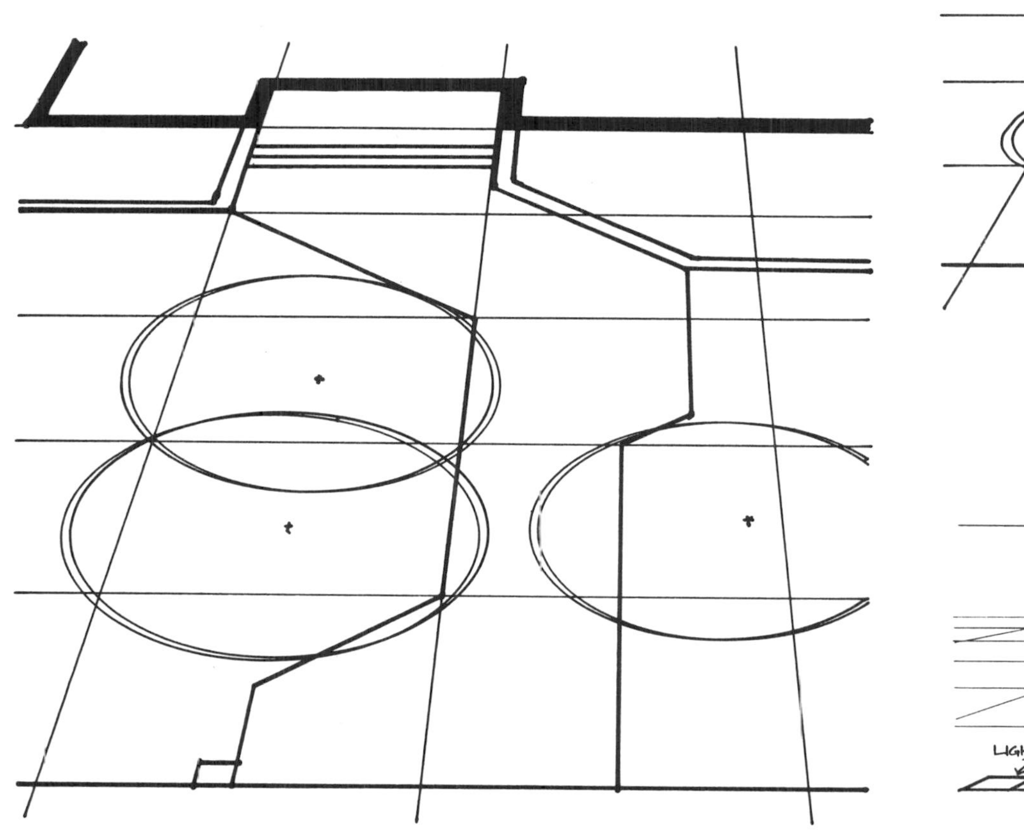

3. Transfer the gridded plan data onto the perspective grid, using the heavy ground line as a locational guide. Note from the sequence of perspective grids shown how the gridded lines become very compressed as you move from looking directly down on a space to standing on the ground plane looking into that space. This makes the plan view lines look foreshortened.

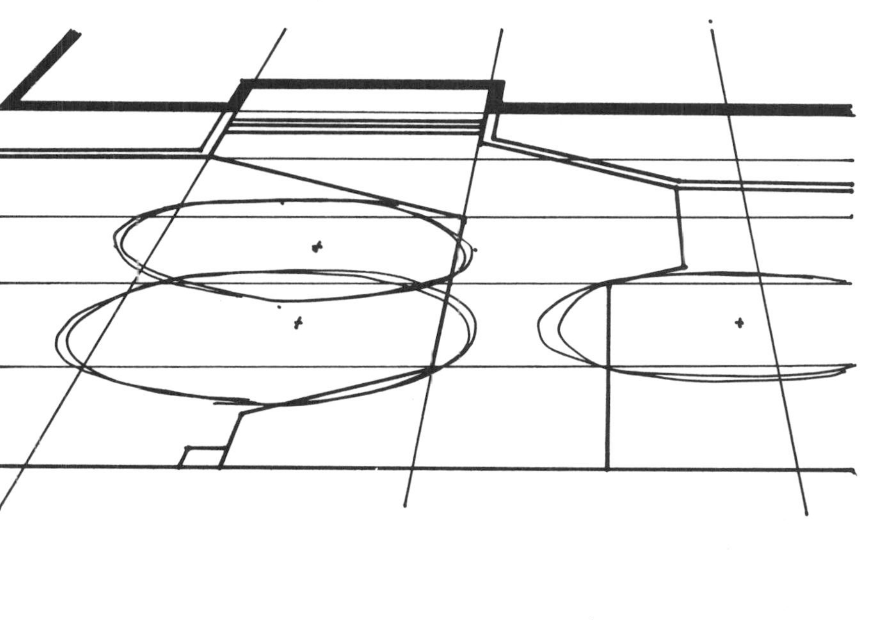

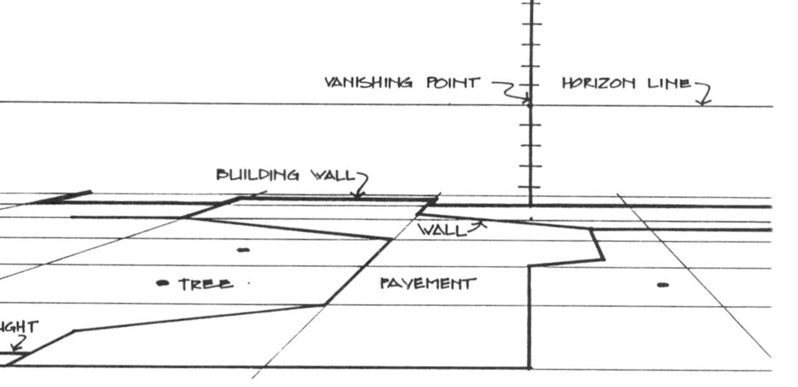

4. Once the foreshortened lines are on the perspective grid, draw vertical lines from the corners of raised objects. Calculate their height by using the proportional method of the vertical measuring line (Appendix I). Finish the outlines of built objects by obeying the rules of one-point perspective.

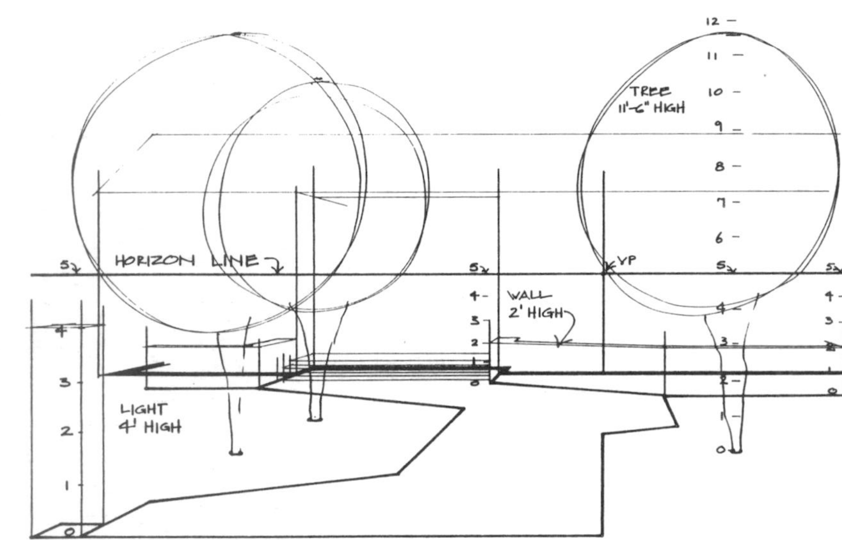

5. Add some fast people and then redraw on an overlay, omitting all hidden and construction lines.

6. Using these principles, try exercise 42.

Quick One-Point Perspective to Study a Plaza Space

VANISHING POINT

HORIZON LINE

Medium: Felt tip pen on smooth paper

Two-point Perspective

One-point perspectives are good for streetscape views and other lineal spaces, but they tend to be static and very specialized. More dynamic representative views are obtained with two-point perspectives.

Instead of one, there are now two vanishing points, the left vanishing point (LVP) and the right vanishing point (RVP). Assume that you are drawing some simple boxes with square corners. There will be only three types of lines.

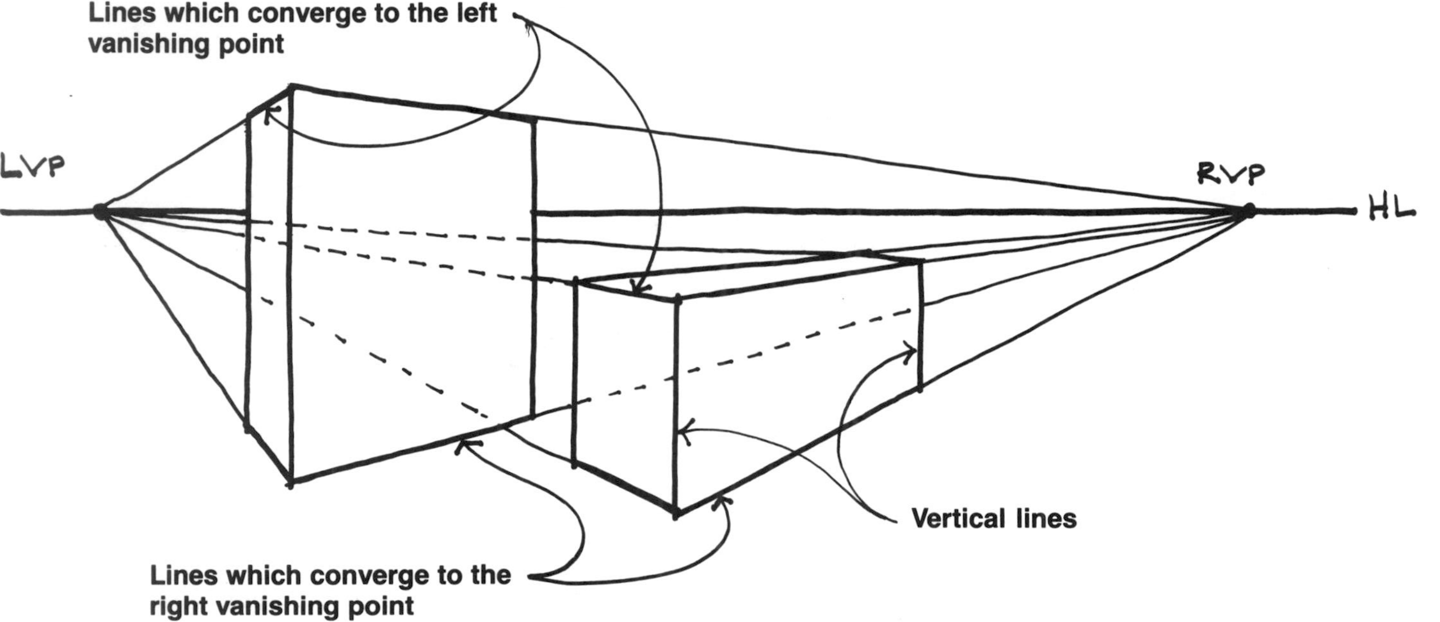

Unlike one-point perspectives, there are no horizontal lines except at the horizon line. An important fact to remember is that all parallel lines on the same plane or object surface vanish to the same vanishing point.

Try exercise 43.

Perspective Charts for Two-point Perspectives

One of the fastest ways to draw reasonably accurate two-point perspectives is to use a prepared chart.

Sketching on an overlay, the designer can develop three-dimensional ideas by following ground plane grid lines, just as with the one-point charts.

Similarly, when transferring plan view data to perspective charts, it is necessary to make a scaled grid on the plan first.

The next step is to make two intersecting lines on the plan. These are heavier than the other lines.

The two heavy intersecting grid lines on the plan are then used as a reference by matching them to the two heavy grid lines that pass through the zero on the chart.

You must select the position of these heavy lines on the plan. Where you put them will determine the point of view for the perspective. So you need to adjust them to provide the most effective message.

Some quick trial-and-error preliminary sketches will give you a clue to the most desirable view point. (Appendix II contains useful field of vision plan overlays and instructions for their use with selected Lawson charts. They can be used to quickly determine the appropriate point of view.)

Do exercise 44.

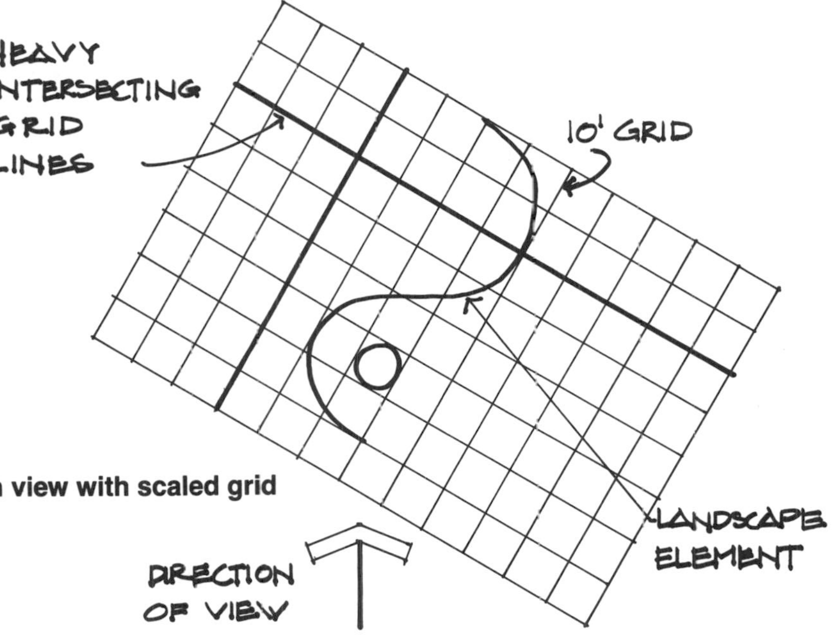

Plan view with scaled grid

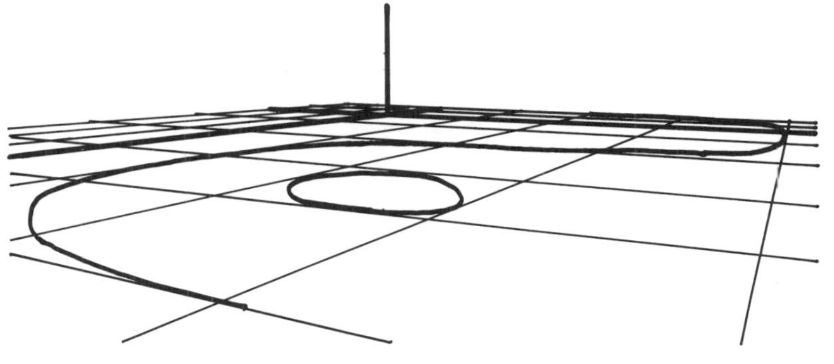

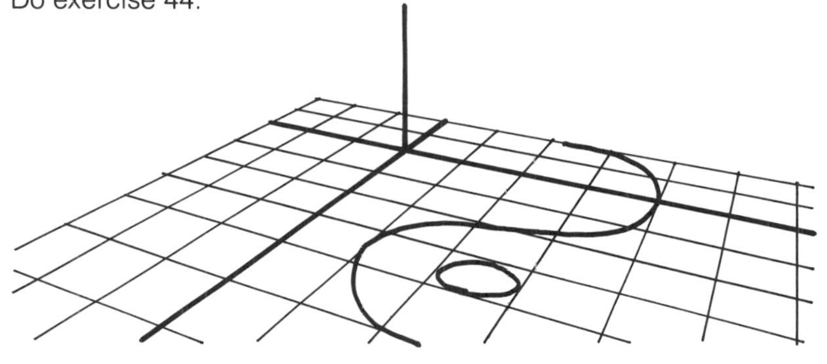

Perspective views

Once the ground plane data is transferred to the chart, the height of objects must be determined. The fastest way is to use the proportional method (see pages 159–161). Any point on the ground plane to the horizon line will be the same height. On Lawson chart 5, it is five feet. Simply use multiples or fractions of this distance to get heights of objects.

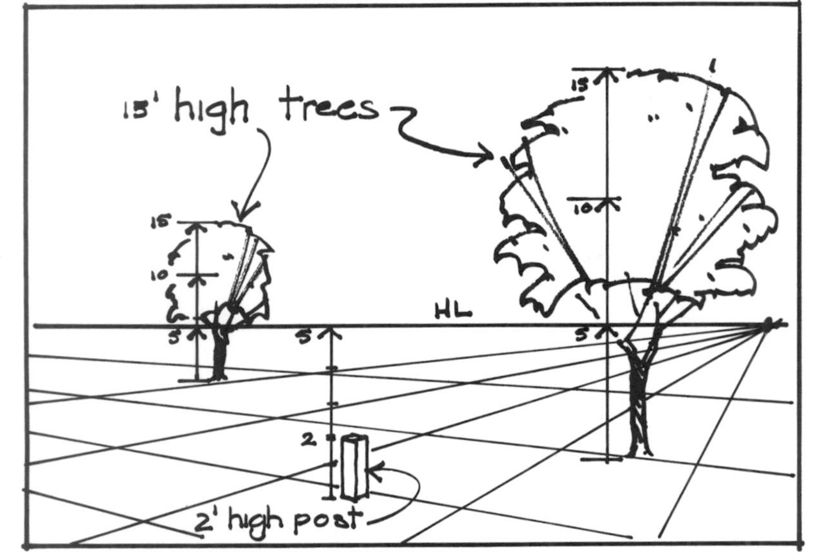

If more accuracy is required on heights, use the vertical measuring line. See Appendix I, pages 183–185 for instructions.

Do exercise 45.

Practice form manipulation by adding for overhangs, ledges, and other like elements and by removing for notches, indentations, and the like. Constantly obey the two-point perspective rules of convergence to one or the other of the vanishing points.

Do exercises 46 and 47.

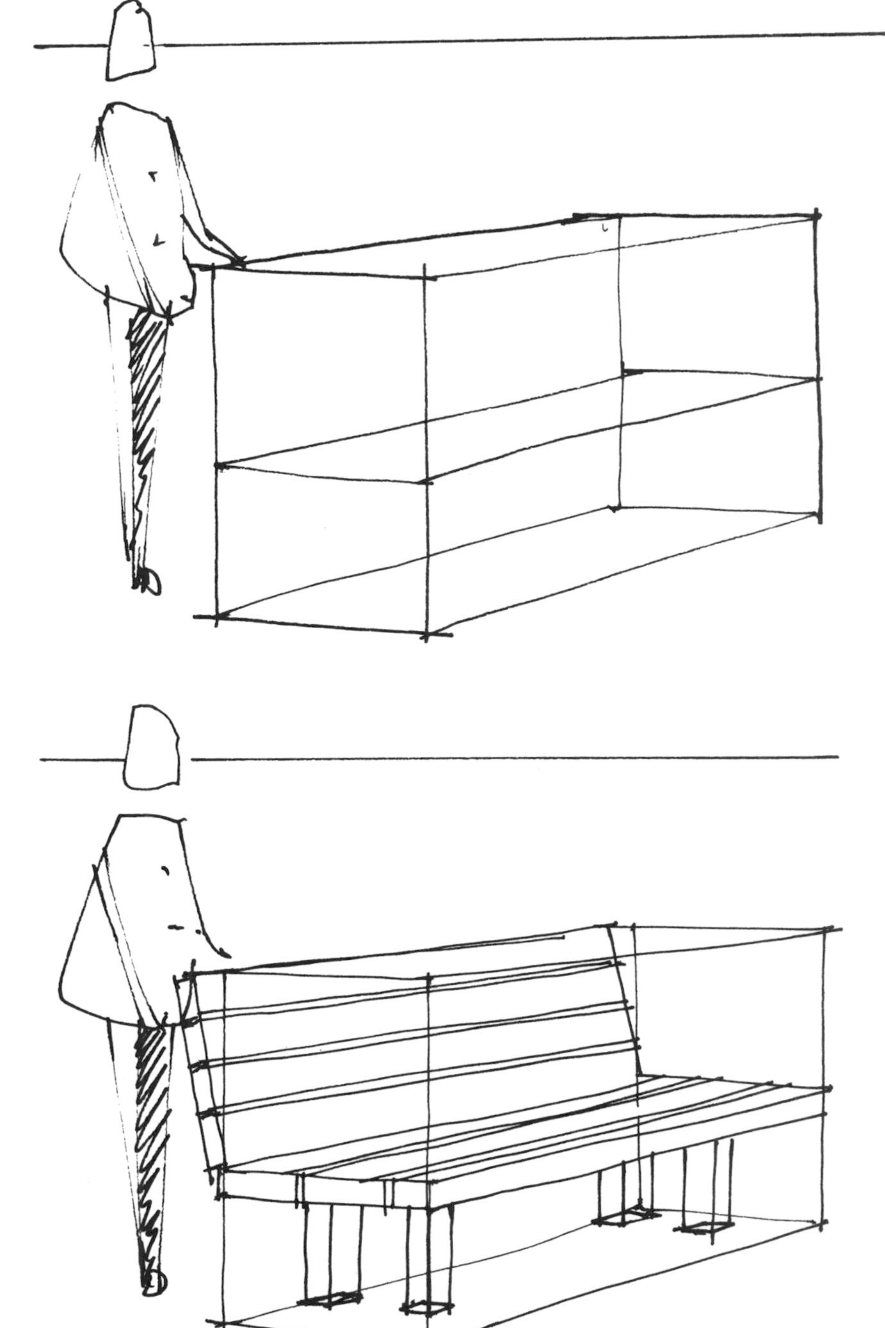

Composition

Composition is a key factor in communicating the spatial message. The following five pages demonstrate some important principles of how to arrange elements, highlight focal areas, and achieve a balanced and interesting composition.

Consider:

1. Foreground, middleground, and background.
2. Overhead plane, ground plane, and vertical plane.
3. Overlapping and foreshortening.
4. Contrast and tonal balance.
5. Light quality, shade, and shadow.

After studying these ideas, try exercises 48 and 49.

Foreground, Middleground, and Background

A mix of all three will create a greater sense of depth or distance.

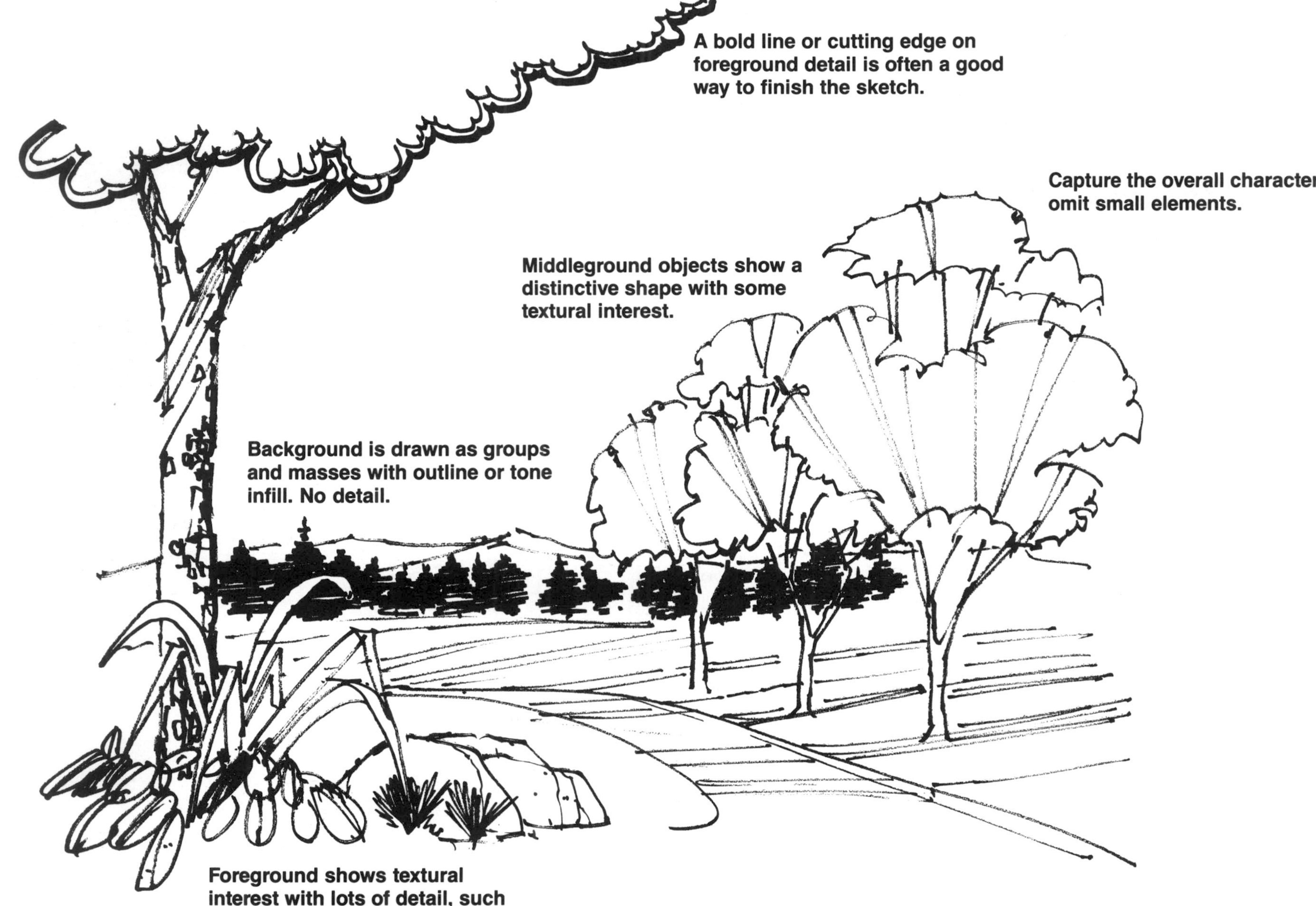

Medium: Felt tip pen on smooth paper

Overhead Plane, Ground Plane, and Vertical Plane

A balance of all three planes conveys a greater sense of spatial organization.

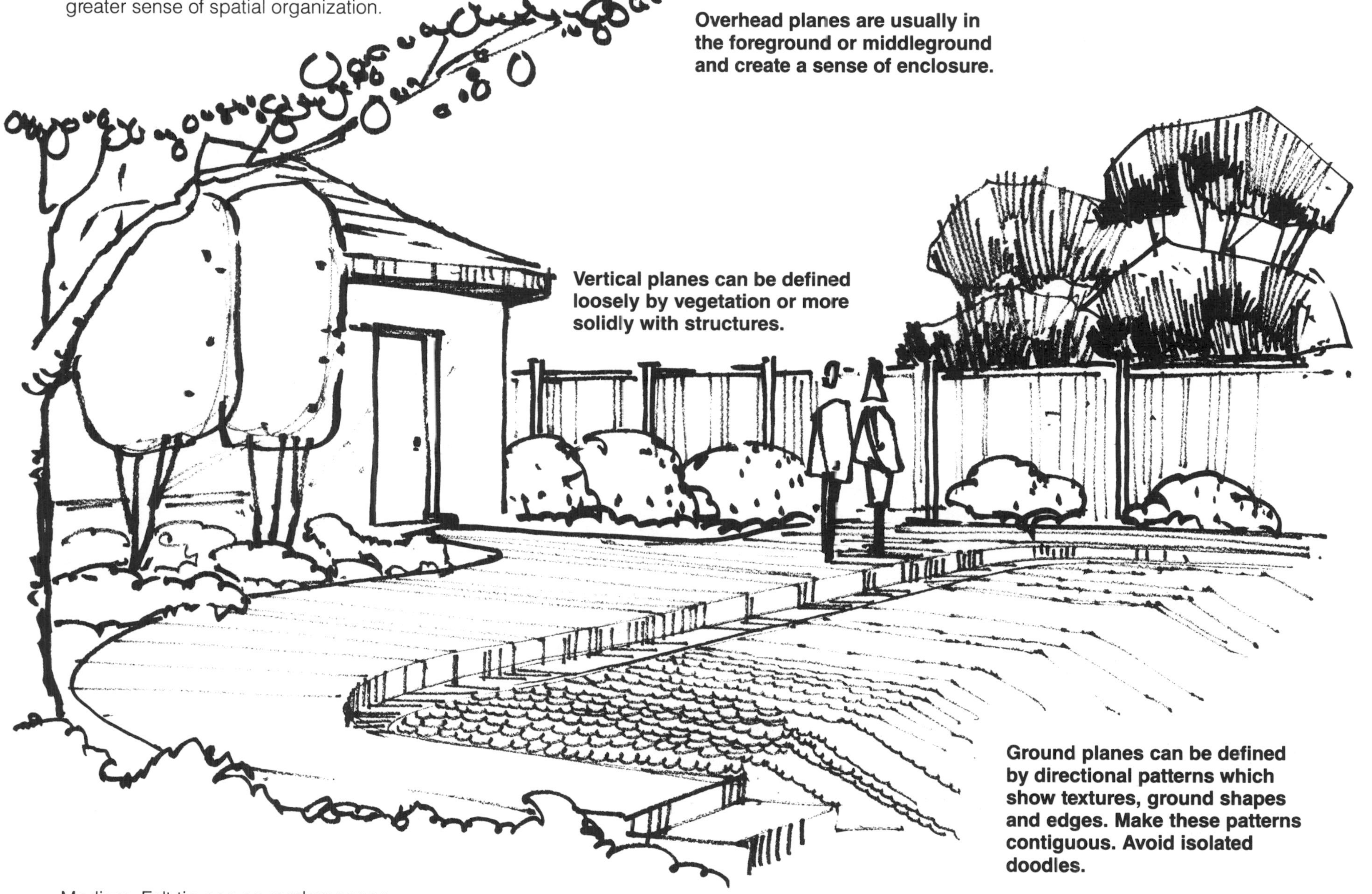

Medium: Felt tip pen on marker paper

Overlapping and Foreshortening

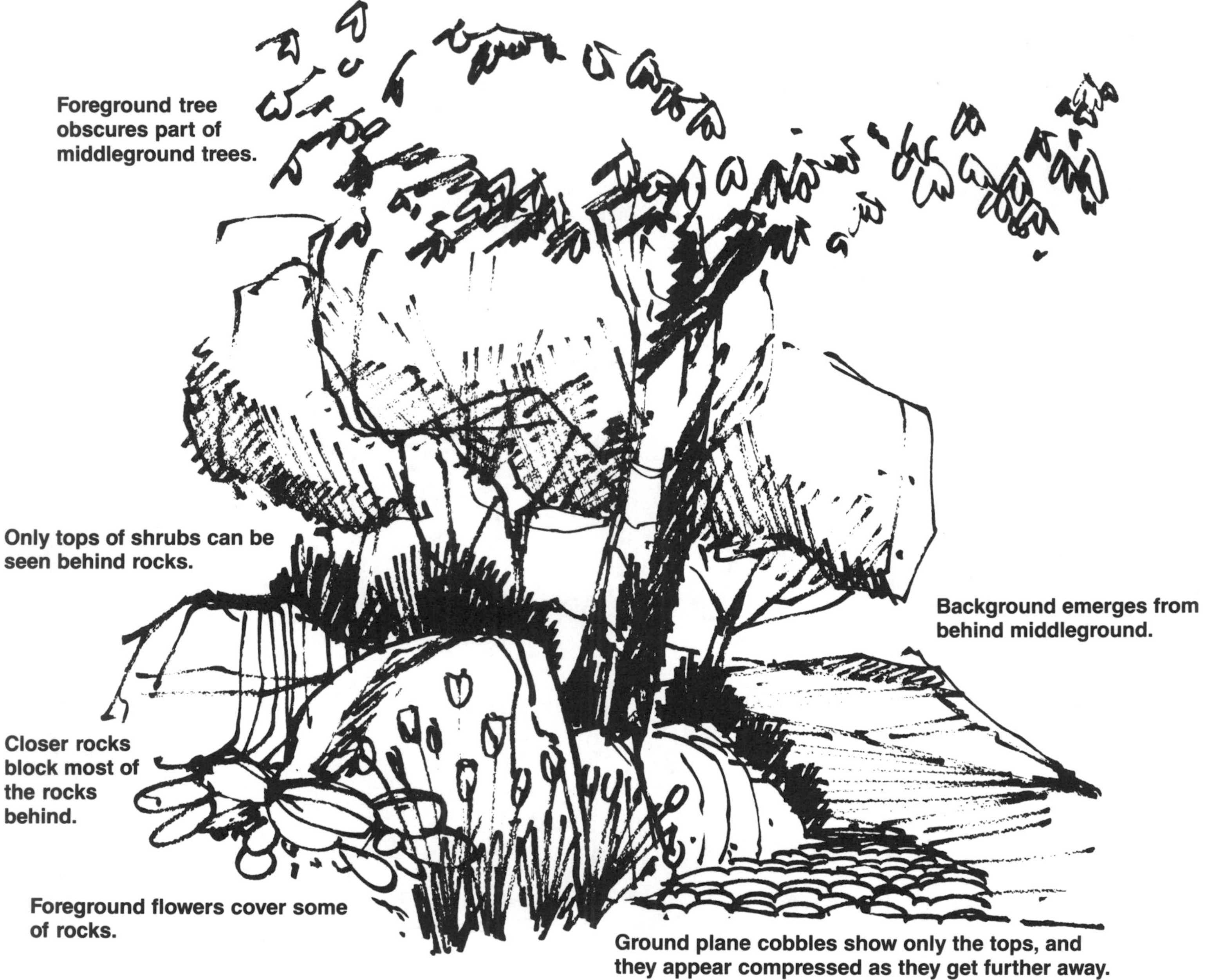

Medium: Felt tip pen on marker paper

Contrast and Tonal Balance

Strive for a balance between black areas, white areas, and grays or toned areas.

Medium: 2B pencil on smooth paper

Light Quality, Shade, and Shadow

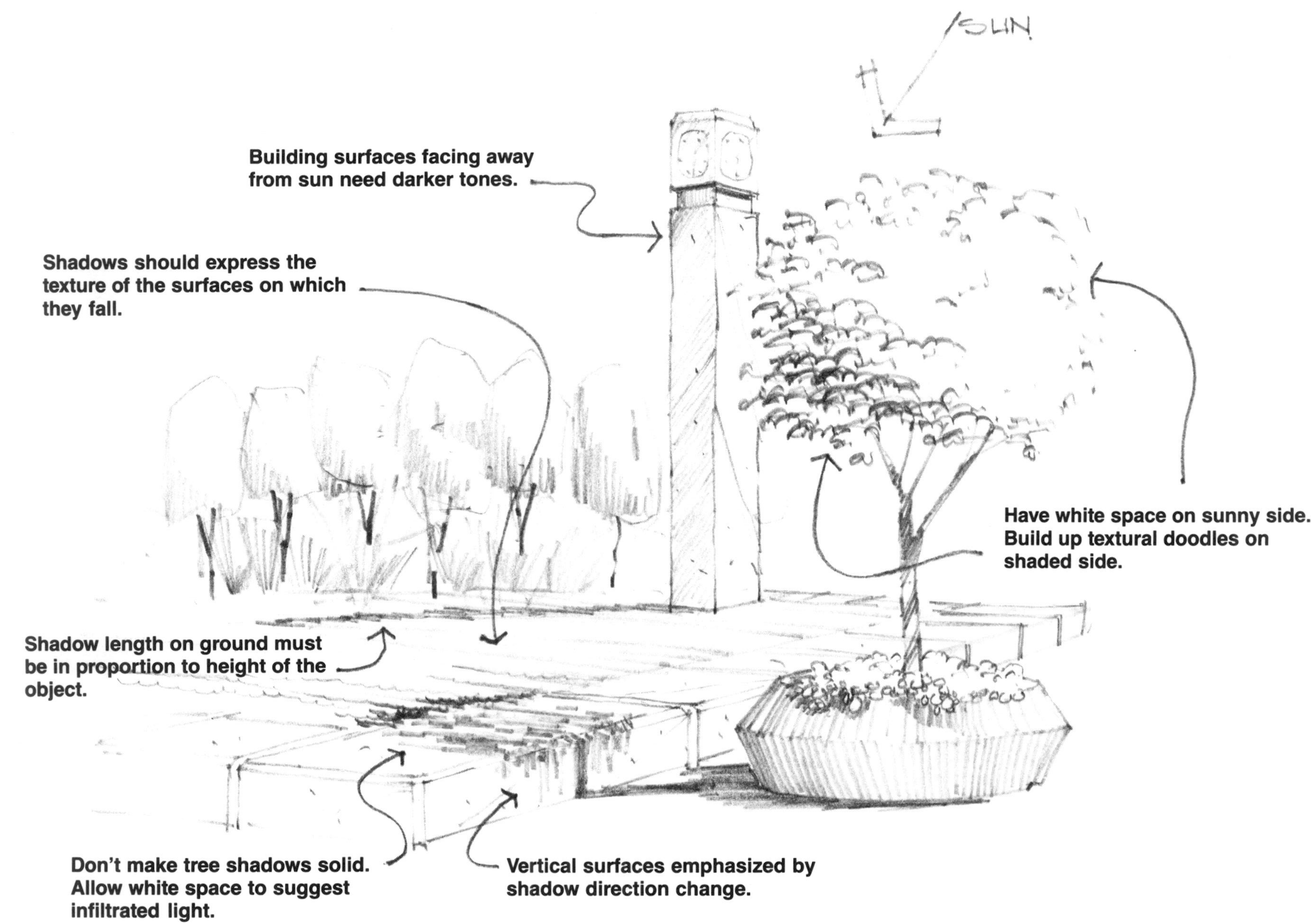

Perspective and Composition Examples

Overview

An overview can be a realistic viewpoint in mountainous areas. It allows the designer to show most of the plan elements.

The darker tones near the center of the sketch emphasize the zone of interest. These transist to white space near the edges.

Bird's-eye View
Although the bird's-eye view is less realistic than an eye-level view, it is possible to show more of the site.

The focal zone has more detail and higher contrast.

Eye-level View
A natural eye-level view of the same space shows good use of foreground, middleground, and background elements.

People emphasize the functional qualities.

Refined Pencil Sketch

Marker Sketch

The thick marker strokes abstract the foliage and emphasize light quality.

Darker background trees give form to the very light middleground vegetation.

Focal zone

Horizontal shadows follow the landform variations.

Note the cluster of ground plane lines, leaving some white areas.

Appendixes

Use of the Vertical Measuring Line on Perspective Charts

One-point Perspective

1. Draw base of object on ground plane.
2. Select an edge that vanishes to the VP and erect object vertical lines at each of the two corners.
3. Follow the base edge back to the horizontal ground line which intersects the zero.
4. Erect a vertical guideline at that intersection.
5. Select the desired height on the VML and draw a horizontal line across to intersect the vertical guideline.
6. Join this intersection with the vanishing point and extend (if necessary) to intersect the object verticals.
7. Draw a horizontal line from the front intersection to form the top of the object.
8. Erect the remaining verticals that are going to be visible.

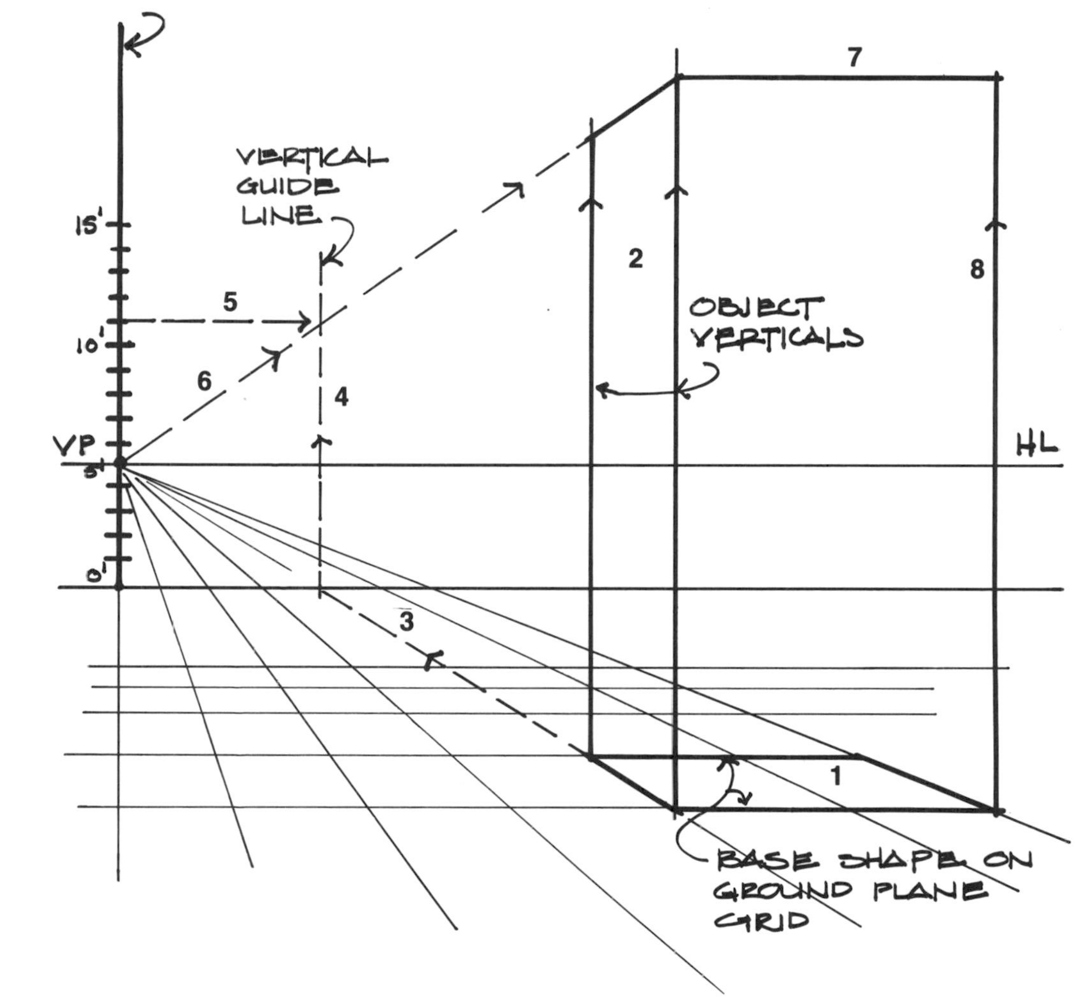

Two-point Perspective

1. Draw shape on ground plane.
2. Draw verticals from the two corners of one base edge.

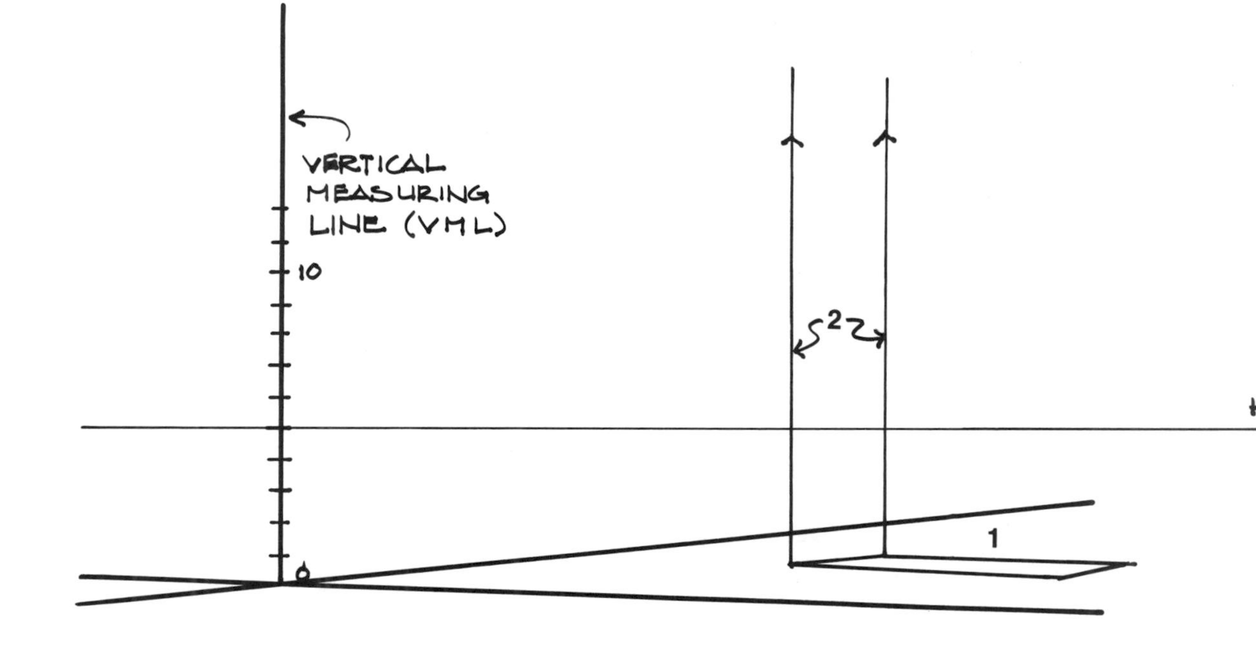

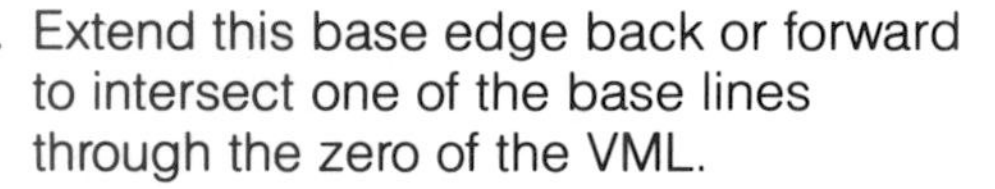

3. Extend this base edge back or forward to intersect one of the base lines through the zero of the VML.
4. Draw a key vertical from this intersection with the zero base line.

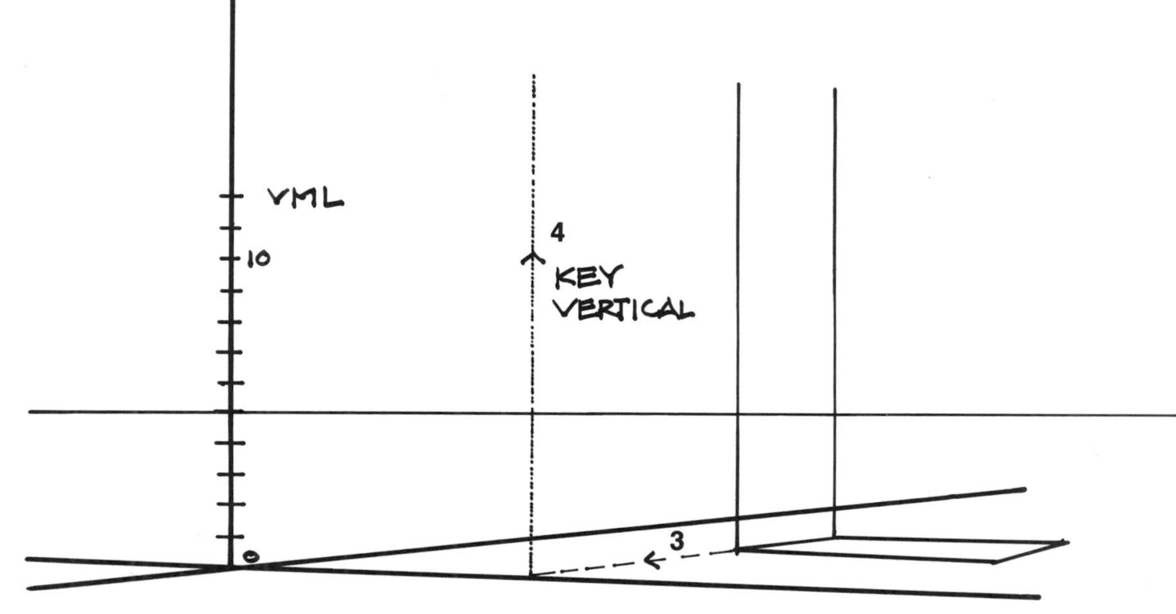

5. Determine which VP this zero base line goes to.
6. Connect this VP with the desired height, mark on VML, and extend (if necessary) to intersect the key vertical.
7. Connect this intersection with the opposite vanishing point and extend (if necessary) to intersect the verticals from the original base edge.

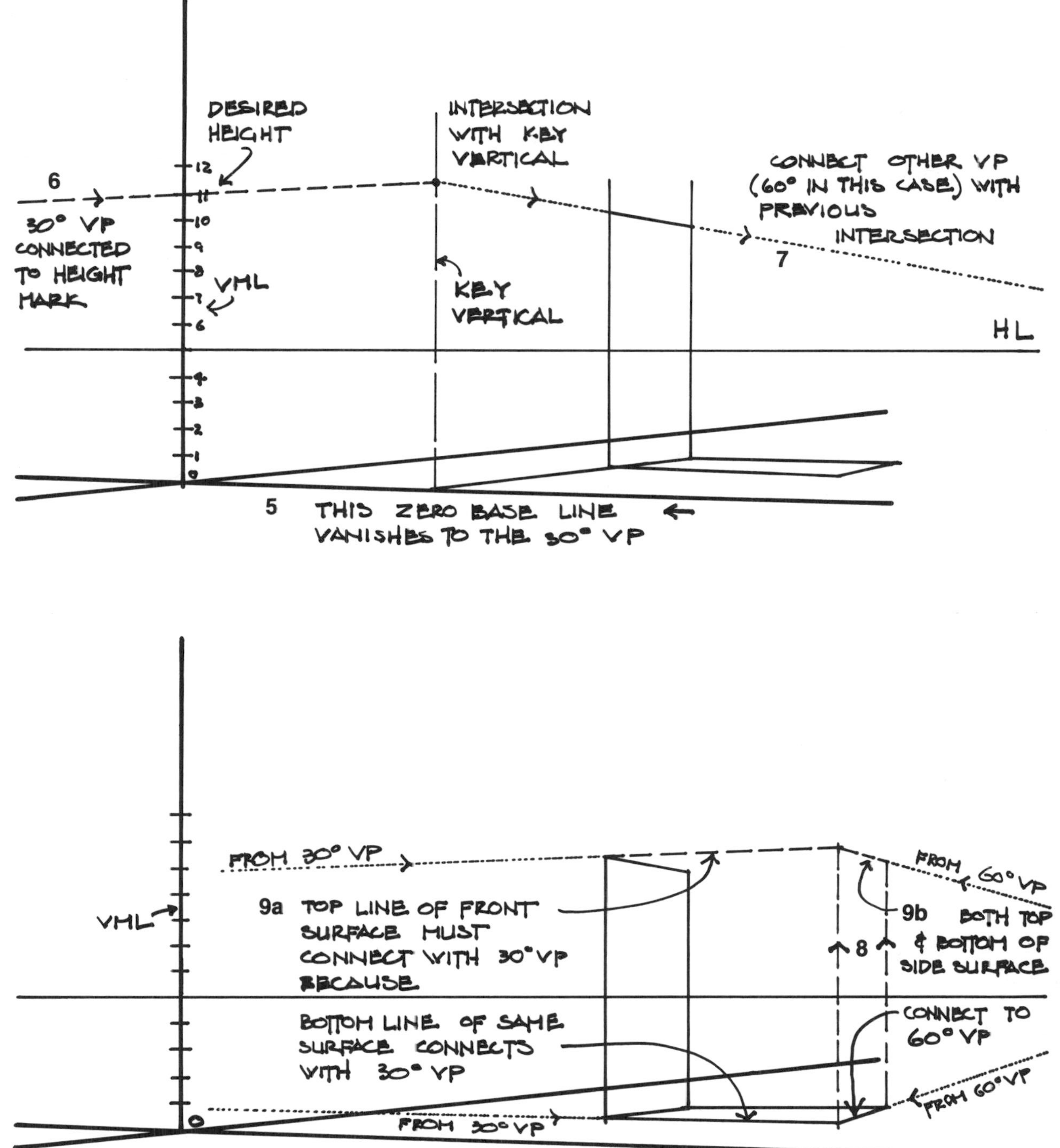

8. Construct the remaining verticals from the other corners.
9. Draw in the remaining top lines of the structure (a and b), making sure that the top and bottom lines of the same surface follow the same vanishing point.

Field of Vision Diagrams

The following diagrams are plan view representations of selected Lawson perspective charts. They show:

- The ground plane with a five-foot or ten-foot grid pattern.
- The station point (SP) with direction of view.
- The two heavy ground lines which intersect at the vertical measuring line (VML) on the perspective drafts.
- The field of vision contained within the edges of the chart (dashed line).

These diagrams are very helpful in setting up the perspective point of view from a completed plan. Follow these steps:

1. Select an appropriate chart. Base this on the angle of view (45°, 30°/60°, 60°/30°) and the desired eye line (five feet or twelve-and-a-half feet.)
2. Run a print of your plan and draft a grid onto it in red. Use a ten-foot grid for charts 6 and 7. Use a five-foot grid for charts 2 and 3. On large-scale plans, you may need to draw a one hundred-foot or fifty-foot grid (the eye lines will then be at fifty feet and one-hundred-twenty-five feet, respectively.)
3. Select the field of vision diagram (see following pages) which matches the chart selected. On a sheet of tracing paper or Mylar, redraw the diagram at the same scale as your plan.
4. Overlay this field of vision diagram onto your plan, keeping the grid lines on both sheets parallel and matching. Move it around until you have the important plan elements located and composed where you want them within the perspective field of vision.
5. Mark where the two heavy intersection ground lines occur on your plan and redraft them as heavy cross lines on the plan. Locate the station point.
6. Transfer the "footprints" of your plan elements onto an overlay of a perspective chart. Use the two heavy lines to guide location of these elements within the ground plane perspective grid.
7. Once you have the "footprints" located, use the vertical measuring line (Appendix I) or the proportional method (pages 159–161) to get heights of all elements.

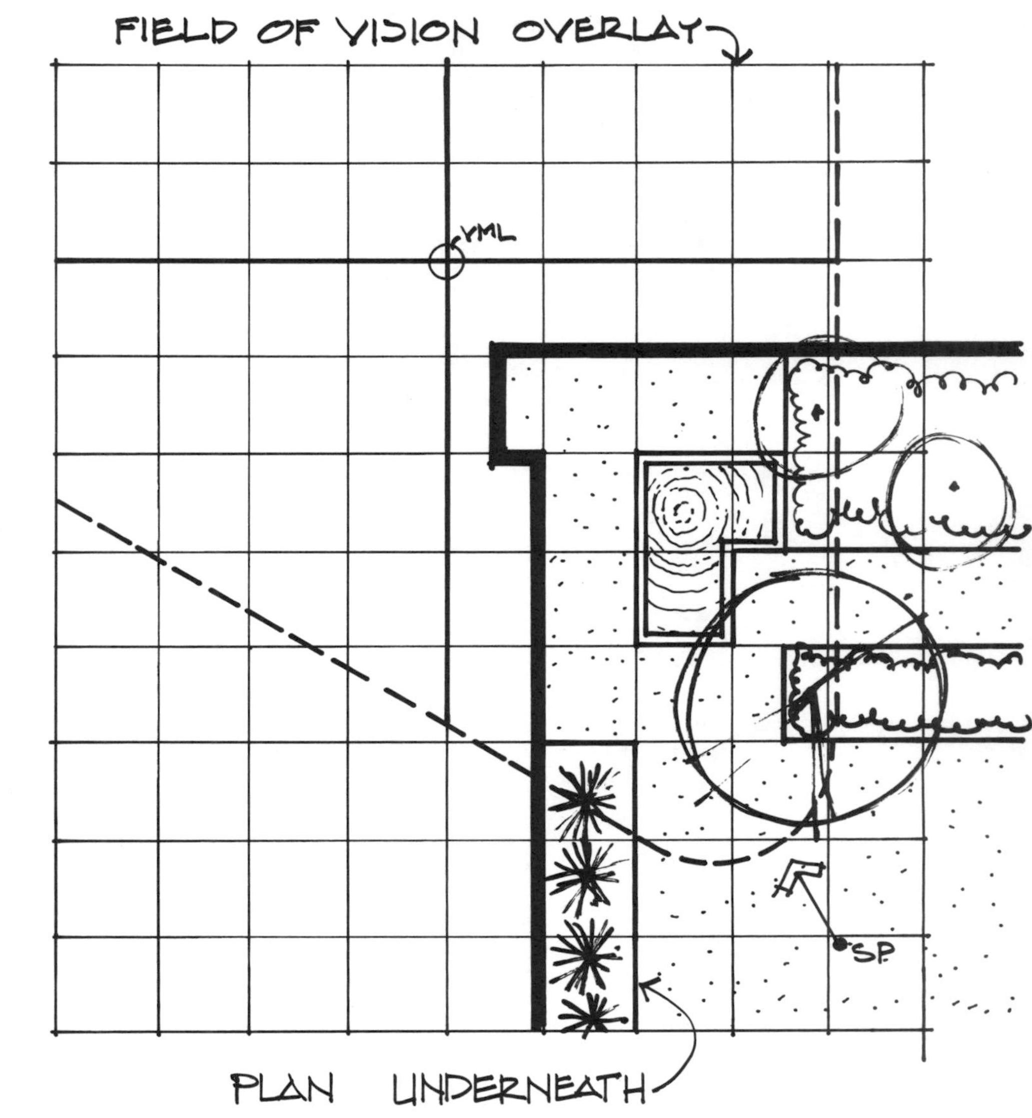

Field of Vision Diagram for Lawson Perspective Charts 3 and 7

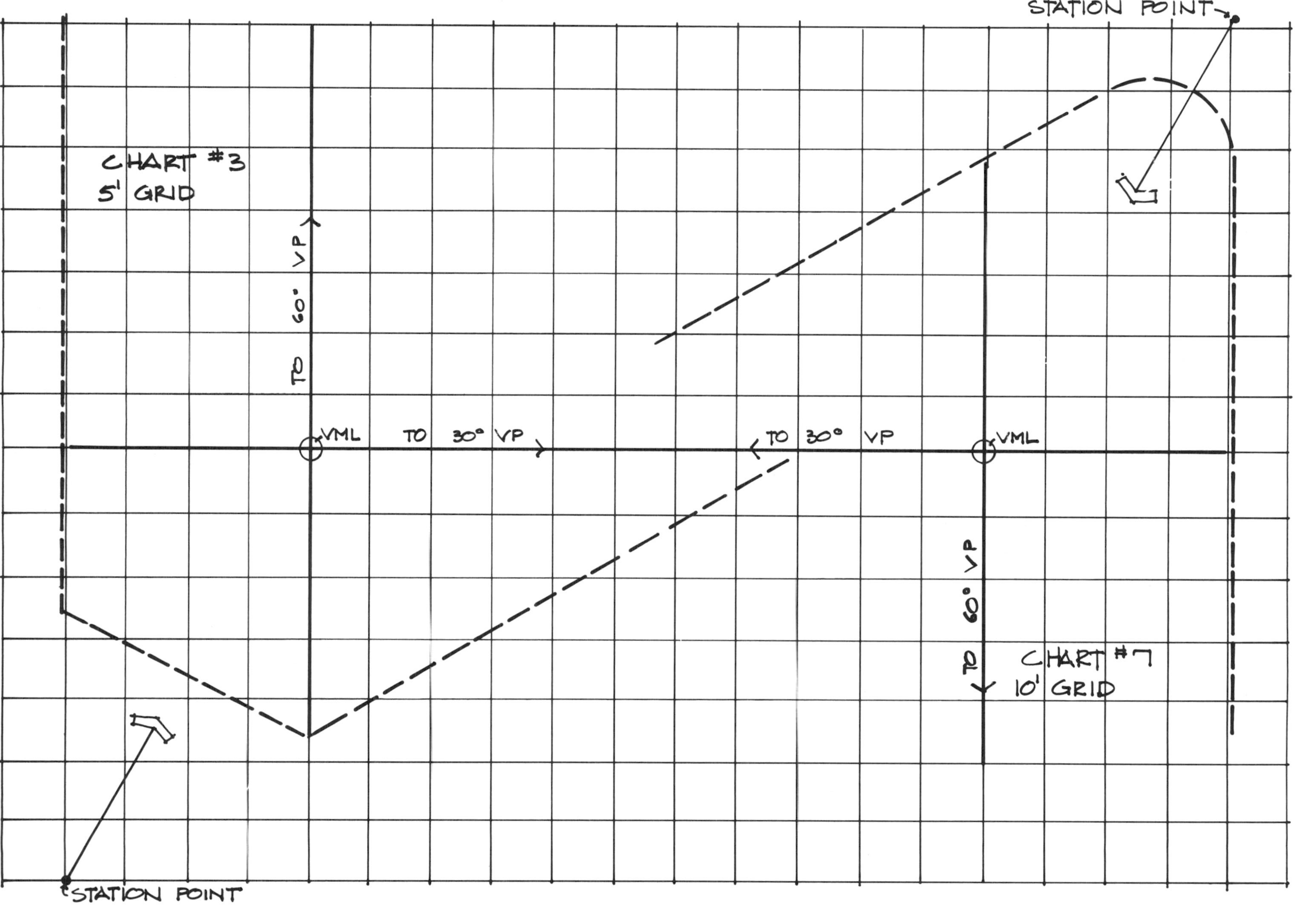

Field of Vision Diagram for Lawson Perspective Charts 2 and 6

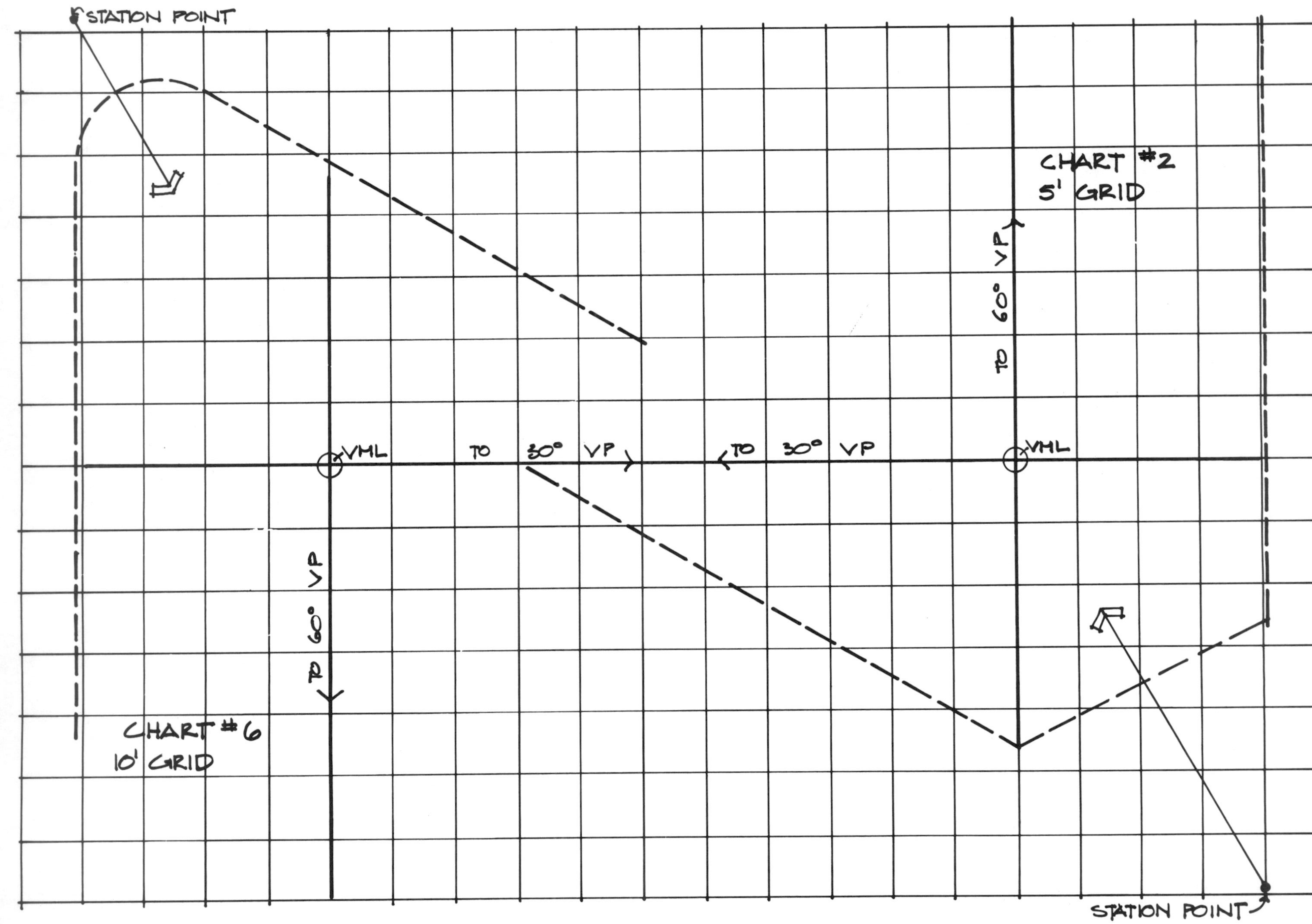

Nontraditional Perspective Techniques

Perspectives from Slides of a Site

This technique allows you to very quickly trace complex site details. The obvious disadvantage is that it is of no use when the buildings or major elements to be drawn are not already existing on the site.

One-point Photograph with Charts

1. Take several photographs, keeping the line of site perpendicular to the main architectural facade. The ground between you and the building should be level. Try to keep the camera about five feet off the ground. Before leaving the site, identify a horizontal element on the building which is about five feet off the ground.

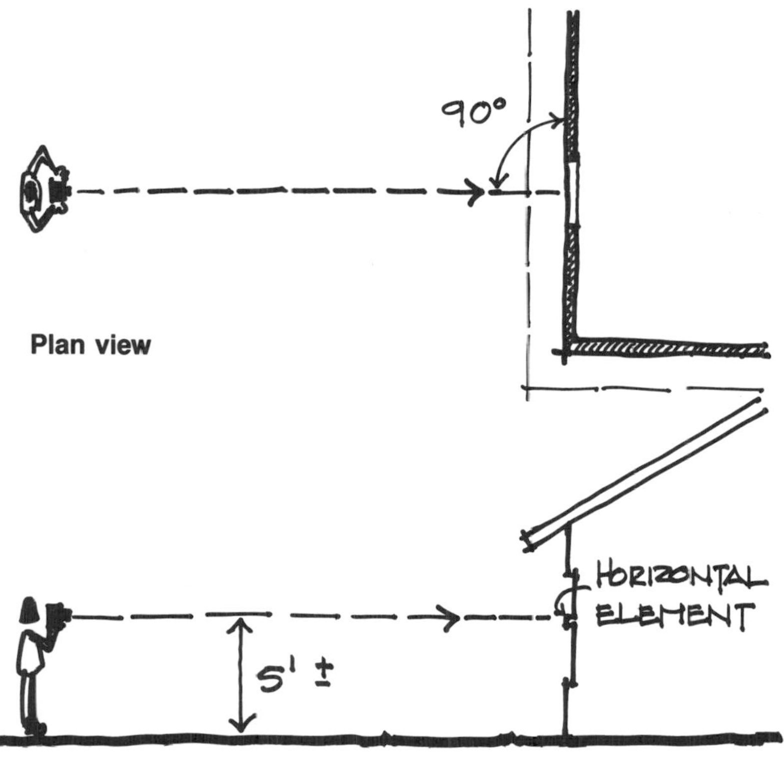

Plan view

Elevation

2. Project the slides onto a one-point perspective chart with a five-foot horizon line. Keeping the five-foot HL and the five-foot building element aligned, move the projector closer or further away to get the desired size. Now adjust the chart left or right to position the building where you want it.

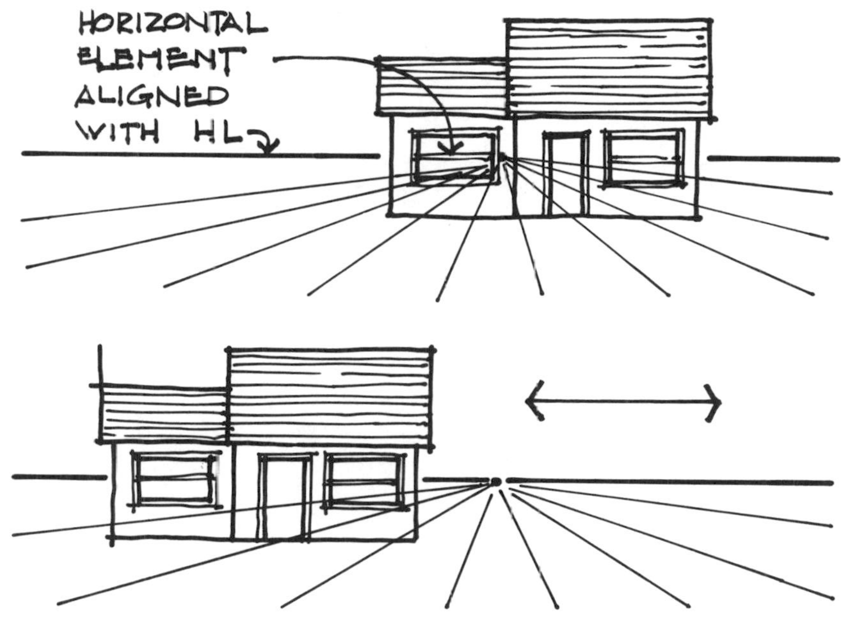

3. (Not shown) On a piece of tracing paper attached over the chart, trace the essential outlines of the building. Before removing it from the wall, add the HL and the vanishing point.
4. (Not shown) Place the chart and your traced overlay on your drawing table. Add landscape improvements using the chart as a guide.

Similar steps can be used to draw a quick one-point perspective from an architectural elevation. You may first have to redraw the elevation at a smaller or larger size to fit the chart in the desired location.

Two-point Photograph with Charts

1. Take several photographs with the line of site at about 45° and 30°/60° from major architectural facades. As with one-point photographs, keep the camera at the same level as the five-foot elements identified on the building. To give greater choice of view, move around the building and take pictures at various distances from it.

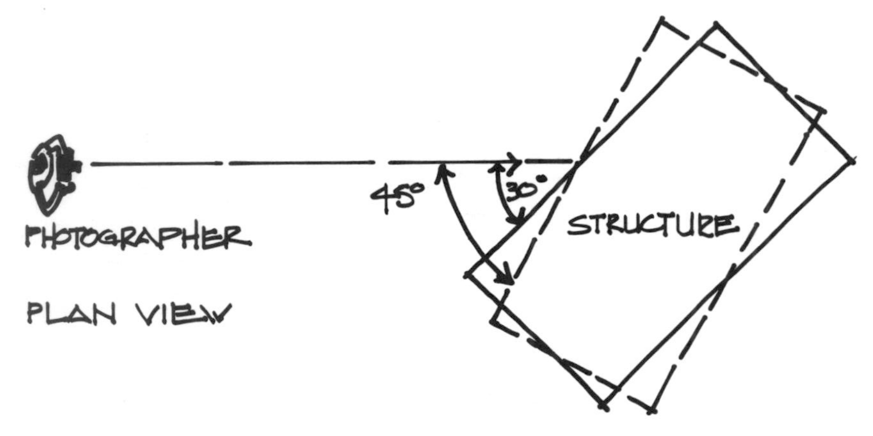

2. Project the two-point slide directly onto the appropriate two-point chart. Always keep the known five-foot building element lined up with the horizon line on the chart.

   Adjust the image in order to get vanishing lines of the projected image to match those of the chart. Use these hints.

   Enlarge the image size if:
   both sets of image vanishing lines vanish at steeper angles than the chart lines.

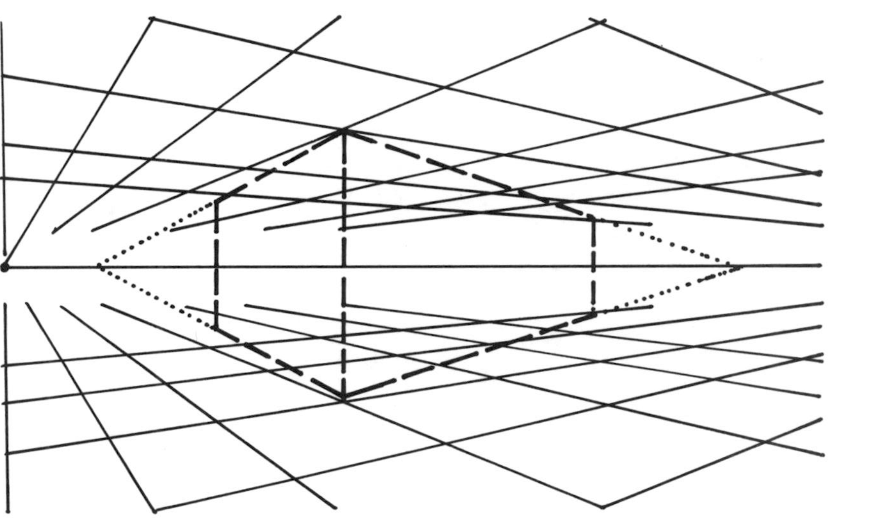

Reduce the image size if:
both sets of image vanishing lines vanish at flatter angles than the chart lines.

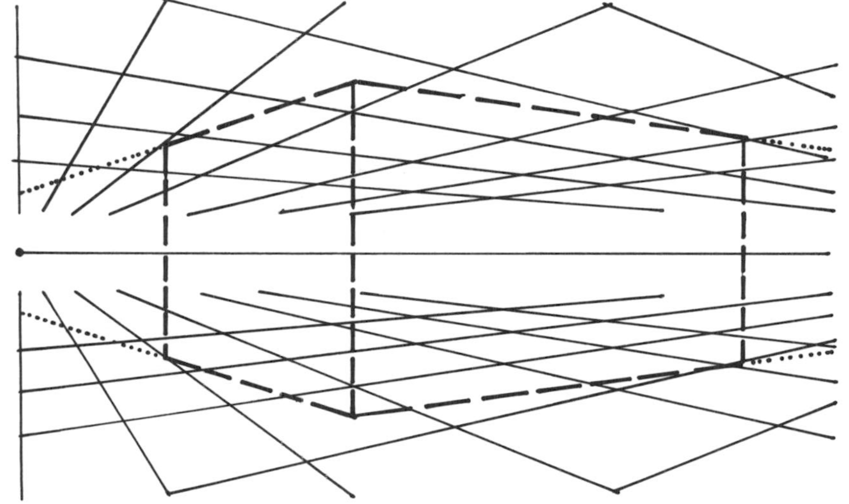

Move the image to the **left** if:
the lines of the image vanishing to the left vanish at a steeper angle than the chart lines and if those vanishing to the right do so at a flatter angle than the chart lines.

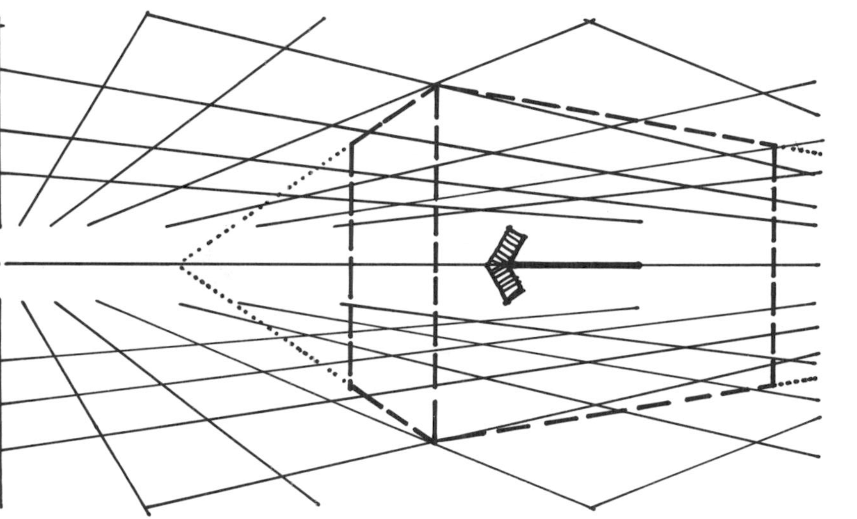

Move the image to the **right** if:
the lines of the image vanishing to the right vanish at a steeper angle than the chart lines and if those vanishing to the left do so at a flatter angle than the chart lines.

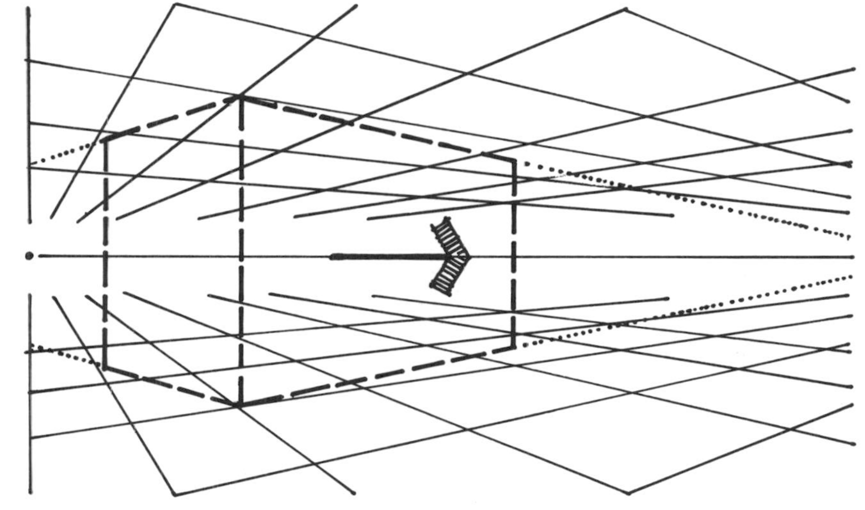

3. (Not shown) When the lines match, place tracing paper over the chart and trace the essential building outlines. Add the horizon line and a mark where the vertical measuring line crosses it.
4. (Not shown) Place the tracing paper and chart on your drawing table. Add landscape improvements, using the chart as a guide.

Perspectives from Slides of a Plan

1. Take several photographs at various angles to simulate a bird's-eye view of your plan. Frame the plan to fill the viewfinder.

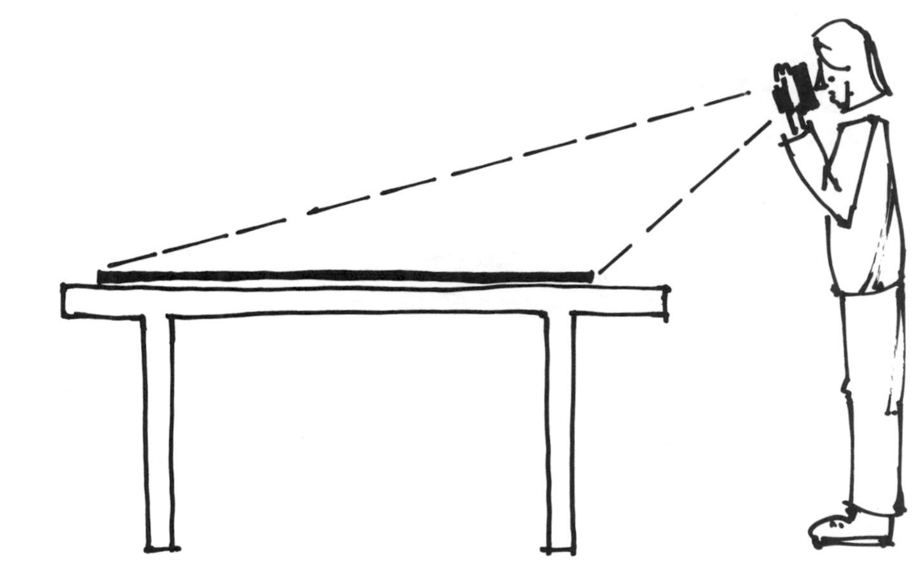

2. Project the slide onto a sheet of tracing paper and adjust the image size for tracing. This will be much easier if you can set up a reverse projection where the slide is in the projector backwards and is projected onto the back side of a clear glass surface.

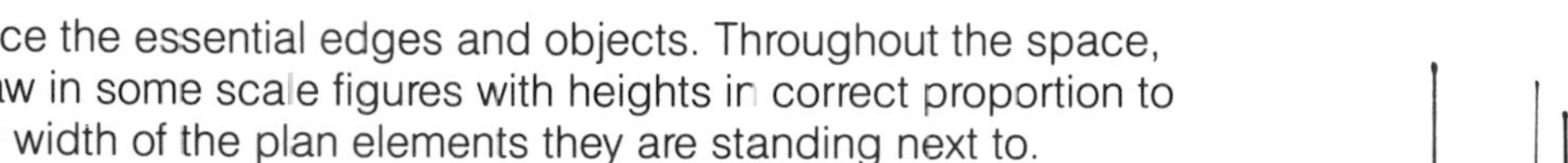

3. Trace the essential edges and objects. Throughout the space, draw in some scale figures with heights in correct proportion to the width of the plan elements they are standing next to.

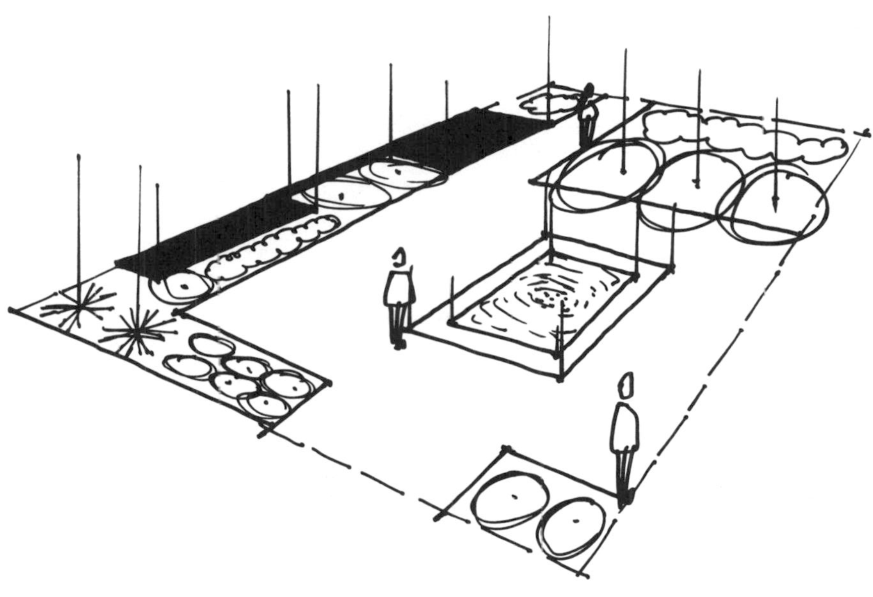

4. Project vertical lines from all important corners and use the proportional method to get correct heights of all objects in the space.

Computer-aided Perspective

Preliminary Plan

Starting with a preliminary design, you can follow the simplified steps on the next three pages to see the potential of the computer in perspective graphics.

Medium: Pencil on tracing paper
30% of actual size

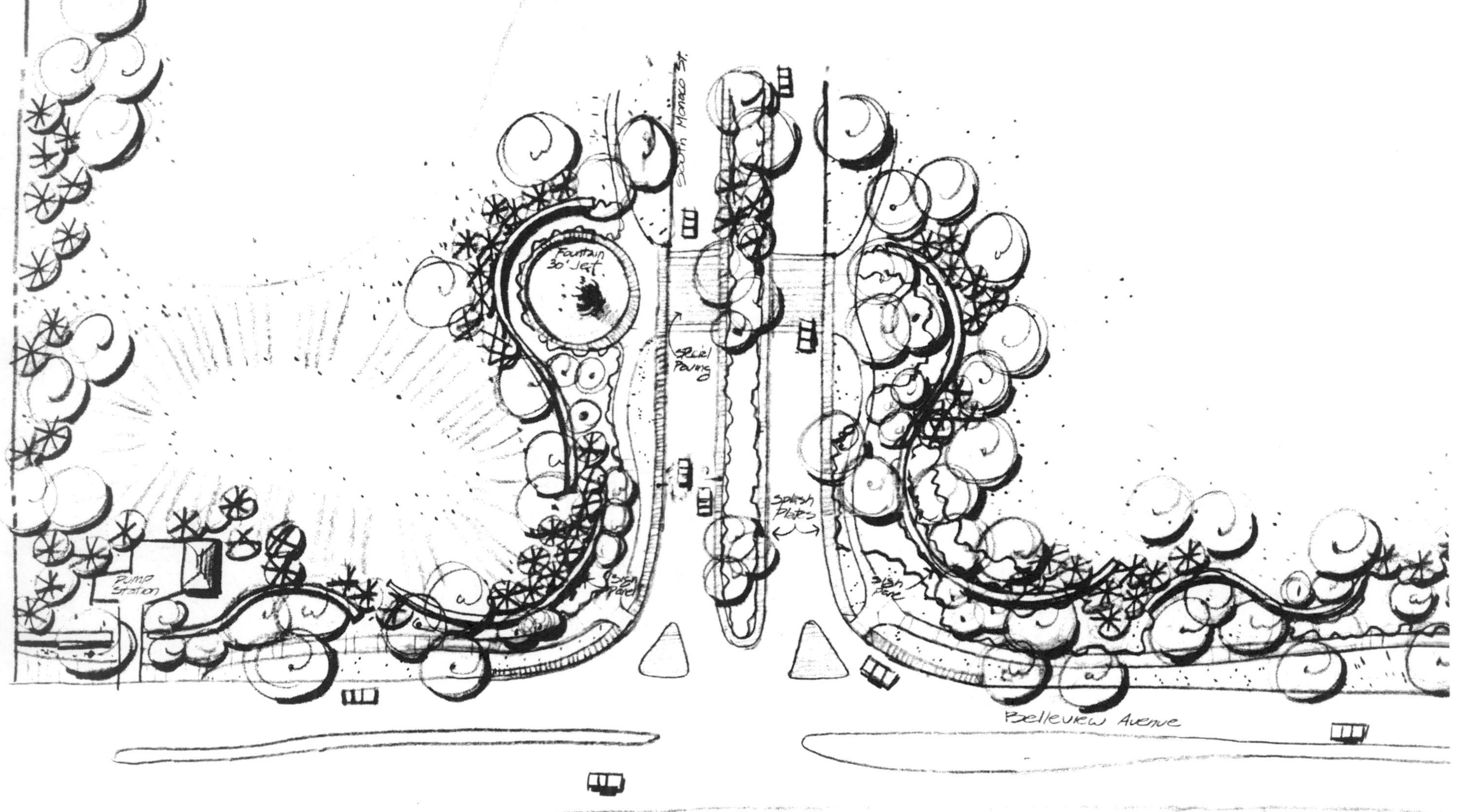

Gridded Overlay on Preliminary Plan

If the plan data is not already programmed into the computer, this is the first step. Start by laying a grid over the plan data, then select a viewpoint (V). The viewing height, topographic data, plus the heights of the fountain, walls, and other structures are now entered into the computer.

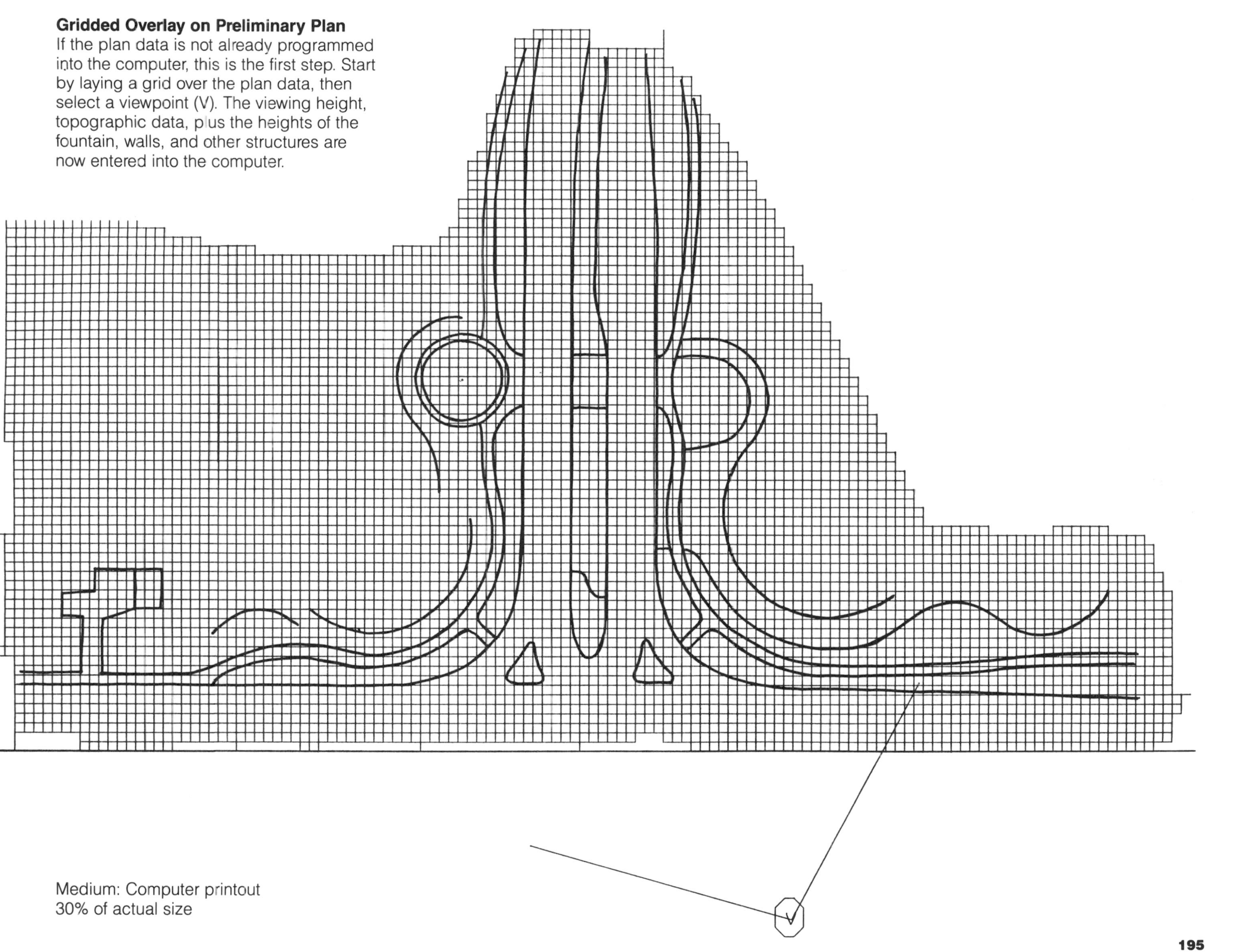

Medium: Computer printout
30% of actual size

Gridded Perspective View

Select the desired size of the perspective printout, which shows the vertical elements in true perspective. In this program, the printout of the perspective grid utilizes simple sticks to show the heights of structures.

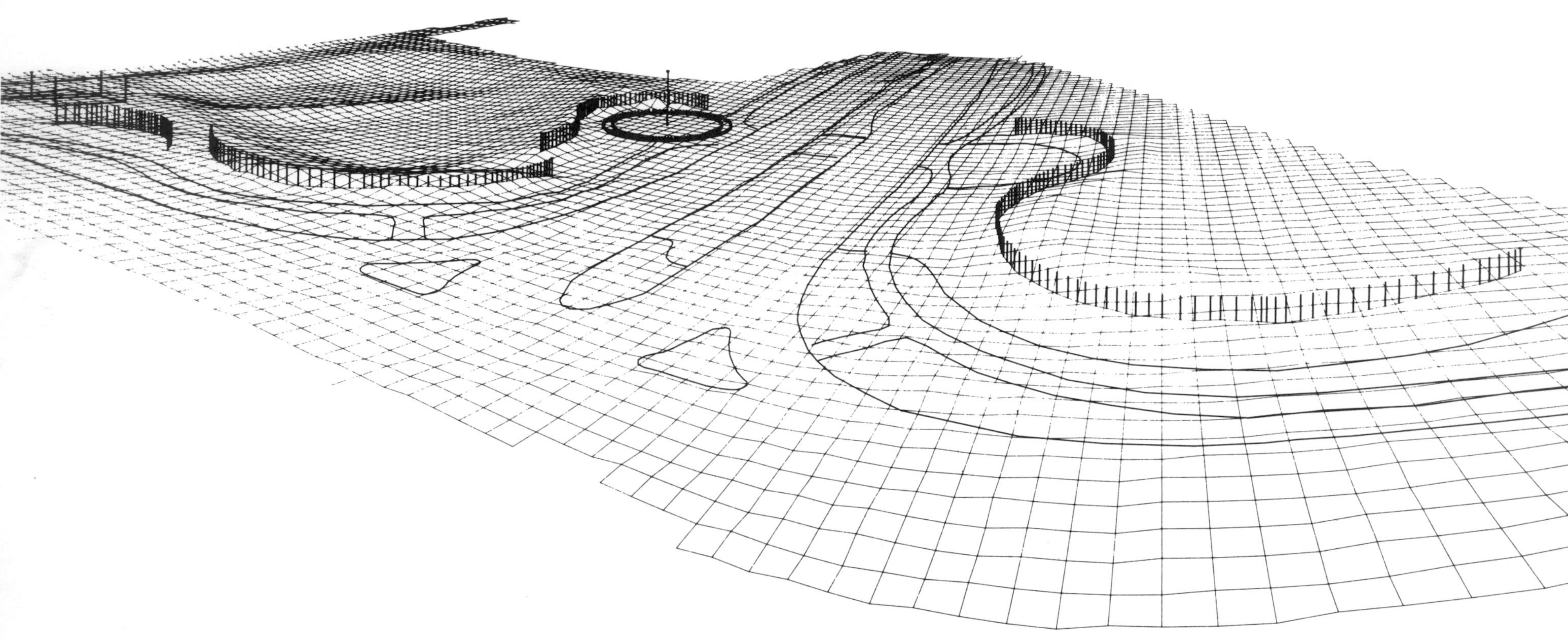

Medium: Computer printout
30% of actual size

Finished Perspective

The perspective printout may need to be enhanced by the graphic artist. The example shown here was sketched using a vellum overlay on the printout grid shown on the previous page.

More sophisticated programs are available in which realistic shapes are printed out directly from the computer. For some purposes, very little or no manual enhancement would be needed. These capabilities, once relatively expensive, are becoming less so and are being used in some landscape architectural offices.

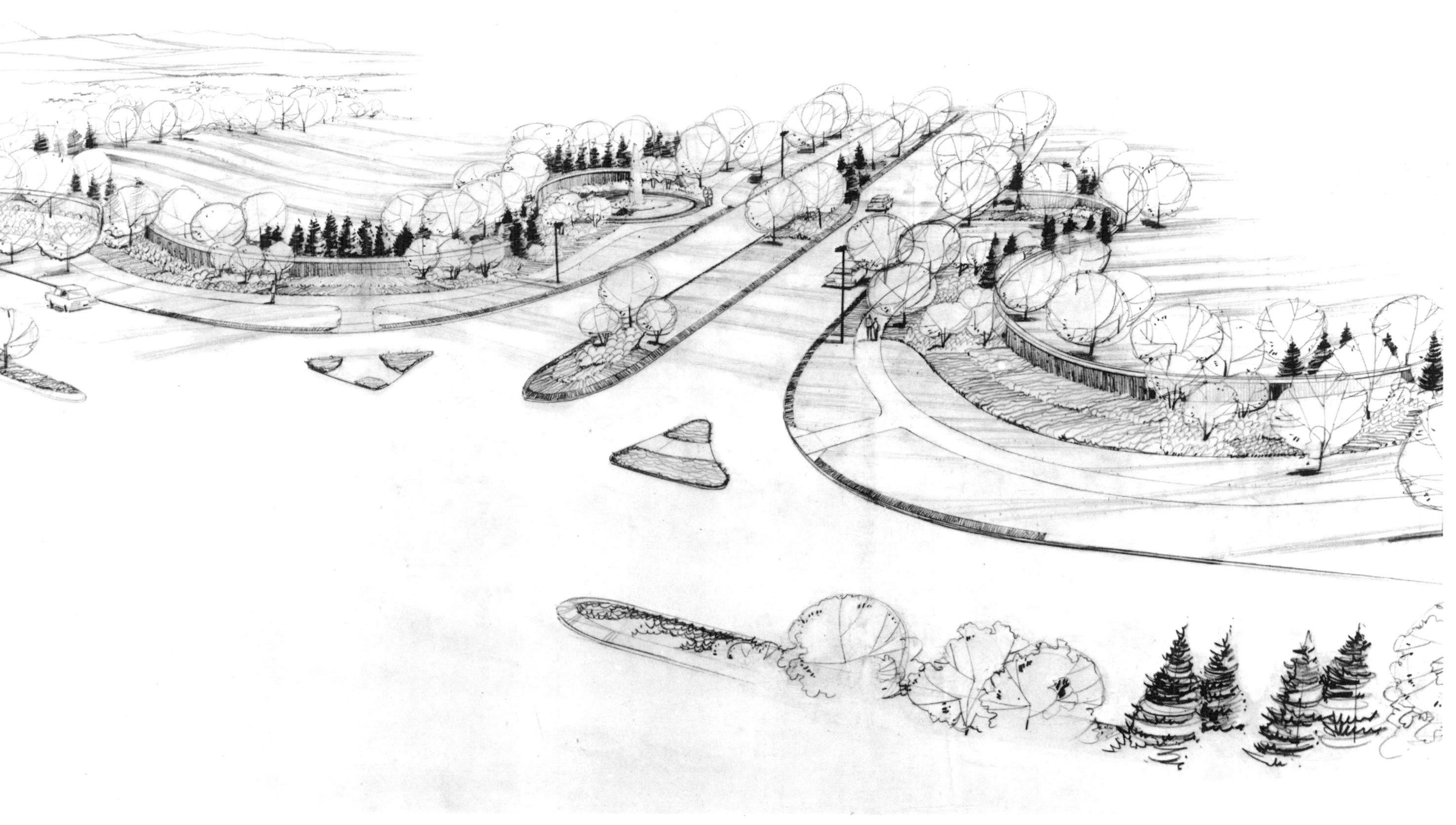

Medium: Pencil on vellum
30% of actual size

Exercises

Whether you are working in a structured classroom situation or just wanting to pick up some ideas on your own time, it is a good idea to have some sequenced organization to your efforts in learning about landscape graphics. For the most part, these exercises follow the text sequence. But you should feel free to alter that sequence to suit your individual needs and skill level. The exercises have been designed with the assumption that the reader may have no previous formal graphics training. Skip ahead to the more challenging exercises if you have had drawing experience.

Some landscape graphics are expressed through free, open-ended techniques such as sketching. Others, such as drafting, are quite the opposite—demanding precision and exacting control. Most landscape graphics require a combination of these "loose" and "tight" approaches. So that you don't get stuck in one or the other of these grooves, it is recommended that you practice different types of exercises simultaneously. For example, it could be a good idea to keep up regular additions to a sketchbook, picking from exercises 1–14 while at the same time following a sequence of drafting, lettering, plan symbol, and perspective exercises.

Chapter 9, on perspective, refers to exercises 39 through 49, suggesting when to try specific exercises. It is important to follow the recommended sequence by matching the text with the exercises. They progress from simple to more complex, with each exercise depending on skills learned in the previous one.

Be creative and invent your own exercises. Those shown here barely scratch the surface, but they will get you started and can reveal new possibilities.

Freehand Drawing

Exercises 1 through 14

A free hand that is willing to sketch makes for a freer mind that is able to evaluate design ideas. It matters less what or even how you draw than whether you draw with frequency and confidence. Keep a sketch tool and small pad handy and make drawing a habit. There are many opportunities every day to indulge in creative doodling. Use the times when you happen to be sedentary but not in a situation demanding your undivided attention: on hold on the telephone, waiting for an appointment, commuting as a passenger, during television commercials. Some people become so at ease with doodling that they can continue sketching automatically while attending to some other important matters.

Use the following exercises as a way to get started in this exciting habit. You will quickly progress beyond them, developing your own style and favorite subject material. Refer to Chapter 2 for descriptions of the appropriate materials and techniques.

1. Freeform shapes
On an 18 × 24-inch sheet of tracing paper, draw a series of freehand circles and blobs of different sizes and shapes. Make some single-line and some multiple-line. Felt tip pen.

2. Long straight lines
Place a series of dots on either side of an 18 × 24-inch sheet of tracing paper. Connect them horizontally and diagonally, keeping the lines as straight as possible. Felt tip pen.

3. Short straight lines
Using several different kinds of smooth sketching tools (soft pencils, felt tip pens, sketch pens), create an interesting freehand composition of straight lines. All lines should be drawn with speed and have strong endings. Do not move finger joints. 9 × 12-inch sketch or marker paper.

4. Boxes and angular objects
Trace or invent a composition of straight-sided shapes which could represent buildings, plazas, walls, and other architectural elements. Make positive connections at all corners and draw with confidence. Allow some shapes to penetrate others. Pencil or felt tip pen on tracing paper.

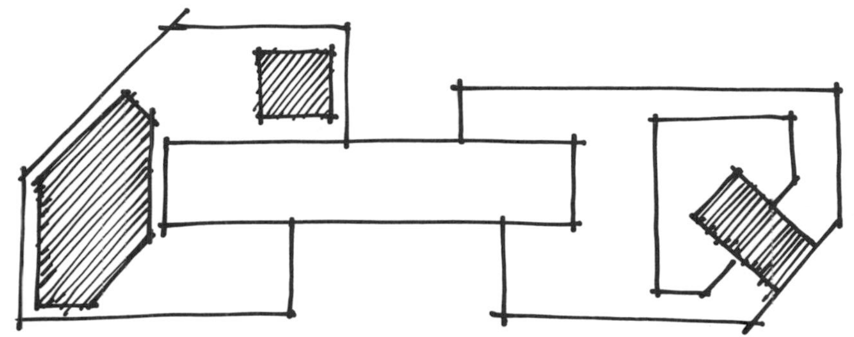

5. Simple line drawings
Use a series of free-flowing yet confidently drawn lines to show essential edges and shapes. Loose line sketches can be effective design development drawings. Choose one organic object (fruit, flower, leaf) and one simple mechanical object and create a line drawing. Do not use shading or toning. Felt tip pen on 9 × 12-inch marker paper.

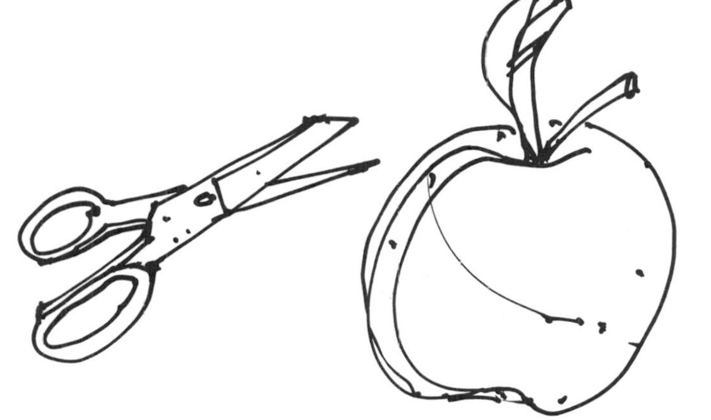

6. Continuous line drawings of man-made objects
A free-flowing appearance is obtained by shaping an object with a continuous line using body joints in harmony. Keep the pen or pencil in constant contact with the paper. Lift and shift position only to avoid excessive doubling up of lines.

Find several simple manufactured objects and fill the page with continuous line sketches. Suggested objects: pencil pointer, set of keys, scissors, shoe, and hat. Use lines to represent edges, indentations, protrusions, and contours. Felt tip pen or soft pencil on 9 × 12-inch sketch or marker paper.

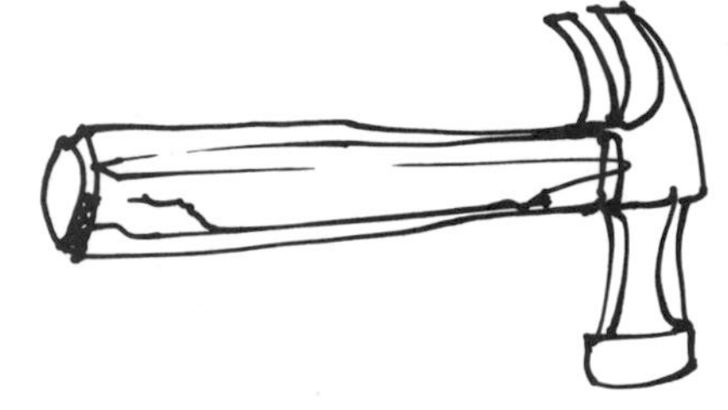

7. Tone and light quality
a. Draw the outline of two long rectangles 1 inch wide and 6 inches long. In one box, use a soft graphite pencil or stick to create an even gradation of tone from shiny black on the left to white on the right. In the other box, use a felt tip pen or a sharp pencil to create a tone of crosshatch lines which are very close and dense on the left and open white on the right.

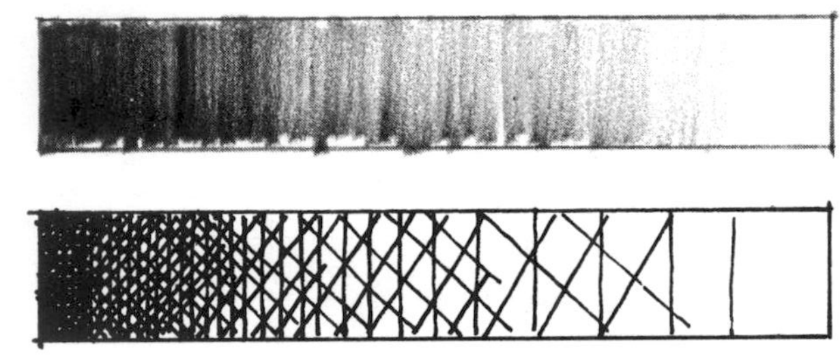

b. On the same sheet draw at a larger size (about 2 inches) the four geometric objects shown below. Note the light direction with an arrow and try to capture the shape by using the smooth tone change on two objects and crosshatch toning on the others. Pencil or felt tip pen on 9 × 12-inch sketch or marker paper.

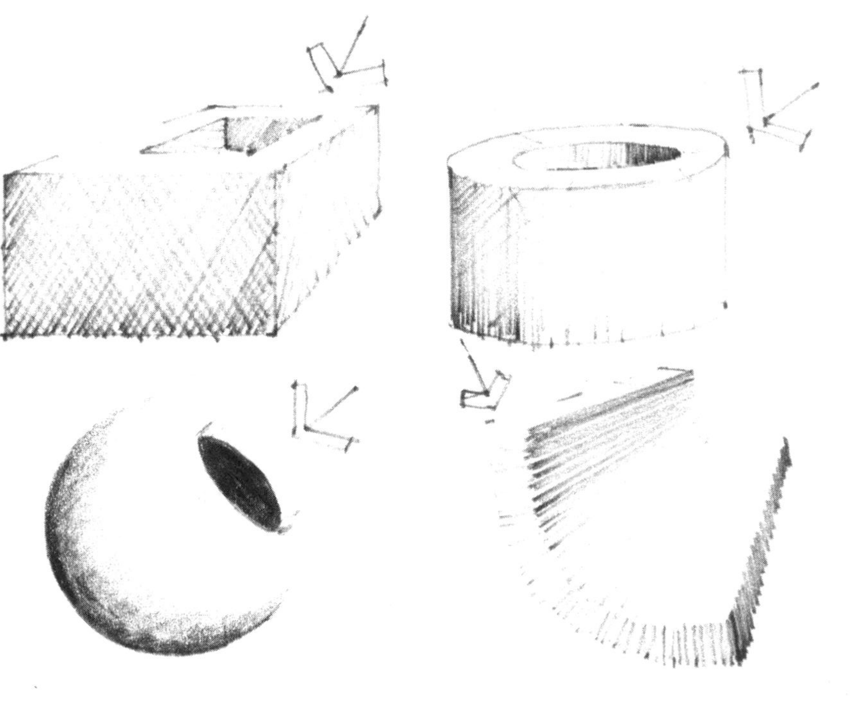

8. Pure tone drawings with no outline
a. Choose a simple solid object or a glass object and make a tone-only drawing with no outlines. Use change of tone to suggest edges, shape, and light quality. 6B pencil or graphite stick on 9 × 12-inch sketch paper. Try another object with a flat-tip sketch pencil.

b. Find a black-and-white photograph. Turn it upside down and copy the tone variations using a build-up of crosshatching. Do not outline the shapes or edges. Felt tip pen or fountain pen on 9 × 12-inch sketch paper.

9. Line expression
Using a 6B pencil, felt tip pen, or sketch fountain pen, draw a series of lines across the page—deliberately trying to vary the width and the darkness of the line.

6B lead holder

Fountain pen

Felt tip pen

This is accomplished by varying the pressure and/or rotating the pencil as you draw to move it from a wide edge to a narrow edge.

a. Now draw a representation of ground plane landform in perspective view composed of a series of continuous lines. Exploit your sketching tool to get the full range of line weight and to provide interesting zones of emphasis.

b. Draw a series of rock groupings or outcrops in perspective view (see Chapter 8). 9 × 12-inch sketch or marker paper.

10. Textural perspective
Copy six of the line doodles shown in Chapter 6 page 92 or Chapter 8 page 149. Draw a single short doodle then next to it show a build-up of the doodle to make a texture. Expand the textural zone, but allow white non-textured areas to remain intermixed with the tone of texture. Let the textures evolve into a specific material on the ground plane (grass, cobbles, flagstone) or a vertical object (tree trunk). Try to capture the principle of textural perspective. Felt tip pen or fountain pen on 9 × 12-inch marker paper.

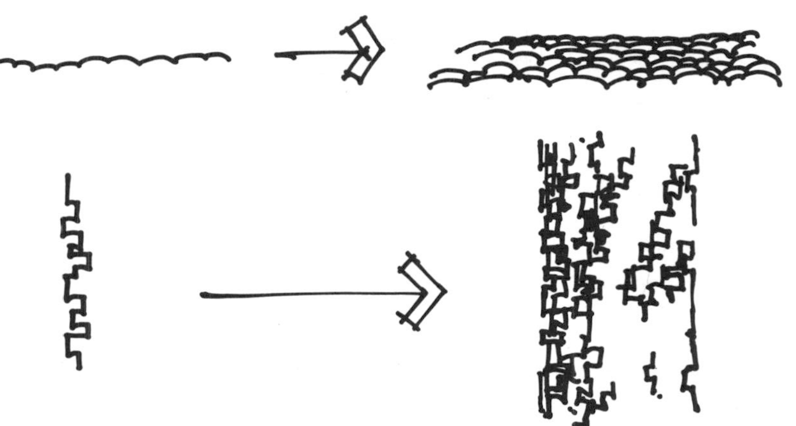

11. Fast trees
Practice drawing mid-ground trees copied from Chapter 8.
a. Five-second trees. Fill a 9 × 12-inch sheet with trees and shrubs showing form only. Be very loose and quick. Relate them all to the ground in some way. Felt tip pen.

b. Thirty-second trees. Fill a 9 × 12-inch sheet with trees that have a hint of texture or light quality in addition to portraying form. Make some with easy doodles and others with quick-stroke technique. Spend no more than thirty seconds per tree. Felt tip pen.

c. One-minute trees with shading. Fill two sheets of 8½ × 11-inch Mylar with deciduous and evergreen trees. Use three different tools: a 6B pencil, a graphite stick, and a flat-tip sketch pencil. Copy from Chapter 8. Establish an imaginary sun direction first; then quickly apply graphite strokes to capture shaded areas and overall form. Each tree should take less than one minute. Keep them about 3 inches tall with a ground connection.

d. Two- to three-minute trees with texture. Using felt tip pen or fountain pen in 9 × 12-inch paper, draw a number of trees and shrubs which have more textural or shading detail than do the thirty-second trees. Do some with only branching texture. Spend no more than two to three minutes on each tree. Capture light quality. Strive for a loose edge with white space penetrating, a contrast of clustered lines and open white spaces, and a directional meaning or consistency to the lines.

12. Perspective arrows
Invent a series of arrows which have different shapes, direction change, and a three-dimensional quality. Assume a light direction. Be creative. 9 × 12-inch material, any medium.

13. Fast people
Draw two rows of fast people copied from Chapter 8. Keep all eyes on the eye lines. Vary size and character. 9 × 12-inch surface, any medium.

14. Automobiles
Using the techniques in Chapter 8, draw a car or truck in perspective view. 9 × 12-inch surface, any medium.

15. For marker lettering, set up light pencil guidelines for four rows of 1½-inch high lettering and two rows of ¾-inch-high lettering. Leave a ½-inch gap between rows. Choose a light-colored marker and fill the rows with words. Outline with double outline method shown in Chapter 2. All must be freehand. 9 × 12-inch marker paper.

16. Do a second sheet with the same set-up but with different words and styles copied from Chapter 2 page 44. Set up the marker words, but do not outline. Overlay with a 9 × 12-inch sheet of marker paper and outline with felt tip pens. You may use a straightedge for the verticals. Other lines must be freehand.

Concept Drawings

Exercise 17
17. On 12 × 18-inch or larger marker paper, use felt tip pens and colored markers to prepare a hypothetical concept diagram. Use many different functional symbols and organize them in a cohesive composition. See Chapter 3 for symbol ideas.

Choose one of these activity areas and transform the ideas listed into abstract graphic symbols.

Park
Public road
Main entry
Automobile circulation
Parking areas (several)
Information center
Play equipment area
Picnic areas
Beach/swimming zone
Concession building
Change rooms
Open play area
Nature center
Pedestrian trail system
Forested areas

Urban mall
Shops
Seating areas
Barriers
Information kiosk
Bus drop-off zone
Parking areas
Fountain area
Performance/entertainment area
Pedestrian access from parking
Automobile access
Conflict areas
Clock tower

Pencil Drafting

Exercises 18 through 21
All pencil drafting exercises are to be done on 8½ × 11-inch vellum. See Chapter 4 for materials and methods.

18. Draft a set of five horizontal lines for each of the leads HB, H, and 2H. Make the lines 5 inches long, ¼ inch apart with 1 inch between each set. Make all these lines very dark and even. Draft a fourth set of five lines, very lightly, with a sharp 4H. On the remainder of the sheet, use the compass to scribe four circles of different sizes, using H lead. Set up the sheet as shown.

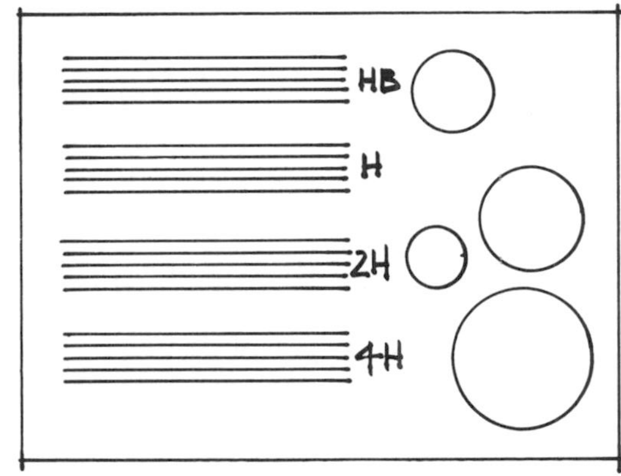

For exercises 19, 20, and 21, draft most of the lines first with a very light 4H lead; then go over them firmly with an H lead.

19. On the left side draw a 3-inch square. Divide the top and the left side into six ½-inch divisions. Draw three lines parallel to the base at the ½-inch divisions on the left side. Then draw 45° diagonal lines through the remaining ½-inch marks.

On the right side draw a 3-inch square. Draw two 45° diagonals. Divide each side in half and connect these points with 45° diagonal lines. Draw a second square by connecting the intersecting points of the two sets of diagonals. Again, divide the sides of the second square into equal parts and connect the division points by 45° diagonal lines. Draw a third square by connecting the intersecting points of the last set of diagonal lines and the first diagonal lines drawn. Set up the sheet as shown.

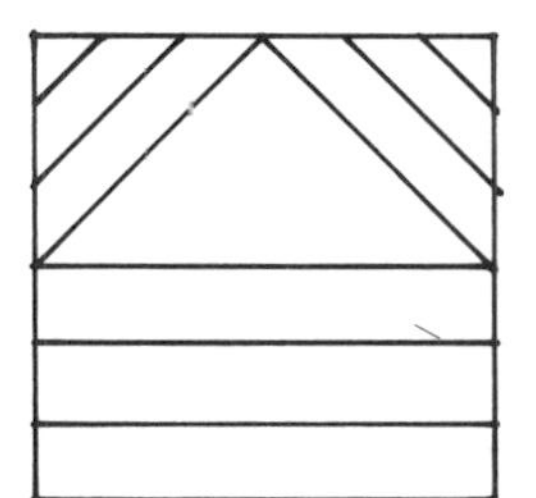

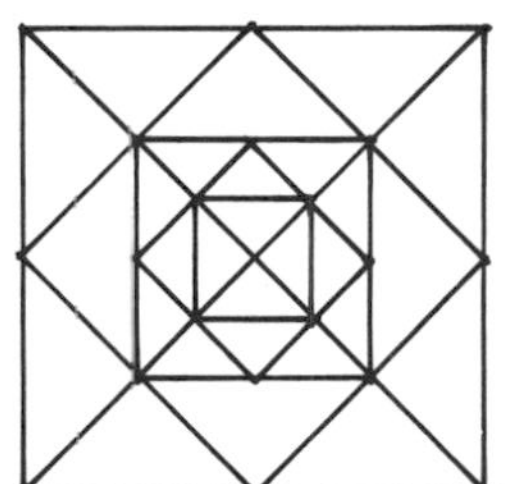

20. First, construct a hexagon. On the left side of a sheet, draft cross lines A B and C D, using very light 4H pencil lines. With this intersection as the center, scribe a very light circle guideline with a 1½-inch radius. Again with light 4H lines, draft the six lines touching the outside of the circle using the 30°/60° triangle. Draft the finished hexagon with a dark, sharp H lead.

On the right side of the sheet, draw a 3-inch square with vertical and horizontal center lines. Draw 45° diagonals to these center lines ½ inch apart, as shown. Then draw two concentric semicircles on each side of the vertical center line with 1½-inch and 1-inch radii. Intertwine the diagonals and semicircles. Set up the sheet as shown.

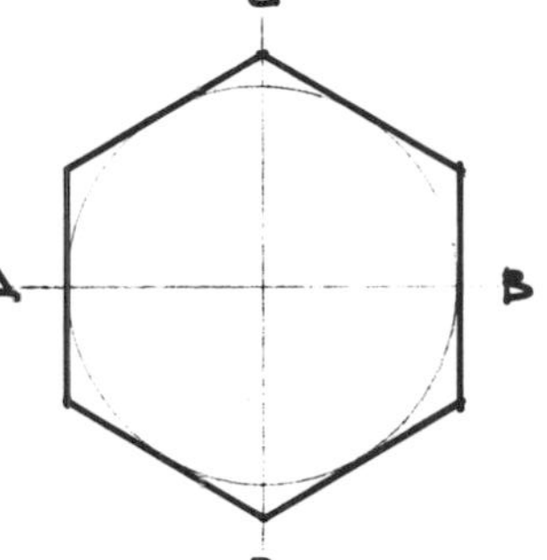

21. Expand the landscape plan features shown below to fill an 8½ × 11-inch sheet. Copy approximate shapes and relative sizes. Do not measure dimensions. Draft straight lines with the T square and triangles. Draft the trees and walk curves with a circle template. Draft the freeform curve with the flexible curve. Draw the dashed contours, shrubs, and evergreen trees freehand.

Ink Drafting and Use of Scale

Exercises 22 through 25
All ink exercises should be finalized on Mylar. You may set up the shapes with pencil on vellum for tracing with ink on Mylar.

22. Trace the construction section in Chapter 7, page 127. Omit labels and leaders. Try to reproduce the variety of line widths shown.

23. Reading the scale
On a sheet of 8½ × 11-inch vellum, draft in pencil four 9-inch long lines about 2 inches apart. Place a small vertical line at the left end of each line. Use the following scales:

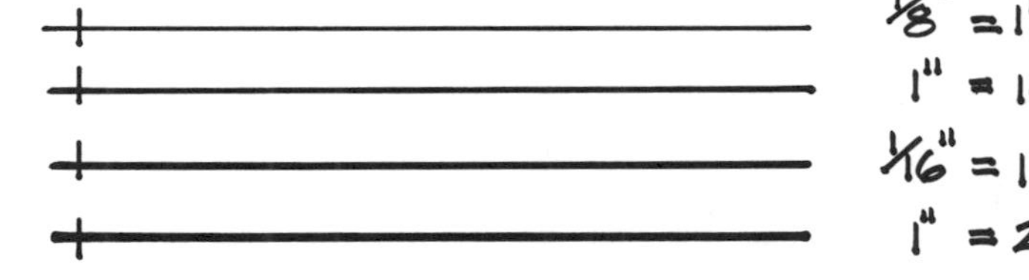

On each line, draft small vertical lines at each of these measurements from the left end of the line:

3′, 10′-6″, 18′-6″, 25′, 39′, 53′, 68′

Place a sheet of Mylar over the top and use four different pen sizes to redraw each horizontal line. Then use a 0 or 00 tip to trace the vertical lines.

24. Scale Change
Redraw this house plan at a scale of ⅛″ = 1′-0″. Draw the walls 6 inches thick. Indicate doors as a single outside line and windows as a double inside and outside line as shown. Ink on Mylar.

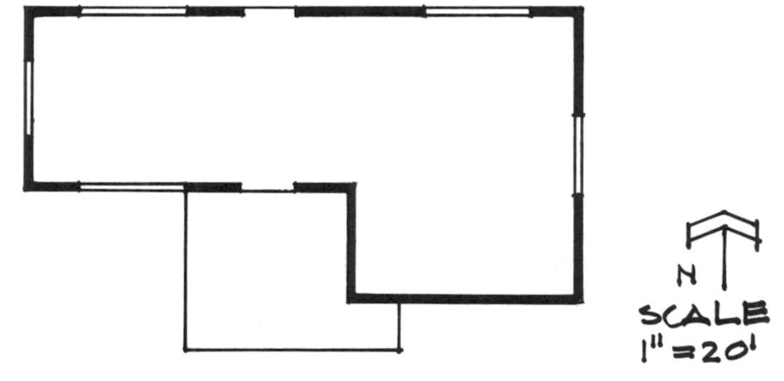

25. North indicators and graphic scales
Fill a sheet with north indications and graphic scales copied (not traced) from Chapter 4. Ink on Mylar, 8½ × 11 inches.

Lettering

Exercises 26 through 28

All pencil lettering is to be done on a vertically aligned 8½ × 11-inch sheet of vellum, using 1½-inch margins with 4H to set up guidelines and 0.5 mm pencil with HB or H lead to make the letters. Dust lightly with the dry cleaning pad before starting.

26. Set up 3⁄16-inch spaced guidelines. Use alternate rows. Letter two rows each of Is, Es, Os, As, and Bs.
Study the shapes shown in Chapter 5. Letter the alphabet in upper case (capitals), then in lower case, then copy the numerals.

27. Set up three 2-inch by 5½-inch blocks of guidelines. Leave an inch between each block. The top block should have guidelines of 3⁄16-inch (setting 6, 3⁄5 row).

The center block should have ⅛-inch guidelines (setting 8, center row). Letter every second row. Medium size.

The bottom block should have 3⁄32-inch guidelines (setting 6, center row). Letter every second row. Smallest size.

Fill the blocks with full sentences copied from a book.

28. For practicing with prepared letters on 8½ × 11-inch vellum or Mylar set up four or five widely spaced light lines to be used as base guides. Invent different titles for each line, using transfer letters and Kroy lettering (if available). Cover transfer letters with clear tape.

Presentation Plans and Symbols

Exercises 29 through 35

29. Fill a page with eight to ten different deciduous trees. Choose the fast outline symbols. Pencil on vellum, 8½ × 11 inches.

30. Repeat exercise 29, choosing some trees with foliage texture and some trees with branching patterns. Felt tip pen on 9 × 12-inch marker paper.

31. Do exercise 29 again, choosing evergreen trees and shrubs. Ink on 8½ × 11-inch Mylar.

32. Create a cohesive composition of ground plane materials to include bermed landform, grass area, three ground covers, three paving patterns, two types of rock groupings, and some water. Ink on Mylar, 8½ × 11 inches, with 1½-inch margins.

33. Create a composition of three buildings, a road, two vehicles, several evergreen trees, and several groups of shrubs. Add shadows and roof texture. Pencil on vellum, 8½ × 11 inches, with 1-inch margins.

34. Create a composition of deciduous trees, evergreen trees, shrub groups, an architectural pool or fountain, and two different paving patterns. Show overlapping and layering. Add shadows and a graphic scale. Felt tip pen on 9 × 12-inch marker paper.

35. Create a plan of a naturalistic area which has deciduous tree groups, evergreen tree groups, shrub groupings, a simple structure (deck, shelter, bridge), paving for pedestrian use, water (both quiet and moving), rocks, and a ground plane texture to tie it together. Integrate a title, north indication, and scale. Include shadows. Ink on Mylar. Suggested sizes: 12 × 18 inches using a 1″ = 10′ scale and 18 × 24 inches using a scale of ⅛″ = 1′-0″.

Sections

Exercises 36 through 38

36. Copy one of the sections from Chapter 7. Pencil on 8½ × 11-inch Mylar.

37. Draw a section through the plan on the right. The thick arrow through the bridge and plaza indicates the cut line. Enlarge it from 1″ = 10′ to ¼″ = 1′-0″ for both horizontal and vertical scales. Include people to show function. Felt tip pen on 9 × 12-inch marker or butcher paper. Use drafting tools to set it up, but final copy should be freehand.

38. Invent a section of your own imaginary landscape. Include structures, water, trees, shrubs, rocks, and people. Suggested environments: play area, urban plaza, fishing pier, botanical gardens, zoo. Felt tip pen on 12 × 8-inch marker paper or butcher paper.

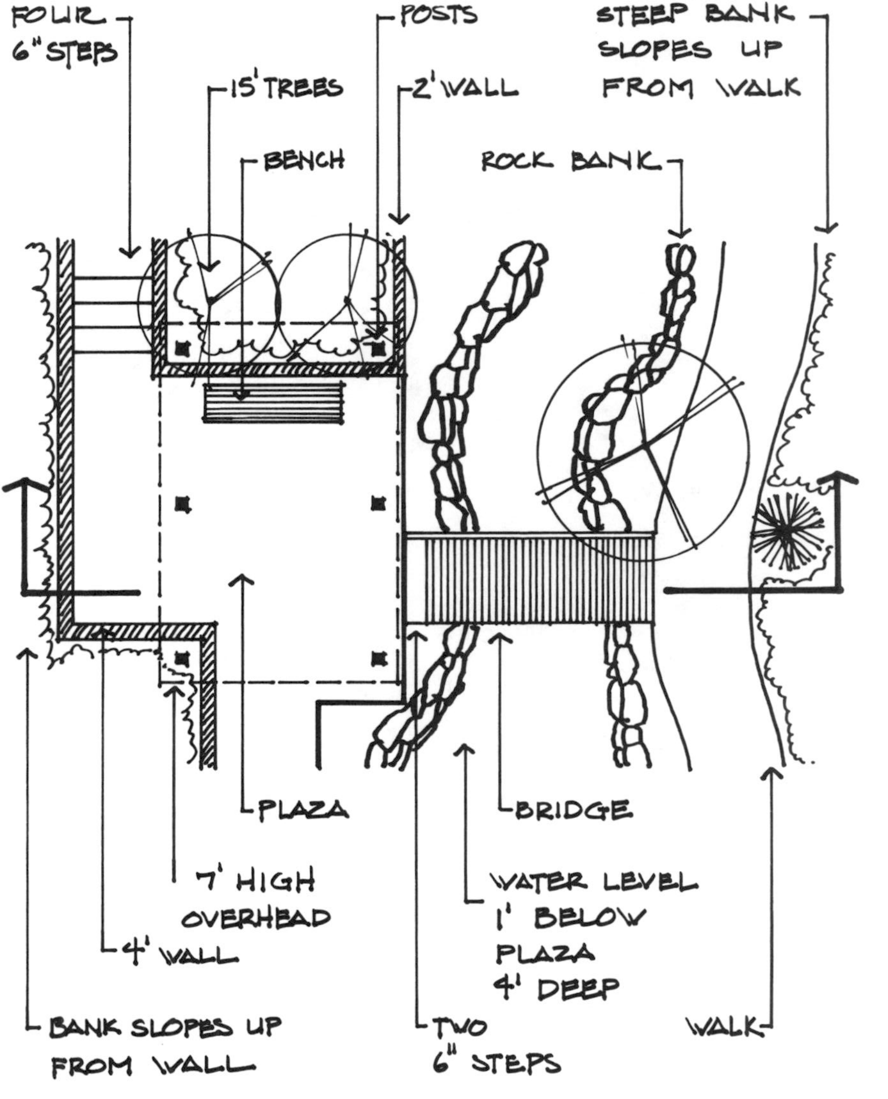

Perspectives

Exercises 39 through 49
39. Using a 6B pencil on tracing paper (any size), draw what you perceive to be a realistic view of things.

a. You are standing, looking down the middle of a set of railway tracks which go straight across an endless, flat desert as far as the eye can see. No trains are coming.

b. You are standing about 20 feet away from the front of a courtyard space looking into it. The three walls are all 20 feet long and 10 feet high.

40. Cubes in one-point perspective
Drawing freehand, use soft pencil or felt tip pen on 18 × 24-inch tracing paper. Draw a horizon line with a vanishing point. Place squares of various sizes all over the sheet, keeping all sides horizontal and vertical. With light lines, connect corners to the vanishing point. Estimate where the back side of the cube will be in order to retain the cube-like appearance. Draw in the back side; then draw heavy lines for the visible edges.

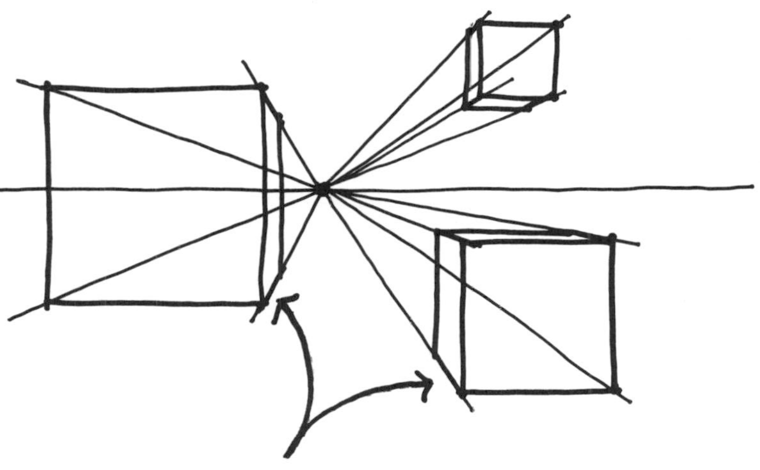

Don't make these lines too long. In perspective, the cube will look foreshortened.

41. Draw a one-point perspective of the courtyard shown below using the proportional method and the scale method described in Chapter 9. An 18 × 24-inch sheet of tracing paper or vellum will be suitable. Follow steps 1 through 9 on pages 160, 161. Begin by placing the horizon line exactly 2½ inches above the GL 20 line. The walls will be one-and-a-half people high. At step 8, the vanishing point must be placed 10 feet to the right of the left side of the space. After placing 10-feet markers along the GL 20, join them to the VP. Find the ground lines using the scale method. Now transfer the plan data to your perspective ground plane grid. Find heights at corners of objects with the proportional method. Add entourage, such as plants, people, and a fountain. Trace all this onto a sheet of marker paper or butcher paper omitting all hidden lines.

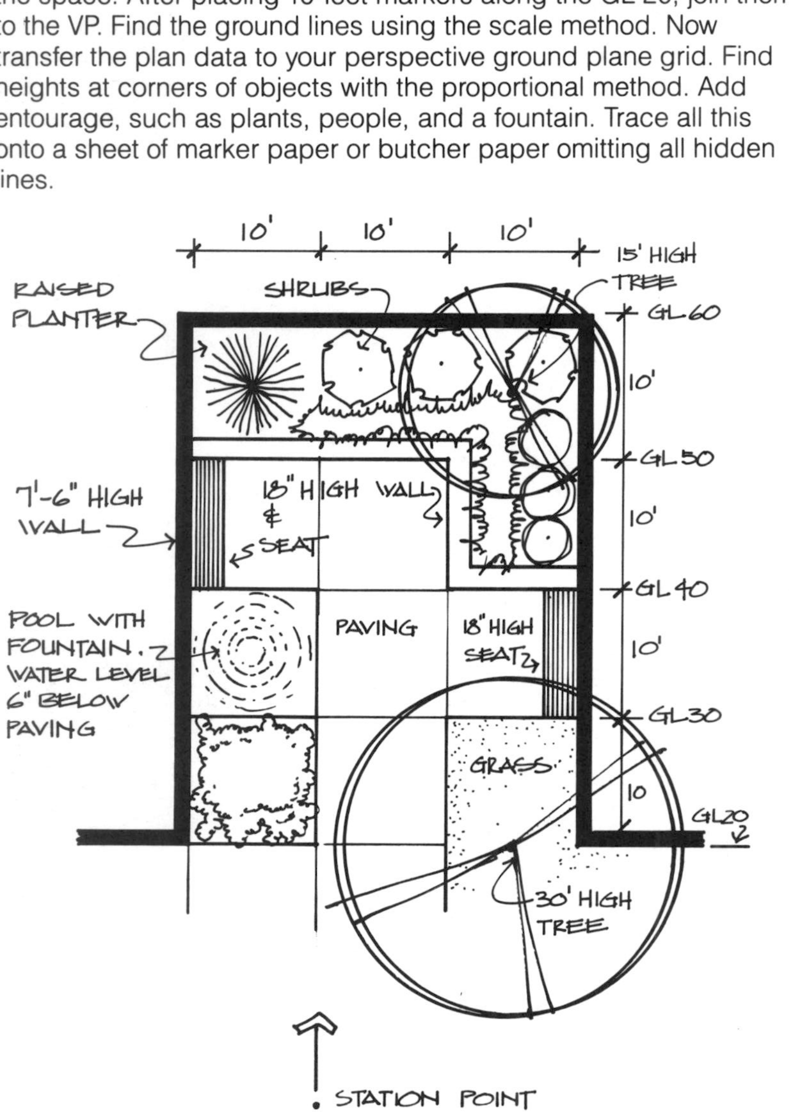

42. Using Lawson perspective chart number 8, or its equivalent, draw a one-point perspective of this plan view pool space. Keep it to simple outline forms but add people and some fast trees. 19 × 24-inch marker paper.

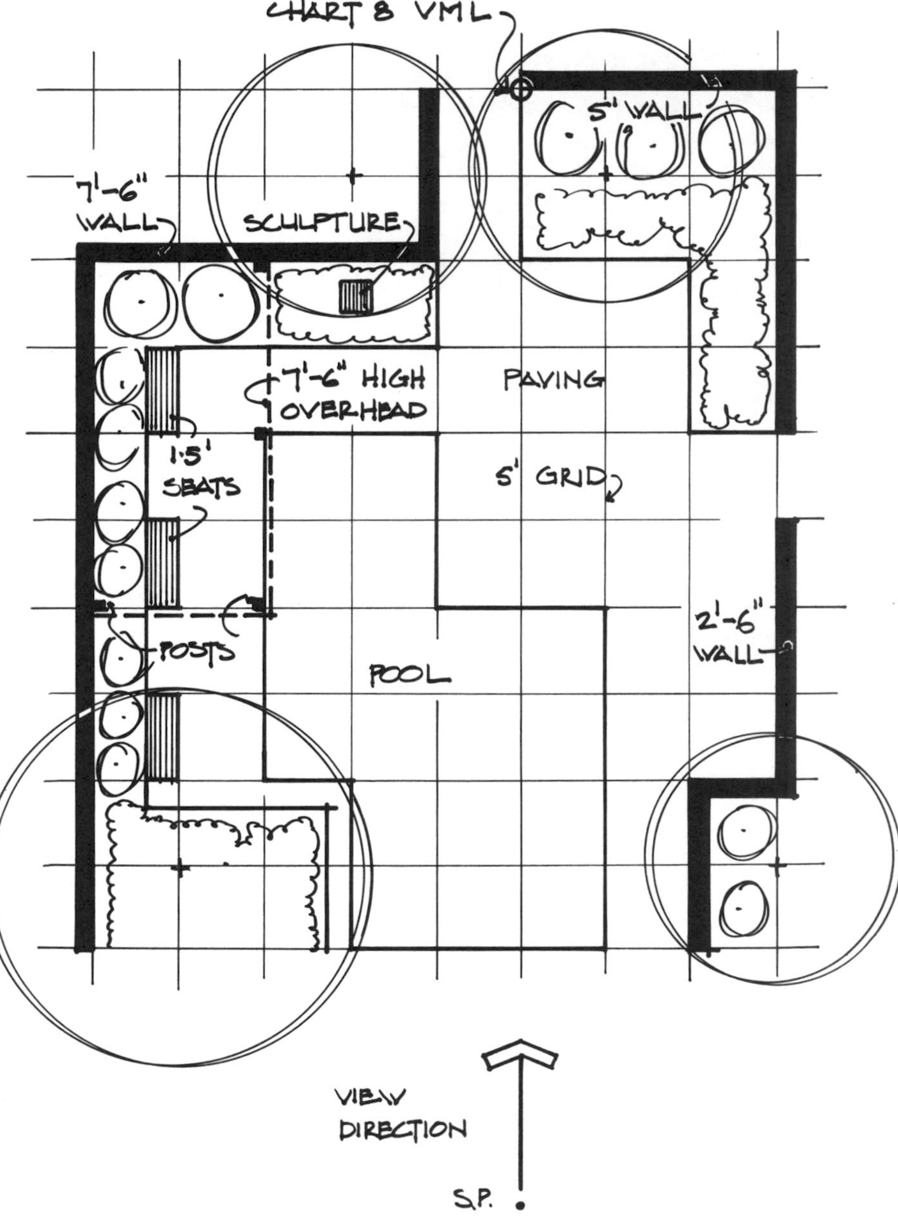

43. Freehand boxes in two-point perspective

Use 18 × 24-inch tracing paper. Draw a horizon line with a dot near the left side of the paper for the left vanishing point (LVP) and another dot near the right side of the paper for the right vanishing point (RVP). With a T square and a pencil, quickly draw a series of straight lines which radiate across the paper from both vanishing points.

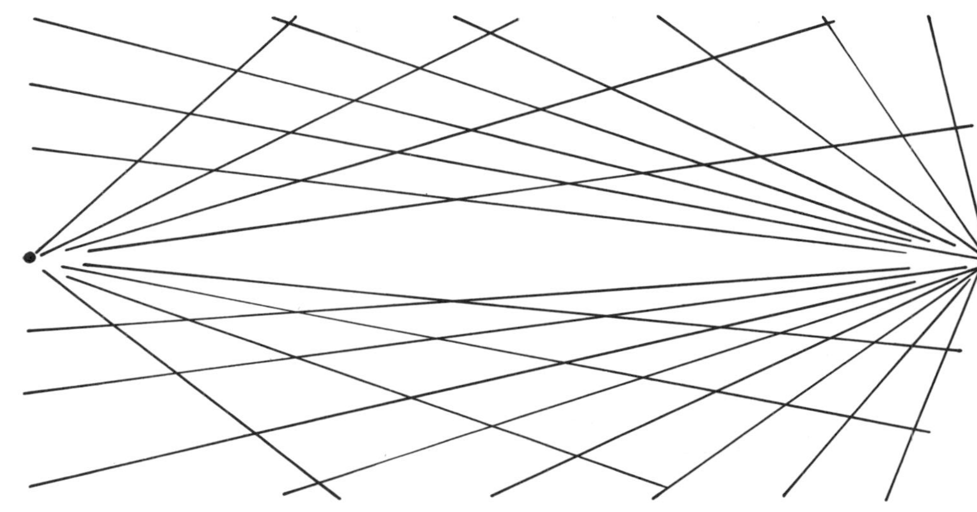

With a felt tip pen draw a number of solid boxes which follow the principles of two-point perspective.

Objective: To understand the three types of ines of simple two-point perspective.

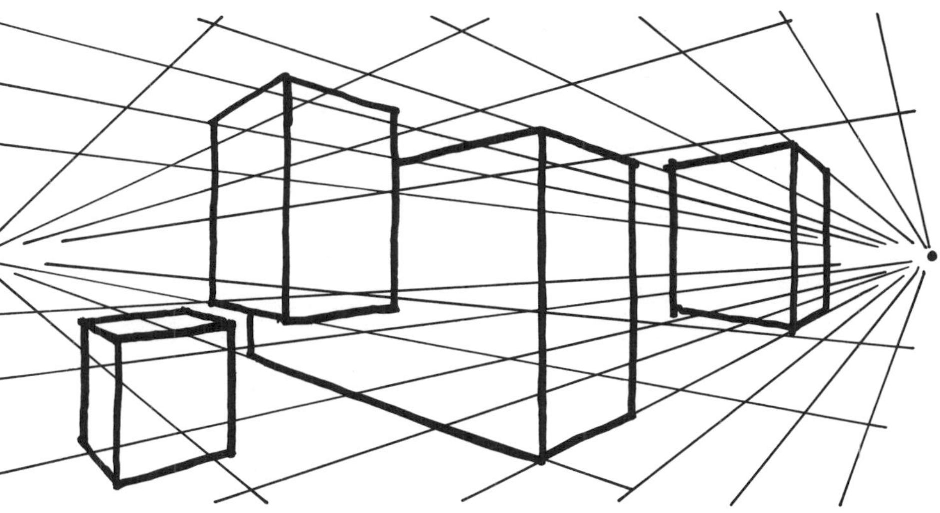

44. Ground plane patterns

Transpose these plan view patterns onto the ground plane of Lawson chart 3 or its equivalent. For the circle, first draw a 10-foot square on the ground plane and mark the midpoint (5 feet) on each side. Then draw diagonals from corner to corner. Place a mark a little less than a third the distance from the corner to the center on each diagonal. Connect the marks in a smooth ellipse.

Objective: To understand the relationship between a plan grid and a compressed ground plane in a two-point perspective chart.

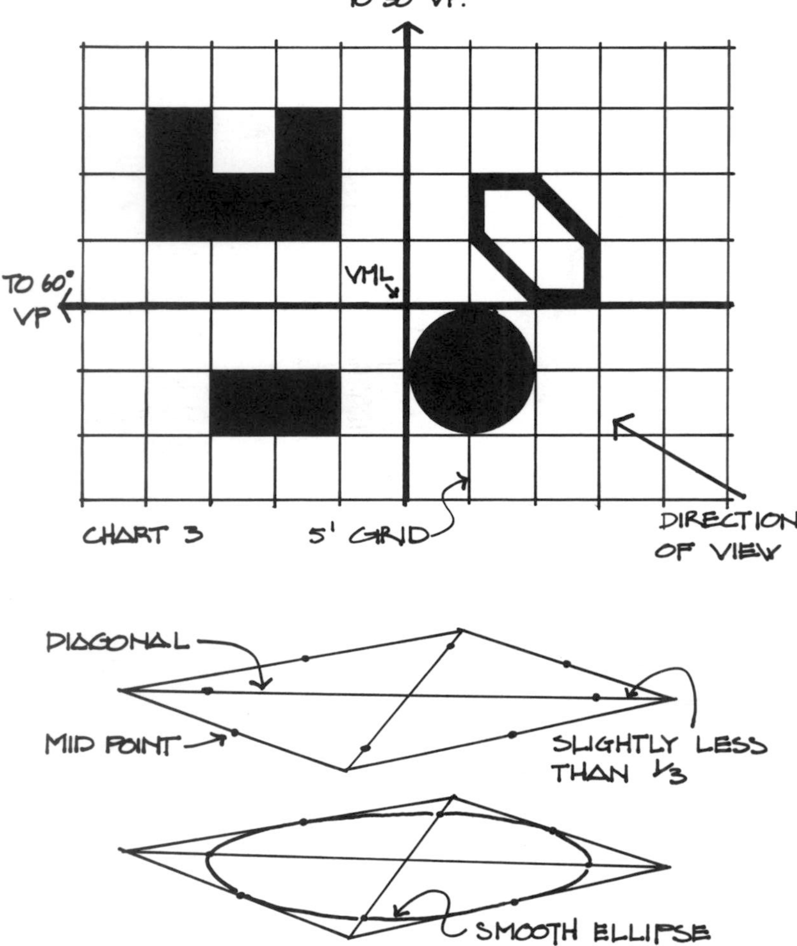

45. Flag poles

Using an overlay of tracing paper on Lawson chart 6, or one like it, locate flag poles on the ground plane. Find their heights by using the vertical measuring line. Since all poles stand directly on one of the heavy base lines, use a simple one-step process. First draw a light vertical line from the pole base. Now determine to which vanishing point the base line vanishes. Connect that vanishing point to the desired height on the VML and extend (if necessary) to intersect the flag pole vertical. Mark the height and draw in the pole. Before removing your overlay, add 10-foot ground plane grid lines.

Objective: To show simple one-step use of the vertical measuring line to find heights in two-point perspective.

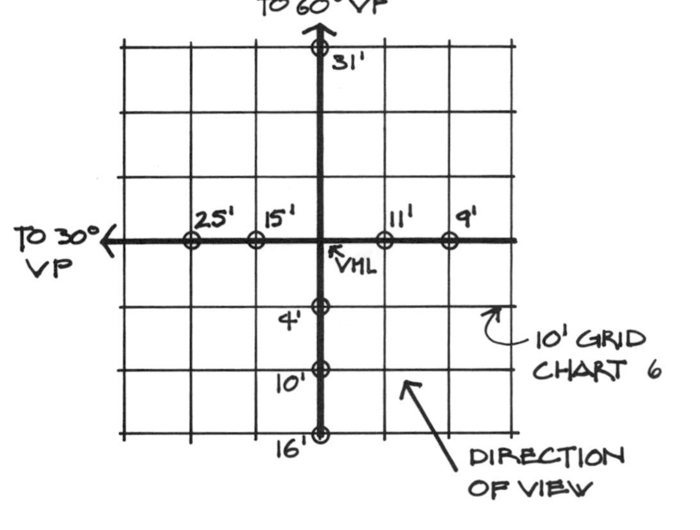

46. Geometric forms
Use an overlay of tracing paper on Lawson chart 6 (or a comparable one). Follow the nine steps described in Appendix 1 pages 184, 185 to draw the boxes at their correct height. Start with the 15-foot high box. To draw the round pool, first draw the ellipse on the ground plane as described in exercise 44. Now project an increment of 1 foot down from the zero of the VML. Use this to construct a 20-foot square 1 foot below the ground plane pool. Add the new ellipse and erase the hidden lines.

Objective: To practice using the vertical measuring line to find heights of simple 3D objects.

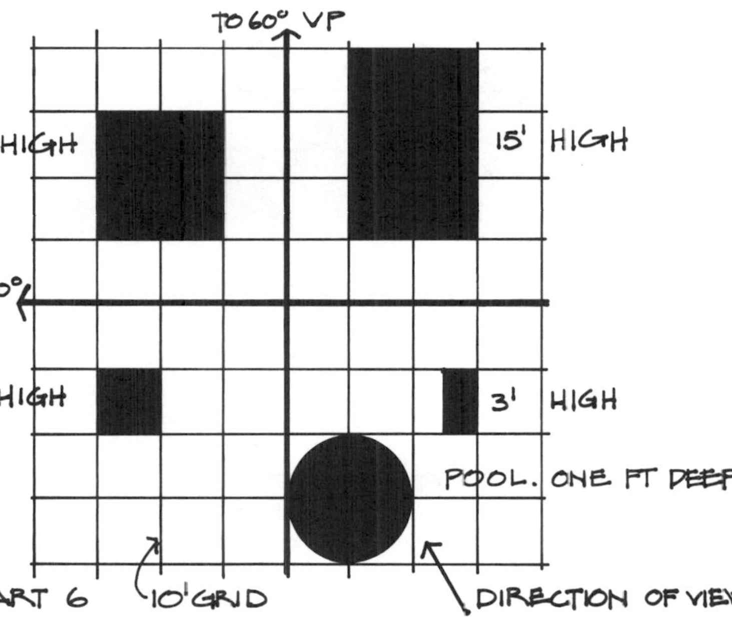

47. Walls
Draw a perspective view of the three walls shown on this plan. Use Lawson chart 2, or another similar one. Block out the shapes and several people then trace onto 9 × 12-inch marker paper adding textural symbols to show wall material and some ground plane grid lines.

Objectives: To practice the use of the VML with curved and angled objects. To show an indication of materials. To draw people in a 12.5 feet eyeline sketch.

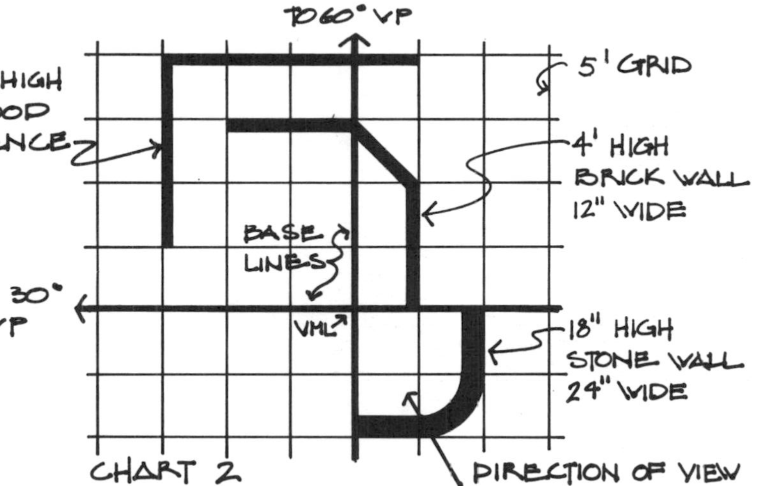

48. Rural landscape
On an overlay of Lawson chart 5, or one like it, invent a rural landscape composition to include trees, shrubs, ground cover, pavement or walkway, a small built element (wall, bridge, seat, deck) and people. Incorporate the principles of composition described on pages 171–181. Sketch size 12 × 18 inches; felt tip pen on marker paper or pencil on Mylar.

Objectives: To practice drawing vegetation and landform. To study the principles of composition.

49. Waterfront
Using Lawson chart 6, or a comparable one, draw a quick perspective of the plan shown here. Include people. Choose simple symbols for trees and shrubs. Add quick indications of doors and windows. Block it out in pencil on any medium, then trace it freehand onto a sheet of tracing paper with felt tip markers, omitting all hidden lines. Sketch size: 18 × 24 inches.

Objectives: To integrate all aspects of two-point perspective. To practice simplicity and speed.

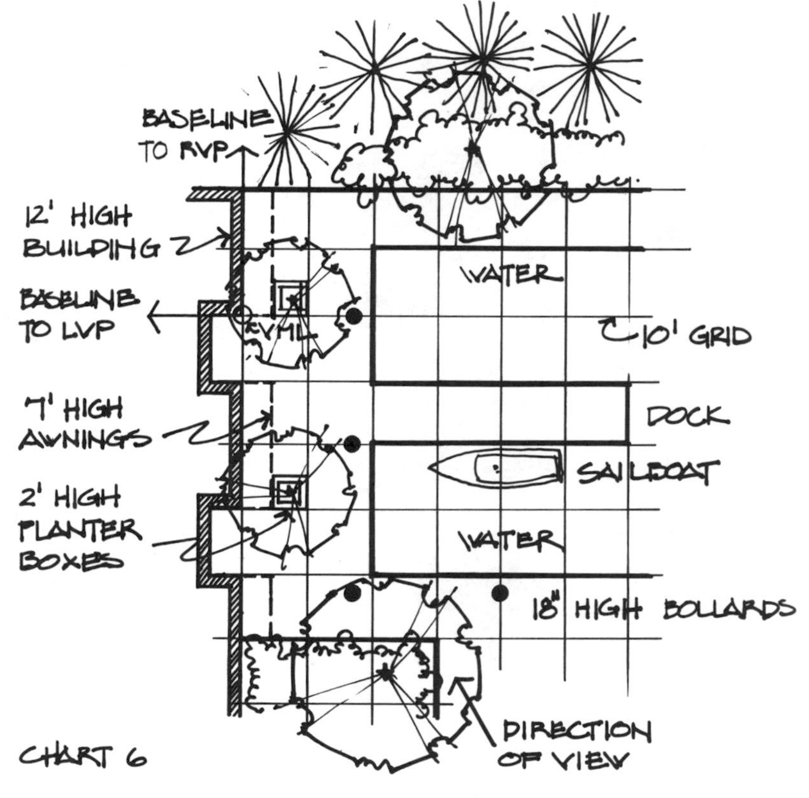

Bibliography

Ching, Frank. *Architectural Graphics*. 2d ed. New York: Van Nostrand Reinhold, 1985.

Doyle, Michael E. *Color Drawing. A Marker/Colored-Pencil Approach*. New York: Van Nostrand Reinhold, 1981.

Evans, Larry. *Illustration Guide for Architects, Designers and Students*. New York: Van Nostrand Reinhold, 1982.

Hanks, Kurt, and Larry Belliston. *Draw! A Visual Approach to Thinking, Learning and Communicating*. Los Altos, California: William Kaufmann, 1977.

Laseau, Paul. *Graphic Thinking for Architects and Designers*. New York: Van Nostrand Reinhold, 1980.

Lin, Mike W. *Architectural Rendering Techniques. A Color Reference*. New York: Van Nostrand Reinhold, 1985.

Oliver, Robert S. *The Sketch*. New York: Van Nostrand Reinhold, 1979.

Szabo, Marc. *Drawing File for Architects, Illustrators and Designers*. New York: Van Nostrand Reinhold, 1976.

Walker, Theodor D. *Perspective Sketches*. 3d ed. Mesa, Arizona: PDA Publishers Corporation, 1975.

Walker, Theodor D. *Plan Graphics*. West Lafayette, Indiana: PDA Publishers, 1975.

Wang, Thomas C. *Plan and Section Drawing*. New York: Van Nostrand Reinhold, 1979.

Wang, Thomas C. *Pencil Sketching*. New York: Van Nostrand Reinhold, 1977.

Wang, Thomas C. *Projection Drawing*. New York: Van Nostrand Reinhold, 1984.

Wang, Thomas C. *Sketching with Markers*. New York: Van Nostrand Reinhold, 1981.

Metric Conversions

inches	cm	feet	meters
1/16	0.16	1	0.3048
1/8	0.32	2	0.6096
3/16	0.48	3	0.9144
1/4	0.64	4	1.219
5/16	0.79	5	1.524
3/8	0.95	6	1.828
7/16	1.11	7	2.133
1/2	1.27	8	2.438
9/16	1.43	9	2.743
5/8	1.59	10	3.048
11/16	1.75		
3/4	1.91		
13/16	2.06		
7/8	2.22		
15/16	2.38		
1	2.54		
2	5.08		
3	7.62		
4	10.16		
5	12.70		
6	15.24		
7	17.78		
8	20.32		
9	22.86		
10	25.40		
11	27.94		
12	30.48		

To convert feet to meters,
multiply number of feet by 0.3048.
For example, to convert 25 feet to
meters, multiply 25 by 0.3048 = 7.62 meters

Index

Senior Editor: Julia Moore
Associate Editor: Victoria Craven-Cohn
Designer: Jay Anning
Production Manager: Hector Campbell
Set in Helvetica Light